Praise for *The Rediscovery of George "Nash" Walker*

"The life and accomplishments of George Walker have long been underappreciated. Atkinson's work is an important contribution to the literature about Black musical theater of a century ago. The documentation is exhaustive and the illustrations are superb. Congratulations!"

— Thomas L. Riis, author of *Just Before Jazz: Black Musical Theatre in New York, 1890 to 1915*

"The fact that there has never been a proper biography of George Walker is sort of insane. In the history of Black American popular culture, he is the definition of seminal. We're fortunate that Daniel E. Atkinson has now tackled the project with thoroughness, insight, and verve. Current scholars can learn from this book, and future scholars will build on it."

— John Sullivan, contributing writer, *The New York Times Magazine*

"The careful and creative research in this page-turning and beautifully illustrated biography demonstrates how much we can know about the glorious and tragic life of a deeply important African American genius. This is a major contribution to the study of race, of business, of popular culture, and of the larger US history in which Atkinson impressively contextualizes Walker's story."

— David Roediger, Foundation Professor of American Studies at the University of Kansas and author of *How Race Survived U.S. History: From Settlement and Slavery to the Obama Phenomenon*

"This fascinating book shines a light on one of the lesser-known but most consequential Black entertainers of the early twentieth century. Why haven't we heard more about him? Probably because he lived a rather short life and has been in the shadow of his more famous partner, comedian Bert Williams. Immaculately researched, Atkinson's account brings George Walker and his world vividly to life, following the talented Black singer and dancer as he fought for Black equality in the oppressive Jim Crow world that was America in the early 1900s."

— Tim Brooks, author of *Lost Sounds: Blacks and the Birth of the Recording Industry, 1890–1919*

"Atkinson's book contributes to the field of theater and performance studies by restoring Walker to his rightful place in the annals of drama. Atkinson makes a case for taking Walker seriously as a caretaker and a superintendent of Black expressive culture and by extension Black musical theater during the long nineteenth century in the US."

— Eric M. Glover, author of *African-American Perspectives in Musical Theatre*

"The attention that [Atkinson] gives to Walker's frustration with the limited lane available to Black artists (only comedies, no love stories) as well as the difficulty black composers had in being paid for their songs grant insight into the racism of the period. The book spotlights the diligence—the hard work—required not only to create a production but also to tour it. Indeed, the fact that several collaborators stopped working because of exhaustion is a signal of the tremendous challenges that they faced."

— Harvey Young, editor of the *Cambridge Companion to African American Theatre*

The Rediscovery of
George "Nash" Walker

The Rediscovery of George "Nash" Walker

The Price of Black Stardom in Jim Crow America

DANIEL E. ATKINSON

SUNY PRESS

Cover credit: "Bon Bon Buddy," June 1908, J. Rosamond Johnson Foundation. Used with permission of K. Mélanie Edwards.

Published by State University of New York Press, Albany

© 2025 State University of New York

All rights reserved

Printed in the United States of America

No part of this book may be used or reproduced in any manner whatsoever without written permission. No part of this book may be stored in a retrieval system or transmitted in any form or by any means including electronic, electrostatic, magnetic tape, mechanical, photocopying, recording, or otherwise without the prior permission in writing of the publisher.

Links to third-party websites are provided as a convenience and for informational purposes only. They do not constitute an endorsement or an approval of any of the products, services, or opinions of the organization, companies, or individuals. SUNY Press bears no responsibility for the accuracy, legality, or content of a URL, the external website, or for that of subsequent websites.

EU GPSR Authorised Representative:
Logos Europe, 9 rue Nicolas Poussin, 17000, La Rochelle, France
contact@logoseurope.eu

For information, contact State University of New York Press, Albany, NY
www.sunypress.edu

Library of Congress Cataloging-in-Publication Data

Name: Atkinson, Daniel E., 1974– author.
Title: The rediscovery of George "Nash" Walker : the price of Black stardom in Jim Crow America / Daniel E. Atkinson.
Description: Albany : State University of New York Press, [2025] | Includes bibliographical references and index.
Identifiers: LCCN 2024053706 | ISBN 9798855803167 (hardcover : alk. paper) | ISBN 9798855803174 (ebook) | ISBN 9798855803181 (pbk. : alk. paper)
Subjects: LCSH: Walker, George W., 1873–1911. | African American entertainers—Biography. | African American theater—History. | Vaudeville—United States—History.
Classification: LCC PN2287.W2395 A94 2025 | DDC 792.02/8092 [B]—dc23/eng/20250117
LC record available at https://lccn.loc.gov/2024053706

Contents

List of Illustrations   vii

List of Abbreviations   xi

Acknowledgments   xiii

Introduction   1

Part One: The Start

1. Growing Up Radical: 1865 to 1891   7
2. Partners in Double Consciousness: 1892 to 1893   21
3. Go East, Young Men: 1895 to 1896   37
4. Honing the Act: 1896 to 1897   53

Part Two: The Stride

5. Cake Walks and Culture: 1898   77
6. As I See You on the Stage: 1899 to 1900   97
7. "Only Just Butting In": 1900 to 1902   117

8. Broadway, the Hard Way: 1902 to 1903 — 141

9. "I Needn't Be Scared of No King": 1903 to 1904 — 165

10. The Royal Strut: 1904 to 1905 — 185

Part Three: The Struggle

11. The Abyss: 1905 to 1907 — 201

12. "Bon Bon Buddy": 1907 to 1908 — 233

13. Who's Leavin' Who? 1908 to 1909 — 259

14. You Never Miss the Water . . . : 1909 to 1911 — 285

15. . . . 'Til the Well Runs Dry — 311

Appendix — 325

Notes — 347

Bibliography — 397

Index — 403

Illustrations

Figure 1.1	"The Rediscovery of George (Nash) Walker."	12
Figure 1.2	"Arcade Minstrels."	19
Figure 2.1	"Xavier Pené and His Dahomeyan Amazons."	32
Figure 3.1	"Dora Dean: The Sweetest Gal You Ever Seen."	40
Figure 3.2	Jesse Shipp.	43
Figure 3.3	Sissieretta "Black Patti" Jones.	45
Figure 3.4	"Oh! I Don't Know, You're Not So Warm!: Comic Song and Refrain with Coon Parody."	48
Figure 4.1	Ernest Hogan.	54
Figure 4.2	"All Coons Look Alike to Me: A Darkey Misunderstanding."	55
Figure 4.3	Hyde and Behman's advertisement.	63
Figure 4.4	"Williams and Walker, Two Colored Men."	64
Figure 4.5	"Darkest Vaudeville."	68
Figure 4.6	"A Lesson for Society Cake Walkers."	69
Figure 4.7	"A Hot Coon from Memphis: Coon Gossip."	71
Figure 4.8	"The Hottest Coon in Town."	72
Figure 4.9	Cake Walk No. 2.	73
Figure 4.10	"Enjoy Yourselves."	74

Figure 5.1	"Cake Walks and Culture."	80
Figure 5.2	Robert (Bob) Cole.	86
Figure 5.3	Ada Overton circa 1900.	87
Figure 5.4	"I'm a Cooler for the Warmest Coon in Town."	94
Figure 5.5	"He's Up Against the Real Thing Now."	95
Figure 5.6	George Walker circa 1898.	96
Figure 6.1	Advertisement, Gilmore's Auditorium.	99
Figure 6.2	"The Medicine Man."	105
Figures 6.3a–k	Series of George Walker circa 1900.	112–14
Figure 7.1	Green Henri "High G" Tapley.	121
Figures 7.2a–j	Character study of Bert Williams and George Walker from Act I of *Sons of Ham*, 1900.	122–23
Figure 7.3	"Miss Hannah from Savannah."	125
Figure 7.4	"My Little Zulu Babe."	126
Figures 7.5a–c	Character study of George Walker in drag from "My Little Zulu Babe."	127
Figure 7.6	Sylvester Russell.	130
Figure 7.7	"Good Morning Carrie."	133
Figures 8.1a–e	The Medicine Man and Cake Walk scenes from act 1 of *In Dahomey*.	143–45
Figure 8.2	Shylock and Rareback on the road to Gatorville, act 2 of *In Dahomey*.	146
Figures 8.3a–b	Rareback as the Zulu Chief with Shylock in the Caboceers scene, act 3 of *In Dahomey*.	147
Figure 8.4	Jerry Nashville Walker, president of the Colorado African Colonization Company.	148
Figure 8.5	"I'm a Jonah Man."	151
Figure 8.6	"Williams and Walker 'In Dahom[e]y Company' 1904."	155

Figures 8.7a–b	Rotographs by Cavendish Morton of Aida Overton Walker and Ada Guiguesse, London, circa fall 1903.	159
Figure 8.8	"Ada Overton Walker."	163
Figure 9.1	George Walker aboard RMS *Aurania*, April 28, 1903.	167
Figure 9.2	"The Real Cake-Walk by Real Coons."	170
Figure 9.3	The Grand Lodge of Ancient Free and Accepted Masons of Scotland, Lodge Waverley, no. 597.	180
Figure 10.1	"Me an' da Minstrel Ban'."	188
Figure 10.2	"Williams and Walker Glee Club."	197
Figure 11.1a–b	Publicity photographs of George Walker and chorus in the stage production *Abyssinia*.	218
Figure 11.2	Accompanying illustration for "What Williams and Walker Think of the Clansman."	224
Figure 11.3	Aida featured prominently in George's article "The Real 'Coon' on the American Stage."	225
Figure 11.4	"I'll Keep a Warm Spot in My Heart for You."	227
Figure 12.1	Nash Walker in his "Bon Bon Buddy" raiment.	238
Figure 12.2	"Abyssinio," 401 Indiana Street, Lawrence, Kansas, as it appeared in 2018.	240
Figure 12.3	Still from act 2 of *Bandanna Land*.	244
Figure 12.4	"Bon Bon Buddy, the Chocolate Drop."	248
Figure 12.5a–b	"The Merry Widow Waltz Performed by Negroes, Mrs. Ada Overton Walker and Mr. George Walker in the Famous Dance."	252
Figure 13.1	The Frogs I.	263
Figure 13.2	The Frogs II.	264
Figure 13.3	"The Last Williams and Walker Company—'Bandannaland'—Field Day, Boston, Oct. 1, 1908."	266

Figure 13.4	"Aida Overton Walker in Male Attire Singing 'Bon Bon Buddy.'"	276
Figure 13.5	"Miss Walker as Salome."	277
Figure 14.1	*Mr. Lode of Koal Song Album.*	289
Figure 14.2	"That's Why They Call Me Shine."	301
Figure 14.3	Possibly the last surviving photograph of Williams and Walker, circa late summer 1908.	303
Figure 15.1	"Castle Lame Duck Waltz."	315
Figure 15.2	Bill "Bojangles" Robinson and Alice Myers in front of a home that he purchased for her in Lawrence in early September 1926.	321

Abbreviations

CIO	*The Inter Ocean* (Chicago)
INF	*The Freeman* (Indianapolis)
LDG	*Lawrence Daily Gazette* or *The Daily Gazette* (Lawrence, Kansas)
LDJ	*Lawrence Daily Journal*
LDJ-W	*Lawrence Daily Journal-World*
LDW	*Lawrence Daily World*
LJG	*The Jeffersonian Gazette* (Lawrence, Kansas)
LWW	*Lawrence Weekly World*
NYA	*The New York Age*
NYT	*The New York Times*
TPD	*The Topeka Plaindealer*
TSJ	*The Topeka State Journal*

Acknowledgments

The folks who were vitally helpful along the way:

Marla B'darla, Jeanne Klein, Raj Rana, Tom Rafiner, Andrew Erdman, Katie Armitage, Traci Wilson-Kleekamp, Ada Danelo, Gabriel Skoog, William Tuttle, Michael Grigoni, Sheridan Reiger, K. Mélanie Edwards, Robert Kimball, Brent Campney, Tim Brooks, Louis Chude-Shokei, Deborah Willis, Alex Hassan, Deborah Dandridge, Shawn Alexander, Paul Gardullo, Eric K. Washington, Chuck Haddix, Edgar Tidwell, Clarence Lang, Jennifer Hamer, Thomas Riis, Sarah Gilmore, David Gallagher, Lisa Ruth, Richard Martin, Levi Fuller, Philip Schuyler, Meagan Hennessey, William "Moreland" Bates, Karimah, Robert Cooper, Camille Forbes, Sarah Smarsh, Joellen Elbashir, Herbert Martin, Sister Virginia M. Dowd, Thomas Morgan, David R. Roediger, Laurel Sercombe, Monica Davis, Reginald Robinson, Kerwin Young, Howard Wiley, Mellonee Burnim, Marc Cary, and Ahmad Jamal.

Introduction

Although Afro-American accomplishments between emancipation and the First World War were numerous, many—too many—have in fact been lost to history. The following narrative *was* among them and represents a small sample of the underappreciated cultural wealth of the first generation of professional Black artists. That vanguard generation endeavored to market Black cultural products within existing White systems that had been completely inaccessible a generation earlier. In doing so, they left a record of achievement that has yet to be fully integrated into the American historical record. Among them, George William "Nash" Walker was one of the most outstanding. His ability to persevere with aplomb, lifting as he climbed, made him one of the most beloved and circumstantially controversial members of the vanguard generation.

More than a cautionary tale of a dream deferred, the arc of Walker's short life exemplified the Gilded Age, as he rose from poverty and obscurity to the height of fame and infamy. He, like others of his generation, personified the potential of the United States and simultaneously fell victim to its hypocrisy. Like all those who believed there was no demerit in being Black and operated as such, Walker paid dearly when he could no longer leverage his talents for high pay from White audiences or maintain control of his intellectual property and Black cultural products.

Because most of the information for this book was gathered from the recollections of Walker's contemporaries, the story is theirs as much as his. Their communal experiences, individual reflections, and ideas permeate whenever possible and are a direct analogue to the current struggle for Black cultural and intellectual sovereignty and solidarity in the United States. Therefore, the following text contains a plethora of information that is not included in any of the six biographies of Walker's partner of nearly eighteen years, Bert Williams, nor the handful of cursory texts devoted to his wife, Aida Overton Walker. With that in mind, one must take popular tropes of the self-made man, do-it-yourself, and the like with a grain of salt. Although Walker was at the center of the collective gaze of his generation, it was the community around him that empowered his philosophy, actions, and legacy. That is how Walker operated, and this text follows suit. His life's work was an unprecedented attempt to assert Black personhood despite continuous and unrelenting institutionalized White supremacy. That caveat must be understood if we are to learn from the sins of our founders and appreciate the true potential of Black people. Understandably, Walker was extremely private, and little about *him* has survived beyond scattered bits of trace information for which an inventory was made, resulting in this most exhaustive account of his life and those of several of his contemporaries, from poverty to posh and, unfortunately, back again.

 The narrative structure of this book stems from Walker's love letters to Lawrence, Kansas, his hometown, as well as two manifestos: "The Real 'Coon' on the American Stage," from the August 1906 issue of *The Theatre* magazine, and "Bert and Me and Them," published first in *The New York Age* on Christmas Eve, 1908, and in the Chicago *Inter Ocean* shortly before he retired from the stage. In those manifestos, Walker left the breadcrumbs that make up the major pivot points of the story. When combined with surviving digitized newsprint and the thoughts of his contemporaries, it serves as the launch point to an entirely new vein of scholarship devoted to the major Afro-American players at the dawn of the modern age. That said, despite diligence, patience, work-arounds, and triangulations, large gaps persist. Where and when they do, I have done my best to surmise what I believe happened and state that. Therefore, this is not an all-inclusive effort, nor do I claim to be the most knowledgeable scholar of the material presented in the narrative. Simply put, it is the best I could do with what was available to me. Warts and all, its value as documentation of the Afro-American experience is beyond reproach. Ultimately, I hope that future research will shed light on events that are currently unknown or partially known so the stories of the vanguard generation can eventually be faithfully documented without artistic license or compromise.

 Although Walker and his contemporaries were as modern and progressive as their White counterparts, their fight for liberty took its toll and left its mark. Then, as now, the circumstances in which Black artists were expected to operate insisted that the most talented were not necessarily representing the best and brightest that Black communities produced. Rather, the best among those who were acceptable to the White power structure and were to operate within very clear and distinct boundaries. With that in mind, the tangible value of this collection of ancestral experiences can help young Black people to think beyond individual, short-term gains and see themselves as conduits and ambassadors of culture rather than self-made individuals who are looking out for them and theirs alone. With the encoded legacy of Jim Crow still doing its work to keep Blacks in a secondary condition, unless deemed useful by the operators of the power structure, this narrative is a testament to the power of community and proof that the tradition of adapting cultural products to the whims of conspicuous White consumers is not necessarily the best way forward. As a ninety-two-year-old Eubie Blake (1883 to 1983) said in an interview for the television series "All You Need Is Love" in 1977, "We're the only racial people in the world, sir, that throw away heritage." Nevertheless, it is never too late to change if one can still see oneself in the ancestors. If so, then one's descendants can do the same, and they, too, will act accordingly and continue to speak our names, preventing a second, final death. Therefore, the integration of our ancestors' experiences into the collective consciousness can foster a genuine sense of belonging for the only cultural group in the United States that cannot declare a specific point of origin or a language beyond its borders. Still the source of popular culture, the industries that depend on Black entertainers and athletes host very few Black people in positions of power and long-term influence, two issues that Walker's generation attempted to address. Call it hustle, swagger, poise, or repose, they had it, and so do we. All we need to do is remember where and whom we come from, and we, too, can become our ancestors' wildest dreams.

A Word on Usage

This text utilizes the contemporaneous term *cake walk* as two words, unless quoted differently; the English spelling of *theatre*, unless quoted differently; and the term *Afro-American* out of solidarity with other New World members of the diaspora rather than *African American*, unless referring to someone born on the continent. Within the text, all references to Colored people, Black people, Negroes, Coons, and the like are used interchangeably and will be treated as proper nouns unless in a quotation.

Part One

The Start

Chapter 1

Growing Up Radical

1865 to 1891

> We want our folks, the Negroes, to like us. Over and above the money and the prestige is a love for the race. We feel that [to] a degree we represent the race, and every hair's breath [*sic*] of achievement we make is to its credit. For first last and all the time we are Negroes. We know it, the race knows it, and the public knows it and we want them to keep knowing it.
>
> —George W. Walker[1]

Throughout a nearly two-decade run of unprecedented success, impeded by withering institutional sabotage, bias, and managerial theft, there had always been a way forward for the indomitable Williams and Walker. They knew what was at stake and took action when almost no one else would to improve social conditions for Black people in the United States. That is, until that fateful moment on the evening of February 22, 1909, just offstage at the Masonic Theatre in Louisville. As partners, Bert Williams and George Walker had been the ringleaders of the vanguard generation of professional Black artists in the United States. However, circumstances had changed, and George Walker had to face facts; his ability to compensate for the demerit of Jim Crow was possible only through his sound mind and his ability to leverage his body's expression of Black cultural products in a world that was hungry for Black culture, but not Black people. Despite his best efforts, rumors about his deteriorating condition had spread for weeks.

Now a nervous wreck, the once idolized specimen of the sporting man finally admitted the truth to his best friend and partner: "Well, Bert, I'm going to leave you." To keep from crying, Bert Williams turned his head and said, "No, you're not. I'm going to leave you," as he shuffled onstage to the roar of a cheering audience.[2]

Although his admission was largely symbolic because forces had been at work for months to destroy the company, it was Williams's first act as a solo artist and Walker's final act of partnership. Thus began the end of Williams and Walker and the vanguard generation's hold over their space as tastemakers and trendsetters. However, for a short period, circumstances, luck, and the resilience of the human spirit allowed for a few to find a little space for themselves and a few others. A man of his time and one of the brightest of his generation, George Walker was well prepared by his elders in a unique social environment, his hometown, Lawrence, Kansas. There, his irrepressible spirit was nurtured until he was bound and determined not to let the sacrifices of his ancestors go to waste as he and his contemporaries personified their wildest dreams. They were the generation who called on all who were able to "Lift Every Voice and Sing."

Lawrence

The inspiration for George Walker's desire to elevate Afro-American life and culture came directly from his childhood in "Bleeding" Lawrence, Kansas, shortly after the close of the Civil War. Although the term was established more than a decade before his birth, it was still fresh in the hearts and minds of Lawrencians who lived through the border war with Missouri prior to the war between North and South. Lawrence was established in part with abolitionist principles in mind and had been lauded as a haven for Black people since 1854. An important station on the Underground Railroad for formerly enslaved Africans, Lawrence was the launch point of John Brown's raid on Harpers Ferry, Virginia, in 1859. It was also the site of Quantrill's Raid, the culmination of the border war with Missouri in 1863, when most of Massachusetts Street in the city center was burned by guerillas and nearly two-hundred people were massacred.[3] In Lawrence, Walker was immersed in a unique atmosphere in which the reality of Blackness in a White world was on display as well as glimpses of the potential of Black liberty. However, the town also manifested its own version of the national discomfort with Africans and their American descendants, commonly referred to as the "Negro problem." Afro-Americans understood the sliding scale of morality of Whites toward Blacks throughout the country and knew that most of the White people who worked vehemently to end slavery did not endorse the idea of full citizenship for Black people or having them as neighbors. Therefore, Kansas revealed itself to be more anti-Black than antislavery, and Lawrence was its saving grace, although not free of problems associated with racism from otherwise well-meaning people. To that end, from an Afro-American perspective, Lawrence was the lesser evil in a largely demonic world, and any Black person who thought differently was little more than a nail to be hammered by a White person who was asserting their "inalienable right" to do so. As Lawrence began to fill with Black refugees from slaveholding states from the mid-1850s through the end of the war, some denizens who embraced the idea of being on the right side of history simultaneously acted on the wrong side of the moment with little to no consequences. Nevertheless, when compared to neighboring municipalities, Lawrence was unique. With the help of some charismatic elders, young George Walker grew to understand how to effectively navigate the hypocrisy of the American social order, so that he could use the institutionalized underestimation of Blackness as a source of power to subvert and dismantle its stigma in the United States.

George Walker's maternal grandmother, Sarah Hayden (1834 to 1907), was born in Boone County, Kentucky, and was the property of a local farmer, either John Brady or Isham Majors, who moved her to Harrisonville in Cass County, Missouri. While in bondage, she gave birth to two children, Sanford in 1856 and George's mother, Alice, on January 11, 1857. It is likely that both children were fathered by a man named Spencer who was born in Virginia and lived on the neighboring Hayden plantation. Spencer likely died before Sarah and her children stole away during the Civil War.[4] While on the run, she gave birth to another son, named William, in 1865 at a refugee camp at Blue Mound, Wakarusa Township, and they all made their way to Lawrence on New Year's Day, 1866. Soon after, both Sarah and Alice took in laundry and worked as domestics.[5]

George Walker's father, Jerry Nashville Walker, was the third of six children born to Alfred and Eva Walker on May 25, 1847, in Talladega, Alabama. The Walkers were the property of Dr. James Simmons, a local physician, but obtained their freedom before emancipation.[6] Nashville left Talladega at the age of fourteen and served as a body servant for several officers on both sides of the Civil War. After the war he drifted to Texas, then to Lawrence in July of 1867, where, early on, he acted as a guide for buffalo hunters. Eventually, he earned the respect and admiration of prominent Black families in the area, particularly Charles (1817 to 1892) and Mary (1835 to 1915) Langston, the grandparents of Langston Hughes (1901 to 1967).[7]

Details are unclear as to how Nashville Walker and Alice Hayden met, and there is no indication that they were ever married or raised their only child jointly. Regardless, their son, George William Walker, was born on July 15, 1872, in Lawrence.[8] By that time, Nashville had become a porter at the Eldridge House, Lawrence's finest hotel on Massachusetts Street. Given his Civil War experience as a body servant, he was uniquely qualified for the unusually conspicuous and coveted position.[9] During his childhood, George lived with his maternal family on Mississippi Street between Fourth and Fifth Streets in northwestern Lawrence and moved to 1100 Pennsylvania Street in 1888 when he was sixteen. Alice spent some of George's childhood working as a domestic in Pueblo, Colorado, and he spent some time there with her as early as 1881.[10] He later recalled,

> How well I remember, when but a mere boy, my dear, good mother left home and went west to find employment from which she could make money and send home to my grandmother to help her support me. How well I remember grandmother's delight when messages, accompanied with money, would come from my dear mother. Then when mother would return home to joys and delights there were in our humble little home, when I used to sit and listen to the wholesome conversation between my mother and grandmother, and how they used to teach me to tell the truth, and be honest and make a good man, and be of usefulness in the world.[11]

Perhaps Alice helped to inspire her son to be a performer. In the spring of 1884, she played the lead role in a well-received yet unprofitable production of *Queen Esther* at the local Bowersock Opera House.[12]

Although the quality and quantity of contact between father and son is unknown, Nashville Walker truly understood the kind of world his son inherited:

> When my boy was born, I began to think. I wondered what the future held for him. While it was true that slavery was now a thing of the past, it was also true that my race had a most

terrible struggle to face in that there was but little hope for opportunities in a land still rife with bitterness and race hatred, with no chance for education and conditions but little better than they were before the war, excepting that slavery was now voluntary rather than forced. I had managed to pick up a little education myself, having studied diligently, and could read and write to a considerable extent.[13]

Likewise, his sense of Black nationalism was a major influence on his son. Later in life, Nashville told an interviewer,

> Southern white people like the Negro—even love the Negro—in his capacity as a domicile, frolicsome, light-hearted, laughing, faithful servitor. The affection between the "old families" in the south and the "old black folks" is marketed and quite touching. For that matter, the general fact is that the white man, in his capacity as a superior, has a *weakness* for the Negro, but the moment the Negro assumes to exercise the equality he was presumably given by law, the white man flies into a rage. We have, therefore, the extraordinary condition of a race that was remarkable for the faithfulness and docility of its service for 250 years and for the affection its faithfulness and docility inspired in its masters, in one generation of freedom becoming, so it feels and believes, a hatred, abused and browbeaten people, constantly menaced with death and torture. And the Southern white man can hardly discuss the situation calmly; he flares and chokes with rage and turns upon the Northern white man who protests against terrible acts of reprisal and asks, hideously, *"What would you do, if your wife or daughter was ravished by a black fiend?"*[4]

Unlike his father, George remained illiterate until early adulthood, preferring to hone his skills on the streets of Lawrence. He displayed his burgeoning musical talents and entrepreneurial spirit at age five when he established the town's first bootblack stand, a common occupation for poor children, particularly those who had little access to other forms of work in factories or on farms. George made the most of his prospects by singing, dancing, and selling papers along with shining shoes. As part of a growing Black presence in town (about 17.5 percent in 1877), he conveniently located himself outside the Eldridge House, where his father worked.

12 | The Rediscovery of George "Nash" Walker

Because Nashville Walker was well-liked, most people referred to George as little or young "Nash." However, the town's gentry also remembered him as a "ragged street urchin" and "one of the most worthless and pestiferous little 'niggers' that ever lived in Lawrence," monikers that many retracted after he became famous.[15] Young Nash sometimes partnered with Cornelius Carter (ca. 1872 to 1944) to shine shoes, and between them they carried a bottle for moistening their rags with a bold label that read "Nigger spit rots shoes; we use water." He was also known for stuffing a whole pie in his mouth and letting people crack walnuts on his head. During that time, his grandmother began to call young Nash her "Chocolate Drop."[16]

The education young Nash gained through his experiences on Massachusetts Street and by observing his father's interactions with elite Whites at the Eldridge afforded him unprecedented visibility in Lawrence and access

Figure 1.1. "The Rediscovery of George (Nash) Walker." *Source: Evening World* (New York), November 1, 1905, 11.

to some liberties that were otherwise denied to most Black children. As a result, he took little to no interest in attending school, although he fondly recalled the Chapel School during his adult life.[17] Instead, he spent most of his days hustling for money, getting into mischief, and sowing the seeds of his future as an elite performer. During that time, he was a sometime porter for Abe Levy, an amateur performer who operated a haberdashery at 821 Massachusetts Street and became a lifelong friend.[18] The elder Nashville Walker moved to Denver in 1879. He became a porter at the Alvord House at Eighteenth and Larimer Street and established the Colorado African Colonization Company, an institution that was dedicated to repatriating Afro-Americans to Liberia, on March 11, 1885.[19]

During Nash Walker's childhood, Charles Langston, a former abolitionist who was deeply involved in local Republican politics, operated a grocery store on Massachusetts Street in Lawrence, less than two blocks from the Eldridge House. With such a small degree of separation from the Langstons, young Nash learned there was real work to be done on behalf of Afro-Americans and that his lack of liberty in the United States was simply an opportunity disguised in work clothes. He was especially close in age to the Langstons' daughter, Carolyn (Hughes Clark, 1873 to 1938), mother of Langston Hughes, and "used to loaf around music stores when he ought to have been at work," where he learned some music from her brother, Nat Turner Langston.[20] Young Nash also "sung in the pool halls for a living" and in Black-owned businesses operated by Mark Freeman as well as Daniel and Curtis Stone's saloon on North Vermont Street.[21] William Allen White worked at the *Lawrence Journal* in 1887 and later recalled that "Nash was the singanddanciest [sic] colored boy in Lawrence . . . Nash used to come around and sing and we gave him a bit of lunch."[22] In 1917, he also remembered,

> Nash never tried to kill us. But he sat at the reporter's desk and grinned that incandescent smile of his while a drunken printer with a long-bladed knife came in one mid-night, while Nash was sharing our lunch, and chased us all over the room, out into the business office and through the [stockroom]. Nash certainly had a sense of humor and the thought of a printer killing us, who had no special grievance other than that we had asked him for a quarter he had borrowed, while good and virtuous [burglars] whom we had libeled and slandered, had failed to wing us—the subtle humor of that situation certainly did give Nash a few merry moments.[23]

The Ways of Minstrelsy

Along with hustling and performing near the Eldridge House, Nash likely attended several of the minstrel shows that played in Lawrence. Minstrelsy had been the benchmark for popular entertainment in the United States following the advent of T. D. Rice's Jim Crow dance in 1828. Tradition has it that Rice observed a disabled enslaved man's walk in a stable that inspired him to buy the man's clothing, blacken his skin with burnt cork, and perform his version of it along with the song "Jump Jim Crow." Rice's imitation was extremely successful and marked the beginning of what would become a worldwide fascination with blackface minstrelsy. Eventually, the term "Jim Crow" became synonymous with the body of legislation that was aimed specifically at excluding Afro-Americans from equal access to the Bill of Rights for the majority of the twentieth century. As a result of Rice's successful exploitation of Negro stereotype, minstrelsy became a fad that metastasized into a tradition of exaggerated, out-of-context mockery under the cloak of satire that endured throughout George Walker's professional life and beyond. The result was that White audience members were spoon-fed a highly curated and idealized atmosphere for the Negro that had little to do with reality; Black humanity was showcased as something to be begged, borrowed, and bemused for profit for everyone but Blacks. Therefore, some young Black people of that generation were compelled to test the limits of their liberty on a daily basis, often at their own peril. Contained in it was a "damned if you do, damned if you don't" kind of existence in which the minstrelized images of sexually dysfunctional, dimwitted, fearful, superstitious, and petty Negroes tried myriad ways to fit into the White world but could not. By extension, their failing attempts were to be met with laughter tinged with condescension disguised as pathos.

 Central to the institution of minstrelsy was the notion that, no matter how bad things were or seemed to be, Blacks were happy with their lot in life and accepted the "natural order" of things. This was evidenced by the stereotypical compulsion to break into song and dance at seemingly every opportunity, especially if there was some work to be done or if a more serious matter should take precedent. In that atmosphere, the virtue of Whiteness was confirmed and reaffirmed simply by comparison. To make matters worse, Black performers were almost entirely excluded from the commercial gains associated with minstrelsy because most minstrel performers were immigrants from Ireland. Therefore, in the hands of White practitioners, many of whom had little or no access to Black culture, the incompleteness of minstrel stereotypes was imprinted into the cultural fabric of the Western world. Any successful attempt to the contrary was an exception to the rule rather than a precedent or benchmark for future generations to build upon toward lasting equity. The effect was devastating, and Black performers have been burdened with its legacy in perpetuity in the United States.[24]

Given that minstrels, managers, and advance agents often stayed at the Eldridge House, young Nash could have readily obtained free tickets from them or the newspapermen across the street who received complimentary tickets in exchange for local promotion. Moreover, young Nash participated in the noonday parades down Massachusetts Street that preceded the performances. In early January of 1881, when he was nine years old, Nash led the parade for McIntyre and Heath's Great Southern Minstrels during a terrible windstorm. As remembered by James McIntyre (1857 to 1937) some forty years later, "In our parade that day in Lawrence, a little negro was carrying one of the banners in the street parade. The wind picked up the banner and the little negro and blew them clear across Massachusetts Street. . . . It was 'Nash' Walker. He made his start with us that day."[25]

Nash also remembered those developmental moments with fondness. Traditionally, interactions with working performers provided the kind of tutelage that could not be learned in any school. Further, performers were among the first Afro-Americans to assert their liberty in three important ways; they traveled relatively freely and chose their profession and their sexual partners. Theirs was a new, worldly perspective that was admired by some and despised by others as they ferried news between somewhat isolated Afro-American communities throughout the South and Western territories.[26] For Nash and many of his contemporaries, it was an enticing proposition and a potential vehicle to financial and cultural independence that, given the alternative, was a path with less resistance.

The most important Black minstrel to visit Lawrence during Nash Walker's childhood was Billy Kersands (ca. 1842 to 1915), who appeared regularly at Liberty Hall (renamed Bowersock Opera House after 1882) from July 1873 through August 1890 with C. W. Pringle's Original Georgia Minstrels.[27] As one of the few Black performers who bucked minstrel traditions by not using burnt cork, Kersands was known for wearing outlandish outfits and stuffing things into his abnormally large mouth when he wasn't singing, dancing, or telling jokes. While it remains unclear whether Walker met Kersands in Lawrence when he was a child, they eventually became very good friends, and many of the earliest photographs of George Walker in costume show a remarkable similarity in his appearance to Kersands. Furthermore, Kersands often encouraged talented young people to pursue their dreams of transcendence via the stage, something George also did throughout his professional life. It is also possible that young Nash made the acquaintance of the Hyers Sisters, Emma Louise (ca. 1857 to 1901) and Anna Madah (ca. 1855 to 1929); the latter was briefly married to George Freeman, a local cornetist.[28] The Hyers Sisters were supremely talented singers and offered a unique theatrical experience beyond the novelty of minstrelsy. Several of their productions also included Sam Lucas (1840 to 1916), the first Afro-American to play Tom in *Uncle Tom's Cabin*, which was presented in Lawrence on March 2, 1882. As reported in the *Lawrence Daily Journal*, "the songs, dances and rapid transformations by Sam Lucas during an intermission were received with universal applause."[29]

Adolescence

As Nash Walker approached his teens, he entertained University of Kansas students, leading to his selection as the cheerleader for the Phi Delta Theta baseball club, where he earned twenty-five cents a day and "accompanied them upon many of their escapades."[30] He and his friends George Hart (1872 to 1918) and Cornelius Carter also spent a lot of time exploring all sides of life as typical truant boys, which included run-ins with Officer Jim Monroe, whom Nash gave "many a hot chase down the alleys 'just off' Winthrop [Seventh] St."[31] Known for his foot speed, his future partner, Bert Williams (1874 to 1922), once recalled, "Why, way back in Kansas, when the larder got low, Walker would go out in the wheat fields, start a rabbit, and run him till his ankles caught fire, and, while the rabbit was burnin' up, grab him."[32]

Through it all, there were plenty of reminders of the reality of Blackness in the United States, especially when Pete Vinegar, George Robertson, and Ike King were lynched on June 9, 1882, at the Kaw River Bridge, where young Nash and many other children liked to swim.[33] Although he was likely not present at the lynching, he certainly heard about it as a cautionary tale of the lack of Black access to liberty even in the safe haven of Lawrence. Nonetheless, as an adult he regularly expressed unwavering love for his hometown:

> Having been born in the town of Lawrence in the State of bleeding Kansas, it was my good fortune all of my life to be associated with white children who had never been trained to look at the complexion of the human skin with suspicion, therefore I can truthfully say, that they have no race or color prejudice, against me. And, as a child I played with white children and was treated

merely as a child and treated other children as children usually treated each other. We played and frolicked about the town of Lawrence together and that was all there was to it. Having left Lawrence at a very early age to seek my fame and fortune in the world . . . I have had to battle against a prejudice called, race prejudice. This prejudice I have not found to be a superstition at all, but a misconception of the truth, for all humanity is one and the same.[34]

Like in other US towns, Lawrence's newest residents were compelled to establish their own separate places for worship. In spring 1883, what was to become Warren (Ninth) Street Baptist Church was purchased. The limestone church provided a much safer place for the expression of ideas, creativity, spirituality, and humanity than one might dare to express in the outer world. Nash Walker's maternal relatives were members, and his mother regularly sang solos during services. Along with traditional worship, the church hosted Charles Langston's Inter-State Literary Society in 1898, where political and social topics were discussed in secret.[35]

Young Nash took part in his fair share of mischief, some of which was reported in local papers. In 1889, when he was seventeen, he and Will Copeland (1872 to 1939) were convicted of stealing tobacco and $2.55 from Zook's Grocery, a popular gathering spot for young Black men. They were given six months each in the "Hotel de Love" (the county jail, colloquially named after Sheriff Love) and put to work on the rockpile. When reflecting upon his youth, he once wrote, "I must admit that I know of only two good things concerning myself. First: I have never been in state prison. Second: I don't know why I haven't."[36] Eventually, Nash waited tables in Lawrence and tried his mettle in Leavenworth and in Kansas City, where he sold the *Kansas City Star* and *Times* newspapers on Fifth Street.[37] During his time there, he befriended Joe Howard (ca. 1879 to 1961), a future vaudevillian who became famous for the hit song "Hello! Ma Baby." At the time, Howard was a destitute runaway; Nash brought him back to Lawrence to live and even paid for his music lessons.[38]

Quack College

Quacks, fakirs, hucksters, and medicine men were commonplace in the late nineteenth century, particularly in the rural towns of the western states, where townspeople were somewhat isolated and hungry for entertainment as well as a cure for their various ailments. If they were lucky, they got both. More often, they were hoodwinked at best or sickened by the "Doc's" concoctions at worst, after the quack was long gone and likely pulling the same flimflam on unsuspecting townies somewhere else. Despite the inherent dangers of the profession, the itinerant lifestyle appealed to young Nash, who desperately wanted to leave Lawrence and make his mark. He later wrote,

> There were many quack doctors doing business in the West. They traveled from one town to another in wagons, and gave shows in order to get large crowds of people together, so as to sell medicine. When a boy, I was quite an entertainer. I could sing and dance, and was good at face-making, beating the tambourine and rattling the bones. I was not lacking in courage and did not hesitate to ask the quacks for a job. First one and then the other hired me. When we arrived in a town and our show started, I was generally the first to attract attention.[39]

He also later recalled, "The first money I ever earned doing what we now call a vaudeville turn was on a wooden platform for Dr. Blank's Cure-em-While-You-Wait Dandelion Tonic. For the songs and dances I got 25 cents and took the rest in tonic."[40] Lawrence's eastern Kansas location made it a mainstay for the most ambitious hucksters of the region, and Abe Levy may have introduced Nash to a Black quack named Doc Warwick.[41] Young Nash struck out with him as a barker, the person who attracted patrons with jokes, songs, dances, and fast talking in anticipation of more excitement to come. At first, the young greenhorn was frightened of Warwick's anatomical charts, and explanations from the "Doc" only made things worse. However, soon after joining Warwick's wagon, Nash appeared in a song and dance role on the corner of Fifth and Main Streets in Kansas City, where he had previously sold papers. He did so well that Warwick took him on a tour of several eastern Kansas towns.[42] Upon his return to Lawrence, Nash expanded on what he learned and worked to further distinguish himself as the best dancer in town.

Likely, in the spring of 1889, Nash left Lawrence for Chicago, where he found no work as a performer. To support himself, he took odd jobs as a porter for a saloon and may have been a bellhop at the Great Northern Hotel:

Figure 1.2. "Arcade Minstrels." *Source: Lawrence Daily Journal*, December 8, 1891, 4.

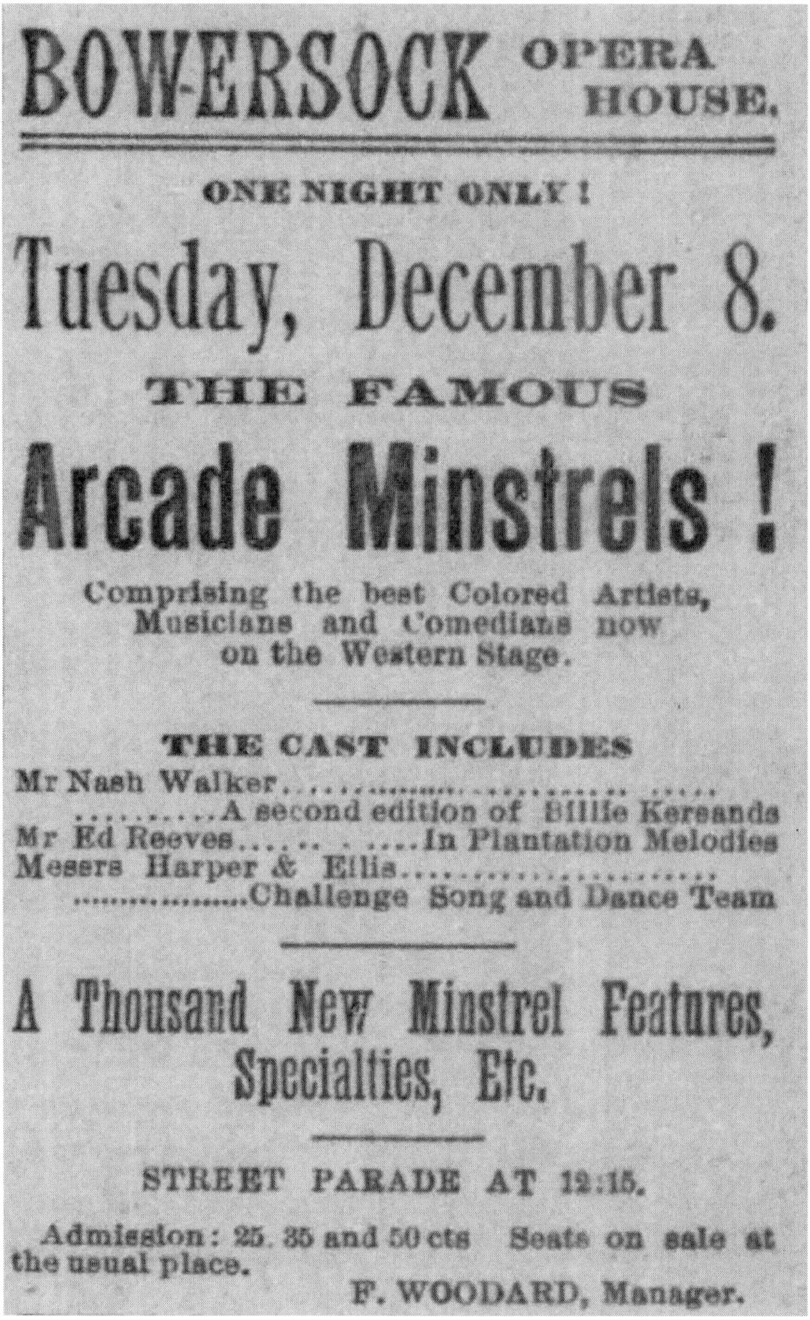

BOWERSOCK OPERA HOUSE.

ONE NIGHT ONLY!

Tuesday, December 8.

THE FAMOUS

Arcade Minstrels!

Comprising the best Colored Artists, Musicians and Comedians now on the Western Stage.

THE CAST INCLUDES

Mr Nash Walker................................A second edition of Billie Kersands
Mr Ed Reeves....................In Plantation Melodies
Messrs Harper & Ellis..........................Challenge Song and Dance Team

A Thousand New Minstrel Features, Specialties, Etc.

STREET PARADE AT 12:15.

Admission: 25, 35 and 50 cts   Seats on sale at the usual place.

F. WOODARD, Manager.

> I was working in a Chicago theatre as one of the scene shifters. It was there that I got into the habit of dancing to every air that I heard played by the [orchestra]. When the warm weather came along in Chicago, they used to help the business along by giving amateur night performances, when any person was allowed to make his or her appearance for the entertainment of the crowds. I used to stand in the wings and laughed myself sick at them, but I never had any intention of trying myself, though I was a good dancer.[43]

A report in the *Lawrence Daily Journal* indicated the saloon where George worked gave roof-garden performances every night, and one night each week was set apart as "amateurs" night. However, he may have first performed at a dime museum operated by C. E. Kohl and Middleton, where the amateur acts were notoriously bad. Nevertheless, success was elusive, but that did not diminish his resolve. Having survived a crash course in the basics of the theatre business, stage work, and what the public wanted to see, he had nothing to lose and pressed on.[44] Although Chicago was pivotal to the development of his business acumen and prowess as a performer, lack of regular work forced him to return to Lawrence.

In December of 1891, nineteen-year-old Nash Walker got his first big break in Lawrence with the Arcade Minstrels, named for the Arcade Saloon, where he was billed as "The Second Coming of Billy Kersands." They paraded down Massachusetts Street in the afternoon and performed banjo solos, guitar, and mandolin duets that night. Newspapers urged audiences to "go see Nash Walker and Jessie Hunter in their sporting song and dance," while the *Times-Observer* wrote, "So far Nash Walker has been their star, and it is said that he came as near imitating a monkey as a man could come to it."[45] Although successful, he knew that his fortune was to be made somewhere other than his beloved Lawrence, a place where he sought refuge to rest and recharge throughout his life.

Chapter 2

Partners in Double Consciousness

1892 to 1893

Following the success of the Arcade Minstrels, Nash was hired by a quack named Dr. Waite for fifty cents a night. The job also called for men to stand on his chest and sometimes to stab him with pins.[1] He remembered, "My experience with the quack doctors taught me two good lessons: that white people are always interested in what they call 'darky' singing and dancing; and the fact that I could entertain in that way as no white boy could, made me valuable to the quack doctors as an advertising card."[2] He stayed with Waite's organization until they reached San Francisco, likely in early 1892. At the time, it was a rambunctious place where violence was common and one could easily end up in a life-threatening situation without much effort. As George recalled, "the Westerners were good-hearted, but a bit rough and ready. I had to rough it, and rough it I did."[3] Likewise, San Francisco's come-what-may atmosphere embraced the Industrial Age shift from a rural-farm-based ethos into urban modernity to a greater degree than more established cities in the East. Fueled by a busy port, full of travelers, sailors, and merchants who had money to spend, the city hosted hundreds of bars and theatres where enterprising young entertainers could test their mettle. With sixty cents in his pocket, George went to several theatre managers to look for work, and when he found none, he wandered to Market and O'Farrell Street. There, he later recalled, "came the advent of my life. As it was, here I met my partner, Bert Williams. We decided to double up and do a vaudeville stunt."[4]

Enter Bert Williams

Egbert Austin "Bert" Williams's (1874 to 1922) foreign birth into a Bahamian family of both African and European heritage facilitated a philosophical detachment from the Afro-American experience that allowed objective observation, interpretation, and personification of Black humanity on stage that no White minstrel could duplicate. After his family left the Bahamas and settled in an established Afro-American community in Florida when he was a child, Bert quickly learned to navigate between two different yet inexplicably intertwined worlds. Somewhat free of the cultural baggage of minstrelsy, he possessed a bit of an advantage as an interpreter and delineator of the Afro-American experience, which he exploited throughout his life:

> Along the street where we lived there were outdoor booths, where old colored mammies sold sweet potato pie. It used to be a favorite haunt of mine, for I loved the pie they made, but I never had money to buy any, so I would begin at the first booth in the row and go up and gaze at the counter of pies.
>
> My mouth would begin to water, and my eyes would get big, and sad looking, and I'd try to mesmerize a pie—why, I guess I almost cried with internal longing and mental hunger, but after I had begged with my eyes long enough the owner of the pies would say; "Bless you' heaht, honey, aint yo' had no suppah?"
>
> "No'm," I'd say, still looking starved and pathetic. Then I'd get a big slice of good old sweet potato pie.[5]

Bert's success inspired him to continue to develop his skills, while his natural shyness compelled him to maintain a certain measure of personal distance. After the family relocated to Riverside, California, he became a master of observation and continuously absorbed the Afro-American experience as lived by the people he encountered. According to his friend Booker T. Washington (1856 to 1915), "I have noticed him standing about in a barber shop or among a crowd of ordinary colored people, the quietest man in the whole gathering. All the time, however, he was studying and observing, enjoying the characters that he saw around him and getting material for some of those quaint songs and stories in which he reproduces the natural humor and philosophy of the Negro people."[6] In time, Bert's ability to elicit pathos, sympathy, and empathy allowed him to take his audience on an emotional rollercoaster ride. He later remarked, "The sight of other people in trouble is nearly always funny. . . . The man with the real sense of humor is the man who can put himself in the spectator's place and laugh at his own misfortunes."[7]

Unfortunately, few details of the first three years of the budding partnership survive. Likewise, the details of Bert and George's initial meeting vary, depending on who recalled it as well as when and to whom the story was related, but it was likely on March 31, 1892.[8] Shortly before he met George, Bert had performed in logging and mining camps along the West Coast with three White men. He reached San Francisco "without a stitch of clothing" and burned his ragged raiment to avoid a confrontation with the police.[9] According to Bert, he was about to begin a tour with a minstrel show he was stage managing and was tasked with finding an end man. Finding no success, he decided to engage the first Colored man he met. When he made it to Market and O'Farrell Street, Bert saw a young, short man wearing a corset coat, a jockey hat, and a club with "a set of teeth like an ivory grove."[10] He further explained, "We came together almost by accident. . . . I asked him where I could find a certain fellow that I wished to get for the opposite end to me. We could not find him, and then I turned to George and said: 'What's the use of looking any longer? You're the right man, anyhow.' And he surely proved to be."[11] George recalled meeting "a gaunt fellow over six feet of orange hue and about 18 years of age, leaning on a banjo, haggling with a manager," who hired him at seven dollars a week.[12]

He also remembered how they determined the order of their billing: "At first it was 'Me and Bert'—that is to say, in the beginning it was Walker and Williams. After a while, my all too-troublesome modesty maybe gave Bert a chance to flip a quarter (or maybe a nickel), to see whose name should be first on the bill. That is how it became Bert and me. How it remained Bert and me is a catalog of strenuousness—I mean the first part is."[13] Although Bert later claimed to have recruited George for Martin and Selig's Mastodon Minstrels in California, no evidence survives. However, there was an aggregation called Martin and Selig's Colored Minstrels that toured California's Central Valley and coast during the fall of 1893. Bert described the company as a small, wagon-driven, integrated group of Black, White, and Mexican performers. He said they stayed with that troupe for five months at eight dollars a week, although they were paid only three times.[14] The spartan circumstances on that tour called upon Bert to double on a brass horn and George on the snare drum in the band for parades.

Their first engagement was at Gibbon's Hall, San Jose, on September 19, 1893. That night, the show bombed, and they were forced to improvise. George remembered, "[Bert's] appearance got him a big laugh, and we did some dancing and I tried to make fun of him about going to the theatre, and the crowd warmed up to us." They sang "See Yer Colored Man," most likely with Bert playing banjo and George singing and dancing.[15] At the time, Bert was more polished than George, who had yet to develop as a singer and was quite self-conscious. Their friend and collaborator James Weldon Johnson (1871 to 1938) noted that "at the time[,] George could not sing alone, he faked along with B[e]rt for years."[16]

The company worked its way south and performed in Redlands, a farming community adjacent to Bert's adopted hometown of Riverside, before they began their return northward. A period source mentioned that Bert and George were part of a trio and quartet made up of the Black members of the cast. One member was Bert's roommate, "Griff" Wilson, a contortionist who took ill and returned to San Francisco early. Another account named acrobats Walter Hill and William Sweet in a quartet with Bert and George that performed in Riverside, likely on an off night when the company was in Redlands.[17] However, the show was not well received. To the "small audience of disgusted spectators" in Hanford, "It was the poorest excuse for a minstrel show at this city has witnessed for several years," and the show was stranded.[18] Bert and George found work at the only theatre in town before setting out again with a local hog farmer and would-be theatrical manager. That too failed, and their manager regularly called on his son at the family farm to sell hogs to make payroll, until the farm was reduced to twenty hogs, which forced the show to close. Shortly after, they made their way back to San Francisco, as one reviewer put it, "sadder, poorer, and wiser."[19] Times were trying, but the new partners developed a mutual respect and admiration that lasted the rest of their lives. Although there were still many more salad days ahead, each lesson learned from their experiences illuminated their path toward unprecedented success.

Following their first tour, Bert and George worked as dishwashers in a San Francisco restaurant and entertained their coworkers in the kitchen after work. One night, Jack Cremorne, a prominent vaudeville manager on the Midway, heard them and gave them a trial turn and a job as janitors. Rivaled only by the Bella Union, the Midway was a second-floor venue at 771 Market between Third and Fourth Streets where drinks were sold in the smoke-filled auditorium every night. The Midway played host to "many a knock-down, drag-out brawl—along with some exciting new dance fads."[20] According to George, "we went on at 1:30 p.m., and were quite satisfied if committed to come off at 4 a.m. We gave a continuous performance by ourselves." They became regulars and earned "enough to buy ham and eggs."[21]

At the time, Black people were a novelty on stage like nearly everything in vaudeville. Although directly related to minstrelsy, vaudeville was a more varied form of entertainment in which anything new that provided a shock or a laugh or tugged at the heartstrings was included. Programs could contain music, comedy, child and animal acts, recitations, high drama, opera singers, acrobats, dancers, comedians, "freaks," strongmen, marksmen, and others. Moreover, vaudeville theatres appealed directly to working-class and immigrant clientele, unlike typical opera houses, so raunchy humor, often based on stereotypes of various ethnic groups, cross-dressing, gender-bending, and the inversion of cultural norms, was commonplace. Because Blacks were limited to the balcony, "Nigger Heaven," if allowed at all in vaudeville theatres, minstrel humor proliferated, and most acts lasted between ten and twenty minutes. Performers could present a dozen times a day, and often a person could purchase a cheap seat and stay as long as they wanted. Because of the variety, short acts, and quick changeovers, Mark Twain's popular notion on San Francisco weather became the motto: "If you don't like what you see, wait a few minutes."[22]

Vaudeville theatres were ripe with free information, and George later recalled,

> About this time a question began to agitate our gray matter. It came of going to see the work of other actors, white and colored, as came out our way. We noticed that colored men had to be comedians and athletic comedians at that. Headstands, flip-flaps, and such "stunts" made up a large part of their performance. And we noticed that white performers came serenely on, spoke at peace serenely and marched serenely off to the office and serenely took down four or five times what the colored man's exertions yielded. So we figured: the white man gets the desired results without perspiring—why?[23]

The situation inspired George to dream of new spaces for Black art and control of Black cultural products:

> When we were not working[,] we frequented the playhouses just the same. In those days black-faced white comedians were numerous and very popular. They billed themselves "coons."

Bert and I watched the white "coons," and were often much amused at seeing white men with black cork on their faces trying to imitate black folks. Nothing about these white men's actions was natural, and therefore nothing was as interesting as if black performers had been dancing and singing their own songs in their own way.

There were many more barriers in the way of the black performer in those days than there are now, because, with the exception of the negro minstrels, the black entertainer was little known throughout the Northern and Western States. The opposition on account of racial and color prejudices and the white comedians who 'blacked up' stood in the way of the natural black performer, and petty jealousies common among professional people also greatly retarded the artistic progress of the Afro-American.

. . . Black-faced White comedians used to make themselves look as ridiculous as they could when portraying a "darkey" character. In their "make-up" they always had tremendously big red lips, and their costumes were rightfully exaggerated. The one fatal result of this to the colored performers was that they imitated the white performers in their make-up as "darkies." Nothing seemed more absurd than to see a colored man making himself ridiculous in order to portray himself.[24]

A Fortuitous Fair

By the time Bert and George made it back to San Francisco from their first tour, there was a new buzz in town about a Midwinter Fair slated to be open from January 27 to July 4, 1894. The fair was intended to duplicate the success of Chicago's Columbian Exhibition of 1893. The local captains of industry and San Francisco's town fathers hoped to end a crippling recession and bring vitality to the Barbary Coast à la the days of the forty-niners. Modeled after the Paris fair of 1889, the wildly successful Chicago offering commemorated the four hundredth anniversary of Christopher Columbus's "discovery" of the New World. It was the largest event of its kind in the United States to date and showcased monuments to nationalism, ingenuity, industrial technology, and consumerism. Chief among the exhibits was a garish display of White supremacy provided by the spoils of the British and French colonial empires, notably a display of Dahomeyans from French-controlled West Africa (present-day Benin and Nigeria) in a zoo-like enclosure. The man behind the exhibit was a French-born huckster named Xavier Pené, who spent most of his life as a trader in West Africa.[25] Due to objections from the Protestant town mothers of Chicago, the Dahomeyan Village was separated from the official fairgrounds by a railroad line. Designed to embody all the sinful pleasures of the era, much like a sideshow at a circus, the exhibits offset much of the cost of the opulent buildings on the fairgrounds.

Like blackface minstrelsy, the purpose of the Dahomeyans was to provide an atmosphere where White people could both eat their cake and have it. Several requirements that fit the anthropological beliefs of the day were used to construct a "faithful" representation of a Dahomeyan village, including portrayals of military maneuvers, savagery, inverted gender roles, and religious rites, along with jewelry to be sold in the gift shop.[26] As a result of contractual and institutional inequities, the Africans and their Afro-American comrades seized opportunities to transform the situation into a theatre of resistance and, in some cases, outright defiance. Following complaints from Ida B. Wells (1862 to 1931) and Frederick Douglass (1818 to 1895), among others, a Colored People's Day was scheduled for August 25, 1893. While it was deemed a sufficient compromise by the fair organizers, Afro-American activists viewed it as an empty gesture. In response, Douglass seized the opportunity to do what he did best: tell White people about themselves via a detailed explanation of the hypocrisy of the status quo through every newspaper that would print his opinion.[27] Among the dozens of promising young Afro-Americans who participated in Colored People's Day were James Weldon and J. Rosamond Johnson (1873 to 1954); composer, playwright, and comedian Bob Cole (1868 to 1911); and Douglass's secretary, the poet Paul Laurence Dunbar (1872 to 1906), whom Douglass introduced to the composer Will Marion Cook (1869 to 1944). Although he could not have known it at the time, Douglass's gesture of fellowship provided a connection that reverberated throughout the twentieth century and beyond. In keeping with the momentum that began with the writers of the so-called slave narratives, and emboldened by the collective experience of the first migration, Dunbar composed "We Wear the Mask," a treatise on the limited palate of choices open to Afro-Americans, shortly after Douglass's death in 1895:

> We wear the mask that grins and lies,
> It hides our cheeks and shades our eyes,
> This debt we pay to human guile;
> With torn and bleeding hearts we smile,
> And mouth with myriad subtleties.
>
> Why should the world be over-wise,
> In counting all our tears and sighs?
> Nay, let them only see us, while
> We wear the mask.
>
> We smile, but, O great Christ, our cries
> To thee from tortured souls arise.
> We sing, but oh the clay is vile
> Beneath our feet, and long the mile;
> But let the world dream otherwise,
> We wear the mask![28]

The arrival of the Dahomeyans for the 1893 fair coincided with a terrible omen. A man named Ussugah, who may have been the chief among them, died shortly before reaching Ellis Island at 5:30 p.m. on May 2, 1893. When his compatriots sang to mourn his loss, they "had to be restrained by the employees for decency's sake." They were hustled to a Chicago-bound train, and Ussugah was buried in the potter's field at Green-Wood Cemetery in Brooklyn.[29] Chicago newspapers extended a similarly cold welcome to the Africans, who were wholly unprepared for the weather, lack of hospitality, and racism. On top of the poor reception, Xavier Pené did not engage well with the press. *The Inter Ocean* reported, "They say the natives are not very pleasant people to get along with, but they are angels when compared with the man who does not care a blank for newspaper mention."[30] However, the Dahomeyans did their best to comply under the inhumane conditions. By September, the impending cooler fall weather and their treatment on the Midway inspired the Dahomeyans to return home rather than remain in the United States for the coming Midwinter Fair in San Francisco.[31] However, their presence was so desired that Director General Michael H. de Young traveled to Chicago to meet with Pené to finalize a deal that called for him to acquire more Dahomeyans so "the international character and success of the California Midwinter Exposition [was] assured."[32] In the meantime, Afro-Americans, including Bert and George, were hired as placeholders. As fate would have it, the brief, seemingly innocuous encounters between Africans and Afro-Americans would for a short period of time fuel a cultural juggernaut, in which the new partners would be at the leading edge for nearly two decades.

Ragtime: The "New" Music

Although Afro-American culture was largely unknown to White America and the music was very limited within the fairgrounds, Chicago's 1893 fair provided an opportunity to make a lasting contribution to American popular culture. Along with the official debut of all things fashionable, mechanical, and industrial at the Chicago fair, a uniquely Afro-American contribution made an unscheduled and unofficial entrance from underground. Ragtime—an exciting, "new" music where melody and harmony were expressed through interwoven, improvised, syncopated rhythms and counterpoint—was heard by Whites en masse for the first time in the bars and bordellos along Stony Island Avenue. According to the sociologist Monroe Nathan Work (1866 to 1945), "as far back as 1875 Negroes in questionable resorts along the Mississippi had commenced to evolve this musical figure, but at the World's Fair in Chicago 'ragtime' got a running start and swept the Americas, next to Europe, and today the craze has not diminished."[33]

The distinction between *inside* and *outside* of the fairgrounds was important because it exemplified the burden of postemancipation Afro-American life. On the inside, especially on Colored People's Day, an operatic interpretation of *Uncle Tom's Cabin* composed by Will Cook was featured along with classical adaptations of "plantation melodies" from the Fisk Jubilee Singers, Standard Quartet, Hampton Quartet, and others.[34] Those meticulously curated performances were meant to serve as marketing and fundraising tools to demonstrate the potential of recently emancipated Afro-Americans to White elites. Clear diction was paramount, and all arrangements adhered strictly to the Western classical tradition as to not draw the ire of White patrons. Via the minstrel tradition, syncopated rhythm had grown in popularity among White theatregoers, so it was selectively included in many of the carefully curated pieces. Unfortunately, acceptability was the prime concern, over merit or legitimacy, so the syncopation was quite tame, and the repertoire was limited to so-called plantation melodies, hymns, and patriotic and minstrel songs. As a result, the cultural disingenuousness of Jubilee ensembles became the preferred vehicle of Afro-American ambassadorship and upward mobility among those who had the means to attend Black-serving universities.[35]

Outside of the fairgrounds, there was ragtime, a multilayered, polyrhythmic, and heavily syncopated expression that encouraged virtuosity and highlighted the uniqueness of a given practitioner's ability to improvise into and out of familiar and unfamiliar melodic tropes. In its "natural" environment, ragtime paid little attention to the needs, wants, and desires of White patrons in favor of glorification and control of the moment and cultural potency. To that end, ragtime was a far more genuine and honest expression of the Afro-American experience than much of what was allowed on the fairgrounds. Despite official oversight aimed to prevent it, ragtime pioneers including Scott Joplin (1868 to 1917), who appeared with the Texas Medley Quartet, and pianists Jesse Pickett (1875 to ca. 1910), Shepard "Shep" Edmonds (1876 to 1957), and others were seen and heard by White people for the first time. Despite its lack of inclusion, the music took Chicago's White fair patrons by storm.[36] According to Will Cook, "the public was tired of the sing-song, samey, monotonous, mother, sister, father sentimental songs. Ragtime offered unique rhythms, curious groupings of words and melodies which gave the zest of unexpectedness."[37]

With real potential for popular influence and unprecedented amounts of money from this "new" music, ragtime practitioners unofficially became the favored cultural ambassadors of the Afro-American diaspora over the jubilee ensembles. Intrinsically, the music and the people who created it were uniquely suited to convert the system's built-in underestimation of Black ingenuity into an advantage and to, in George's words, "gently [pry them] loose and from the cash box" to build wealth.[38] The next step involved bringing the music to the marketplace and keeping as much of the money in Black pockets as possible. Another "catalog of strenuousness," as George described it later in life.[39]

The popularity of ragtime at the Chicago fair revealed the overriding conundrum for Black musicians for generations to come: The music as expressed within the emerging Afro-American tradition had to be entirely different from what was translated, transposed, fixed on a sheet of paper, and sold to consumers whose closest proximity to Black culture was the minstrel show and the remote control of White exceptionalism. As with all products of Afro-American culture, an important distinction emerged between ragtime as *lived* and ragtime as *sold*. Ragtime as sold, much like jubilee, was designed to be accessible as a novelty to Whites, to be played the same way every time as in the Western classical tradition. That measure of success meant the intricacies and complexity of rhythm and harmony that were heard in the traditional setting had to be simplified for the sake of accessibility and profit. Ragtime as lived was played in such a way that it was recognizable as one piece or another but could be infinitely varied at the whim and pleasure of its practitioner, much like its more influential descendant, jazz, which followed the same basic philosophy of expression. James Hubert "Eubie" Blake, the longest lived of the original ragtime practitioners, discussed the virtuosity of Black musicians in his hometown of Baltimore: "These men were what they used to call 'piano sharks.' These guys could play! And only one of that group (that I know of), Shout Blake could read music. The rest of them couldn't read, but they could all play in any key."[40] As with their jazz descendants, ragtime practitioners were conduits of a craft that called on them to be at the top of their game, adaptable, charismatic, and willing to express themselves under duress or threat of bodily injury. The ragtime music buyer knew little to nothing of the reality faced by Black musicians; they mostly wanted new, syncopated music that was foreign, but not so foreign as to be too difficult or offensive. The sheet music that was sold to consumers outside of Afro-American culture facilitated an environment where the player did not improvise in cyclical, interlocking patterns. Instead, the music was made linear, like a march, with a clear introduction and strains with a verse and chorus. Although some White players took ragtime seriously after developing a sincere fondness for it, the music was designed specifically for conspicuous consumption, with its "otherness" being its chief selling point. Within a few years of its introduction, ragtime sheet music would be printed on an industrial scale. As a result, Afro-Americans could participate in the free market and earn money from their cultural and intellectual products despite the zero-sum ideology of the United States in which any prosperity for Afro-Americans was viewed as a net loss for Whites. Regardless, for a hungry young generation of Black entrepreneurs, the environment was ripe for testing the yet-to-be-defined limits of their liberty for the first time in history. One unintended result of Colored People's Day at the Chicago fair was that the many young Black performers began to build a social network. Some of them would soon become tastemakers, often with problematic results that paid dividends for generations, far beyond the short-term financial benefits enjoyed by the original composers and performers of ragtime.

"Sham" Dahomeyans and "Real Coons"

The site for the Dahomey Village within the San Francisco Midwinter Fair's 160 acres in Golden Gate Park was chosen with care.[41] However, it needed to be stocked with a reasonable facsimile of Africans until Xavier Pené could return with authentic replacements. Bert and George were among them and eagerly accepted the first paying opportunity to leave the smoky, violent halls on the Midway. Almost too good to be true, they did next to nothing and said even less, which afforded the partners plenty of time to come up with a plan of success for their future. Local papers understood the ruse and published updates of the "real" Dahomeyans' journey until they arrived on May 25, 1894, just before the village reopened on May 29, which signaled the end of George's easiest job to date.[42] He remembered,

> Having had free access to the fairgrounds, we were permitted to visit the natives from Africa. It was there, for the first time, that we were brought into close touch with native Africans, and the study of those natives interested us very much. We were not long in deciding that if we ever reached the point of having a show of our own, we would delineate and feature native African characters as far as we could, and still remain American, and make our acting interesting and entertaining to American audiences.[43]

Figure 2.1. "Xavier Pené and His Dahomeyan Amazons, Cal. Midwinter Expositi[on]," Isaiah W. Taber, Photographs of the Dahomeyan Village at the California Midwinter Fair, 1894. *Source:* Turner Collection, Special Collections and Archives, University of California, San Diego. Used with permission.

However, the representation of the Dahomeyans in San Francisco papers was in lockstep with Chicago a year earlier: no objective context for the public to interact with the "other," other than to cement the myth of White supremacy. At least one of the Dahomeyans, a man named Tevi, spoke English, French, and German, which surely facilitated meaningful, brief exchanges between the real and the sham Dahomeyans. In meeting those people, Bert and George experienced majesty, sovereignty, and beauty from an African point of view. The Dahomeyans' lack of acknowledgment of White exceptionalism or superiority was wholly new to the duo, and it would inspire them for the rest of their lives. Intrinsically, Bert and George saw an opportunity to expose the theatregoing public to a new world of possibility that could eventually sow seeds of cultural sovereignty. The fundamental component of their strategy was to inspire a new way of thinking among unsuspecting audience members to give rise to reasonable doubt in the accepted notion that the difference between the races was due to Black deficiency. Understandably, it was to be accomplished subversively, hidden within humor and pathos, and implemented slowly over time. Unfortunately, their time with the Africans was short, and by the end of July 1894 the Dahomeyans made their way to Los Angeles, and the partners returned to the grind on the Midway.[44]

In the earliest days of the Williams and Walker partnership, George was the comedian and Bert the straight man.[45] Although their roles would change, they regularly revamped and refined their act, keeping what worked and discarding what didn't. Night after night, they performed and watched others perform in front of audiences that could've attempted to lynch them, as happened twice during their partnership, or showered them with their hard-earned and sometimes ill-gotten gold. The two learned how to read an audience, adapt, and rely upon each other in all environments, and a bond of friendship developed that was soon to become the stuff of legend. As reported by Uncle Rad Kees in the Indianapolis *Freeman*,

> I'm thoroughly convinced that in those days, when ten pennies bought for both a "mincess" pie, when one ham sandwich was a feast for two, and when you could easily tell when both were home by seeing either's shirt hanging on the line—those were the halcyon days! Brothers never stuck closer together, sweethearts were never more loyal to one another, and the cruel winds that have blown many a sad tale of sorrow and sadness only found

them tight and tighter together. As friends, husbands, brothers or wives, they were but one. To hit either meant to kill both, for they could be seen in joy and in misery, in poverty and in pain, sticking, yes, tighter than glue, and with that sturdy, unswerving bulldog tenacity they hung on and on together.[46]

Essential to the developing relationship was the reciprocating component of their personalities. George was feisty, impatient, and full of braggadocio, while Bert preferred to find a middle path or an outright workaround for many of the problems they faced. "Walker was different," according to composer and lyricist Alex Rogers (1876 to 1930), a friend and future collaborator:

> He had not the educational advantages nor the breeding of Williams, but there was a native shrewdness in Walker that made him a very good businessman: that was coupled with an honesty that bespoke a very fine character. George Walker was one of the most generous men and the fairest, squarest dealer in a business transaction that I have ever known. He had the cleverness to see an advantage and to take a legitimate stand for it, but he never took an unfair advantage of anyone.[47]

The differences in their individual temperaments, personalities, and overall approaches to the expression of the human condition allowed for a versatility and refinement of tactics that most other Black performers lacked at the time. Further, their differences played to their collective strength and aided them in their flexibility as they struggled to make space for their names in American households like their White contemporaries. Their bond grew by the day because they knew that there were hazards at every turn and they were stronger together than as individuals. During the early years, they made their own fun when they weren't working, often engaged in a game of smut. Bert remembered,

> Many of my closest friends in those old days were boys about my own age who used to think that I was wonderful. They would hang around until I finished my work at night and then we'd all go over to my house and play cards. No, not for money.

I'm sure the gambling spirit was there and was only not made manifest *because we had no money.*

Instead, we had a sooty plate that we smoked up over the lamp; and the loser of each hand had to smear a daub of soot on his face as a penalty. Then we kids would sit around and howl at the grotesque appearance.[48]

Between games of smut, the small community of young performers discussed their aspirations late into the night. George later recalled how they set out to break the mold:

How to get before the public and prove what ability we might possess was a hard problem for Williams and Walker to solve. We thought that as there seemed to be a great demand for black faces on the stage, we would do all we could to get what we felt belonged to us by the laws of nature. We finally decided that as white men with black faces were billing themselves "coons," Williams and Walker would do well to bill themselves the "Two Real Coons," and so we did. Our bills attracted the attention of managers, and gradually we made our way in.[49]

As "Two Real Coons," Bert and George were not the only Black performers to exploit their "realness" as a drawing card for their performances. Comedian Ernest Hogan (1865 to 1909) performed under the moniker "The Unbleached American," and Matilda Sissieretta Jones (1868 to 1933) went by the name "Black Patti" to signify her Blackness as well as her vocal similarity to the Italian opera singer Adelina Patti. Therefore, when White people paid to see their minstrel-style cooning, they also received Black-curated entertainment, full of universal examples of the human condition told from a uniquely Afro-American perspective. Although still a relative newcomer, George believed the stage could create a wellspring for a new, more accurate perception of the children and grandchildren of the recently emancipated. His dream was simple: Black performers, via superior talent and critical mass, could wean the White theatregoing public off minstrelsy and send what he called "cushion-foot coons" into another profession.[50] Now with a partner, George began to build his network, and together the partners honed their act in anticipation of reaching the top. As remembered by Harrison Stewart (1883 to 1918),

[. . . To] my old friend George Walker, who has sat up many a night telling me of the methods used by him to elevate himself to the high position he now holds, which has been an inspiration to me at all times:

Since becoming a comedian my motto to success has been:

> Tho our professional road looks muddy
> Let us never cease to study
> You try hard and so will I
> To be headliners before we die.[51]

Chapter 3

Go East, Young Men

1895 to 1896

Road to Los Angeles

After their dismissal from the Dahomey Village in the spring of 1894, Bert and George performed at Jack Cremorne's Midway off and on until the late summer of 1895. They then made their way to Los Angeles in early November, where, through Cremorne, they made the acquaintance of Gustav Walters, who managed the Orpheum circuit of theatres. As luck would have it, Charles Schimpf, the manager of the Los Angeles venue, was in a pinch. One of the acts had failed, and Walters needed someone to fill space in the program until another, more established act could be found. Luckily, the desperate young performers were present and available to snap up the opportunity to earn forty dollars a week. Listed in the *Los Angeles Times* as "Williams and Walker, Singers, Dancers and Comedians," their three-week trial began on November 18, 1895. They made an unexpected hit, which resulted in a 50 percent raise and an extension to six weeks as a featured act. (Billy) Clifford and (Maud) Huth were the headliners, earning $300 a week, and Bert remembered their eyes popped out of their heads when Clifford showed them $300 in gold.[1]

Although the duo was inexperienced, they advantageously appeared second to last on the bill. The *Times* declared, "Their act was really better than 75 percent of the performances for which the Orpheum pays from $200 to $400 weekly."[2] The *Herald* reported, "Williams and Walker, the versatile black-face comedians, are regarded by many as the cleverest buck and wing dancers of the day. They accurately picture that careless easy-going colored gentleman of the south who would rather dance than eat." The characterization of the performers as "black-face" is a bit misleading because George never wore burnt cork and Bert wouldn't begin to blacken his face for another two years. Rather, it was signification of their Blackness, still a rare thing on American stages.[3]

By December 1, Williams and Walker had begun to tinker with their formula with an adaptation of "Hawkshaw the Detective" and introduced the fin de siècle "possum" dance, a buck and wing.[4] While in Los Angeles, Bert and George became acquainted with Joe Hodges and Nina Launchmere, a popular Black song and dance act. According to fellow vaudevillian Tom Fletcher (1873 to 1954), Launchmere said, "Hodges was so impressed with the kind of act they were doing that we had a talk with them and asked them if they would like to come east. Bert Williams said, 'OK by me,' and turned to his partner and asked, 'How about it, Nash?'"[5]

By the end of their run at the Orpheum on December 28, 1895, Williams and Walker were at the top of the bill, and the public began to take notice. Even the matinees were standing room only; as *The Herald* noted, "From the entrance of Williams and Walker to the closing somersault of Granto it is encore after encore."[6] In particular, Williams and Walker's dancing differentiated them from the other "coon acts" without resorting to low or vulgar minstrel clichés. Their "up-to-date" performances, complete with "real coon" flair, were particularly appreciated. As reported in *The Herald*, "they have the natural Negro dialect and put all the snap and go into their work that might be expected from the excitable Negro working on the levee. . . . They have made a distinct hit here and their work is of the cleanest possible description. The fact that they are colored men no way detracted from their success in Los Angeles."[7] The *Los Angeles Times* chose to remark on their depth: "They demonstrate their versatility . . . by playing the bones, tambourine and banjo with a strong darky flavor, and manage to keep things lively while they are on."[8] The early success in Los Angeles inspired Bert and George to expand their enterprise into composition and the eventual control of their publishing rights as well as the royalties generated from the sale of sheet music. Bert's songs showed a lot of potential to produce ancillary income, especially when the two danced in front of Los Angeles audiences. Inspired by their growing popularity, they looked east to Chicago and New York, the big time.

"Dora Dean" Is Obscene

One of Bert's early successes was a rag titled "Dora Dean," "the hottest gal you've ever seen." He composed the piece in July of 1895, and it was dedicated to Dora "Dean" Babbage (1872 to 1949), of the team of (Charlie) Johnson and Dean, former members of Sam T. Jack's (1852 to 1899) Creole Company.[9] According to the ragtime composer Joe Jordan (1882 to 1971), "In fact, she was what they called a feminine scissor. . . . When she walked in, the room caught on fire!"[10] Bert's innate subtlety painted a more modest picture, but the sentiment was shared:

> Say, have you ever seen Miss Dora Dean?
> She is the hottest gal you've ever seen
> I'm a-goin' by and make this gal my queen
> Next Sunday mornin' I'm goin' to marry Miss Dora Dean.

There is no evidence that Williams and Walker had met Johnson and Dean yet. Likely, Al Anderson, a seasoned San Francisco–based Black performer told them about her.[11] Also, during their time in San Francisco, George befriended Hugo V. Schlam, a press agent and would-be music publisher, who reportedly "showed [George] what [agents] could do."[12] "Dora Dean" was published in February 1896 by Broder & Schlam in San Francisco and generated modest returns in Los Angeles. When Clifford and Huth left the Orpheum, Bert and George gave them the song to introduce Williams and Walker to White audiences in the East. Moreover, George understood the idea that, as Black men, Williams and Walker's rights to their intellectual properties were either negotiable or nonexistent. However, if a White publisher had a stake in their success, their rights were likely to be protected to a much greater extent. Further, they wouldn't have to sweat to do it because the White man who protected *his* stake would in turn protect *theirs*. Times being what they were, and with the new profitability of ragtime, barely two months elapsed before a blatant copy of the song was released via a rival composer and publisher, resulting in an unprecedented lawsuit.

Spanning two years, the trial to determine ownership of "Dora Dean" began on April 8, 1896, in San Francisco. Hugo Schlam asserted that Charles Sydney O'Brien (ca. 1872 to ca. 1900), a well-known saloon musician in San Francisco, stole the music and part of the words to create a strikingly similar song titled "Ma Angeline," published by the Mauvais Music Company, also

Figure 3.1. "Dora Dean: The Sweetest Gal You Ever Seen," Broder & Schlam, New York / San Francisco, 1895. *Source:* Author's collection.

of San Francisco. Bert's version was copyrighted four days after O'Brien's on February 10, 1896, because he waited for permission to use Clifford and Huth's likeness on the cover. Despite this, the language in the papers favored Williams and Walker and suggests a guiding hand from George via

Schlam. The *San Francisco Call* described O'Brien as "a comical little man of exceeding blackness," whose "appearance on the street suggests that he had just stepped from an end chair at a minstrel performance" and that "burned cork would never change his complexion."[13] Regardless, the judge labeled "Dora Dean" "of doubtful character and unclean" and wanted to throw the entire case out due to its suggestive imagery of a buxom Black woman. At issue was the line "She's the hottest thing you've ever seen," which implied a sexual overtone and, therefore, was not subject to copyright. Although he showed a clear favoritism for the lighter-skinned Bert, the judge refused to enjoin the plaintiffs, and his ruling stated that both songs were in effect twins that both companies had equal rights to. Litigation continued, but the original ruling was largely maintained on June 1, 1898, in the United States Circuit Court. However, Schlam secured copyright privileges for the melody alone, and O'Brien was deemed a pirate.[14] Although a financial dead end, it was a partial victory for Bert and George and an invaluable lesson on the rules of monetizing Black cultural products. The publicity of the trial ensured that the names Williams and Walker were being openly discussed all over the country, and they didn't have to perform, embarrass themselves, or break the law to do it. Also, the controversy extended the life of the composition and inspired new discourse on the commercialization of Black sexuality, something that everyone other than Black people was free to exploit.

George referred indirectly to this case and his relationship with Schlam when he discussed the development of his business acumen and navigating the perils of White gatekeepers:

> We studied the white man's methods first, then our own limitations, and on our own deductions planned a future. For instance, we realized that the prime motive with Mr. "Eddie" is the coin. Well, we wanted it, too, but we could not go straight to the mint as he; so we did the next best thing—let him take the "Jew" on the money and took for ourselves publicity, which is as good as a certified check in this business. Well, when Mr. "Eddie" had given us all the publicity he knew how, we gently pried him loose from the cash box, and then called some bigger manager to see how easy it was to graft on Williams and Walker, and repeated the performance. Thus we attained our present growth.[15]

Although White composers had no such caveat to hamper their liberty in the free market, Bert's composition showed that the policing of Black bodies extended to Black thoughts and imagination, especially if they affected the sanctity of White sexual norms. Likewise, Bert and George demonstrated that they could exploit the commercial appeal of syncopated rhythm, comical situations, and frolicsome melodies that formed the basis of the burgeoning ragtime craze, so long as the lyrical content was acceptable. Consequently, their "realness" and talent also made them a regular target for piracy from "fake coons" who had neither the talent nor insight of Williams and Walker. It was their hope that audiences could learn to see the difference and demand the real thing from the growing swath of Black performers who were on the scene and ready to game the system. With a product that could neither be stolen nor duplicated, Bert and George knew that audiences could be compelled to demand "real coons" or nothing at all. Moreover, they counted on the idea that their ability to generate income would smooth over the indiscretion of their ambition among White gatekeepers in the industry. It was a theory and practice that George would implement for the rest of his life, lifting as he climbed.

Goin' to Chicago

Hodges and Launchmere provided the duo's first positive validation from seasoned Black performers who knew what it took to be successful in the East. Moreover, they were the first major connection in a social network that was essential for future success. After a small taste in Los Angeles, Bert and George walked away from a guarantee of sixty dollars a week at the Orpheum and joined an eastbound medicine show for eighty dollars a week. However, the journey was fraught with difficulty. The first major stop was Denver, but the show was stranded short in Cripple Creek, where trouble was brewing in the boom town's mining community.[16] As Bert gently described the situation to his friend, theatre critic Lester A. Walton (1884 to 1965), "the medicine man developed a case of 'cold feet,' however, and the team went to Chicago, not any too natty in appearance; neither had they been any too familiar with the dinner table."[17] The quack's "cold feet" was due to some miners who objected to Bert and George's fancy clothing. Fearing confrontation, the "Doc" abandoned his own show and the eighty-dollar debt the partners owed him, which left them at the mercy of the miners, who demanded they disrobe in exchange for burlap sacking before they were allowed to move on. Fortunately, Bert and George found jobs at the Topic Theatre in town, and they saved a little money.[18]

Eventually, they made it to Chicago in rags, likely in early February of 1896, "with $2 for two and [we] ate up six-bits worth at the first restaurant." Shortly after pawning everything but their costumes, they were picked up by Walter J. Plimmer, who ran the Theatrical Exchange.[19] Likely through Hodges and Launchmere, they became acquainted with a few of the local Black performers who participated in Colored People's Day at the Columbian Exposition of 1893 and began to find modest success in the city. A pivotal connection was made with Jesse Allison Shipp (1864 to 1934), who was appearing in John Isham's (1866 to 1902) *Octoroons* at the time. Shipp was an experienced actor, writer, and stage manager who had worked with the Primrose and West Minstrels, a White company. Even at this early stage, the quality of his work was only surpassed by his imagination, and, according to theatre critic Sylvester Russell (1864 to 1930), "he [spoke] incessantly without tiring or even growing tiresome."[20]

Figure 3.2. Jesse Shipp. *Source:* Photo by White Studio ©Photographs and Prints Division, Schomburg Center for Research in Black Culture, New York Public Library. Used with permission.

John Isham's *Octoroons* was built upon the success of his previous employer Sam T. Jack's *Creole Burlesque Show*. In 1890, Jack, a White man, was the first to successfully exploit the talent of Afro-American women in the chorus of his show at his theatre near the corner of Madison and State Street.[21] Jack hired several Afro-American actors such as Billy Jackson, Irving Jones (ca. 1874 to 1932), Fred Piper, and Johnson and Dean. The most senior was Sam Lucas, who may have suggested the implementation of a female chorus, which included his second wife, Carrie Melvin. With veteran performers and an all-female chorus, the *Creole Burlesque Show* supplanted the traditional plantation backdrop for one that reflected post-emancipation, urban "Darkies" while expanding the traditional minstrel interplay between an end man and a female interlocutor. According to James Weldon Johnson, "it was the start along a line which led straight to the musical comedies of Cole and Johnson, Williams and Walker, and Ernest Hogan."[22]

In the winter of 1895, Isham took the knowledge gained from Jack and formed the *Octoroons* and *Oriental America* shows, composed largely of very light-skinned Black people who might be considered (in the nomenclature of the day) Creoles, Octoroons, high-yellow, Redbones, and other monikers to denote their racial liminality. An essential component of an Isham show was a very loose plot that featured elite Black performers, from operatic sopranos to rifle twirlers and dancers of all sorts. Due to their recent connection with Jesse Shipp, the heart of Isham's cast—the Hyers Sisters, Tom and Hattie McIntosh, Belle Davis (ca. 1873 to 1938), Mattie Wilkes (1875 to 1927), the Mallory Brothers, the Halliday Sisters, and several others, including the composers Will Cook and Will Accooe (1874 to 1904) would soon become the foundation of the Williams and Walker company.[23]

Following Shipp's introduction, Bert and George attempted to combine forces with Bob Cole and Billy Johnson (1858 to 1916), an ambitious songwriting team and comedy act from Sam T. Jack's show.[24] The move was one of George's first attempts to cash in on the publicity gained from "Dora Dean" and call "some bigger manager [Isham or Jack] to see how easy it was to graft on Williams and Walker."[25] Paired with young dancers Stella Wiley, Bob Cole's former wife, and Mattie Wilkes or Belle Davis, they failed to impress audiences. It was then that the partners learned one of the harsh lessons of the vaudeville circuit: Their success in Los Angeles was not guaranteed in Chicago. Regardless, Bert and George collaborated with Cole and Johnson on the moderately successful song "Baby Will You Always Love Me True?," George's first documented performance in drag.[26] Shortly after, Cole and Johnson left Jack's aggregation for Sissieretta Jones's

Figure 3.3. Sissieretta "Black Patti" Jones. *Source: Saint Paul Globe*, January 3, 1897, 10.

Black Patti's Troubadours, another company that hosted several future cast members of the Williams and Walker company among its ranks.

One surviving story of Bert and George's early days in Chicago tells of a short time they spent with a German-born carpenter named Herman, which immediately followed their failure with Cole and Johnson. Broke and at the mercy of an unsympathetic landlady, the partners packed up their single, damaged trunk and hit the streets. Soon after, they noticed a carpenter's shingle on a building, and George quickly came up with a plan to leave the trunk at the shop to be repaired. That way, the trunk would be kept in a secure location for free, and they would still have access to its contents while they looked for work. It was a flawless plan, until the carpenter saw through their ruse into the disheveled reality of their homelessness. To their surprise, Herman was kind and said, "You boys come here tonight[,] and we make out somehow. You sleep on my workbench: I only have this little couch here." Eventually, they found a little work and made enough money to repay Herman. At night, when they weren't working, "they supped on beer and liverwurst, with rye bread and onions. Then the boys would play a little music and the three would have a game of pinochle."[27]

Although engagements were infrequent, they appeared at the Oxford, Imperial, Lyceum, and Chicago Opera House throughout the spring of 1896. Their act went over well, but not well enough, so they remained itinerant. Eventually, they wound up in Detroit at the Wonderland Theatre during the week of July 19.[28] With nothing to lose, they decided to bury their act and switched roles, with George appearing as the as the straight man and Bert as the comedian. However, vaudeville audiences would not accept Bert's natural honey-bronze complexion in that role, and he was expected to don burnt cork. His only previous experience wearing cork was shortly before he met George, and it was a disaster because he had an anxiety attack during the first ensemble number and unintentionally made a hit. According to Eileen Southern, "the sweat of distress poured down his face. His makeup ran in streaks of alarming perpendicular zebra effect. When the end man fired his funny question at Williams, the novice's eyes opened in terror and beads stood out on his forehead. He couldn't remember his lines. In dismay, his mouth flew open. The house roared. 'If Ah says anything, those folks'll laugh at me.' Williams backed out into the wings."[29] With trepidation, Bert tried blackface for the second time in his career and performed his newest composition, "Oh, I Don't Know, You're Not So Warm." In bittersweet irony, he was a huge success on each occasion. However, with George beside him, his anxiety abated, and in that moment the foundation for the Williams and Walker formula was established. Further, "Oh, I Don't Know, You're

Not So Warm" became their first signature hit, largely due to Bert's natural penchant for observation and lyricism:

> I had a girl, and her name was Pearl,
> I thought her heart was mine;
> I gave a French dinner,
> For I thought I was a winner,
> I'd have bet my life 'gainst a dime.
> I told her how I lov'd her,
> But she said she'd not be mine; then I told her I was sweller,
> Than any other feller,
> But this was her reply . . .

The song was based on Bert's observation of a young woman who let her suitor down the hard way in Chicago. According to Bert, she said, "'Oh, I don't know, you ain't so wahm.' And he wasn't, for she proceeded to do him then and there until the patrol wagon came. I went home, sat down to the piano, and in about 10 minutes the song was there. That night we sprung it on the audience, and it made a hit."[30] George's willingness to switch to the straight role and play to Bert's natural comedic timing increased Bert's comfort level, which allowed him to hide more of his true self from the audience. He remembered, "Nobody was more surprised than I was when it went like a house on fire. Then I began to find myself. It was not until I was able to see myself as another person that my sense of humor developed."[31] Now that he had a partner to augment his growing ability to compartmentalize and contextualize, he became another person while under the mask. Bert was tall, handsome, inquisitive, and elegant, whereas the mask was slow, shuffling, and susceptible to all manner of chaos from the company he kept, facilitated by George. Likewise, Bert's dancing, influenced by Charles Hunn, was the stuff of legend.[32] As Bert recalled of his early days in California as a young minstrel, "one night I slipped on a smooth board while doing my stunt, one foot sliding forward in a clear fashion and I just escaped falling backward. The audience laughed and clapped to the echo, and I repeated it. I found it such a hit at every performance that I practiced it everywhere I went, and I suppose I will always use it."[33]

Although George had been a comedian since childhood, he continued to get laughs in the straight role and played it for the rest of their partnership. As described by Arthur Ruhl of *Colliers Weekly*, "each of these men is an artist in his own vein . . . with the big man compelled to trust the superior worldly wisdom of the other, and yet always vaguely aware that he is being

Figure 3.4. "Oh! I Don't Know, You're Not So Warm!: Comic Song and Refrain with Coon Parody," words and music by Bert Williams, Charles Sheard, London, 1896. *Source:* Author's collection.

'done.'"[34] Pending finances, George's new dude persona inspired his inner Beau Brummel as he interpreted the Zip Coon "Learned Scholar" trope of the minstrel tradition to counter Bert's version of the "Happy Darky," Jim Crow. Essential to Bert's manifestation of double consciousness was his subtle way of differentiating Bert Williams the man from the character he played by featuring himself out of costume on the covers of his sheet music. As more hits came, the partners began to sell their songs to more established, White acts to drum up some publicity among White people who would never hear their music otherwise.[35] Nevertheless, the duality of Bert and his mask would prove controversial among his family, contemporaries, and subsequent generations of Black performers who understood the context yet despised the practice.

During the first week of August 1896, Williams and Walker were booked at the Harrison Park Casino in Terre Haute, Indiana. While passing through Louisville, they busked in a saloon at Sixth and Green Streets and passed a hat around at Abe Robert's dance hall located at 500 Sixth Street before they caught a break.[36] According to George,

> We had gone from Chicago to Louisville and were trying to make it a round trip without being at all impeded by accumulated treasure. Now, we were long on leisure and found some white professionals who were also the possessors of some spare golden moments; so we mixed counsel with them, and the upshot was we all decided to devote a week to mending our health at West Baden, and to give a "commonwealth" show one night during the week so as to meet the bills incident to the mending.[37]

Along with that motley aggregation, Bert and George made the fifty-mile trek to West Baden, Indiana, where they secured a booking at the opera house under the name of the Willis, Clark, Roof Garden Vaudeville Company. They performed on August 18 and 21, 1896, to packed houses, and, fortuitously, Thomas Canary (of the New York firm Canary and Lederer) was there and promised to book them in *The Passing Show*, a three-act extravaganza. In the meantime, George and Bert returned to Chicago as planned and performed in a children's show at Ferris Wheel Park from September 8 to 12, when, according to Bert, "we got a telegram from [Canary] saying that 'if we could get to New York' by September 14 we could have an engagement in '*The Gold Bug*.' If we could get there! As if we wouldn't have crawled there on our knees!"[38]

Road to New York

The Gold Bug, a three-act play about interracial mixing, was due to open at the Casino Theatre on Broadway and Thirty-Ninth Street. However, it was plagued with delays and incompetence to the point that the producers referred to it as a "stop-gap" and wanted to cut their losses, hence the telegram to Williams and Walker. By the time they arrived, the production was in freefall and there were no costumes for the cast. To compound the problem, George Lederer, the other half of Canary and Lederer, thought Williams and Walker were mediocre and the wrong color for the production. With another failed audition, Bert and George had exhausted their only prospect in New York, and the play opened without them on September 21, 1896. As a consolation, they were offered menial positions at the Casino. The show was so bad, *The New York Times* asserted, "It was as heavy as lead," and the following day they were "rediscovered," as George later put it.[39] Their second chance was facilitated by Truly Shattuck (1875 to 1954) of the vaudeville team Leslie and Shattuck, who were performing with Hodges and Launchmere at the Standard Theatre on Broadway and Thirty-Third Street. Shattuck met Williams and Walker on the train to New York, heard them sing "You're Not So Warm," and was smitten, despite their dilapidation. Following her matinee performance on the opening night of *The Gold Bug*, Shattuck strolled up Broadway with her partner and the White, would-be ragtime composer Charles Trevathan. When they reached the Casino, about six blocks from the Standard, she remarked,

> Do you know, there are two colored boys who have just come to town who are musical geniuses in their way? Miss Leslie and I heard them singing on the train coming from 'Frisco. They were singing one song called, "Oh, I Don't Know, You Ain't So Warm," that would set New York crazy if it ever gets to the footlights.
>
> But the poor boys can't get anyone to give them a chance. They're down on their luck, they haven't a penny and when I met one of them on the street yesterday and asked him how things were going, he told me they were so broke that they had both gone to work as chore boys behind the scenes at the Casino.[40]

Reportedly, Trevathan excused himself and walked directly into George Lederer's office, where he was in the "depths of despair" over the impending failure of *The Gold Bug*. Trevathan asked, "Have you got two colored boys here who are working as messengers? If you have, bring them in here and let them get busy on that piano. I hear they've got a great song." Later known for his coon song compositions, Trevathan possibly thought of the down-and-out partners as a source for new material, a common tactic of

White composers of ragtime and subsequent Afro-American musical styles.[41] When Williams and Walker appeared five minutes later, they did not disappoint: "'Heavens!' cried Lederer after hearing one verse [of "Oh, I Don't Know . . ."], 'if I could only work these two boys into the piece tonight[,] they might save the show.' But it was too late to have an orchestration made of the song before the curtain went up. The 'Gold Bug' was produced without the assistance of Williams and Walker [opening] night and scored one of the most disastrous failures in the history of that theatre."[42] Because of the disastrous opening night, Bert and George were thrown in as a last-ditch effort. However, the uniquely Afro-American, syncopated music that Bert composed proved to be an impediment for the orchestra and, rather than meet the challenge, they threatened to quit. Lederer recalled that when the house musicians saw the score, they all but declared a strike because the music was a "jigsaw puzzle to the[m]."[43] The music was different and therefore deficient to the establishment, but, against all odds, Williams and Walker scored the only hit of the unabashed failure and subsequently "caught the town."[44]

As in Los Angeles, Williams and Walker were reluctantly added to the show and were burdened with the task of saving Canary and Lederer's folly, at a discount of course. For those in attendance on the second night of *The Gold Bug*, it was probably the first time they had ever seen Blackness on stage outside of the minstrel tradition. Coupled with the growing momentum of the ragtime craze, "The Real Coons" had arrived in New York at the perfect time. Nevertheless, their excitement was tempered with a dose of reality when the show promptly closed because the problems of the first night remained unaddressed. Years later, George recalled, "*The Gold Bug* closed in a week—in spite of us. But it lived long enough for us to make the needful impression." Lederer recalled, "It was the first time I had ever seen a musical moke team stop a show and they stopped '*The Gold Bug*,' that night until they eventually gave out physically."[45]

The success of Williams and Walker's brief appearance at the Casino led to a booking with strongman Eugene Sandow's *Olympia* show at the Columbia Theatre. They did well, and the *Brooklyn Daily Eagle* reported, "On[e] novelty was the sketch of Walker and Williams, two negro comedians, who made a decided hit in New York during the summer. Their buck and wing dancing was the quaintest and most curious that has been seen in Brooklyn for many a day. The same may be said for their jokes, which while not humor of the most refined sort, were much preferable to the stereotyped repartee of the ordinary sketch team."[46] After a week with Sandow, Williams and Walker went to Boston with Peter Dailey's *A Good Thing* company for a week at the Hollis Street Theatre.[47] Cast as a servant and waiter in the second act in a New York Bowery auction room, they were listed in the *Boston Post* as "Walker and Williams." Regardless, they had survived the Casino disaster and achieved modest success in two of the largest cities in the East.[48] At the close of their engagement, they returned to the Casino in anticipation of more work and found some at Harris' Musee Theatre in McKeesport, Pennsylvania, some twenty-five miles south of Pittsburgh. An all-female minstrel troupe was booked with David Montgomery and Fred Stone as the featured end men, but the two men refused to appear after they learned of the unconventional makeup of the show.[49] As printed in *The Pittsburgh Press*, when Harry Davis learned of the loss of his end men, he telegraphed his New York booking agent, who told him that he had "two good colored men" who could fill in. Having never booked Black performers before, Davis rejected the idea. Likely at George's urging, the agent called long distance to press his case, and Davis hired them begrudgingly. After they arrived, Bert and George made such an impression that Davis sent a glowing dispatch back to the agent. They performed in the olio that night and made a hit for the third time when no White option was available.[50] Despite the circumstances, they earned enough money to complete their journey back to New York, where they would soon take advantage of another do-or-die moment.

Chapter 4

Honing the Act

1896 to 1897

"All Coons Look Alike"

Coinciding with Williams and Walker's new success in New York, the so-called "coon song craze" had taken hold of popular culture since the unofficial debut of ragtime at the Chicago World's Fair in 1893. Essential to exploiting the fad was the streamlining of minstrel stereotypes into single, one-off situations of chaos, strife, and yet, somehow, deserved pain for the involved "Coons" onstage. More important, the source of strife was usually the actions of other Coons and never White people or the Jim Crow power structure. As reported in the *Washington Times*, "the songs, when written by Negroes, as a great many of them have been, are written to order, and in accordance with a preconceived idea of what the 'coon' song ought to be."[1] Between 1896, the year of *Plessy v. Ferguson*, and the end of the First World War, the coon song captured the public's fervent hunger for all things "authentic" relating to Black life and Black people, which required a certain amount of curation and cultural ambassadry from Black performers in order for them to earn a living with a measure of dignity. Therefore, the public hunger for "real coons" made for a double-edged opportunity that was ripe for Black performers who were well schooled in the tactics of double consciousness.

The earliest coon song hit, credited for sparking the craze, was "All Coons Look Alike to Me," by Ernest Hogan, in 1896. Born Ernest Reuben Crowdus in Bowling Green, Kentucky, "The Unbleached American" was an accomplished singer, dancer, piano player, stage manager, and comedian as a teenager.

Figure 4.1. Ernest Hogan. *Source: New York Clipper Annual*, Frank Queen, 1898, 184.

Chorus:

All coons look alike to me
I've got another beau, you see
And he's just as good to me as you, nig! ever tried to be
He spends his money free I know we can't agree
So, I don't like you no how
All coons look alike to me

Honing the Act | 55

Figure 4.2. "All Coons Look Alike to Me: A Darkey Misunderstanding," words and music by Ernest Hogan, published by M. Whitmark & Sons, New York / Chicago, 1896. *Source:* Author's collection.

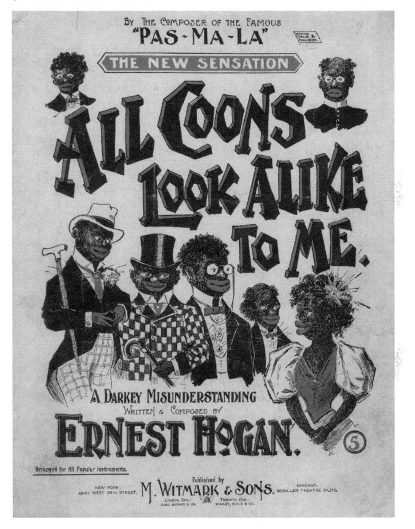

Presented with an accessible syncopated rhythm, the song captured the White public's attention like nothing before, to the tune of $100,000 in sales during its first three years.[2] On the go-round, Hogan exposed a thoroughly modern method to jiggle nickels out of White folks' pockets without ever having to interact with them. On the come-round, the "free market" success of "All Coons" rectified the unfortunate tradition of catering

Black cultural products to the desires of those who did not matter beyond their purchasing power. Hogan and his contemporaries had to contend with what they believed would be a temporary compromise, and he expressed regret for the unintended influence it had on popular culture. As his friend Tom Fletcher remembered,

> During those days the economic situation among colored people was very bad. After Hogan had written the number it was too late to be sorry for it. It was a tremendous hit. Colored shows blossomed like mushrooms and they all made money. Soon white minstrels and all shows of that period were using the song and it was sung and whistled all over the country. And of course songwriters, white and colored, jumped aboard the bandwagon and "Coon Songs" became the rage.[3]

Unfortunately, "All Coons" affirmed unfavorable stereotypes of Afro-Americans that, when reproduced ubiquitously in other compositions over two decades, did not allow ragtime to endure in perpetuity as a profitable vehicle for Black composers. Likewise, due to the inaugural popularity of the song, many historians label Hogan as the "father" or "inventor" of ragtime. In reality, he was simply the first to reap the benefits of marketing a Black cultural product for conspicuous White consumption. Hogan was neither the first to write the music down nor the best composer that Afro-America had to offer, but that did not matter to a public that saw him as the singular source of a "new" music. Right away, Hogan understood the consequences and felt uncomfortable with the moniker "father of ragtime," and later lamented to Fletcher, "Son, this song caused a lot of trouble in and out of show business, but it was also good for show business because at the time money was short in all walks of life."[4]

By the closing decade of the nineteenth century, ragtime could be heard in the back rooms of cafés, juke joints, bars, and houses of ill repute in any city in the United States where Afro-American musicians were working. Seemingly overnight, ragtime was in demand in every place that Blacks were not allowed except in a domestic capacity. Since most White people had little to no substantive knowledge of Black life outside of the minstrel show, the stereotyped "authenticity" of coon songs became the benchmark and expectation that Black composers were forced to contend with if they wanted to work. Their lived experience was entirely different than what was sold, and it was only permissible if White publishing houses also profited from the fad.[5] However, Ernest Hogan, Bert, George, and the rest of their generation spent their professional lives trying to bridge the gap. As a vehicle for both liberation and subjugation, George was aware of the possibilities and pitfalls of capitalizing on Black cultural products: "At that stage of the development of Williams and Walker, we saw that the colored performer would have to get away from the ragtime limitations of the 'darky,' and we decided to make the break, so as to save ourselves and others."[6]

Cake Walk: The "New" Dance

Aside from their interplay as partners, Williams and Walker's most endearing feature to White audiences was their ability to dance and make it look as easy as a "cake walk," in the twisted, contemporary sense of the term. With its roots firmly planted in traditional West African ring dances, the cake walk originated in the antebellum South, where it functioned as a vehicle for subversion. Typically, an individual or a couple would parade, strut, improvise, or walk slowly and erect between two parallel columns of other dancers, imitating or parodying courtly European dances such as the gallopade or quadrille. As a couple walked down the line, utilizing their charisma and skill, they sought to best other couples in competition for a cake, judged by plantation owners or their guests. As with most Afro-American products in a traditional or lived setting, one's individuality, humor, and the glorification of the moment served as a marker of cultural mastery while providing a much-needed break from the struggles of daily life. Those skills were put to work on stages wherever they performed as professional entertainers.[7] As described by Aida Overton Walker (1880 to 1914), George's future wife and collaborator, in the *Indianapolis News*,

> Think of moonlight nights and pine knots and tallow dips, and of lives touched by the hardness of toil, for there was sunshine in the hearts of those who first danced the cakewalk. . . . A little flirtation—just a little flirtation—is a prime requisite.
>
> It must be borne in mind that your partner has much to do with the prospects of winning a prize. So I say, smile sweetly at your partner. Whatever you do, no matter how intricate the dance, don't forget him. Always have a pleased expression, a half-smile, at least. Be happy, for the original cake walkers were glad in the light of the moon when their work was done. Be

joyous, then, and don't dance with a partner that is too serious to smile as though he meant it.[8]

Despite the public's growing hunger for "authentic" coon specialties, both ragtime and the cake walk incorporated nontraditional elements for White acceptability and profitability. Understanding how to exploit the social context allowed Bert, George, and hundreds of their contemporaries to act as cultural ambassadors often out of context in front of audiences that did not care to understand the dance's original function or its history. Likewise, the press struggled to generate objective commentary on Black cake walking and relied on such words as "eccentric," "clumsy," "grotesque," and "queer" when referring to its uniquely Afro-American characteristics that were new to the White public.[9] However, they were almost unanimous in declaring Williams and Walker the kings of the new dance fad because, like Ernest Hogan, they were at the right place and time and were inoffensive. As one critic in Boston wrote about Bert's dancing in 1909, "he just wiggles his legs, crooks his knees, falls over his feet, bends his back." George's athletic and flashy approach was fitting of his new Beau Brummel persona, which inspired fellow Lawrencian and vaudeville performer Essie Whitman (1882 to 1963) to call him "the greatest strutter of them all."[10]

Dusky Dukes of Manhattan

When Bert and George established a foothold in New York, the Black population was quite small but had grown steadily since the great purge following the Draft Riot in 1863. That year, the Enrollment (or "conscription") Act was passed, and mostly Irish immigrants rioted from July 13 to 16, resulting in the deaths of more than 120 people, most of them Afro-Americans, along with eleven lynchings.[11] The partners quickly found their way to Sixth Avenue, where there was a newly established community of Black people. They rented a small, fifth-floor apartment on Sixth between Twenty-Sixth and Twenty-Seventh Street that was owned by John B. "Jack" (1853 to 1942) and Edward (c.1849 to 1899) Nail. The Nail brothers operated what was arguably the most fashionable and respectable Black bar and eatery in the city and a liquor store, at 450 and 461 Sixth Ave, respectively.[12] Consequently, "Coontown" became a wellspring for the codified and artistic Black presence in Manhattan. Its proximity to the Tin Pan Alley publishing houses on West Twenty-Eighth Street between Fifth and Sixth Avenues made the neighborhood an ideal location for Black composers to create and privately refine their ideas before attempting to monetize them via White publishing houses and theatres.

By mid-October of 1896, Bert and George were hustling in New York and building their network of fellow composers, musicians, and performers of all stripes from their apartment. Around that time, George Lederer introduced Williams and Walker to Will A. McConnell, manager of Koster and Bial's, one of the most successful vaudeville venues in New York. Bial had recently booked La Belle Otero at $1,750 a week, but she was ill and was replaced by the Martinetti pantomime company at $2,000 a week, and they promptly failed as well. With options waning, and possibly due to the recommendation of Harry Davis in Chicago, Bert and George were given a chance, albeit half of one. Although the third choice for the spot, they made the most of their debut at Koster and Bial's on October 25, 1896.[13] As reported in *The Inter Ocean*, "until Mr. Bial could get another attraction he decided to put in Williams and Walker in a big cake walk. About twenty other 'coons' were engaged. Williams and Walker were paid $200 and the others $200, a total of $400 a week. Yet it was a knock-out, and eventually played to more money than any other attraction before or since. Although the first night was a bit rough, the first week brought in $14,000," and Koster and Bial quickly discovered they had a discount tiger by the tail.[14] According to Jesse Shipp, Williams and Walker's act had changed little since he last saw them in Chicago a few months earlier:

> When I arrived in New York and saw what a hit the boys had made, I was very much surprised: not that I didn't think they both had ability, because I knew they had; but with us in the Cole and Johnson show they had not even pleased. Here they were doing the very same songs and they were a riot. Evenings after the show we would all go up to their room on Sixth Avenue and talk shop. . . . Often when I arrived for a talk or a visit the boys would be just sitting there, the two of them playing "smut" and laughing like kids.[15]

Now that they had a community and a hit act in New York, it was time to make moves toward what George called "velvet."[16] Bert remembered,

> Walker generally arranged the contracts. He was suave; one of those oily fellows, and so persistent. Walker used to insist on

> having things decided his way—Our way. In a business deal where the other party decided against us, I was usually willing to consider it settled rather than argue. Not so with Walker. He would talk on and on. "Arguing" he called it, and little by little the other side would begin to be convinced. Eventually you would have to believe that Walker was right. He had the methods of a diplomatist.[17]

At the time, George's costume, consisting of a box coat, pointed shoes with spats, and a gambler hat, was at least a year old and likely being toted about in the same single trunk that he and Bert had used since San Francisco. His impatience, fueled by ambition, may have gotten the better of him, and he was caught shoplifting in late October of 1896,

> Walker . . . says he saw a pair of trousers hanging in front of the store, and absentmindedly threw them over his arm, forgetting to pay the man for them. He was promptly arrested and taken to court where he pleaded guilty of theft. He was discharged, much to the surprise of the prosecuting attorney, who demanded to know the reason.
> "He'll have to go back and steal the coat and vest before I can make a suit out of the case," was the reply.[18]

George's saving grace must have been that he was half of a popular act and leveraged it for leniency and a better contract. After all, he couldn't get caught stealing clothes if he had the cash to pay for them and was focused on growing his act. The incident was never discussed again, and with a new contract under his belt, George promptly expanded the act and his wardrobe. Jesse Shipp remembered, "George Walker was then developing and showing signs of the very decided business ability that he had. He was the business head of the team and he never tired of it. Business was meat and drink to him. With the prolonged stay at the variety theatre, they were able to move to better quarters and enjoy the sartorial indulgence for which Walker, at least, was famed. Walker not only loved clothes, but he became quite a dandy."[19]

By December of 1896, Williams and Walker's cake walk was one of the most popular acts in New York, and they shared the top of the bill with the French singer Yvette Guilbert. According to *The Sun*,

There are but two couples, and as the cake is not in evidence the walkers promptly get down to business. One pair holds the floor at a time, and the man's manners are in strong contrast. One chap is clownish, though his grotesque paces are elaborate, practiced, and exactly timed, while the other is all airiness. It is a revelation to most observers to see so much of jauntiness in one human being. . . . The airy man's attire is gorgeous. Pointed shoes, tight trousers, red and white striped shirt front, and shining silk hat are not a bit out of harmony with mock diamonds that are as big as marbles, and of other near there is a smile that for size and convincingness is unequaled. Away up stage he and his partner bow and curtsey, she with utmost grace, he with exaggerated courtliness. Then down day trip, his elbows squared, his hat held upright by the brim, and with a running gate that would be ridiculous were it not absolute in its harmony with the general scheme of airiness. With every step his body sways from side to side, and the outstretched elbows see-saw, but the woman clings to his arm, and this grand guest of entries is prolonged till the footlights are reached. There a turn at the right angles brings another elaborate curtsey before the two pass along parallel to the footlights. Here he faces the audience, and no lack of grace comes from his unusual position in walking. The smile is thus in view throughout the promenade, and, if anyone could doubt that is a dandy of dandies, it should be an effective dispeller. Its expressiveness is only limited by the Negro's face, and it is genuine in large degree, also the sparkling eyes belie it. The other chap's rig is rusty, and his joints work jerkily, but he has his own ideas in high stepping, and carries them out in a walk that starts like his companions, but that ends at the other side of the stage. Then the first fellow takes both women, one on each arm, and, leaving the other man grimacing vengefully, starts on a second tour of grace. Even then he walks across the front of the stage with that huge smile wide open, and then off, leaving the impression that he's had a pretty good time himself.[20]

Within a very short period, George became the benchmark for the sporting man on the American stage regardless of color. His friend Lester

Walton described George as donning his raiment only a few minutes before going on as well as "strutting before the glass for hours and studying every movement with the idea that each had a meaning of its own was what made this well-known stage character famous."[21] In total, they worked thirty-eight consecutive weeks at Koster and Bial's and by the end of their run were earning $350 a week. Shortly after, they appeared at Proctor's Theatre, where they combined forces with Hodges and Launchmere, who were excellent cake walkers as well. The Williams and Walker star was rising, and they were asked to perform at charitable benefits with increasing regularity. The exposure to new audiences allowed them to rub elbows with the theatrical elite in the city and find new mules for their growing catalog of compositions.

As "Real Coons," Williams and Walker had distinguished themselves from the rest. The *Brooklyn Daily Eagle* reported, "Their cakewalk has the real flavor of the darkeys which white performers in the blackface find it so hard to get."[22] The growing success inspired George to book the duo in London, and he sent word home to Lawrence that he and Bert received their first photo spread in the February 20, 1897, issue of *The Standard*.[23]

In the session, George was still sporting a tan box coat, possibly inspired by Billy Kersands, and Malacca cane that had been his signature outfit for a couple of years. More important, it is the first group of images where he wore a monocle, an integral component of his dandy persona until 1904.[24] By early March, Williams and Walker were featured players at Hyde and Behman's with McIntyre and Heath, whom George had not seen since his minstrel banner days on Massachusetts Street in Lawrence. Now stars in their own right, Williams and Walker expanded the cake walk portion of their act to seven couples.[25]

The London Flop

To date, only a few Black acts had made the trip across the pond, including Harry Callendar's Minstrels around 1884. With trepidation, Bert and George boarded the transatlantic steamer *Lucania* bound for Liverpool during the week of April 11, 1897, for an engagement at the Empire Theatre in Leicester Square, London. Early on, reports falsely indicated that they made a hit.[26] However, Bert remembered, "[We] went on immediately after the ballet, and promptly died. That taught me to know better than to try to follow a ballet."[27] Moreover, Bert and George had so thoroughly curated their act

Figure 4.3. Hyde and Behman's advertisement. *Source: Brooklyn Daily Eagle*, March 7, 1897, 18.

Figure 4.4. "Williams and Walker, Two Colored Men," *The Standard*, vol. 15, no. 391, New York, February 20, 1897, 16. *Source:* Author's collection.

to be both entertaining and inoffensive to White audiences in the United States that almost nothing translated. George described the effect of their work on an English audience:

It was different from New York, but after a while we got used to them and they got used to us. We had to explain all about it, what we were and what our act was and where the joke was, too! After the first few nights I used to go on and say something like this: "Ladies and gentlemen, we will endeavor to give you impersonation of two real coons, as we say in America, meaning two genuine blackies. We shall sing as you might hear our people singing in the South and Southwest of our country. One of our songs is entitled, 'Oh, I Don't Know, You're Not so Wa'm,' meaning, 'Oh, I'm not so certain, you are not so many, you are not so great.' We shall also do some buck-dancing, or, as you call it, a regular darkey hoedown." After I said all that a few nights the Englishman began to get used to us. They would come a second time watching for our jokes, and you'd see them watching for the jokes they remembered. "Wait a bit, he's going to do it," they would say; "he's going to say something right jolly in a moment; now it's coming; now, ah!—there you are; isn't that capital; isn't it great?" Then the friends would bring their friends, and we got to know our audience. They always wanted the same things over again, being in this particular entirely different from an American audience which always demands something new.[28]

In a London restaurant after a performance, they encountered a pair of curious Virginians. George's recollection began with a question from one of the "gentlemen": " 'You fellows are niggers, ain't you now? But damme[d] if you look it!' I don't know how he knew we were American Negroes anyway. London is full of Africans, Indians and such like." Bert joined in: "T'was funny how they ended up. . . . We got [to] talking and one of them finally said, 'Well, if all niggers were like you now—but we haven't got 'em over there.' I told him I could give him the addresses of a bunch more at home like us, but he wouldn't wait."[29] As usual, before they said a word, Bert and George's mere presence upended social norms and the usual stereotypes that most White Americans harbored. It was conceivably too much to bear for the curious Virginians, who were intrigued by their uniqueness yet afraid to see them as the beginning of a Black critical mass.

Aside from the occasional interaction with fellow Americans and excursions to Paris on off days, their first London experience was scarcely mentioned after the fact. George told the *Los Angeles Times* that they simply left a telegram with specific directions to deliver it at the time they were supposed to go on: "Very sorry, but have gone home."[30] Back in London, *The Era* reported,

> Now we are told that Messrs. Williams and Walker are returning home "disgusted with their treatment," and that "they have a way of quietly but effectually squelching American acts in London by putting them on before anyone is in the house." . . . London audiences are pampered with the latest novelties from all quarters of the globe, and only the fittest survive the test that all are put to without regard to nationality. I have seen a great deal of this "coon" business and black-face comedy both in England and America, but never yet saw any "gentlemen of colour," either real or imagination, who could cause the laughter that little George Le Clerq does in *Black Justice* and similar sketches, or who could do better all-around "Nigger" turn than Mr. Eugene Stratton, clever American artists are fully appreciated in London.[31]

Bert and George left Liverpool aboard the RMS *Majestic* on May 19, 1897, arrived in New York Harbor on May 27, and almost immediately they were back on the boards at Koster and Bial's to make some quick cash before the end of the season.[32] In July, George traveled to Lawrence for the first time since he left with the medicine show in 1892. Although local journalists were excited to see "Nash," they were astounded by his success. As reported in the *Lawrence Weekly World* on his twenty-fifth birthday,

> There was a Lawrence boy in this town who did not amount to much. His parents thought him lazy and his companions were sure that he would go to the bad. The boy for his part was always confident that he will do something. Just what [they] did not clearly understand. He was always into some kind of mischief and was ready for anything that came along.
> That boy was Nash Walker.
> No one has been expecting any good from him, so this article will be a surprise. Nash left this city and went on the stage. He struck his gait in minstrelsy and is today one of the best in this country. He is drawing a salary of $75 per week and his journeyings across the country are veritable triumphs. He is up-to-date and everything and as clever as they make them. He

has lost his boyish ways and is now a man among men, a credit to his race and the pride of his friends.

You can't always tell what's in a boy to see him loafing around town in his earlier years. Nash Walker gave no promise of greatness, but it was in him and he came out.[33]

In keeping with the aristocracy of the Gilded Age, Nash brought twenty-one suits and made three changes a day during that week. He bragged about his contract with Hyde and Behman's show and brought his photo spreads from *The Standard* and *The Musician* as well as an advance copy of *Leslie's Weekly* from July 22, in which Williams and Walker were featured in a select class of performers from Isham's *Octoroons*. His mother and grandmother were living in Colorado, following Alice's marriage to Frank Myers in 1894, so he did not see them.[34] Instead, Nash spent some time at the home of Reverend Albery Allson Whitman. Essie, the second of four daughters, remembered cooking greens when Nash offered to sponsor her and her older sister Mabel (1880 to 1942) for a tryout in New York. Reverend Whitman declined.[35] All told, Nash Walker's first trip home in five years was a triumph, and seemingly everyone in town reveled in his newfound success. It was the first of a yearly ritual for him throughout the rest of his life, much to the joy of the town's denizens. However, there was much work to do, and he returned to New York to build on the success of the previous season.

On August 22, the *American Woman's Home Journal* published a series of photographs titled "The Cake Walk as It Is Done by Genuine Negroes." The series of seven images featured Williams and Walker with Belle Davis and Stella Wiley, who may have been George's girlfriend at the time.[36] Both Wiley and Davis were in Isham's *Octoroons* when Bert and George debuted in Chicago a year and a half earlier and were likely paired with them in their failed audition. It is possible that the *Journal* photo session was initiated for promotional purposes at the start of the run at Koster and Bial's, as evidenced by the older costumes, and the poses match well with the earliest description of the act in the December 3, 1896, edition of *The Sun* before the act was expanded.[37] Although Wiley and Davis were in New York at that time, it is more likely that the session took place while the partners were in Chicago, around the time of their audition for the *Octoroons*, prior to their switching roles in Detroit in July of 1896. That may be the reason for Bert's natural skin tone and the coat that he wore only in their earliest days. Once established in Manhattan, George sported the

Figure 4.5. "Darkest Vaudeville," *Leslie's Weekly*, July 1897, 52. *Source:* Author's collection.

Figure 4.6. "A Lesson for Society Cake Walkers." *Source: American Woman's Home Journal*, August 22, 1897, 12.

same coat on the cover of "A Hot Coon from Memphis," his first known composition in collaboration with Bob Cole, released at the end of 1897, as well as the gambler hat that he stopped wearing in December of 1896. "A Hot Coon" hosted several hallmarks of the new genre—"Coon" in the title, a reference to heat that implied a sexual overtone, and the mystery of "A straight haired yaller nigger" who was brimming with the uniquely American brand of confidence of the time.

Verse I:

Have you heard the latest news that's giving all the coons de blues
It's all about a gentleman of color,
He's just landed in the town, and he's doing things up brown,
All de colored population's in a furor,
He done cut an awful swell 'mongst de high-toned colored Belles
Every darkie's eyes in town done opened wide,
And dis coon[']s got lots of tin
He's done bought up all de gin,
De coons all shout as down de street he glides.

Chorus:

He's a hot coon from Memphis you will hear them cry
A hot coon from Memphis when he passes by,
A straight haired yaller nigger cuts but mighty little figure when they run against dis hot coon from Memphis

Verse II:

At de swell cafés he dines it makes the other coons eyes shine
The white folks show dis hot coon partialty
He calls on Astors and Depews
His neat card they don't refuse and dats done roused de colored animosty
Every coon's done brought a gun done brought razors, by the ton not a five-cent piece is this hot coon's life worth
Some night while he's asleep, I spec' down on him dey'll creep
And blow dis high strung coon clean off the earth.[38]

Figure 4.7. "A Hot Coon from Memphis: Coon Gossip," words by Bob Cole, music by George Walker, F. A. Mills, New York, 1897. *Source:* Author's collection.

Hall Studios produced most of Williams and Walker's early photographs as well as tobacco cards that showcased baseball players, celebrities, and fads, of which the cake walk was the latest. Because Williams and Walker were so closely associated with the dance, they were the obvious choice for promotional material. The popularity of the series became stock images used to promote cake walks, the old South, and all manner of products. George knew that he and Bert needed to "[take] for ourselves publicity, which is as good as a certified check in this business," and the plan continued to work.[39] American Tobacco also produced five large, colorful, true-to-life images for Old Virginia Cheroots that featured the young dancers, which paid promotional dividends for years.[40] A prolific source of promotion was a set of postcards that was issued by Franz Huld for the US and European markets. Although low fidelity, they were purchased by the thousands and confirmed Williams and Walker as the supreme cake walkers everywhere they were sent.

Figure 4.8. "The Hottest Coon in Town," American Tobacco card, circa 1895 to 1898. *Source:* Author's collection.

Figure 4.9. Cake Walk No. 2, George Walker, Belle Davis, Bert Williams, and Stella Wiley. *Source:* Courtesy of Case Auctions.

By mid-September of 1897, Williams and Walker were scoring at Pastor's Twenty-Third Street Theatre, where they tried to make a hit with some new songs, like "Enjoy Yourselves," but audiences only wanted to hear "You're Not So Warm." Next, they appeared with Hyde's Comedians in a sketch titled "The Upper Ten and Lower Five of Blackville" during a tour of the East and Midwest.[41] While on tour, Williams and Walker announced that they were to appear in *In a Policy Shop; or, 4-11-44* in the 1898 to 1899 season as leaders of their own company. Simultaneously, George acquired most of the cast of Isham's *Octoroons*, managed by the Mallory Brothers, Frank (1864 to 1917) and Edward (1865 to 1920), following the decline of Isham, likely due to syphilis.[42] With George's goal of having his own show in sight, it was vitally important that his small company sustainably grow into an elite and lucrative wellspring of "real" Black culture. Although unknown at the time, the coming year and season would prove to be their best, most profitable yet.

Figure 4.10. "Enjoy Yourselves," words by Dave Reed Jr., music by Charles B. Ward, T.B. Harms & Company, New York / London, 1897. *Source:* Author's collection.

Part Two
The Stride

Chapter 5

Cake Walks and Culture
1898

Cake Walk Double Crossover

Between December 1897 and January 1898, the New York press reported that William K. Vanderbilt, one of New York's famed "Four Hundred" elites, performed the cake walk at exclusive house parties and "led in magnificent style, introducing many new steps and graceful glides that brought applause from the guests" to the strains of "All Coons Look Alike to Me."[1] Once news spread of the "Four Hundred" slumming to the level of the lowly cake walk, prominent and enterprising Black walkers from the Midwest and East issued challenges to Vanderbilt and other aristocrats who also took up the dance. The Black challengers all knew that White people did not know or care for the dance's cultural context or the requisite merit to walk with style, so they jumped at the chance for some real, easy money. When Bert and George read the news of Vanderbilt's "success" as a cake walker, George saw an opportunity to gain some free publicity and arrest control of a Black cultural product in a public setting. The New York *World* reported their conversation while they were dressed in coat and tails in the smoking room at the Douglass Club at 114 West Thirty-First Street:

> "See here Bertie," said Mr. Walker, "here's Willie K. Vanderbilt going in for cake walking."
> "He's not so warm," languidly returned Mr. Walker.

"He'd better stick to railroads and yachts and horses and"—explained Mr. Walker, himself getting warm.

"Oh, I don't know," answered the indifferent Mr. Williams.

"But I do!" retorted Mr. Walker. "Cake walk! Why, Willie K. couldn't walk for a doughnut! But he's got a name, d'ye see, Bertie, he's got a name, and he'll be cutting us out of engagements. Why managers will be falling over each other. But I'll tell you what we'll do, Bertie, we'll challenge him and we'll do him in a week."

"It's a shame to take the money," said Mr. Williams, "so make the stakes small, George."[2]

The following morning, Bert, George, and their valet Alfred strolled down Fifth Avenue, and upon reaching Vanderbilt's Petit Chateau at the corner of Fifty-Second Street, they requested a personal audience with him. The butler reported that "Mr. Vanderbilt was busy smoking and entertaining some callers, and he would not be seen, but he would carry any message to Mr. Vanderbilt that they were pleased to give him." Their only recourse was to hand the butler their written challenge and try again later:

To Mr. William K. Vanderbilt

Corner of Fifty-second Street and Fifth Avenue

New York

Dear Sir:

In view of the fact that you have made a success as a cake-walker, having appeared in a semi-public exhibition and having posed as an expert in that capacity, we, the undersigned world-renowned cake-walkers, believing that the attention of the public has been distracted from us on account of the tremendous hit which you have made, hereby challenge you to compete with us in a cake-walking match, which will decide which of us shall deserve the title of champion cake-walker of the world. As a guarantee of good faith, we have this day deposited at the office of the New York World the sum of $50. If you purpose providing to the public that you really are an expert cake-walker we shall be pleased to have you cover that amount and name the day on which it will be convenient for you to try your odds against us.

Yours truly,

Williams and Walker[3]

Following the attempt, they retired to the Douglass Club smoking room for an hour and continued their conversation:

> "What about that answer from Willie K.?" asked Mr. Williams, pulling out his watch.
> "My dear Bertie," replied Mr. Walker, "we have called on Mr. Vanderbilt once. To do again would not be the proper thing. We will send Alfred for his answer."[4]

Upon Alfred's arrival, the butler informed him that Vanderbilt was still smoking, and at 5:30 that evening, the answer was the same:

> "Still smoking," mused Mr. Walker at midnight in the Progress Club's supper-room [at Fifth Avenue and Sixty-Third Street].
> "Smoking," echoed Mr. Williams, "but he's not so warm."[5]

Despite Vanderbilt's indifference, George made further use of his contact at the New York *World*, and, a week after, "Cake Walks and Culture" was published. Presented as a "careful philosophical analysis of cake walking as dance and an art, which are important contributions to literature," the article featured drawings of Williams and Walker and the Vanderbilts for emphasis and an explanation of what was about to unfold:

> That Mr. Vanderbilt's cake walking exhibitions and the singing of the "coon songs" is a direct infringement upon Messrs. Williams and Walker's accomplishments there can be no doubt. But they display no jealousy. They show no petty selfishness, on the contrary, they are pleased that the fashionable world should take a lively interest in the form of relaxation that is distinctly American.
> Though flattered by Vanderbilt's effort, Walker wanted it known in plain terms that, "Mr. Vanderbilt suffers from the natural disadvantage of his training and environment."[6]

Figure 5.1. "Cake Walks and Culture." *Source: The World* (New York), January 23, 1898, 33.

Next, George made his first public statement of Black cultural sovereignty in the headline "Mr. Vanderbilt Not Likely to Succeed as a Cakewalker—He's Not to the Manner Born." His blaze-bravado and willingness to publicly leverage Blackness as a cultural currency was unprecedented and may have been the first time anyone, let alone a member of the Four Hundred, was taken to task on the points of Afro-American excellence in a public setting:

Of course, a cake-walker is born, not made. While we welcome Mr. Vanderbilt as an amateur and a member of the best society, yet he should know that he is not the manner [sic] born, and probably never will achieve the distinction he might obtain in some other and less conspicuous walk of life.

His ball, of which we hear so much, will doubtless be a grand and gorgeous affair. Naturally, we are glad to see how the "400" are taking up rag songs, and especially cake-walking.

That is bound to be the feature of this coming ball.

We should like to aid Mr. Vanderbilt in any way we can to make the cake-walk a thorough success. I may say we promise not to evince any chagrin if all the honors go to the host on that occasion.

I wonder if Mr. Willie Vanderbilt smiles naturally? If he really hopes to reach a worthy eminence as a pedestrian he must know how to smile, for that is absolutely characteristic of a cake-walker par excellence. It is his business to smile, as if he really meant it.

Then, his toes must be off the ground. Perhaps Mr. Vanderbilt does not know that. Also, he should have patent leather shoes on, or at any rate have a good shine.

And there's another thing—a good cake-walker must be not only a high stepper—and I presume all in Mr. Vanderbilt's set are—but he must also know the flat foot step. Now, that's where he'll need help, for he'll need a good heel action at the great ball so as to get the real spring heel-and-toe steps.

But the real thing is to be a rag-time walker, something that these cushion-foot coons never can be, even if they live to get white hairs. Mr. Vanderbilt was not born a coon. He can't help that. But it's what he will miss when it comes to his big hoe-down.

I would just like to have a mangle with Mr. Vanderbilt, I would. Failing that let him study the suggestions of Mr. Williams, my partner, and consult the pictures illustrating the graces of cake-walking, for which we and two young ladies posed.

Observation and diligent practice should enable Mr. Vanderbilt to positively electrify the spectator, no matter how swell the function. Of course, that will require grace. I don't insinuate that a member in good standing of the most exclusive circle of metropolitan society does not possess that qualification. It also requires experience, and Mr. Vanderbilt is gradually acquiring that. It wants perfect knowledge of the multitude of steps, both plain and fancy. It necessitates poise and swing, and above all a perpetual smile, in order to become a prize cake-walker.[7]

Because of the tradition of begging humanity, utilized in the so-called slave narratives and other Afro-American manifestos well into the twentieth century, George's directness, likely perceived as arrogance, surely ruffled feathers. His use of "swing," a rhythmic concept employed ubiquitously in subsequent generations to denote the most fundamental and mysterious (to White people) aspects of syncopation, may have been a first in print. Further, his right to cultural sovereignty *by birth* and Vanderbilt's reciprocal lack of membership in the Black race had been an effective tactic to justify the subjugation of non-Whites since the colonial period. Astutely, George used the same tactic to subvert and invert social norms, and Bert's uncharacteristically direct contribution followed suit:

> Mr. Vanderbilt, unfortunately not being able to accept our challenge to a competitive cake walk, I am glad of this opportunity to present some suggestions and advice, remember with some illustrations pertinent to his coming ball and cakewalk.
>
> Of course, the music is a very essential part of a cake-walk. It must have the right swing so it must carry you along, you know, or it will not give the necessary inspiration.
>
> It will not do for Mr. Vanderbilt to rely on any Hungarian orchestra or Wagner quartet. He must have real harmony and action, plenty of action; none of this jerky, high-fangled music, but just melody.
>
> Here in the North even children learn to walk as soon as possible can get on Thompson Street and listen to the strains of a hand organ; but I don't suspect Mr. Vanderbilt, all tied up with the restrictions of wealth, ever had these early advantages, which every pickaninny came by naturally.
>
> Grace and an easy carriage come just as natural as the coon kid as melody and pattering do. They are just born in them—a different inheritance. With a little cultivation dancing and cake walking become almost an art with them.

> We (meaning the firm of Williams and Walker) are not merely cake-walkers by any manner of means. We have developed our natural qualities and race characteristics until we have become the most-talked-of colored comedians in the world. I don't say this boastfully, but only as expressing our regret that Mr. Vanderbilt did not see fit to accept our challenge. He might have learned a few things not dreamed of in his philosophy. We have been abroad, in London, Paris and all the continental cities, besides traveling all over the United States.
>
> Now Mr. Vanderbilt, we understand, is trying to emulate us. Besides cake-walking, he has been singing our coon songs—"Oh, I Don't Know," "Miss Maria Johnson" and our latest success, "I Don't Like No Cheap Man." Our songs have become the recognized cake-walk music, as it is perfectly natural that he should imitate us.[8]

Without mincing words, Bert and George declared the cake walk a dance of action and conviction that stemmed from a uniquely Afro-American experience and that no amount of pedigree or schooling could change that. To stir the pot, Bert's reference to Hamlet's lament to Horatio, "There are more things in heaven and earth, Horatio, than are dreamt of in your philosophy," subtly declared that he was far more comfortable on either side of double consciousness than any member of the Four Hundred.[9] The ploy worked well enough to compel Vanderbilt to downplay the challenge, "The challenge tickles Mr. Vanderbilt immensely and he remarked last night that he was having lots of fun out of his being a cake walker, but he would not accept the challenge, as he had no desire to be classed as a professional."[10] After the publication of the article, a few adventurous and ambitious elites sought the duo's instruction and companionship. When they returned to their western tour with Hyde's Comedians, George gifted the song "I Don't Like No Cheap Man" to McIntyre and Heath, now their contemporaries.[11] During a short break after the Los Angeles engagement, Bert likely traveled to San Francisco for the conclusion of the "Dora Dean" trial, and Nash made his way home to Lawrence, where the homefolk were eager to revel in his success:

> Nash Walker, who is spending a few days, in this city, has probably made more fame for himself than any other man,

black or white, who has gone out from here . . . Walker has done enough to make any town proud of him and when he comes back home he is always sure of a royal welcome. He has the best press notices of any man who has been in the show business. He is a master of dialect and singing and many of the most popular airs have been composed by himself.

Mr. Walker is a good deal of a sport. He dresses flashingly but as he earns all kinds of money no one begrudges him the goodtime he's having. He looks well fed and happy.[12]

Several local papers mistakenly announced that Nash planned to delay his departure to compete in a cake walk with local champions Doc Brown (1835 to 1905) of Kansas City and Dandy Bud from Independence on Decoration Day. However, George was under contract until the end of the season and had to rush back. Some Lawrencians were so upset that a telegram from Williams and Walker and a statement from Nash's mother were published in the *Lawrence Daily World* to calm things.[13] Following disbandment, the partners appeared in vaudeville throughout the summer. Then, *she* walked in.

Enter Ada Overton

When Ada (Reed) Overton was added to the cast during the summer of 1898, it was clear that she was a star in the making, and shortly after, she and George became an item. Ada was born on February 14, 1880, at 112 Thompson Street in Manhattan.[14] Her parents, Moses C. Overton (1856 to 1882), a waiter, and Pauline (Whitfield) Overton (1861 to 1910), a dressmaker, were born near Elizabeth City, North Carolina. Moses's family was large, somewhat prosperous, interracially mixed, and had emancipated members as far back as the colonial period. Pauline's early years were likely in bondage, but at some point both parents made it to Manhattan and were married on October 13, 1877. Unfortunately, Moses died when Ada was two, and Pauline subsequently married Miles Reed (b. 1845) when Ada was still a small child.[15]

Because her mother was an accomplished dressmaker, young Ada was always dressed in the latest style. At a very early age, she distinguished herself as Little Ada Reed when she danced on the sidewalks of Manhattan. In similar fashion to young Nash in Lawrence, James Weldon Johnson credited Ada with popularizing child performers on the city's streets. Eventually, she recruited three other girls and choreographed their act on her family's front stoop. Their success attracted the attention of an organ grinder, who noticed that when Ada and her friends followed him from block to block, they made money at each stop. Soon they began working together regularly, and her mother, Pauline, allowed it as long as they never went beyond a predetermined distance from the house, at which point the grinder divided the money, treated the girls to ice cream and candy, and returned them to the stoop. The act became so popular along Sixth Avenue that the police agreed to provide traffic control if they moved along after one song. Eventually the act was relegated to side streets when the traffic in front of the Park Theatre on Thirty-Fifth Street and Broadway became gridlocked. When Ada was around ten years old, her mother forbade her from busking and enrolled her in the Thorpe dancing studio on Seventh Avenue between Thirty-Fourth and Thirty-Fifth Streets. When Ada was thirteen, theatrical manager A. M. Palmer attempted to place her in the *1492* show at the Chicago World's Fair in 1893, but her mother did not allow it.[16]

Ada completed Mrs. Thorpe's program in her late teens and had a short stint with Isham's *Octoroons*, where she showed real star potential, but her singing was lackluster. Shortly after, she was engaged with her former partners from her sidewalk days in Black Patti's Troubadours, the top Black aggregation at the time in *A Trip to Coontown*, the first major Black production in the United States. Ada was allowed to join the cast under the condition that her mother be added as wardrobe mistress.[17]

Shortly thereafter, Ada was paired with Grace Halliday (1874 to 1906) in a sister act following the death of Grace's actual sister. According to James Weldon Johnson, the show's producer, coauthor, lead actor, and stage manager, Bob Cole, hired Ada because he believed that she could eventually learn to sing at an acceptable level. However, her singing did not improve quickly enough during the season, and she was fired. Nevertheless, critic Sylvester Russell, who was rather conservative with his praise, saw her at Miner's Bowery Theatre in New York on September 6, 1897, in Isham's *Octoroons* and declared her "the greatest girl dancer," and proclaimed that *A Trip to Coontown* was "too legitimate to be criticized."[18]

A Trip to Coontown was very successful until a row developed between managers Voelckel and Nolan and the multitalented Cole, who played Willie Wayside, a White tramp, and his partner, Billy Johnson. At the time, Cole was one of the top performers in the country, regardless of color, and believed his pay should have reflected his status. When it became clear that no raise was coming, he left the company with his intellectual property, and

Figure 5.2. Robert (Bob) Cole. *Source: The Colored American Magazine* 9, no. 3 (November 1905): 634. Beinecke Rare Book and Manuscript Library, JWJ A +C7195.

Figure 5.3. Ada Overton circa 1900. *Source:* Schomburg Center for Research in Black Culture, New York Public Library.

management took him to court. Ultimately, Cole retained ownership of his work, but he was blacklisted for a time, which exacerbated what Sylvester Russell called a "nervous temperament." Shortly thereafter, his partnership with Billy Johnson dissolved along with the show. It was no small loss, and Cole's somewhat successful experience protecting his liberty traumatized young Ada, and she promptly retired from the stage after she was fired.[19] However, her talent was such that would-be agents and managers wanted her to return. According to Tom Fletcher, "as a dancer she could do almost anything, and no matter whether it was buck and wing, cake walk, or even some form of grotesque dancing, she lent the performance a neat gracefulness of movement which was unsurpassed by anyone. Those of us who can actually remember her, are pretty well agreed that she was a Florence Mills and Josephine Baker rolled into one."[20]

The following season (1898), Grace Halliday became engaged to Williams and Walker's new stage manager, Frank Mallory of the Mallory Brothers, formerly of *A Trip to Coontown*, who was tasked with recruiting a sister act. Ada was intelligent, sophisticated, beautiful, well-trained, supremely talented, and fit the bill better than anyone else at the time. Unfortunately, Mallory's assurances to her that the Williams and Walker Company was a new kind of Afrocentric organization that was destined for unprecedented success fell flat, and she refused. That is, "until [she was] summoned by Cupid, disguised as George Walker," although it reportedly took several attempts. Some historians falsely associated Ada with the American Tobacco Company cake walk photo session, but it took place at least two years before she joined the Williams and Walker cast.[21] Regardless, in short order, Ada became a third, silent partner in the expanding Williams and Walker organization. Despite her addition, the show was only passable and lacked refinement. Fully aware, George set out to augment the show by adding every high-caliber specialist act available, most of which came from the faltered *Octoroons* cast. Meanwhile, the dynamic pair of talented Black artists, Will Cook and Paul Dunbar, were creating a new show for Williams and Walker that would set the standard of excellence for Black shows in the coming decade.

Clorindy

Fortuitously, Frederick Douglass's introduction of Will Cook and Paul Dunbar at the 1893 World's Fair facilitated a partnership that lasted for the rest of Dunbar's short life. Their first collaboration, *Clorindy; or, Origin of the Cake Walk*, was intended to establish a sense of Black ownership of the new cake walk fad, "from plantation to palace." Bert and George contributed seed money for the project and introduced Cook to their manager, Will McConnell. Williams and Walker were the intended stars, but their contract with Hyde and Behman prevented their participation, so Ernest Hogan was cast as the star and impromptu stage manager.[22]

According to Cook, the script was finished rather quickly. Dunbar worked at a near-superhuman level, which inspired him to meet the challenge presented by his supremely talented collaborator. Both men were independent and opinionated, which gave them a quarrelsome reputation among other performers. Cook, especially, was a loner, and his feisty personality was his greatest asset and, in many ways, his greatest liability. Long before he met Dunbar, he did everything in his power to equip himself with all the necessary tools to write Afro-American operas with sensitivity and humor that highlighted the uniqueness of the culture. Likewise, Dunbar was fresh off his first major publication, *The Uncalled*. His use of dialect to describe and emphasize the reality of Black life in the United States afforded him a new kind of Afro-American celebrity, previously the exclusive realm of his former employer, Frederick Douglass. Their work ethic and personalities matched well, and the partners developed a great respect for George's sense of cultural sovereignty and knack for business. Cook recalled the similarities between George and his mentor Antonin Dvorak:

> [George's] has been the greatest influence in the development of modern, Negro music. At twenty-eight he could not read a note and could hardly read his name, yet day and night he talked Negro music to his people, urged and compelled his writers to give something characteristic. Each year he wanted bigger and better things. He engaged the best Negro voices in the United States and their success in ensemble singing was as great in London, Paris and Berlin as in New York, Boston and Chicago. Dvorak would have been proud to know such a man. In all reverence—Dvorak-George Walker. They had high ideals and they showed the way.[23]

Everyone involved knew what was at stake and that any opportunity to express Black culture in such a new way was going to be a singular one, subject to White acceptance. However, the changes they sought were understandably incremental, so minstrel tropes permeated the play. With that in mind, Cook set out to create music that was unmistakably and unapologetically Black, which triggered his mother's reaction to "Who Dat Say Say Chicken in Dis Crowd?," his "most Negroid song": "Oh, Will! Will! I've sent you all over the world to study and become a great musician, and you returned such a *nigger*!"[24] Cook's mother graduated from Oberlin College and firmly believed that Black composers should strive to Western European ideals to ensure their financial and, by extension, cultural success. As a path of less resistance, many ambitious Afro-Americans prescribed European pursuits for their children and needed convincing that Black humanity was a thing of beauty all its own that was commercially viable and worthy of respect. Considering the social conditions for most Black people at the time, their fear of the potential consequences of willfully exposed Black humanity was justified.

Under the direction of Ed Rice, *Clorindy* opened on the rooftop of the Manhattan Casino on July 4, 1898, with Ernest Hogan as the lead. The show remained at the Casino for six weeks as part of "Rice's Summer Nights" before it was taken to Boston, where it split into two companies, likely because Cook and Dunbar wanted first-class booking with Williams and Walker as the stars and Rice wanted the production to tour vaudeville houses exclusively. Hogan signed on with Black Patti's Troubadours for the coming season.[25] Having fulfilled their contract with Hyde and Behman, George assembled a new cast of specialist performers to insert into a loose plot, à la John Isham, that was linked together via Bert and George's interplay. As George remembered in 1908,

> We had increased our act quite a bit by now, so we contracted with [Will A. McConnell] to start the season to begin in September [1898]. Thus came our first show "The Senegambian Carnival." It consisted of vaudeville acts and we put on Will Cook's "Clorinda" for an afterpiece. We had a bill of colored acts that looks good yet. There were that Malory Brothers, and Brooks' musical act; Ed Goggin[s] and Charles Davis, acrobats; Hodges and Launchmere, singing and dancing; Black Carl, the magician, and Bert and me. Now, would you grudge real money to see that aggregation? This was the beginning of the [Bert and me and] "them" part of the combination.[26]

George had boasted of a first-class, Broadway-caliber production for months, and on September 5, 1898, Williams and Walker's *Clorindy* premiered at the Boston Theatre. With Cook, Dunbar, Shipp, and Overton giving their input, Williams and Walker took their first, best shot.[27] The show's plot featured Dollar Bill (Bert), a Southern levy roustabout who had recently won $30,000 in the Louisiana Lottery. In his travels, he ran across Silver King (George), a confidence man. As Dollar's self-appointed adviser, Silver persuaded Dollar to part with some of his winnings as payment for his consultation as they made their way north. The production culminated in a grand cake walk and Dollar Bill's ascension into Darktown society.[28] As the first vehicle under their leadership, the *Senegambian Carnival* allowed Williams and Walker to showcase their unique chemistry as they introduced well-seasoned, successful vaudeville acts between their skits. The first of two acts presented singing, dancing, solo specialties, and gymnastics. The second act was Cook and Dunbar's *Clorindy*, billed as "the best exposition of the ability of colored people to reach the highest standard of entertainment."[29] Audiences were both surprised and thrilled by the prowess of Afro-American performers in what was at the time a revolutionary theatrical spectacle.

After closing in Boston, the company appeared for one night on the Casino Roof Garden in New York and in Philadelphia. Following a critically successful yet financially moderate week in Cincinnati, management canceled the engagement in Buffalo in late September, and they were left stranded. When reached for comment, Will McConnell said,

> We came to the conclusion that there was little money in going through the country this season for the purpose of building up a reputation that might be valuable in years to come. Accordingly our engagements to appear at the theatres where the box office schedule is rather high, have been canceled, and when we resume it will be at the "popular priced" houses, where the local managers tell me a colored company ought to be exceedingly popular and profitable.[30]

The layoff infuriated George, but during that time Jesse Shipp introduced him to the Hurtig Brothers, Benjamin (1864 to 1909) and Jules (1868 to 1928), and their cousin Harry Seamon (ca. 1865 to 1938), "commission merchants" who had an office on West Sixth Street in Cincinnati. George struck a deal with them on the spot to keep the company together, continue the fight for access to first-class houses, and remove McConnell's hands from the cashbox.[31] Bert's valet, Thomas Ernest "Chappie" Chappelle (1886 to 1977), remembered, "Bad luck seemed to follow us around that season, come to think of it. We were stranded twice. The weather was very hot and in addition we followed Primrose and West around the country. They must have picked up whatever money there was."[32]

When the company made it to Philadelphia and reopened at the People's Theatre in early October under Hurtig and Seamon, George and Ada introduced "The Hottest Coon in Dixie," Ernest Hogan's former piece in the show.[33] Because the song was originally written with George in mind and echoed his earlier effort, "A Hot Coon from Memphis," he and Ada mesmerized audiences:

> When I go out to stroll away,
> I wear my Regent suit,
> Put on my silk plug hat so gay,
> My necktie is a beaut',
> Put on my gloves and cane in hand,
> I wander down the way,
> Whenever I meet some merry beaux,
> Here's what the darkies say,
> Behold the hottest coon,
> Your eyes e'er lit on,
> Velvet ain't good enough,
> For him to sit on,
> When he goes down the street,
> Folks yell like sixty,
> Behold the hottest coon in Dixie.[34]

Shortly after George and Ada became an item, Bert met Charlotte "Lottie" Thompson (1866 to 1929), a widow eight years his senior from Chicago. She was the granddaughter of Henry Mitchem, a Scotsman, and Casa Mitchem, a Cheyenne woman. Her mother was reportedly the only Black woman who was ever admitted to the Convent of the Sacred Heart in Chicago. However, Lottie was raised mainly by her godfather, John Jones, a famous abolitionist and a member of one of the most prominent Black families in the city. She attended Northwestern University and studied to be a teacher but likely did not finish. Her first professional stage work was in Baltimore with a vaudeville quartet for six months before she met Bert, who promptly asked her to join the Williams and Walker Company. In *Clorindy*, she sang Dunbar's "Jump Back, Honey, Jump Back" during the first act. Although she had passion for the craft, Lottie never set the stage afire like Dora Dean Johnson, nor did she dazzle audiences with her skill like Ada. Rather, she seems to have had a genuinely introverted sensibility that appealed to both audiences and Bert. She quickly became his rock and remained so for the rest of his life.[35]

Newly invigorated, the tour resumed at the Academy in Washington, DC, Will Cook's hometown. Both he and Dunbar were present at opening night, and the *Evening Times* declared, "If enthusiasm could have raised the roof off[,] the managers of the theatre would have had to postpone tonight's performance."[36] *The Morning Times* raised the stakes: "Only the first-class theatres will be played, and lovers of novelty will be given a chance to learn that the colored race has a music that, far from being a burlesque, is as high class in its way as any that has been given us by the schools of Europe."[37] That socially dissonant aspiration was only partially true because most theatre owners did not want to book Black acts in their houses despite the company's potential to draw large audiences and profits. Unfortunately, the company was stranded again at the end of the engagement, likely over a dispute with new management over booking.

While the company laid off for two weeks in Philadelphia, George and Bert took a train to New York, where they found their former managers Hyde and Behman in a bind. The stock company's production of *The White Rabbits* at the Park Theatre had disbanded, and that inspired George's growing penchant for dealmaking. He needed money to keep his production afloat, and Hyde and Behman needed a quality act for a few weeks. In the end, George received the financing he needed and agreed to repay it by filling the hole left by *The White Rabbits* with Williams and Walker. Not wanting to repeat Bob Cole's experience, George used the money to purchase *The Senegambian Carnival* outright from Lederer and McConnell on October 12, 1898. To fit smaller vaudeville stages, a condensed, forty-minute version of the show that featured new, secondhand scenery of a corridor of a palace with a wide stairway in the background was utilized. They opened at Proctor's in Manhattan and then moved through several other venues through the first week of December, first at $250 per week; by the time they closed, their fee had increased to $350 per week.[38] The *New York Dramatic Mirror* noted,

> The first scene was laid on a steamboat pier in Louisiana, the second on a New York street and the third in a grand ballroom, with a stairway reaching up into the flies. This was probably the most elaborate setting ever given a production of this kind, and the

colored folks seemed to revel in it. A profusion of red incandescent lights and calciums and a splashing fountain helped to make this scene effective. The entire company made their appearance by walking down the staircase and the effect was dazzling.[39]

Figure 5.4. "I'm a Cooler for the Warmest Coon in Town," Words and music by Williams and Walker, Joseph W. Stern, New York, 1898. *Source:* Frances G. Spencer Collection of American Sheet Music, Arts and Special Collections Research Center, Moody Memorial Library, Baylor University, Waco, Texas. Public domain.

Figure 5.5. "He's Up Against the Real Thing Now," words by Edward Furber, music by Bert Williams, Joseph W. Stern, New York, 1898. *Source:* Author's collection.

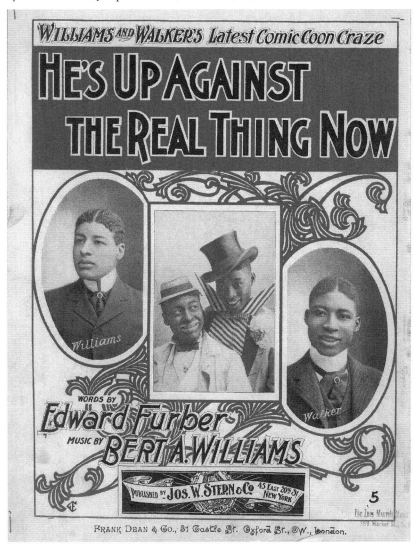

Once up and running again, Bert and George continued to make refinements as they composed and performed their original music, including "I'm a Cooler for the Warmest Coon in Town" and others that were published by Joseph Stern. Although the first half of the season was rough, things were looking up, and *The Senegambian Carnival* was renamed *A Lucky*

Coon when they opened at the Park Theatre, Brooklyn, on December 11, 1898. Following their stint in New York, Nash spent Christmas in Lawrence with his mother and grandmother and brought several photographs to be displayed at Dick Brother's drug store on Massachusetts Street.[40] As exhausted as he must have been, the season was only half over. Regardless, he had a company of sixty people who depended on him, and, despite his problems with management, he was determined to make it a success.

Figure 5.6. George Walker circa 1898. *Source:* Author's collection.

Chapter 6

As I See You on the Stage

1899 to 1900

A Lucky Coon

Williams and Walker opened 1899 at the Dewey Theatre in New York, where the show had been lengthened with new features and renamed *A Lucky Coon*. Bert and George made a hit with "Why Don't You Get a Lady of Your Own?" Chicot, the reviewer for the *Morning Telegraph*, objected to the ostentatious production and declared that he wanted a real Coon show, not a Black and tan.[1] Hurtig and Seamon thought it worthy to include a bit of hyperbole in the fluff packets they sent out to local newspapermen where the company performed: "Last season at the command of the Prince of Wales they appeared before them at their mansion Marlborough (Blenheim) Palace. The prince and his guests were so elated and pleased at their performance that he personally gave Williams and Walker an autographed letter thanking them for entertaining him and his honored guests."[2] Also, in a folio of songs from the show, Bert and George were depicted on the cover "coaching W. M. Vanderbilt for cake walk" and "appearing before the Prince of Wales," among other descriptions of merit. Although propagated by Hurtig and Seamon for promotional purposes, neither happened. If either were true, Williams and Walker would have been the toast of high society in London and New York. Also, a nondisclosure agreement surely would have been in effect, as was the case when New York's "Four Hundred" crowded their apartment for private lessons before a large event in Saratoga a year earlier. More important, it showed that Hurtig and Seamon were willing to stretch the truth and test limits to promote the exploits of their stars.[3]

When the company made it to the High Street Theatre in Cincinnati on March 2, 1899, Fred Neddermyer's Orchestra refused to play with Will Cook as conductor and quit in protest. Bert attempted to explain the situation to the audience, as the theatre's manager tried and failed to relieve the tension, so the music was furnished by cast members Mazie Brooks and Charlie Alexander on violin and piano. Cook conducted out of principled spite.[4] When the company made its way to the Great Northern Theatre in Chicago, the management did not want Williams and Walker to stay at their related hotel despite the fact that George had once worked there as a bellhop. To discourage their patronage, a demand of twenty-five dollars a night was made. However, at $400 a week, Bert and George had become the top-earning Black performers in the country and paid the fee, an act of defiance they would repeat with regularity for the rest of their lives. Despite the row, Lottie Thompson, Ed Goggins, Maggie Davis, and many other of the company's top performers were from Chicago, and eventually it became a second home to the Williams and Walker company. They were never Jim Crowed in the Windy City again.[5]

Another sign of the company's arrival to the "big time" was the new baseball team. However, despite their optimism at the close of their return engagement in Philadelphia in early May of 1899, the Williams and Walker team was humiliated by Black Patti's team 28 to 13.[6] Undeterred, they made their way to the Academy of Music in Washington, DC, where *The Times* commented on the Williams and Walker formula:

> It is merely stated that "A Lucky Coon" gives ample excuse for the introduction of those specialties which have always been a feature of the Williams and Walker entertainments. Incidentally, one or two of the incidents written in are supposed to give the senior member of the firm opportunity for the class of work at which he excels, while plenty of chance is provided for such songs, dances, choruses, and cake walks as the Negro is known to do to the best advantage.[7]

The Evening Star focused on the patrons: "The two galleries were packed to suffocation, and the lower floor was well filled, the applause being almost constant in the enthusiasm of the colored people present being of hilarious and contagious kind."[8] Unfortunately, Williams and Walker's success in Washington, DC, was short-lived. A cold snap hampered attendance in playhouses citywide, and the company was left stranded again. At that time,

Figure 6.1. Advertisement, Gilmore's Auditorium. *Source: Philadelphia Times*, April 30, 1899, 27.

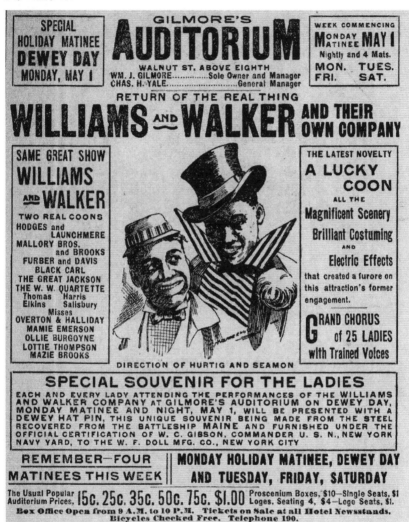

Jesse Shipp replaced Frank Mallory as stage manager.[9] Bert's valet Chappie remembered, "We were stranded again in Washington. Somebody tried to attach the costumes, but each of us grabbed a couple of trunks and claimed they were ours. Then we had them in our rooms and managed to hold onto them."[10] Once back in New York, the company closed the season at the

Dewey Theatre. At the end of the engagement, a policeman attempted to stop their show because it violated the Mazet rules that prohibited secular performers from wearing costumes on Sundays. As reported in the *New York Journal and Advertiser*, "he desisted when it was explained to him that 'black face' is the complexion in which Williams and Walker regularly eat and sleep, as well as act, having been born in the same."[11]

George's first season as a leader tested his still-developing business acumen, but his resolve ensured a measure of success. By season's end, he had raised capital first to buy and then again to keep the show. They endured a protesting orchestra and others that refused to perform their music and upgraded their management and salary. The tour was profitable, and rather optimistically the partners further tested the waters to see how much liberty their newfound success afforded them. While enjoying the high life at the St. Cloud Hotel café on Forty-Second and Broadway, Bert, George, and possibly their manager Sam Tuck or writer and performer George Cohan "agitat[ed] polite society to much inquiry" when the unusually assertive Black men arrived and acted as though they belonged there. Some patrons left, but future US Representative Edwin Underhill inquired, and when he was told who they were, he replied, "I suppose we'll be gettin' Cole an' Johnson up here in glad clothes next."[12] Shortly thereafter, Bert and George spied a pair of summer cottages in Elmhurst, Long Island, at a popular theatrical retreat. A deposit had been paid and they had cash on hand to cover the balance. However, the deal was canceled after the developers learned that the would-be purchasers were Black. Word quickly spread to the resident actors in the village, and "every obstacle [was] put in the way of their completing the purchase." Incensed, Sam Tuck vowed to purchase the lots himself and then turn them over to Bert and George, but, wisely, the issue was dropped.[13]

In early June of 1899, Nash took the train to Lawrence and caused a stir on Massachusetts Street with his nickel-plated Pierce bicycle, complete with freewheel mechanism and coaster brakes.[14] After a few days, he hurried back to New York to marry Ada. On June 22, Reverend Dr. Bishop, of St. Philip's Church, performed the ceremony, and the reception was held at the newlyweds' apartment.[15] The *Journal and Advertiser* labeled George a "Benedict," a reference to Shakespeare's *Much Ado About Nothing*, in which Benedict, a confirmed bachelor, eventually married the beautiful and independent Beatrice: "There was excitement among the fair sex of the colored population yesterday when they heard that the Beau Brummel of the ebony aristocracy and well-known comedian, George Walker, of the firm of Williams and Walker, had taken unto himself are young and beautiful bride, Miss Ada Overton, who was last season the soubrette of the Williams and Walker company."[16] The rest of the summer of 1899 was spent out of the spotlight. However, Bert and George purchased a "swell yacht" and invited some friends to sail down the bay from Manhattan Beach, but the wind died, and they were stuck. To pass the time, Bert proposed a game of seven-up, and, once the inexperienced sailors were enthralled, a swell rolled them over. While floundering in the water, Bert reportedly yelled, "Say, you fellows. If we are saved remember I have the four-spot for low."[17]

The Policy Players

The "numbers game" had been the basis of minstrel skits for several years as well as Williams and Walker's previous and subsequent vehicles. As remembered by Tom Fletcher, "Policy was a game in those days. The winning numbers were picked after the turn of a wheel, patterned after a roulette wheel. Three spins of the wheel [and] the winning digits were picked. Like this: 3-6-9, or like this: 3-11-33, or 19-29-39. If you had any of those digits on your slip you played, you were the winner. That was called a 'gig.' You were paid four dollars for [a bet of] five cents."[18] Although they copyrighted their new show under several titles, the new stage manager, costar, and head writer Jesse Shipp's insight won out, and the team settled on *The Policy Players*.[19] Williams and Walker were credited with writing it, but they borrowed heavily from Isham's *Octoroons*, as noticed by reviewers in the cities where both companies played.[20] As the most experienced member of the company, Shipp possessed aptitude, skill, and patience that George put to prolific use as they updated Isham's defunct vehicle.

The first of two acts took place on Thompson Street, where Dusty Cheapman (Bert), a lottery fiend, somehow won the lottery. He was introduced to Happy Hotstuff (George), who devised a scheme to manifest Dusty's, and ultimately his own, desire to enter high society. The act concluded in the policy shop, where, following a dream, Happy and Dusty attempted to break the bank with the numbers 3-11-33, a play on the popular choice of 4-11-44. The second act was an elaborate, moonlit scene on the lawn of the "Astorbilt" (a conflation of the Astor and Vanderbilt family names) residence on the Hudson. To gain entrance to a lavish party, Happy and Dusty conned the butler, Mr. Readymoney, and Dusty impersonated the former president of Haiti. As an added attraction, Bert's bull terrier puppy Sonne was given a small part.[21]

Bert and Lottie married on September 21, 1899, just two days before *The Policy Players* opened the 1899 to 1900 season at Hoyt's Theatre in South Norwalk, Connecticut. Although the premise had changed little from the previous season, *The Sun* reported, "Nevertheless, it was amusing, and so crowded with songs and dances which were changed frequently that little matters what the name is that it bears."[22] The *New York Journal and Advertiser* declared it "momentous, because it launched something new and distinctly worthwhile in the realm of entertainment; momentous, because a huge audience uproariously hailed the clever mulatto team as organizers and chiefs of a burlesque company numbering forty-two performers."[23] When the tour moved to Philadelphia's Auditorium for a week's engagement, a row between chorus members Effie Wilson and Joe Smith erupted over a nickel, and Smith struck Wilson with a large stick. She was sent to the hospital and recovered well enough to perform the next day; Smith was arrested and removed from the company. Nevertheless, they earned more than $6,000 and were booked for a return engagement at the end of the season. Next came the Grand Theatre in Washington, DC, where, despite the good-clean image of the company, some local newsmen thought that management had "depart[ed] triflingly—ever so triflingly—from their regular policy." Serendipitously, the sentiment changed after the company found success, but all credit was given to Hurtig and Seamon, not Williams and Walker.[24] Washington, DC, being a "Chocolate City," the audience was especially fervent, and "the New Grand was packed to sardine intensity" with Black patrons. The manager used local police to block the unwanted Black patrons from the orchestra section in favor of Whites, but he failed spectacularly.[25]

Unfortunately, the growing popularity of the company had exposed a fundamental hypocrisy of the Jim Crow ethos; Whites did not want to share space with Blacks at Williams and Walker shows and failed to understand why Black people would revel in the rare opportunity to see a first-class Black show. Likewise, most theatre managers catered to White patrons and enacted policies to subjugate Blacks. Charles R. Douglass (1844 to 1920), veteran of the famous Fifty-Fourth Massachusetts Regiment and son of Frederick Douglass, expressed his frustration in *The Colored American*: "Are we forever to be dependent upon the whites for theatres, hotels, cafés, and stores of all descriptions? Can we ever escape those indignities so long as we continue to flood their pockets with our money and look up to them beseechingly for our every want? I think not."[26]

The situation meant that Black patrons were summarily denied access to the orchestra section in favor of Whites, who often overflowed into the designated Colored area. When that occurred on opening night, chaos ensued. As reported, Nelson E. Weatherless, a Black high school physics instructor, was forcefully ejected from the orchestra section and temporarily charged with disorderly conduct. Regardless, the engagement was profitable, but "Manager Chase had all he wanted of nigger shows." The ordeal was so stressful that his physician recommended a long hunting trip.[27] As it was, the growing number of Black people who attempted to assert their liberty and Whites' growing desire to consume Black cultural products while simultaneously despising Black people exposed a problem that had no logical solution for George. On one hand, Black patrons had champions whom they enthusiastically supported and were desperate for a recreational release. On the other, White curiosity and comfort was expected to be accommodated, and the conspicuous Black presence, even within the rules, was unacceptable. With their eyes on a future prize beyond the immediate concerns of what was essentially a local matter, George understood that the only measure of control the company had to usher in change was from the stage, where all eyes were on them and not in the hands of management and theatre patrons. Once issues of race and Black access to liberty left the theoretical and controlled confines of the stage, the best course of action was to say nothing and quietly move to the next town as the locals dealt with local problems facilitated by the confines of Jim Crow, the real "race problem."

George agreed with Charles Douglass's assertion that "a white man will not stand for color discrimination to the detriment of his pocket book," but he also knew that fighting every fight in every city would surely mean the end of the company and, therefore, the end of progress toward equal access to liberty.[28] Compromises were expected at every level. To boot, when Bert and George stayed in the nicest hotels that were available to them, they were required to eat their meals in their rooms to avoid unpleasant remarks from White guests who would object to their presence. All to avoid a repeat of the humiliation in Cripple Creek five years earlier and the most recent embarrassment at the Great Northern in Chicago earlier in the season. However, they demanded satisfaction and made a game of it. As reported in the *Kansas City Times*,

> The plan pursued by Mr. [George] Harris [Williams and Walker's business manager] was to go to the finest hotel in each city and pick out the finest apartment. Expense was not considered for a minute and whether the proprietor asked for five dollars a day or fifteen dollars a day made but little difference to the

manager and no difference to Williams and Walker. When Mr. Harris explained that the rooms were intended for two colored men, but that they would take their meals in their rooms and could be counted upon to be so quiet around the house that no one would know they were there and the proprietor seldom raised an objection to their coming, especially when he saw that the cost was no object.[29]

Following the successful implementation of the workaround, Bert and George were able to secure the best rooms at the Auditorium in Chicago, the Colonial in Cleveland, the Lincoln in Pittsburgh, and the Narragansett in Providence without incident. Moreover, the compromise of taking their meals in their rooms was included in their press kit for the cities where they performed, along with a sanitized version of their origin story.[30] Williams and Walker were still lifting as they climbed; their plight required subversive, preemptive action to offset the sliding scale of White morality.

Following Washington, DC, came a series of short engagements throughout the Midwest before a return engagement at the Great Northern in Chicago on Christmas Eve, where George made a hit with "The Medicine Man," despite objections from the Society for the Suppression of Ragtime.[31]

Chorus:

Oh, de medicine man.
Wid his grip in his han'.
He's an every lan'.
When he explains about yo' pains
The hair on yo' head will stan'.
Ef' yo' feel kinder sick
Yo'd bettah go quick—
As quickly as you can—
For nobody knows but the medicine man!

On Christmas Day, Sam Tuck organized a banquet at the Lakeland Hotel. Speeches were made by D. E. Russell, manager of the Great Northern Theatre; George H. Harris; Ed Smith; and Bert and George, who recited the original poem "As I See You on the Stage."[32] Despite the incident in DC, the year ended on a high note, and, for the first time, the company

Figure 6.2. "The Medicine Man," words and music by Williams and Walker, Joseph W. Stern, New York, 1899. *Source:* Author's collection.

was scheduled to play the Bowersock Opera House in Lawrence. George was making unprecedented business deals, dressed impeccably, and spent his money as soon as he made it on the people around him. As expressed in *The Freeman*,

> To be a businessman and a gentleman in the theatrical business is almost an impossibility. Mr. Walker was one of the few colored stars who was constantly trying to open new and greater fields for the colored performer—always hiring and holding as many together as was in his power, giving each a fair opportunity of showing what he could do, and always having a smile, a pleasant word and good advice for all, giving at all times a bit of cheer where the heart seemed sad, and ever ready to intercede and demand wherever there was a possibility of advancement.[33]

Despite the cold, Lawrence brimmed with anticipation, as noted in the *Lawrence Daily World*:

> About two hundred of the colored friends of Williams and Walker were down to the train this morning to welcome them home. When the swell colored gentlemen and ladies from New York arrived, they didn't cake walk up the street exactly, but they had the whole street to themselves. The silk ties of the gentleman and the automobile coats of the ladies wear a dazzling sight to their home friends, who hung around the corner long after the party had entered the Eldridge House. Since leaving here a boy Nash Walker has made a prodigious success in life and has won fame that is not confined to one continent. . . . It must be a source of great satisfaction to Nash to come back and receive such a greeting.[34]

The town's fervency was confirmed by the most fully packed house in recent memory. For those who did not buy their tickets well in advance, standing room only was at a premium: "Interest of course was centered in the work of Walker, and hundreds of friends were highly pleased at the way in which he acquitted himself. His 'pardner' Williams, is equally as good a comedian, and the two convulsed the audience with laughter from the beginning to the end of the show."[35]

Lawrence bootblacks were spread all over the house. During the second act, the performance was stopped by Sherman Harvey, president of the Twentieth Century Club, a well-known Black organization. He climbed onto the stage with a handsomely engraved and embossed sterling silver loving cup and presented it to the partners as a token of esteem and appreciation for the prominence Nash brought Lawrence and Black people. At the banquet after the performance, several speeches were given, including one from Sam Tuck, who declared the Bowersock was the best venue for a one-night stand.[36] Following Lawrence, they appeared at the Crawford Theatre in Topeka, where Tuck made a gaffe. Just before showtime, he appeared before the audience and stated that because of the inability of the orchestra to play the music of the show, it would be performed on a solo piano. He then criticized the local musicians who were without their leader, Frank Watson. After the company left town, Tuck sent an apology to the Crawford management, likely at George's request.[37] Surely Tuck believed he was helping, but by making the private thoughts of the company's members public, he only made things worse. Although innocuous, it would not be the last time that the good intentions of management made things harder for Bert and George.

Much like in the incident in DC, the audience in Topeka was estimated to be two-thirds Black, which included two box parties, and many local Whites believed the presence of Williams and Walker served only to exacerbate the so-called race problem. The following day, their lodgings were canceled in Atchison, Kansas, after the manager of the Midland Hotel learned the company was composed of Negroes, so they found accommodations among the local Black families.[38] Following several short engagements came a week at the Creighton-Orpheum, Des Moines, where two thousand people were turned away on opening night. The *Omaha Daily Bee* noted, "George Walker is the presentation of the Negroes' ideal. He possesses a wardrobe of swell garments which he wears with the grace of a Chesterfield."[39]

Following Des Moines, there was a short layoff. With little to do, Bert and George got themselves into a bit of trouble when they met up with an "old friend," likely future cast member James Escort Lightfoot (ca. 1875 to 1964) of Black Patti's Troubadours, who were engaged at the Grand.[40] As the story went, their old friend had a "big bundle on him," and by extension, Bert and George mistakenly thought, "Here's some easy money." Bert remembered,

We suggested a game of dice, played a while and it wasn't long before Walker and I were broke. We made a "raise" from a friend who was standing by and changed the game to poker, congratulating ourselves that "that bundle" was now ours for sure. We started to win, then our stacks went down and we were losers for a while. Pretty soon we started to gain, and were very near even, but our luck was against us for we kept losing, losing, our stacks got smaller and smaller, and we went broke again. Then I went to a friend of mine who kept the drug store across the street, borrowed a five spot from him and we started a game of euchre, but we soon went broke again.

It was now about 7 o'clock in the morning. So Walker and I pawned everything of value we had with us and started in the play "banker and broker." At this stage of the game we would have been satisfied to even get the money back we started with, but we soon went broke again.

By this time, it was a serious proposition with Walker and I, so I asked our friend "could he run?"

He said, "A little bit."

. . . When our friend said he could run, Walker and I looked at each other and smiled sympathetically for our friend. I said, "Alright, will you wait here just one fifteen minutes?"

He said, "Yes," and we hurried out, dug up $200 dollars and returned. We made a $200 side bet, and I couldn't see how Walker could lose his rabbit-chasing abilities of younger days in my mind all the time. . . .

I didn't want to make the race too long, so I made the distance two short blocks . . . I was the starter, and Walker gave all the best of it, but Walker hadn't covered the first block before our friend finished.[41]

Following George's trouncing, the company continued through the Midwest and soon found themselves in Indianapolis. It was their first engagement there since their days with Hyde's Comedians, and the local Black population was primed for a good time. Once again, the orchestra refused to play under Will Cook's baton, and although two members resigned, a compromise was reached and the engagement was successful. On Valentine's Day, Ada's twentieth birthday and the last day of the engagement, George presented her with a horseshoe ring set with turquoise, sapphires, and diamonds. Next, the company returned to Chicago, where they did moderate business because it was a return engagement.[42]

All told, the western tour was a success. As reported in the "Notes from the Williams and Walker Company," regularly published in the Indianapolis *Freeman*, they were "treated royally on their western trip by the colored citizens."[43] However, life on the road for a popular company had some repercussions. The decidedly conservative *Topeka Plaindealer* lamented that, after the company left St. Louis, they were in no condition to give performances at their expected level, and they had letters from several disappointed fans to prove it. Tinged with the recent memory of Tuck's gaffe, the article further asserted that Bert and George epitomized the hypocrisy of "Eastern darkies," and that Black Patti's Troubadours had trouble following them in the West because of the unsavory reputation left by the company. Another article claimed that when the company left Decatur, Illinois, they were rude and arrogant and that some of the men "acted as though other people didn't have any right on earth, and looked at the white people employed at the lunch counter and in the depot as though they wanted to make known for the fact that they held the whites in the most utter contempt."[44] As the company navigated uncharted waters, seemingly everything they did incurred praise on one hand and condemnation on the other. Further, management believed that George's obsession with first-class booking was a solution in search of a problem and that he should've been content with things as they were.

Having returned east, the company played Boston, then short stints in Brooklyn, Manhattan, and New Haven.[45] That spring, the baseball team reformed, and they busily secured opponents to play. Following a 10-to-5 loss in Meriden, Connecticut, a local newspaperman wrote, "Some of the Williams and Walker troupe are thirty-third degree baseball cranks."[46] Despite the rocky start, the company issued a standing challenge to any and all of the traveling companies for a baseball game, "for a purse, for fun or for love," in or around New York City. Potential challengers were told to inquire with chorus member Fred Douglass at the new Marshall-Lett Hotel. At the first Williams and Walker field day on May 8, 1900, Ada won a footrace among the female cast members, followed closely by Odessa Warren (1863 to 1960), and Lottie won the tree-climbing contest. When the festivities continued in New Haven, they held a big sack race.[47] Shortly after, the thirty-two-week season closed on May 12 at the Star in New York, and *The Policy Players* was retired. To keep top members of the male chorus working, paid, and under contract, George organized the Williams and

Walker Quartet, under the direction of William C. Elkins. It was a clever way to prevent poaching of the company's talent, keep their skills in top form, and grow the Williams and Walker brand.[48]

Hotel Marshall, a Black and Tan Oasis

While briefly at home in New York in March of 1900, Bert and George moved into a newly established hotel at 114 West Thirty-First Street that was run by James L. Marshall (1874 to 1925) and Charles Lett.[49] In a similar fashion as the Douglass Club and others, the Marshall-Lett Hotel was established to provide a safe and comfortable environment for the growing "Black and Tan" culture in New York, a uniquely fruitful environment for interracial interaction in defiance of Jim Crow laws. Conversely, it provided some White people with access to Black culture that they could later leverage as "composers" of the melodies and rhythms they heard there, likely for the first time. The Marshall–Lett partnership was short lived, but James Marshall opened another hotel at 127 and 129 West Fifty-Third Street on October 15, 1900. Harlem Renaissance–era painter and writer Richard Bruce Nugent (1906 to 1987) gave an elegant description of the atmosphere at the Marshall: "They would come, all the glittering, plumed ladies of the theatre, the carelessly perfect brown Beau Brummels of stage and song, [everyone] important or aspiring in the entertainment and sport worlds, the young and unknown attracted by the presence of the known and famous, to see and to be seen, to be entertained and to entertain, to mull over the collaborations and to form partnerships, to relax exchange courtesies and ideas."[50] Shortly after the Fifty-Third Street establishment opened, Bob Cole moved in two doors down from Bert and George and installed two floor-to-ceiling bookcases that were stuffed with books on history, art, and culture. When the Johnson brothers took up residence in the back room on the second floor, they installed a piano and worked constantly during the offseason, hidden away from White composers.[51] Likewise, George and Bert's flat became the new gathering spot for up-and-coming Black entertainers. As George recalled in 1906,

> The first move was to hire a flat in Fifty-third Street, furnish it, and throw our doors open to all colored men who possessed theatrical and musical ability and ambition. The Williams and

Walker flat soon became the headquarters of all artistic young men of our race who were stage-struck. Among those who frequented our home were: Messrs. Will Marion Cook, Harry T. Burleigh, Bob Cole and Billy Johnson, J. A. Shipp, the late Will Accooe, a man of much musical ability, and many others whose names are well known in the professional world. We also entertained the late Paul Laurence Dunbar, the negro poet, who wrote lyrics for us. By having these men around us we had an opportunity to study the musical and theatrical ability of the most talented members of our race.[52]

James Weldon Johnson agreed, noting their private, Afrocentric discussions often focused on "the manner and means of raising the status of the Negro as a writer, composer and performer in the New York theatre and world of music."[53] As remembered by Lester Walton, dramatic editor of *The New York Age*,

In looking for entertainment the Vanderbilts and other prominent society people have listened for hours and enjoyed the brand of amusement provided by the colored musicians, and there were times when they tripped the light fantastic—Women and men. Even prominent white men from the South who came to New York sightseeing soon forgot their prejudices as to go to the Hotel Marshall to while away the hours, forgetting temporarily the decorum one is supposed to maintain afflicted with the "social equality" germ.[54]

The importance of the Marshall Hotel as a wellspring for Black artistry in Manhattan at the turn of the twentieth century cannot be overstated. Moreover, it provided a respite for Bert and George from the stress and strain of life on the road, management, fans, and their spouses. Around that time, Bert and George met the composer and future collaborator Alex Rogers, whose initial impression of George was not favorable: "George Walker dresses well, and that's about the best thing he does. He is an exceptionally bad singer, a very tame dancer, and, judging from the language he uses, a very rusty scholar. We claim that in many instances appearance is everything—this is one of those instances, as Mr. Walker has a very extensive wardrobe."[55]

Figures 6.3a–6.3k. Series of George Walker circa 1900. *Source:* Photographs of Prominent African Americans, James Weldon Johnson Collection in the Yale Collection of American Literature, Beinecke Rare Book and Manuscript Library (JWJ MSS 76, box 17, folders 215–17). Continued on pages 113–14.

Figures 6.3i–6.3k.

By nearly any standard, George was still a little rough around the edges, but compared to the ragamuffin who left Lawrence as a barker with a medicine show, he was far and away a sophisticated young man on the make. The actor and writer Sidney Easton (1885 to 1971) certainly appreciated the hospitality at the Marshall facilitated by Williams and Walker: "Man, when I first came to New York, Bert Williams and George Walker took me under their wings. Now, I was about as much out of the country as a blade of grass. When them cats walked into the Hotel Marshall with their fine suits and their studs glistening, I *think* the women passed out. The reason I say *I think* is 'cause I had already passed out from just being there!"[56] In addition, Black and tan culture at the Marshall and other places stimulated creativity and occasionally profit, but Black musicians were normally reticent to unveil new material in public areas before copyright. Richard Nugent recalled how the partners found an unlikely patron in that atmosphere:

> These glittering people would sit around Marshall's telling anecdotes, always willing to entertain when called upon, always being called upon, graciously attracting more and more people. Anna Held, Weber and Fields, would listen while Bert Williams, in his dry, slow voice, would tell of how [Samuel J.] Carter had met him at a bar at 30th Street and Sixth Avenue, and suggested that Williams incorporate into one of his songs he was singing in a show, a verse advertising his Little Liver Pills. Carter even furnished a few rough lines, rhyming rocks and rills with Carter's Little Liver Pills. Williams from his end of the bar had called to Walker at the other and asked him what he thought of the idea. The elegant Walker had had Carter repeat the doggerel several times. Then after an elaborate exchange of repetition with Williams, had pronounced the idea to be a good one. It would cost Mr. Carter three hundred dollars. Mr. Carter had not quite expected that, but there was nothing for him to do except agree. It had all been so public. Walker had then returned to join his cronies at his end of the bar, to continue to busy himself with pleasant conversation and imbibing. Carter had waited around and finally spoke again to Williams about the verse. Williams had again called Walker and again the sartorial Walker had joined them. Williams had asked if Walker had composed a verse yet. For a moment Walker was vague, then inspiration lit his features

and he spoke a first line. ["How does a little liver pill when you're ill know where your liver is? Hmm?"] Williams thought for a moment, then inspiration lit his face and he supplied a second line. ["How does he know the correct way to go? How does he know?"] Walker spoke a third ["He has no eyes to see with,"] and together they chanted a last one, ["He has no legs to walk with."] Then, very pleased with themselves, they repeated the entire verse. And again and again. The creation called for a drink for the house on Williams. Then one for the house on Walker. And another for the house on Carter. And Carter beamed and handed over three hundred dollars. They had sold Carter his own jingle.[57]

Although the song was not theirs, Bert and George's collaborations made the most of their vastly different approaches to the compositional process. While Bert tended to be more pragmatic in his approach, George relied largely on "spur of the moment genius" to construct clever lyrical passages that no one else could come up with.[58] Williams and Walker had finally hit their stride and had become leaders within a small community of Black artists who, like them, believed that they were the catalyst for major social change. However, their newfound celebrity made them targets of the defenders of the status quo who equated all Black progress with White loss. Their success was to be enjoyed, but they knew that a lot more was required to inspire lasting change.

Chapter 7

"Only Just Butting In"

1900 to 1902

"Get Ernest Hogan and Williams and Walker and Cole and Johnson"

The summer of 1900 was spent preparing for the next season's tour, which included Williams and Walker's first trip to the West Coast with their new vehicle, *Sons of Ham*. They also appeared in several vaudeville houses in the East, including Proctor's Pleasure Palace, where they were featured in the "Zulu specialty" skit *The Wedding of King Booloolum and Queen Razzerina*, which eventually became the hit "My Little Zulu Babe."[1] That summer, the heat was stifling, and with that came a high probability of a riot. With growing frequency, White mobs had begun to focus their rage on Black populations throughout the larger cities in the East, and in the dog days conditions were ripe in Manhattan. As if cued by a stage manager, the Anti-Black Police Riot of 1900 found its ignition source. Unfortunately, George and several of his colleagues were among the primary targets of the sadistically ritualistic pathology of White supremacist rage.

As with most "race riots," it began as a "business as usual" transaction that went awry because a Black person who was on the receiving end of the business chose not to participate within the norms, which provided an excuse for violence to preserve the "natural" order. The catalyst event occurred early on Monday, August 13, 1900, outside McBride's Saloon at Forty-First Street and Eighth Avenue in the Tenderloin. Around two o'clock in the morning, a Black woman named May Enoch exited the saloon and waited for her boyfriend Arthur Harris to walk her home. Before Harris exited the saloon, Enoch was accosted by Robert Thorpe, a plainclothes police officer who may have thought she was a prostitute. According to Enoch, Thorpe did not identify himself, which sparked a violent confrontation when Harris exited the saloon and saw a White man with his hands on her. Words were exchanged, and Thorpe hit Harris with his baton, for which Harris stabbed Thorpe three times in his abdomen. The couple fled, and Thorpe was rushed to Roosevelt Hospital, where he later died. The following day, Thorpe's body was taken to his sister's home, where fellow officers, sympathetic mourners, and "those drawn by morbid curiosity" kept vigil.[2] The summer heat, simmering racial animosity, and alcohol consumption inspired a full-fledged riot to avenge the death of the White police officer at the hands of a man whom George's father referred to in a similar, fictitious scenario as a "black fiend" who did not know his place.[3]

By nightfall on August 14, violence had erupted. Hundreds of off-duty police officers and other young White men flooded the streets of the Tenderloin and formed lynch mobs with a fervent desire to *exercise* White liberty by *exorcising* Black liberty, particularly among those who exhibited conspicuous prosperity.[4] As reported in the *New York Tribune*, "there were at one time more than 5000 persons in Broadway. Up and down, into and out of the hotels and saloons, through Herald Square and the side streets, the mob surged and rushed, looking for Negroes. Any unfortunate black man was set upon and beaten."[5] To make matters worse, most police offered little or no protection and even participated in the violence with gusto. James Weldon Johnson recalled:

> When Negroes ran to policemen for protection, even begging to be locked up for safety, they were thrown back to the mob. The police themselves beat many Negroes as cruelly as did the mob. An intimate friend of mine was one of those who ran to the police for protection; he received such a clubbing at their hands that he had to be taken to the hospital to have his scalp stitched in several places. It was a beating from which he never fully recovered.[6]

As the riot reached its zenith, celebrities were called out by name. Johnson remembered, "The cry went out to 'get Ernest Hogan and Williams and Walker and Cole and Johnson.' These seem to be the only individual names the crowd was familiar with." Among the first of the Negro neo-bourgeoisie to feel the wrath of the mob was a fashionably dressed and unaware Ernest Hogan. At half past midnight on August 15, he was standing on a curb on Broadway and twirling his cane as he waited for a cab. As reported in *The Freeman*, "A cry came from 44th St. and Eighth Avenue, and a mob of 500 men, armed with clubs and stones, surged over towards Broadway. Hogan was seen, 'Get the Nigger' was the chorus. Hogan dropped his cane and started down Broadway on a run. The mob followed and for the next three minutes it had a life and death race for Hogan."[7] By the time he reached Broadway and Thirty-Seventh Street, the mob almost had him, but he found an open door at the Marlborough Hotel. A sympathetic police detective kept the mob at bay long enough for Hogan to slip out of the Thirty-Sixth Street entrance, and he escaped in a cab.[8]

News of the riot had not yet made it to midtown when Williams and Walker closed at Proctor's Pleasure Palace at 154 East Fifty-Eighth Street between Lexington and Third Avenues. Bert went home, and George boarded a southbound streetcar on Broadway with Clarence Logan, his private secretary, to meet Hogan in the Tenderloin for a drink. When the car reached Thirty-Third Street around one o'clock in the morning, George and Clarence were singled out, and a dozen men dragged George off the car and beat him. Clarence escaped and ran down Sixth Avenue until he was caught and beaten almost to death. Somehow, he made it to a drugstore and was let in by the proprietor, who promptly locked the door and kept the mob at bay until the police made their way in, which likely saved his life. George was chased to the corner of Broadway and Thirty-Fourth Street, where he ducked into the side entrance of Trainor's Hotel.[9] Fortunately, he did not receive any permanent injuries, made his way home, and never spoke about his experience in public. The violence held sway over the Black population of Manhattan for three terrifying days, making it the worst riot in New York since the Draft Riot in 1863.[10]

News of George's brush with death made the papers all over the country, including in Lawrence. Ultimately, no police were held accountable and no indictments were issued beyond the four men who were arrested for attacking George.[11] In addition to being hunted and marked for death by fellow New Yorkers, George was expected to perform for some of the same people who nearly killed him when the new season started in two weeks. Also, during the riot, the poet Paul Laurence Dunbar was drugged with "knockout drops" and robbed on the night of August 17. Following the violence, Clarence Logan resigned as George's private secretary and was hired by Ernest Hogan in the same capacity. Bert and George continued their engagement at Proctor's Pleasure Palace and then moved to Proctor's Fifth Avenue Theatre for the week of August 21.[12] With the specter of a "tough crowd" looming, Baltimore badman Eli Lucas (1867 to 1918) was hired for extra security. According to Eubie Blake, Lucas was "a bad guy like Jesse James" and wore a large coat to hide the pair of pistols that he carried. A crack shot with either hand, Lucas *was* the "Nigger" who lived in the imagination of most White people, and his job was to individually escort Bert and George, Cole and Johnson, and Hogan to and from their respective theatres for a few days until they were sure that the violence was over.[13]

Sons of Ham

At the start of the 1900 to 1901 season, Ada's mother, Pauline, became the company's head seamstress. Having sewn Ada's outfits since she was a child and being well-known for custom work among prominent performers, she opened a popular dress shop at 110 West Twenty-Sixth Street in 1898.[14] Of particular importance was the addition of Green Henri "High G" Tapley (b. 1875), an outstanding first tenor whom George initially heard as a chorus member of *Quo Vadis* in Chicago during the previous season. His voice was what George liked to call a "comer." Tapley eventually took on Clarence Logan's former secretarial role.[15] There were several departures from the cast, most notably Mattie Wilkes, who signed with Isham's *Octoroons*, and the Mallory brothers went with Isham's *King Rastus* company, now under the direction of John Isham's brother Will, who reverted to minstrelsy. While *Sons of Ham* was in preproduction, an unprecedented second company was established to perform Williams and Walker's previous vehicle, *The Policy Players*. The new company was managed by Sam Corker Jr. (1874 to 1914) and starred fifteen original cast members, including Ben Hunn as Silver King and Walter H. Dixon (1879 to 1917), later dubbed "the dancing conductor" by James Weldon Johnson, as Dollar Bill.[16]

With all-new scenery painted by Joe Physioc, the Jesse Shipp and Stephen Cassin plot for *Sons of Ham* followed the Isham formula that had proved successful since *The Senegambian Carnival*. Tobias Wormwood (Bert), "an awkward, ignorant Negro of a sullen, pugnacious disposition,"

Figure 7.1. Green Henri "High G" Tapley. *Source: The Colored American Magazine* 8–9, September 1905, 500.

GREEN HENRI TAPLEY

and Harty Laughter (George), "a 'dandy coon,' whose disposition [was] all sunshine and whose manners [were] most graceful and refined," were the ringleaders of the hijinks. Along with a supporting role, Jesse continued as stage manager of the large, fifty-member aggregation. Will Cook directed the thirty-member chorus, and the company carried an entire carload of special scenery, lighting effects, and a sixteen-foot cake for a grand cake walk.[17]

Figures 7.2a–j. Character study of Bert Williams and George Walker from Act I of *Sons of Ham*, 1900. *Source:* Beinecke Rare Book and Manuscript Library (JWJ MSS 76, box 17, folders 217–19).

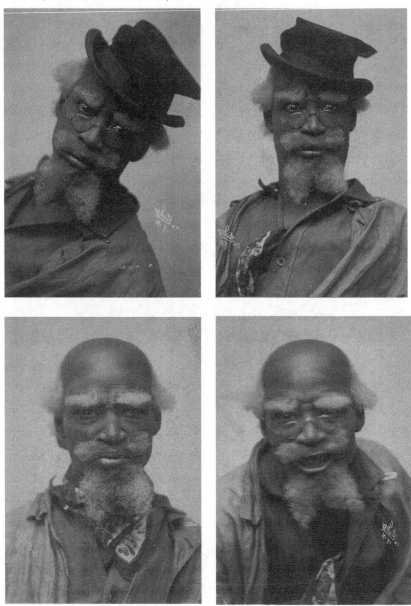

Presented in two acts, the first scene of *Sons of Ham* took place in Swampville, Tennessee, in front of the home of Uncle Ham. Played by Pete Hampton (1871 to 1916), Ham was the elderly father of two students at Riske University, a nod to Fisk University in Tennessee, home of the original Jubilee Singers. The scene featured several elders with fake beards, of which the *Sunday Telegraph* remarked, "they stick out on the face like the old-fashioned bustle, and in no way serve the purpose for which they are intended."[18] Jesse was made up in a wig and eyeglasses, a là the British actor Sir Henry Irving; he played Professor Skitchen, who, in the second scene, hired the two miscreants, Tobias and Harty, as water carriers who kept audiences in stitches. The third scene took place at Riske, and scene four, *In Africa*, provided Ada with her first feature, "Miss Hannah from Savannah." In an attempt to push the envelope, the play included a "love scene," or the approximation of one as allowed for Black actors, but by all accounts, it fell flat. However, no one objected, which indicated that White audiences had warmed to the idea of Black sensuality so that subsequent attempts could possibly allow for a little more realism. The hit of the show came at the close of the first act with Bert and George's "My Little Zulu Babe," with George appearing in drag as the love interest.

The second act opened inside the conspicuously Southern home of Uncle Ham as he prepared for a cake walk given by the students of Riske. Ham had not seen his sons in six years, and just before their arrival in scene two, Tobias and Hearty showed up and proclaimed themselves to be the "Sons of Ham." To seal the deal, Harty devised a scheme to introduce Tobias as a fortune teller and phrenologist, which facilitated Bert's singing of "Phrenologist Coon" and "My Castle on the Nile." George was also featured in his latest dude song, "The Leader of the Ball," as well as "Good Afternoon Mr. Jenkins" and "Elegant Darky Dan," a nod to "Darkie" Dan Dorcas, a fictional Black detective. The third scene featured a lavish ballroom adorned with a fountain and a marble statue.

After three weeks of rehearsal, Williams and Walker debuted *Sons of Ham* on September 17, 1900, at People's Opera House, Mt. Vernon, New York, followed by stops throughout the East, then back to Manhattan for the final two weeks of October where Will Cook and soprano Abbie Mitchell were married.[19] Shortly after traveling from Rochester to Pittsburgh for their appearance at the Bijou, two chorus members, Harry Winfred and George Pickett, presented symptoms of smallpox. They were taken to the municipal hospital, and health officials vaccinated the entire company at the theatre. After two performances, the engagement was closed, and before the end of the next

Figure 7.3. "Miss Hannah from Savannah," words by R. C. McPherson, music by Tom Lemonier, Joseph W. Stern & Co., New York, 1901. *Source:* New York Public Library. Public domain.

day, five more were in the hospital. Once word got out, members of the cast could not walk up Fifth Avenue without causing a scene, so their engagements in Ohio and Kansas City were canceled. Although local health officials wanted the company to quarantine in Pittsburgh, George consulted with the home

Figure 7.4. "My Little Zulu Babe," words by W.S. Estren, music by Jas. T. Brymn, Windsor Music Co., Chicago / New York, 1900. *Source:* Author's collection.

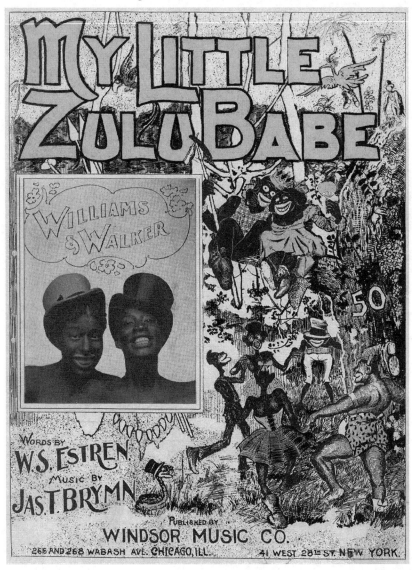

office and arranged for the cast all to be paid before they scattered on November 24. Some returned to Manhattan, where another small outbreak occurred, and others made their way to Cincinnati in anticipation of an engagement on

Figures 7.5a–c. Character study of George Walker in drag from "My Little Zulu Babe," mislabeled as "In Dahomey." *Source:* Beinecke Rare Book and Manuscript Library (JWJ MSS 76, box 17, folders 217–19).

December 9. However, the company took most of December off, reformed in Muncie, Indiana, on Christmas, and closed the year in St. Louis.[20]

The new year of 1901 brought the company to the Midwest. When they made it to Topeka, the Black denizens were ready to pick up where they left off. According to the *State Journal*, "every seat was sold and the gallery door is closed before all the gods had crowded in. . . . The blackest little street urchin was in the gallery and the swells of society were in along with the members of the colored 400. The gallery was decidedly unruly[,] and three policemen tried to keep order there with but partial success."[21] Following Topeka, the company arrived early for the engagement at the Bowersock in Lawrence. Most of the cast took advantage of a day of rest, especially Nash, who visited with his family.[22] The performance was well received, and Nash's success was a bottomless source of local pride: "The fact that Nash Walker, an old Lawrence boy, remembered here as a ragged street urchin, is one of the leaders of the successful company, had much to do with drawing the crowd, but the entertainment was much superior to the average show that comes to Lawrence, and people were well repaid for their presence." Following the show, a reception was given that included members of the Langston family.[23]

The tour continued throughout the Midwest and East, broke attendance records in several cities, and earned a large profit. During the winter and spring of 1901, Will Isham's *King Rastus* company permanently disbanded, which provided new members for the company, most notably Charles Hart (1863 to 1917).[24] Hart and his future partner, Dan Avery (1878 to 1912), would become the stars of Williams and Walker's second company during the following season. Avery, a dancer, took on George's parts, and Hart, a comedian, assumed Bert's parts. While engaged in vaudeville houses, they settled into their roles and eventually were eclipsed only by the original "Real Coons." In December of that year, the *Boston Globe* declared, "Avery and Hart imitate Williams and Walker so closely that you are kept guessing."[25]

The newly bolstered Williams and Walker company opened in Boston for a three-week engagement on May 6, 1901, amid rumors that they'd be making another trip to London during the summer of 1902 with Cook and Dunbar's opera *Cannibal King*.[26] As soon as the company disbanded for the season on May 18, Bert and George's *Cake Walk Carnival* premiered at Keith's, Boston, for a stint before moving to the Manhattan and Philadelphia venues. By early July, the duo was earning $600 a week for twenty minutes of work in top vaudeville houses.[27] On George's twenty-ninth birthday, they opened in Lancaster, Pennsylvania, on the rooftop of the Woolworth building as part of the *Oriental Troubadours*, an amalgamation of the *Sons of Ham* and *A Trip to Coontown* companies, in a Bob Cole sketch titled *The Golf Links*. Bert and George carried the show and provided space for less-refined acts to tighten up for the coming season. It also provided Cole with a bit of relief following his legal battle to retain ownership of *A Trip to Coontown*. According to J. Ed Green, Chicago correspondent for *The Freeman*, George Walker was "the 'Hottest Coon' at present."[28]

A Subversive Path Rarely Taken

Williams and Walker's hard-won fame and profitability allowed them to occupy spaces that were previously forbidden to Black actors, much to the consternation of the White Rats, a professional organization of White thespians.[29] While engaged in Chicago at the end of the season, George and Bert were invited to a reception. After the performance they were driven to an event where they mingled with the city's White elite. A prominent local journalist and two elites approached them and said, "A number of us have been trying to find out what the first remarks of Shem, Ham, and Japheth were when they went out into the world, and what they would each like to have." Believing the man was joking, Bert replied,

> Shem, who was the first white man, was asked what he would most like to have, and he answered: "Lots of wealth, so I could travel and see all the grand sites of this world." Japheth, who was the first red man, was asked what he wanted most, and answered: "Lots of fire water and bullets to kill pale faces." Then came Ham, who was the first colored man. When the same question was put to him, he looked up and smilingly said: "Oh, nothing, only just butting in," and that is what we are doing here.[30]

Bert's clever response rendered the two elite men speechless. For possibly the first and only time in their lives, they were given a dose of reality in both an objective and subjective sense. It was surely something that the Black people who had likely served these men for their entire lives, like George's father, would have wanted to say but almost never would. Despite their discomfort, "the gentleman looked at one another, [took] Williams and Walker by the arm, opened a couple of bottles of wine, at the same time vowing them both jolly good fellows."[31] Had Bert not been a commercially viable performer with growing clout, the reprisal for such an indiscretion could have been deadly, as was nearly the case for George just before the start of the season.

The Rise of Russell

During the 1901 to 1902 season, the critic Sylvester Russel came into his own after J. Harry Jackson left his position as theatrical editor for *The*

Figure 7.6. Sylvester Russell. *Source:* Indianapolis *Freeman*, March 6, 1909, 6.

Freeman and became its New York correspondent. Russell quickly transitioned from a faltering singing career into that of a self-proclaimed expert who used his new sounding board as a bully pulpit to the greatest possible effect.[32] His curt review of the second iteration of *Sons of Ham* was a sign of things to come: "Bert Williams and George Walker are interesting and bound to be good in any sort of coon play, but in a play of this class they're well-known vaudeville specialties should be dropped entirely. The stars simply waltz around the play as two impossible students."[33] Throughout his career, Russell's directness and insights were tinged with an elitism that did not endear him to most actors. However, his consistency and longevity provided a check and balance for some of the more politically centrist publications, most notably the *New York Age*. Nevertheless, his tough-love critiques proved to be a necessary frustration for George and his colleagues, although Russell later revealed that his earliest criticism of Williams and Walker was the nexus for a cordial yet strained relationship that lasted the rest of their lives.[34]

Rocky Road to First Class

At the start of the 1901 to 1902 season, Williams and Walker agreed to extend their contract with Hurtig and Seamon for two more years at $500 a week. This was likely the reason they continued with *Sons of Ham* instead of Cook and Dunbar's latest vehicle. *Cannibal King* had been in development since 1899 and was expected to debut in a Broadway theatre around August 15, 1901, but without Bert and George, it was shelved for another year.[35]

Low-performing songs from the previous season were not carried over, but hits such as "My Little Zulu Babe" and "She's Getting More Like the White Folks Every Day" were retained. Bert continued to score with "The Fortune Telling Man," "The Phrenologist Coon," "My Castle on the Nile," and "When It's All Goin' Out and Nothin' Comin' In." George scored with "The Leader of the Ball" and "When Zacharias Leads the Band," so they remained. Having put in diligent work since her dismissal from the *Trip to Coontown* company, Ada had begun to stand out as a singer with "Miss Hannah from Savannah" and was studying piano. *The Freeman* extolled, "A new departure is the dark soubrette . . . in coon comedy," declaring that Ada was at the forefront, an unusual distinction for a darker-skinned woman. Although marked for areas that needed some improvement, most notably her lack of singing confidence and facial byplay, she was a leader in the company and was about to become a trendsetter in the business.³⁶

For the second year, *Sons of Ham* premiered in Mount Vernon, New York, on September 16, 1901, followed by other Eastern cities, including a week in Brooklyn where demand was so high, the fire department was called in to regulate capacity.³⁷ In Philadelphia, they broke box office records and recorded several songs for Victor Monarch on October 11, 1901.³⁸ Although George was well known to be insecure about his singing, James Weldon Johnson remarked that he "surprised the world" when he recorded "Good Morning Carrie" as a duet with Bert. George earnestly sang lead with a mid-Atlantic accent and slight falsetto break in his voice that matched well with the aspirational spirit of the song. Bert's harmony and contrapuntal banter tied the sections together and added to the earnestness of their comedic delivery.³⁹

Chorus:

Good morning Carrie, how you do this morning?
Was your dreaming 'bout me my pretty maid?
Say look here Carrie, when we gwine to marry?
Long springtime honey, good morning babe

Following Philadelphia, the company moved throughout the East and into the Midwest before winding up in Lexington, Kentucky, where two of the members of the local orchestra refused to play with Williams and Walker's Black pianist, but the rest of the orchestra remained under protest. They closed 1901 in St. Louis, where Sam Tuck declared that business was up 25 percent over the previous year.⁴⁰

The year 1902 began on a decided upswing for Nash as he headed home to Lawrence. Having skipped his yearly trip home to earn some extra money in vaudeville during the previous summer, he took a much-needed break, albeit brief. Chief on his agenda was to locate a suitable lot to build a new home for his mother and grandmother. When the company returned to the road, they played Kansas City and Topeka before the Bowersock, where tickets were nearly sold out by the afternoon on the day of the performance. Seemingly everyone wanted a fleeting moment with good old Nash at the ball after the performance.⁴¹ January ended with the company in Chicago, where Green Henri Tapley married contralto Daisy Robinson (1882 to 1925), who also joined the company. Following

Figure 7.7. "Good Morning Carrie," words by R. C. McPherson, music by Smith & Bowman, Harry H. Sparks Music, Toronto, Canada, 1901. *Source:* Author's collection.

the close of the eastern leg of the tour, the company had a three-day layover in Chicago before they began to move west to Omaha and San Francisco.[42]

While in San Francisco, Bert and George gave a rare candid interview to Guisard, a local White journalist who asked whether *Sons of Ham* was the height of their ambition:

> "No, indeed. . . . But that represents all that the public will at present take from us."
>
> Then I learned where the shoe pinched.
>
> Very gently, without any rancor, Walker explained that the negro is as yet only permitted to entertain the white man as his buffoon. He will not "stand for" pathos, romance[,] and the rest of it, and perforce the colored entertainer must comply with the requirements.[43]

After expressing a desire to play Uncle Tom, George divulged their plans to challenge the many limitations placed on Black actors, while Bert's penchant for subtlety was temporarily relieved:

> Our new piece for next year, "In Dahomey," it may be called, is a little more ambitious. In fact[,] it was a genuine comic opera, written by our colored composer, Will Marion Cook, the lyrics by Paul Dunbar and the book by us, but we have turned it into a musical comedy. But the subject deals—In comedy fashion—with a very vital question to our race, the practical disenfranchisement of the Southern negro. Someday, perhaps, going quietly on in our own little groove, we may do something of which people may say, "that is good, without tacking on that poor little tail—for a negro."
>
> "Do you play the South?" I [Guisard] asked.
>
> "Not yet," the manager [Sam Tuck] interposed.
>
> "The Jim Crow cars, and other inconvenient features, are still in evidence there."
>
> "We play Louisville, Kentucky," and the Walker pearls were again cleaning: "There [are] some of the white fellows [who] will take us for a drink to some third-class saloon and tell us it is the first time negro has been served at the bar. Of course we are grateful, but—how do you feel about it, Bert?"
>
> "I want to be the blackest black nigger God ever made," said Williams.

In sensing Guisard's White supremacist sentiment, Bert seized an opportunity to make things a bit plainer. After all, he aimed to epitomize the idea of what a Black man was to an uninitiated White audience. As with his encounter in Chicago a year earlier, his uncanny ability to provide a stark contrast between the *man* and the *mask* on cue was something Black performers had to perfect if they wanted to remain in the business with a measure of dignity.

When the company closed in San Francisco, *Sons of Ham* was reported to be the most popular show of the season at the theatre.[44] Next, the company moved north on a series of one-nighters. While they were engaged in Portland, Oregon, life imitated art for Bert. As reported, Lottie had recently purchased a Kodak Brownie No. 2 camera to document the western tour. On the morning of April 26, 1902, George, Ada, Bert, and Lottie drove a carriage through Washington Park, when they came across a dry reservoir. Lottie came up with an idea for Bert to climb the Chiming Fountain at the center and pose as a Cupid in his "Phrenologist Coon" costume. Bert rushed back to the theatre, and when he returned, Lottie snapped a pair of images. About that time, a policeman came along, which gave George an idea of his own. "In a spirit of fun, [George] pointed out Williams, [who was] perched out in the center of the big tank, as an apparently crazy tramp, who had been making the most outlandish gestures at them for some minutes past." Lottie verified George's lie when she said, "Yes . . . and he has been swearing dreadfully, too, I think he should be arrested." Bert was promptly arrested, and the three conspirators drove their carriage a couple of blocks away and waited for a good laugh. Caught unaware, Bert began to shout, and that angered the policeman. When they passed George, Lottie, and Ada a few minutes later, the arresting officer heard none of their explanations of the prank they pulled. Claiming that Bert had resisted arrest, the officer stated, "He would take him in if he were Grover Cleveland." The manager of the theatre had to get him out for that night's performance, and Bert did not speak to the conspirators for some time.[45]

Following Bert's brush with the law, the company moved to Seattle, where Bert and George had a three-hour meeting with Sam Tuck at the Butler Hotel to discuss their next vehicle, Cook and Dunbar's *Cannibal King*, now renamed *In Dahomey*. It was an unprecedented three-act production that had the potential to raise the standard of acceptability for serious Black theatre.[46] Following Seattle, the company moved to Vancouver, British Columbia, and then made its way south and west, playing several one-nighters until they reached Pueblo, Colorado, where the old-timers remembered "young Nash" from his brief stints there as a child and went wild when "George Walker" came onstage. Finally, the season ended with two weeks at the Great Northern in Chicago.[47]

Back Home Again in Lawrence

At the close of the season, there was a lot of buzz in the press, mostly speculation regarding *In Dahomey*. Nash made his way alone to Lawrence for a week to complete the purchase of two lots totaling $610 for his mother and grandmother and to take delivery of a colonial-style, mahogany piano from the Bell Brothers of Muncie, Indiana. Located at Indiana and Elliott Street in West Lawrence (Pinkney), the lots were prime real estate in a growing section of town, conveniently adjacent to the home that his grandmother and mother rented, close to the Kansas River. Although he meant to keep a low profile, Abe Levy persuaded Nash to participate in the annual Independence Day parade down Massachusetts Street on July 4 in front of a crowd of 25,000 people.[48] In what would become a tradition for him, Nash recounted his bittersweet experience in a love letter to "the good people of Lawrence":

> I returned to my New York home feeling all o.k. and am extremely grateful to my many friends for the countless and uniform kindnesses shown me during my brief but pleasant stay. I shall never forget Lawrence—I fancy myself again a boy, and the proud possessor of the first bootblack stand of the town I confessed myself proud of that—my first business venture, and even today there lingers pardonable, friendly zealousness of my successor. Well do I recall the days when "Carter and Nash" dispensed shines at so much per shine—dear old Carter—by the way, I rode from Kansas City to Lawrence on Carter's train (I mean Santa Fe train but from his actions one would have believed it the individual property of Cornelius Carter, Esq.) Yet Carter was merely the porter. I was amazed at the change in Carter, he had developed into a great big man, married, and had learned to smoke cigarettes. I left Lawrence in 189[2] to follow my chosen profession, which, since then has carried me into every prominent city of the United States. Have been

feted, wined and dined by the representative people therein but none assumes in mine eye the magnitude of the memories of Lawrence. . . . The fragrant recollection of the time when my father, Jerry Nashville Walker was employed at the Eldridge house, coupled with the fact that I, in years after was welcomed as a guest in the same hotel furnishes food for the reflection that time works changes, strikingly contrasting. I would indeed be derelict should I fail to return my sincere thanks to Manager Malcolm Conn who exerted every influence to make my sojourn a pleasant one. . . . During the absence of my mother, Mrs. Alice Myers, on a visit to friends at Cripple Creek, Colo. [319 E. El Paso Ave.], I had our residence remodeled and refurnished, which more than accomplished my object of surprise, as I had given her no intimation of my intention hence the surprise was the more complete. When I revisit Lawrence next year I shall personally superintend and direct the construction of our completed new home upon my recently purchased property diagonally across from our present domicile according to plans of the most recent ideas of modern architecture.

During my visit I enjoyed the Elks Carnival and was an honored guest of that organization, they confirming every concession and suggestion that tended to enhance my comfort and pleasure, even to giving me the post of honor in the parade, receptions, etc. On the morning of July 4th I was awakened by a complementary visitation of the Indian brass band, which served as a reminder to make it good my promise to participate in the B.P.O.E. parade. Just then Willie Thurston rushed into my apartment yelling, "For God's sake Nash, get up, the white folks are about to parade and you are the only darkey in the procession, so fix up and get right, if you don't we sure will tell you about it after the parade is over and Mr. Donnelly has got you the white horses and trap all fixed up for your special benefit. Please get up Nash." As soon as I could "get myself together" I dispatched a note to Mr. Donnelly setting forth the direct contrast between the white horses and the occupant of the trap, and mildly suggested that black horses be substituted which was readily done. Consulting my watch, I found that I had but ten minutes in which to dress and reached the dining room before the doors closed and as I could not afford to miss a meal, you can use your own judgment upon my affirmation that I reached there in due time. Between explaining my tardiness and fanning away flies, I managed to find time to ask the waitress why the flies were so much in evidence, she responded. "Well Nash, we give them sugar, molasses and all the delicacies they can devour but when a 'ham' is around we lose control of them." Being a "Son of Ham," I readily grasped the point.

I found the trap and black horses awaiting me on the outside and when I took my seat, I was just as happy as a big sunflower, and mentally calculated that had I the bank account of Mr. J. B. Watkins coupled with the pride of Nash Walker, Jr., I would be Monarch of all I surveyed. The parade was a dazzling success . . . I was assigned a position just ahead of the local fire department, but it did not occur to me why I was thusly placed. All along the lines of march I was hailed and greeted by businessmen, ladies and even the children and news boys, with "Go on with Nash," "What's the matter with Nash?," "He's all right." "Who?," "Nash," "Nash you're a hot article," etc. Then it dawned upon me why [they] put the fire department near me (I was so warm). Three cheers and a tiger were given me right royally as we passed the reviewing stand at Elks Hall. Arriving at the park I found a unique form of amusement in progress, the profits derived therefrom being used towards defraying the expenses of the Carnival. A special set of officers (members of the committee of course) patrolled the grounds, arresting the prominent men from the mayor down to the civilian. The "prisoners" were incarcerated in a little 2 x 6 house that served as a jail. Upon payment of five dollars the "prisoner" is given a badge showing the profile of a man behind the bars over whose head is printed "I've been there"—the possession of this badge serving as immunity from a re-arrest. I eluded them until about five o'clock p.m. when with the aid of several Pinkerton detectives, I was apprehended [while] sitting on a flower barrel eating chicken. I was immediately committed and released upon "coughing up" the fiver. I didn't mind paying my "fine" but I did kick because the kids came to the cell and made uncomplimentary remarks about Darwin and his theory and even threw bananas and peanuts through the bars to me. This seemed like too much "monkey business" and had a tendency to remind one of Barnum's circus.

There is some talk of the building a car line from Kansas City, MO, to Topeka, Kas, via Lawrence, but from the bustling activity of Lawrence I would humbly suggest that the track make a loop and run around Lawrence—this remedy will obviate the possibility of inferring with the present perfect (?) streetcar system now so conspicuous by its absence.

Next July I will be accompanied to Lawrence by my wife and my partner, Mr. [Bert] Williams. My partner warns Jim Strode that with his new Bell Bros., piano he has made all Eastern Ragtime pianists emigrate to the far distant and extreme portion of the building and there assuming sitting posture, or in other words "Go Way back and Sit Down."

Cornelius Carter accompanied me on my return as far east as Chicago and finding Chicago a trifle larger than Lawrence, he essayed to count the stories of the Masonic Temple, with the result that he was threatened with spinal meningitis. In vain did I implore him to come to New York, but he said, "No, Nash, if New York City is bigger than Chicago, I'm going back to Lawrence," and he disappeared in the surging crowd.

I feel it a pleasant duty to return my thanks even at this late hour to Messrs. Grant Mull, Lute Lewis, Abe Levy and others who in the days of my boyhood threw many a nickel and dime in my way and gave me substantial encouragement and advice that has proven so beneficial to me. In conclusion I must admit that I know of only two good things concerning myself:

First—I have never been in State prison.

Second—I don't know why I haven't.

Good bye dear old Lawrence

Good bye to the windmill on the hill.

Good bye to the railroad bridge where the boys we used to go swimming.

Good bye to the old [recently demolished] chapel school.

Good bye to the old time horse cars and

Good bye to good old Officer Brock whom I have led in many a race against "time."

Dolce Nella Memoria ["sweet is the memory"]—Geo. W. Walker "Nash" (New York, July 21)[49]

By his own account, the trip was a case study of the Black experience in the White world for the coming century. Nash made a triumphant return home from his most prosperous season yet, visited with old friends, and raised the standard of living for his family. However, it was a reality check, facilitated by children who pelted him with no fear of reprisal or accountability for publicly humiliating him. Although Nash was beloved, George's success brought out a feeling of resentment that some White people in town privately harbored for an audacious young man who never seemed to grasp the, in their view, inappropriateness of his ambition. In many ways, management was the same. Despite it all, his printed love letters to Lawrence provide rare insight into the personality and feelings of an understandably guarded man in ways that exist nowhere else. Further, his admitted vulnerability in expressing what happened to him was in stark contrast to the intent of the event organizers, which must have been embarrassing for them, especially Abe Levy. To their credit, their willingness to print Nash's version of events in three local papers spoke truth to power and their willingness to improve, simply by acknowledging their collective shortcomings, when it came to honoring their favorite, although problematic son.

Chapter 8

Broadway, the Hard Way

1902 to 1903

Summertime Row

Following George's return to Manhattan from Lawrence during the summer of 1902, the partners accompanied Charles Schwab, president of the United States Steel Corporation, to Atlantic City and were seen tooling about in Bert's automobile.[1] Following a two-week engagement at the Brighton Beach Music Hall that featured fourteen chorus members, the company began rehearsals for *In Dahomey* in mid-August and renewed their contract with Hurtig and Seamon with the option for a three-year extension until September 1, 1908.[2]

Once rehearsals were well underway, a row began between Williams and Walker and Ernest Hogan and Billy McClain (1866 to 1950), who accused Williams and Walker of poaching cast members and sent an angry "defi." Cooler heads prevailed, and the cast members in question returned to the fold. However, the purposefully articulate men were misquoted with a false minstrel tinge in the *Morning Telegraph*. Hogan was quoted as saying,

> Ah doesn't clim . . . that Williams in Walker hasn't talent. Ah doesn't say one thing or t'other; but Ah'm a nat'ral bohn comedian. Ah doesn't have to put nothin' on ma face, nor where outlandish costume to git folks to laugh at me. God made me funny, an' that's all is necessary. Three of ma people is back whar

dey belong; but dat ar Leola, dat Hawayun bell, has remained with Mistuh Williams an' Mistuh Walker, who by de way, is one o' des hayar fancy darkies.³

Incensed by Hogan's accusation, Bert reportedly said that if they had acquired any of the Hogan–McClain forces, it was because Williams and Walker offered larger salaries. Likewise, George was angry with Hogan, but also with the *Telegraph* for their ungrammatical representation in the press. It was all an unwelcome distraction from perfecting a first-class, Broadway-caliber show.⁴ George believed that once they were established on Broadway, the air of legitimacy could force the hand of first-class theatre managers throughout the country to open their doors to high-quality Black shows, the first of which would be Avery and Hart's *Sons of Ham*.⁵ If present conditions continued, they would have been relegated to another season of record-breaking attendance in smaller theatres and one-night stands, resulting in lower receipts from more work. That was unacceptable to George, and he readied himself for a long, hard fight.

On August 25, 1902, Grace Vanderbilt hosted a lavish summer ball at her Newport, Rhode Island, estate that was designed to mimic the Midway Plaisance of the Chicago World's Fair. Along with *The Wild Rose* company's "commanded" performance on the east lawn, Bert, Lottie, George, and Ada were engaged to perform as well. That evening, the couples took the train from Manhattan, performed some of their songs, and led a cake walk across the ballroom floor, although no reports mentioned any renewal of a challenge between "Willie" Vanderbilt and Williams and Walker. Upon returning to their hotel, they found a personal check from Mrs. Vanderbilt for $300, a receipt for their hotel, and train tickets for their trip back to Manhattan.⁶

In Dahomey

Following a successful dress rehearsal at the Harlem Opera House, *In Dahomey* opened the season on September 8, 1902, at the Grand Opera House in Stamford, Connecticut.⁷ As with all previous Williams and Walker productions, it took many forms over its run, with a continuously evolving aggregation of songs, dances, cast members, and plot, at least some of which came from *Cannibal King*.⁸ The earliest surviving synopsis of *In Dahomey* is in a program from February 1903:

An old Southern negro, Lightfoot by name, president of the Dahomey Colonization Society, loses a silver casket (jewelry box), which, to use his language, has a cat scratched on its back. He sends to Boston for detectives to search for the missing treasure, Shylock Homestead and Rareback Pinkerton (Williams and Walker). The detectives in the case, failing to find the casket at Gatorville, Florida, "Lightfoot's" home, accompany the colonists to Dahomey. Previous to leaving Boston on their perilous mission, the detectives form a syndicate. In Dahomey, rum of any kind, when given as a present, is a sign of appreciation. Shylock and Rareback, having free access to the syndicate's stock of whiskey, present the King of Dahomey with three barrels of appreciation and in return are made Caboceers (governors of a province). In the meantime, the colonists, having had a misunderstanding with the King, are made prisoners. Prisoners and criminals are executed on festival days, known in Dahomey as Customs Day. The new Caboceers, after supplying the King with his third barrel of appreciation (whiskey), secure his consent to liberate the colonists after which an honor is conferred on Rareback and Shylock, which causes them to decide, "There's No Place Like Home."[9]

Figures 8.1a–8.1e. The Medicine Man and Cake Walk scenes from act 1 of *In Dahomey*. *Source:* Author's collection. Continued on pages 144–45.

Figures 8.1b–8.1e.

Broadway, the Hard Way | 145

Over five months, the company toured the East, and the show evolved continuously as George, Bert, Jesse, and Ada played for growing audiences of Black and White patrons whose expectations and sensibilities were often at odds. Farce or not, Afro-Americans returning to Africa had been a source of public discourse since Abraham Lincoln's administration, only this time it was Blacks who exercised a sovereign choice to leave rather than an ill-informed, insular discussion between Whites to address the "race problem." Although unmentioned, George surely had some inspiration from his father, who was president of the Colorado African Colonization Com-

Figure 8.2. Shylock and Rareback on the road to Gatorville, act 2 of *In Dahomey*. *Source:* Author's collection.

Figures 8.3a and 8.3b. Rareback as the Zulu Chief with Shylock in the Caboceers scene, act 3 of *In Dahomey*. *Source:* Author's collection.

pany and had been working to repatriate Afro-Americans to Liberia since 1885. The elder Walker and his compatriots filed articles of incorporation in June of 1902, and the first voyage was planned for May 1, 1903, to begin settling on a fifty-thousand-acre land grant. Unlike his son, who was working within existing systems to subversively bring about change, Nashville did not believe that the United States' affinity for Black oppression could be reasoned with, let alone be entertained into oblivion. Moreover, the change in location from the South Pacific, as in the original *Cannibal King* script, to Africa speaks to Nashville's influence. To boot, the pomp and circumstance of the entrance of Caboceers in the third act may have been directly influenced by the interactions between Bert, George, and the Dahomeyans at the 1894 World's Fair.[10]

Figure 8.4. Jerry Nashville Walker, president of the Colorado African Colonization Company. *Source: Denver Post*, August 20, 1916, 24.

Although some reviewers thought Williams and Walker shows were too ostentatious, they ultimately received a passing grade, so long as they stayed within the narrow confines of White acceptability. Once established, Bert and George could run wild with satirized speculation of Afrocentric possibilities that were universally entertaining. In that atmosphere, Whites would tolerate the surprise of Black ambition, so long as they were thoroughly entertained and the offending action remained within the confines of the stage. That aside, initial reviews of *In Dahomey* were positive, although what little plot there was caught some theatregoers off guard. Nonetheless, Bert and George kept the audience in a constant state of laughter. Ada and Pete Hampton were lauded by critics, as was Marshall Craig (1878 to 1951), a contortionist from Chicago who was cast as an alligator for the "Road to Gatorville" scene and amazed audiences with his ability to sit on his own head.[11] By far, the most informed reviews came from Sylvester Russell's admittedly heavy hand. The first of three featured consultation from audience members Bob Cole, Billy McClain, and Rosamond Johnson, who were present on opening night, and suggested many of the changes that were implemented in the earliest days. Russell expressed disappointment with the lack of a love scene, but the cast received high marks, and he lobbied for Ada to get more stage time. As before, his opinionated delivery did not endear him to Bert and George. Little did they know that he was just getting started, and, although infuriating, his notions were usually correct, assuming he had access to all pertinent information.[12]

Following the opening, the company traveled to Hartford before a grueling week in Boston, where they gave two performances a day, every day for a week.[13] Next was a week at the Auditorium, Philadelphia, where a young sculptor named Meta Vaux Warrick (1877 to 1968), who had recently returned to her hometown from Paris, likely saw the show. Her sense of Afrocentricity was beginning to awaken following the rejection of her work by White galleries, and she had recently opened a new art studio at 1432 South Pennsylvanian Square. The result was a figurine of George titled "The Comedian."[14]

While engaged in Manhattan, Sylvester Russell saw and reviewed the show again and called George "the greatest swell and cleverest talker of his race on the stage." Although paternalistic, his affection for Ada had grown: "Girls will be girls and Ada Overton Walker is one girl fashioned after many who have become stars and made their fortunes. Her one short historic spasm of modern aristocracy is a little something to marvel at."[15] Russell jumped at the chance to expound on a given subject regardless of who was sullied or minimized in the process. Even so, he gave a high endorsement at the end of this review: "Williams and Walker's aggregation is a big thing[,] and the new comedy is a howling success."[16]

During a series of one-night stands, the *Harrisburg (PA) Telegraph* reported a seven-eighths Black audience and unprecedented sheet music sales during intermissions.[17] Not only had the show proved fertile among Black people in the cities where they played, but the sheer novelty of the show continued to pique the curiosity of White theatrical writers all over the country.[18] Next came a respite from one-nighters in Altoona and in Pittsburgh, where Williams and Walker were the first act to be booked in a number of years due to an agreement among downtown theatre managers to ban Black acts.[19] While the company was engaged in Cincinnati, a young soprano named Laura Bowman (1881 to 1957) was added to the cast. Shortly thereafter, she began a relationship with Pete Hampton, a member of "The Syndicate Four Big Shots" with Sam Corker Jr., Fred Douglass, and Jesse Shipp, who ensured the smooth operation of the company. Although Bowman was already married, she and "Hamp" remained a couple and performing partners until his death in 1916.[20]

While engaged at the Great Northern in Chicago during the second week of December 1902, Bert debuted a new song, "I'm a Jonah Man." Composed especially for him by Alex Rogers, it was the ideal vehicle for his sad-sack, downtrodden, common-man character, who was no one important but somehow had everyone's attention as he lost it all just before he had it:

Chorus:

I am a Jonah, I am a Jonah man
If money growed on trees there ain't no doubt, I'd stay blind
Till the crop run out.
Why am I dis Jonah man, I sho' can't understand
But I'm a good substantial full-fledged, real, first-class Jonah man.

The audience was spellbound. Immediately, it became the hit of the show and Bert's first signature piece, which inspired him to write the publisher to tell them that it was the best song he ever had.[21]

During the new-year break, Nash made a solo trip to Lawrence to complete the purchase of the property on Indiana Street. The only mention of him in the local papers was "Nash Walker just passed in a hack," on January 5, 1903. He rejoined the company in Kansas City three days later.[22]

Figure 8.5. "I'm a Jonah Man," words and music by Alex Rogers, M. Witmark & Sons, New York, 1903. *Source:* Author's collection.

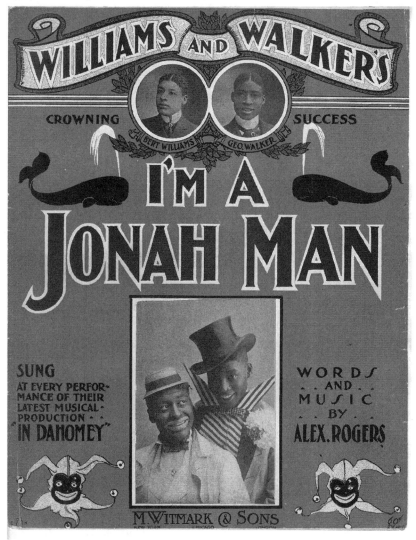

Their arrival had been anticipated for weeks, and posters printed in red and blue were placed all over the Colored side of town. Now a tradition, Ben McRay's B. P. A. lodge hosted a banquet for the company on opening night where silk dresses and tails were the required attire. At the ball, George was in his element and shared fond memories of his early days in Kansas City when he sold newspapers on Fifth Street near where he barked for "Doc" Warrick and discovered Joe Howard.²³ Next came the Opera House and the Bowersock. Nash came a day early and held court on Massachusetts Street before the rest of the company arrived. People lined up as early as four o'clock in the morning outside of Bromelsick's store to secure seats. When the store opened, three windows were smashed, and all available seats were quickly snatched up. The *Lawrence Daily Journal* reported, "A man went to the chart sale today and asked for two seats as near together as possible, to Williams and Walker. On being told that the seats were all gone he asked for two standing rooms as near together as possible."²⁴ Next came Topeka, where they set a record for advance-ticket sales. The *State Journal* reported, "It is no figure of speech to say that the store was black with people while the sale was on. The balcony lasted about as long as a watermelon would. 3/5 of the first floor was sold before the line broke."²⁵

After several one-night stands, there was a short layoff in Chicago, where Bert and George made a point of attending the Smart Set's production of the comedy *Southern Enchantment*, with Hogan and McClain, whom they had publicly quarreled with during the previous summer.²⁶ During the layoff, George returned to Manhattan to check on preparations for their unprecedented eight-week run on Broadway, following a deal with Marc Klaw (1858 to 1936) and Abe Erlanger (1860 to 1930), owners of the New York Theatre and other first-class houses.²⁷ James T. Brymn (1874 to 1946) and Cecil Mack recruited sixty new chorus members in Manhattan, while Shipp and Cook rehearsed them. Satisfied with preparations, George returned to the company on January 31 for their weeklong engagements in St. Paul and Minneapolis.²⁸ Coinciding with their time in the Twin Cities, Sylvester Russell published an article titled "Doctrine of George W. Walker" in *The Freeman*:

> Every cloud has its silver lining. One day the sun shines for you, and the next day for somebody else. Today it shines for Mr. Walker. The gentleman in question is George W. Walker, of Williams and Walker, the most famous team of comedians in America. I choose Mr. Walker for a singular inference. In summing up the deal of criticism of the past year, a vast amount of it fell unintentionally upon him. There was no special cause for this except his defective style of dressing for low comedy. This defect does not mar his ability as an actor, but rather reflects upon the playwrights. But Negro comedies have been put together so much by botchworkers, it is hard to tell who

the authors of any of the plays really are. The quality of acting depicted by Mr. Walker is of such an odd time that there is scarcely any of the writers with whom he has been associated who had the ability to write apart classical and witty enough to suit the requirements of his personality. Mr. Walker is not a low comedy comedian. He will only be able to sustain his reputation in high Negro comedy and classical features.

As the cleverest talker of his race on the stage, what can he say beyond the limits of the botchworkers? What can he do as a faddest when noted composers, who advertise themselves at his expense, fail to write him a song that will make him shine? This song, "On Broadway in Dahomey," is very clever to be sure—considering who wrote it. Mr. Walker may well be styled "The Colored Fashion Plate." He excels everybody in style, his ways are rich and his language unapproachable. His dances are sugar-cured tips of aristocracy.

These are the distinct qualifications with which he must mesmerize the people in order to maintain the power of his magnetism.

When Mr. Walker rushed on the stage in his Brooklyn engagement, emblazoned with diamonds, I said to myself, "Now he's in his element." How sorry I am that playwrights do not know enough to keep him dressed up—since he does not seem to insist upon it himself. But never mind; let it go. The young comedy playwrights are doing fairly well—quite as well as the actors.

Playwrights can answer back and say: If actors want to keep dressed up why don't they say so? White actors commission the playwrights to do "thus and so," and this means that both Mr. Walker and the botchworkers will learn to think a little more hereafter. Mr. Walker is not only blessed with accomplishments and success, but he is generally regarded by all his friends and acquaintances as a man of exceptionally good personal qualities.

To add to all of these luxurious blessings, he is the husband of the most talented actress of his race—Ada Overton Walker.[29]

Russell utilized a rare complimentary tone with a hint of optimism within his normal hubris. George's stardom was, by necessity, secondary to Bert's, but there was fertile space for development. However, his potential as an actor was not fully maximized in their current formula, although he dressed better than everyone. Bert, on the other hand, was beginning to attain a high level of artistry while literally, figuratively, and creatively trapped under a mask. Although *clever* was adequate for the partners to shine, *brilliant* could mean the kind of lasting impact beyond their lifetimes that their generation longed for. For the time being, George had to settle with a hit show on Broadway and the pride of providing for his mother and grandmother, who would soon take possession of one of the finest new homes in Lawrence.[30]

The Colored Entrance to the Great White Way

After two weeks in the Twin Cities, the company made its way back to Manhattan for their engagement on Broadway, scheduled to begin on February 18, 1903. In order to secure their booking at the New York Theatre, George devised a scheme to rent it for two months and book themselves exclusively. As expected, the management team of Marc Klaw and Abraham Erlanger was against the idea of booking the wildly popular show on the Great White Way, so concessions were demanded. Although it was a first-class house with a first-class show, tickets were to be sold at second-class prices to not anger the establishment. Once again, the company was expected to contend with the reality of artistic excellence at a discount, simply because they were Black. As Bert expressed,

> The way we've trained for Broadway and just missed it in the past seven years would make you cry. We'd get our bearings, take a good running start and—land in a Third Avenue theatre. Then we'd measure the distance again and think we'd struck the right avenue at last—only to be stalled in a West Thirty-fourth Street music hall with the whole stunt to do all over again. We'd get near enough to hear the Broadway audiences applaud sometimes, but it was someone else they were applauding. I used to be tempted to beg for a $15 job in a chorus just for one week so as to be able to say I'd been on Broadway once.[31]

George's sense of nationalism had rubbed off on Bert enough for him to make a rare public statement that was akin to his partner's shortly before they opened: "My partner and myself have pretty carefully gauged the public taste in the past ten years, and just for once we want to be allowed to paddle our own canoe entirely."[32]

Figure 8.6. "Williams and Walker 'In Dahom[e]y Company' 1904." The photograph was not made in 1904 as the cataloging label states. Likely, the label was created from memory, because Williams and Walker had parted ways with Will Accooe (#29) in 1903 after his demotion from conductor of the first troupe (in place of Will Marion Cook / James Vaughn) and was put in charge of *Sons of Ham* starring Avery and Hart. That company made its debut in mid-April of 1903, and by the fall, when Accooe became fatally ill, he was working on *The Volunteers*, which was supposed to star Dan Avery and Charles Hart, possibly because the first troupe was expected to continue with *In Dahomey* for another year after they returned from England. However, Accooe died in late April of 1904 in Manhattan while the first company was abroad and had been for nearly a year. Also, Marshall Craig (#36) left the cast after the Broadway run in late April of 1903 and never returned. Last, Lizzie Avery (#22) was one of several original cast members who stayed in England to tour with her husband, who was a star of the second company in June of 1904. As such, the photograph was probably made in January or February 1903, shortly before their debut on Broadway. *Source:* Eubie Blake Photograph Collection, Maryland Center for History and Culture. Public domain.

At last, an all-Black show was to be presented on Broadway, albeit, as *The New York Times* put it, "an interesting experiment." As with any unprecedented event, Manhattan was abuzz with excitement, and the company was now larger than ever, with fresh voices and legs. Although the previous five months were successful, it had been accomplished at a grueling pace, and the veterans were glad to stay put for a while.³³ In anticipation of the momentous event, the *Evening World* declared, "A deep chocolate-colored shadow fell athwart the Great White Way." Fortunately, the show did not disappoint elite Broadway theatregoers, and the tone of the reviews followed suit: "They saw the same show that had attracted Eighth Avenue to the Grand Opera House earlier in the season. And they seemed to like it even better than their less critical neighbors had done."³⁴ As reported in the *New York Tribune*,

> All were there! The old first night faces, looking wise; and the critics, "the newspaper chain gang," as the merriest member calls them, sat them down in the seats of the scornful. For there was a feeling abroad that this shadowy invasion of Broadway would bring shadows of blue, and dark would be the way and beset with ragtime which the audience must travel before they could reach repose and refreshment. Perhaps that was the best joke of the performance. For Williams and Walker—somebody will call them sooner or later "the colored Weber and Fields," so it might as well be done now—one spontaneous reading of laughter at their first appearance, and thereafter no doubt could possibly exist that they had vindicated their right to appear on Broadway. The climax was reached when the originator of the chain gang phrase was seen himself to laugh—nay, not only seen, but heard. Of course, a man may laugh and laugh and be a critic: but it's rather mean to, none the less.³⁵

Opening night truly was a sight to behold. *The Sun* reported, "The laughter was so incessant, so noisy that it often drowned the voices of the actors and actresses."³⁶ In an article titled "We Are Broadway Stars," from an unknown newspaper, George spoke about their unprecedented accomplishment with a bit of euphoric candor:

> One night I told a New Yorker I believed we were a warm bunch, and that we'd end up on Broadway sooner or later. He didn't say anything but he just hummed two lines of a song we'd made our first hit with. It was: "Oh, I don't know! You ain't so wahm! Day'd oddeh coons as wahm as you-oo!"
> I've hated that song ever since. Just the same[,] when I saw that man's face in the second row, on our opening night on Broadway, it did me good.³⁷

That exchange likely took place between George and Abe Erlanger early in the negotiation process for access to the New York Theatre. Once in, they took the house like no other show in history. By design, if George shined, Bert sparkled. As if giving a master class, he pulled the audience's emotional heartstrings at will, often without saying a word. *The New York Times* declared, "He holds a face for minutes at a time, seemingly, and when he alters it, bringing a laugh by the least movement."[38] In all, Bert's rendition of "Jonah Man" generated a dozen returns, thwarting *The New York Times*' premonition of a race war due to the presence of a Black company on a Broadway stage and the potential influx of Black patrons. The *New-York Tribune* declared, "Those who had come to scoff were loudest in their applause."[39]

Once applied and amended as necessary, the Williams and Walker formula met with real, tangible success that was undeniable. However, when Black patrons attempted to sit in the orchestra section, they were turned away by force and placed in the balcony. In response to the disruptions on opening night, Klaw and Erlanger issued a notice so "all question of race discrimination is avoided." The lower floor, orchestra, and orchestra circle, all boxes except the top tier, two sections of the dress circle, and one section of the balcony were given exclusively to Whites, which left one section of the dress circle, two sections in the balcony, and the entire gallery for Blacks.[40] Intrinsically, the declaration only worked if there were no Black people present to complain. Estimated at a thousand strong on opening night, Black people saw no reason why they should be Jim Crowed at a Black event, and, according to Harry Jackson of *The Freeman*, "nevertheless they are there at each performance, arriving in, automobiles, coaches, coupes and on foot attired in evening gowns, tuxedos and swallowtails, just the same as the members of the 'white 400.' "[41]

Despite *In Dahomey* being a Black show about Black people going to Africa, Black people were not as welcome as Whites. Nevertheless, the *New-York Tribune* expressed a uniquely progressive point of view on the subject:

> The number of colored people who have presented themselves for admission to the theatre has been a source of astonishment to those who sit in judgment. And all of these colored people have shown the same prime qualification for admission as their white brethren—rectangular strips of paper with green backs. Their argument was irrefutable. But, on the other hand, to admit them to all parts of the house would be to drive away the usual patrons of the theatre, it was felt; perhaps to convert the New York into a colored resort. As Klaw and Erlanger are not yet

quite prepared to take that step, a compromise was affected, and a hard and fast color line drawn within the theatre. The boys who pass the water between acts are the only negroes allowed to overstep this line, and no white person but the manager of the house is allowed to cross in the other direction.[42]

As usual, White comfort won out over the Bill of Rights, and Bert and George were forced to comply. What was a "most remarkable experiment" to some was a possible future to others, and declarations from management could not solve the problem. Black New Yorkers were overjoyed at the prospect and gladly tested the limits of Jim Crow to be a part of the unprecedented event. Aside from a gaffe by Charles Moore, their business manager, Williams and Walker said nothing about the injustice. As things progressed to a head, Bert and George were caught between it all and received criticism in local Black press again for not getting involved. Privately, they continued to assert that a lasting impact could only be achieved from the stage as they compelled audiences to question, argue, and explore while they laughed. In conjunction, the timeliness of their highly curated artistry sparked jealousy among their White contemporaries. Comedian Alf Grant of *Nancy Brown* rushed over from the Bijou to see the show and reportedly said, "That's it exactly. Abraham Lincoln freed the Negroes and Williams and Walker give them work."[43] Despite the stakes, George could not resist another opportunity to stir the pot. Inspired by President Theodore Roosevelt's "coquetting for the negro suffrage," Bert and George dispatched a missive to inform the president that a box was reserved for his use throughout the run on Broadway. Still reeling from the backlash of Booker T. Washington's recent visit to the White House, Roosevelt ignored the invitation.[44]

Aida Outshines the Four Hundred

While *In Dahomey* played to a packed, segregated house week after week, Ada began to blossom as a masterful performer, teacher, and cultural ambassador in the drawing rooms of New York's "Four Hundred," where she charged $100 for four lessons to teach them "how to cake walk gracefully."[45] Shortly before the Broadway debut, Ada Guiguesse (ca. 1873 to 1937), a soprano from New Orleans via St. Louis, was added to the chorus and briefly replaced Abbie Mitchell Cook, who went on maternity leave in mid-March, just before birth of her second child, Mercer Cook (1903 to 1987). With an additional Ada featured in the cast, something had to be done to avoid confusing the audience, and by March 12, 1903, Ada Overton Walker changed the spelling of her first name to *Aida* and retained it for the rest of her life.⁴⁶

Although the new spelling sparked some intrigue, it paled in comparison to Aida's next move, which inspired newspapers all over the country to weigh in on the audacity of her scandalous invasion of a sacred White space. On March 9, 1903, Aida made a solo appearance at Delmonico's, the most exclusive club in the country, which catered only to the Four Hundred. For many, that was beyond a step too far. In reality, she received an invitation from Robert Hargous to appear at a party at the exclusive club for Lady Mary Paget, who was visiting from England. It is possible that Harogus reserved a box early in the run at the New York Theatre and Hurtig and Seamon came up with a publicity stunt to add a little fuel to *In Dahomey*'s

Figures 8.7a and 8.7b. Rotographs by Cavendish Morton of Aida Overton Walker and Ada Guiguesse, London, circa fall 1903. *Source:* Author's collection.

fire. Although their enthusiasm was genuine, the stunt created problems for Aida that were not of her making.

The night of the event began as another dull evening among the Four Hundred that was expected to end in a card game, but Aida's presence transcended the dull into the sublime. Dressed in Irish point lace relieved with blue chiffon, she arrived in her modest brougham, driven by a White footman, and took the arm of Harry Seamon, who escorted her into the exclusive building. As reported in *The St. Louis Republic*,

> As the clock struck 12 Mrs. Walker, who had "done her turn" and wanted to go home, made a final fluttering bow and was about to leave the floor. Then it was that a well-known society leader and squire of dames jumped suddenly from his seat, signaled to the orchestra and, in a trice, had the negro dancer about the waist and was waltzing about the floor with her while the others looked on.
>
> At first the company sat still and gasped; then somebody giggled; and in a moment there was a wild burst of applause. The musicians caught the spirit and the deed was done. Mrs. Walker had been initiated into New York's four hundred and fifty.[47]

Overnight, the normally reserved Aida came to personify the "Negro Problem" in the United States, and for a few weeks she surpassed W. E. B. Du Bois and the recently crowned, first Afro-American heavyweight champion of the world, Jack Johnson (1878 to 1946), in the national press. Regardless, the day after the party, she was the guest of Lady Paget at the Waldorf-Astoria, where she gave a private lesson to a select group of women, as well as a gathering at Mrs. George Law's residence at 10 East Fifty-Fourth Street, attended by Alva Belmont, Mrs. Frederick Neilson, and Barron Knapp-Herr.[48]

Even though the press was aware that she was giving private lessons to elites, neither Aida nor her pupils would divulge any details. Elites were bound by the requirements of their status and were reticent to admit to seeking counsel on matters of culture and refinement from a Black person, let alone a performer. Nevertheless, since "Willie" Vanderbilt's popularization of the cake walk among the Four Hundred back in 1897, it was fashionable to conclude cotillions and parties with a cake walk, and those with ambition always wanted to make a good showing.[49] Further, thanks to the American aristocracy's tether to English nobles like Lady Paget, coupled with Williams and Walker's impending tour in England, Aida's new venture foreshadowed some lucrative side work for cast members. However, anonymity was key, a nuance that was ignored by publicity-seeking management who wanted to exploit the controversy, seemingly at all costs. When pressed to reveal her client list, Aida said, "I cannot mention their names[,] for that would not be right or courteous to the ladies who are receiving instructions from me and who are paying me very well, but they are among the social leaders of New York and Newport and, I might say, London also."[50] For the first time, she was the center of attention, and her new depictions in print reflected her ascending stardom. She was more than just what met the eye, and it was undeniable:

> Mrs. Walker is an artist to her finger tips. She is a decided "brunette," even among her own color. She has a bright face and sparkling, coal-black eyes that stand and twinkle as she sways in the dance. She has a straight black hair that falls in a huge and gorgeous pompadour over one of those eyes. She has the full lips and flashing, white teeth that tell of corn bread fare and a bacon appetite. There may be a suggestion of powder on her nose, but it is the typical nose of her race, and the grace with which she goes through the contortions of the cake walk is typical, too, even if it is a bit more cultivated then that which is found on the average Southern plantation.
>
> But her gowns. There's nothing of the plantation in those. They smack of Paris and are cut in the latest mode with pearl ornaments and chiffon ruffles. Her hat is a Florodora and about her dusky throat hang two long strings of pearls that remind you of the famous Lillian Russell or the Duchess of Marlborough.[51]

The throngs of unflattering press inspired Aida to make a statement from her dressing room at the New York Theatre:

> Really, now, this is astonishing[.] Why should all this fuss be made? I was Mr. Hargous' partner for a waltz, and we cake walked together. It was all very proper and rather good sport, and I found the dinner company charming, you know. My husband was not with me. That is not fashionable, you know. Mr. Seamon was my escort. When I came in they were playing

bridge. Then I sang a bit and danced a bit, and there you are. I was there for an hour or more. No, indeed. I was not entertaining all the while. What was I doing? Oh, chatting—small talk, you know.[52]

In Aida's defense, Lady Paget and Mrs. Law also tried to curb the tide of scandal. An unnamed attendee of the party said, "I call this unmitigated impudence[.] It will teach us to select our entertainers with care. I know the girl is not responsible for the 'hurrah.' It was her manager who brought her to the dinner and who will reap the benefits of this nauseating notoriety. It would be an injustice to our host to say whether he waltzed with the young woman."[53] Philosophically, the incident came full circle when it was finally ascertained that despite Aida's precociousness of dancing her way into the "big house," the elites didn't seem to care: "the Vanderbilts, Sloans, Depews, Astors and other prominent leaders of 'The 400' occup[y] boxes at every performance. Box parties to see 'the colored sensation' at the New York theatre have really become a fad among the swell sets of New York."[54]

The Delmonico's incident was so controversial that upon Robert Hargous' death, two and a half years later, it was still one of the points of interest mentioned in his obituary, despite his long and prosperous life.[55] It was one of several cases where management did what they believed was in the best interest of their clients but simultaneously sabotaged them because reprisals were far more likely to be directed at Aida, Bert, and George than those who created the problem. Further, Aida had little recourse beyond giving an abbreviated and transcribed version of her class that she was then teaching several times a week at the Waldorf-Astoria. With George in intensive negotiations with George Lederer for a run in England, the timing could not have been worse. The situation was ridiculously absurd, and the way forward was prophetically described by W. E. B. Du Bois that same year in "The Forethought" of *Souls of Black Folk*: "The problem of the Twentieth Century is the problem of the color-line."[56] Nevertheless, the show was the toast of New York. With their run soon ending in anticipation of their impending opening in London, it seemed as though nothing could derail the Dahomeyan juggernaut.[57]

Figure 8.8. "Ada Overton Walker," *Royal Magazine* 10 (May–October 1903): 387. *Source:* Author's collection.

Chapter 9

"I Needn't Be Scared of No King"

1903 to 1904

Gone East to the West End

Just before *In Dahomey* closed on Broadway, Sylvester Russell saw the show for the third time and noted that nearly half of the boxes were occupied, the gallery was crowded, and the third balcony was full of enthusiastic Black patrons. He showed a lack of insight when he praised Hurtig and Seamon's piety as managers and downplayed Bert and George's role in maintaining the momentum of the show despite the sometimes harmful actions of management. Still, the significance of their accomplishments to date was not lost: "Judging from serious observations of the people in all parts of the house, I should venture to say that few comedy teams of any race shine more brightly in the eyes of New Yorkers than Williams and Walker."[1] On April 4, 1903, *In Dahomey* closed at the New York Theatre, and the company moved to the Auditorium in Philadelphia, a first-class venue, for a two-week engagement, then returned to New York for the week of April 12, when it was announced on both sides of the Atlantic that the "somewhat strange and daring experiment" would travel to England for an extended run.[2]

Shortly before their departure aboard the RMS *Aurania* bound for Liverpool on April 28, 1903, George sent a telegram to Lawrence and announced that they would open at the Shaftesbury Theatre on May 18. He also told a reporter from the *Morning Telegraph* that he hoped to do a little hunting, which was relayed with a bit of unnecessary minstrelized inflection: "It's jes possible . . . that the Earl of Harewood might invite me up to Heathercote to his shooting lodge naixt fall, and Ah'll be there with the gaudy raiment." For context, the reporter included a list of George's wardrobe: twenty-four business suits, various shades from a bright green to a pattern in checks; seven black frock suits with trousers ranging from robin blue to a new shade of mauve; three gray frock suits; thirty-four fancy waistcoats; six dozen pair of kaleidoscopic silk socks; four dozen pair of gloves from white to rich lavender; six full evening dress suits; and three tuxedos. George's suits for the stage were lined with red and yellow satin, and his gray tuxedo was inspired by the English-born actor William Faversham. Williams was reportedly more pragmatic with his attire, resembling "a ribbon clerk." Aida brought a corn-flour-colored chiffon dress in anticipation of attending the Lord Mayor's garden party in June. The dress was said to be so fetching that it would "cause the Thames to flood its banks if it is ever exhibited in the open." Lottie brought "a gown of watermelon pink crepe de chene quite likely to merit a display head in the London fashion notes of the conservative old London Times." With their minds set on a command performance at Buckingham Palace, Bert reportedly declared, "Ef ah doan make that ole King laugh, ah'll quit de business."[3]

Over one thousand well-wishers saw them off at the pier, and Bert's new $1,800 automobile was stowed in the ship's hold. About a half hour before the gangplank was raised, there was an informal Black and Tan reception, for which Hurtig and Seamon supplied a dozen bottles of Mumm Extra Dry champagne. Everyone put on a brave face, but deep down they were very nervous. As Bert wrote in 1909,

> When we went aboard the ship it was more like Noah loading the ark than a theatrical company starting on a trip they hoped would last a year. All of us, down to the members of the chorus, pushed out our chests and shoved our hats back on our heads and walked up the gang-plank trying to look as if crossing the ocean was an old story. That was the way we *tried* to look, but at least half of us in our hearts felt we might never put our peepers on America again. I suppose we must have inoculated our relatives with the same unspoken fear.
>
> There were more relatives on hand to bid us tearful and apprehensive farewells than I thought we had. They just swarmed around us, and the way they shouted and cried and sang and carried on made me wonder if we hadn't better call it all off and stick to dry land—the land we knew.[4]

Figure 9.1. George Walker aboard RMS *Aurania*, April 28, 1903. *Source:* Collection of the Smithsonian National Museum of African American History and Culture.

Upon departure, Jesse Shipp wanted to hold rehearsals immediately on the main deck. With the 1897 debacle on their minds, the plan was to give all the material a thorough shakedown. If a joke came off as too American, some of the English officers of the ship were to be pressed into service as an impromptu audience. On the last day of the voyage, a dress rehearsal was scheduled for the benefit of the Seaman's Fund. However, there was so much seasickness among the company members during the voyage that they put on a traditional minstrel show instead. According to Bert, "Danged if I didn't get a million laughs on the trip. The company were the whitest looking mob I ever saw. The majority of them had never crossed before and they were *scared* white. In the course of about twenty-four hours, however, they had turned greenish and this color they retained until we landed."[5]

The *Aurania* made landfall in Liverpool, England, on May 5, 1903. Aida mailed a letter to George's mother that detailed the goings on of the voyage, and Will Cook held rehearsals on the train to London's Euston Station. Despite having a reservation at the Cecil Hotel, they found it was rescinded at the insistence of unnamed Americans when they attempted to check in. Cook relayed the incident to an interviewer from the London *Daily News*, who told him, "You will find none of that narrow-minded racial feeling here."[6] The prosperity from the spoils of hundreds of years of colonialism and the novelty of "Real Coons" from the United States created a unique environment that was tantalizing to the members of the cast who had slayed Broadway and were poised to conquer London's West End. Yet the company's excitement was tempered by the unaccomplished task of entertaining another exceptionalist White audience. Failure was not an option, and to squander the rarity of a second chance might have meant years or decades before another opportunity presented itself.

Just before opening at the Shaftesbury Theatre, Bert's anxiety was at an all-time high: "in the ten days of rehearsal and preparation, I never went through so much panic and mental indecision in my whole lifetime. Friends and friendly enemies would come to me one at a time and tell me in great confidence, just what I should and should not do in the part to make a head over there. They had me so worried that I wanted to escape and let the whole thing go."[7] The London press coverage was akin to New York's in emphasizing the production's novelty and uniqueness. Unlike the American press, which focused on more stereotypical depictions of the cast members in photographs and drawings, the British papers featured a wider variety of more dignified imagery.[8] A lot more attention was given to Cook and Dunbar, partially because they were known entities in England and because of Cook's willingness to speak at length to reporters. Other than stock photos and their accompanying blurbs, George was conspicuously absent from press accounts, possibly due to his apprehension and the sourness of their departure back in 1897. Instead, he continuously revised the show on the way to London. Ironically, George chose to remove the cake walk after the run on Broadway because they believed that it had become passé. However, the May 13 issue of *The Tatler* featured an image of George and Aida from "The Tzar of Dixie" with the caption "The Real Cake Walk by Real Coons."[9] Also, the characteristic "Negro dialect" that was common on the American minstrel stage was softened and made a little plainer for English audiences. Bert later remarked, "Once or twice I turned loose a little broad 'coon' talk on them, but they couldn't understand all the words and lost the point of the jokes."[10]

As excitement grew, *The Tatler* commented on the growing presence of smartly dressed Black people in the theatre district.[11] Bert recalled a rocky but successful opening night:

> Things started smoothly. There wasn't a sign of trouble, and as the night went on and these conditions continued, I got more and more nervous. I thought I could feel them saving up all the trouble for the very last. They seem to be enjoying the play, but I knew that wouldn't mean anything if they were just playing 'possum and waiting for the chance to give it to us good.
>
> Then, right in the middle of a quiet spot in the performance, somebody in the gallery started the booing. In about one 'steenth part of a second it seemed that nearly everybody in the gallery was following his lead. For a moment I wanted to turn and run, but just as I was about ready to make a record that would put [sprinter] Tom Longboat to shame, the audience downstairs came to our rescue, and with their applause drowned out the booing and put the gallery to silence . . . I was ready to lie down and rest after that first night's performance. Of course, it had been a severe nervous and mental strain, and we all felt the reaction.[12]

Bert and George had been forewarned that English audiences were known to boo and hiss regardless of the stature of a play. In response, Bert joked that they considered going onstage with armor under their costumes.[13] *The Sketch* described the situation: "Whilst fully admitting the right, legal

Figure 9.2. "The Real Cake-Walk by Real Coons," *The Tatler*, May 13, 1903, 246A. *Source:* Author's collection.

"I Needn't Be Scared of No King" | 171

and otherwise, of the gallery to express its opinion during and after the performance, fact that it is using the right ungenerously and tactlessly is painfully patent. The coloured people must have thought that the offensive interruptions on the first-night displayed a sad lack of good manners, and not only did they startle and disconcert and to some extent paralyze them, but were very displeasing to the more patient parts of the audience."[14]

George remained silent for nearly a year and only discussed the opening night in his annual letter to Lawrence:

> That was a memorable night in the life and struggles of Williams and Walker, for we felt happy that our dream of a national and international reputation had been realized.
>
> The theatre was crowded almost to suffocation and the nerves of all the members of our company were at high tension, almost to the snapping point. Everybody wanted to make good and everybody did make good that first night and the reputation of our company was thoroughly established. That was what made my partner and I happy and we are still happy.[15]

All told, the reviewers were kind but somewhat confused by the foreignness of the show. *The Observer* exclaimed, "It is to be seen, not described," and "The success of the production, at least last night, resulted from its novelty, not of refined nor pleasing character." *The Globe* noted, "The new entertainment at the Shaftesbury is well worth seeing—once. We are not sure that a second visit to it is to be recommended to anybody with nerves. For it is a noisy entertainment."[16] Further, the show was a stark contrast from the minstrel fare that had been the prevailing style for seventy years; *The Globe*'s reviewer noted, "What we really get it is a Negro-American. We do not get the Negro in the rough; we get him with Yankee veneer."[17] The London *Daily News* asserted that Bert was the only person in the play who understood "real" Darkey behavior and thought that any finery was appropriated from European culture. He further noted difficulty understanding the dialect, which denoted the low nature of the show.[18] However, not all reviews expressed discomfort with the show's "New Negro"-ness. The *St. James Gazette* declared, "It will be a pity if the conclusion of 'In Dahomey' is made to undergo any change. At present it is distinctive, in an age when distinction is rare."[19] Because it was such a unique and unprecedented vehicle, the audience was unaware that the show ended at eleven o'clock on opening night. To indicate the show's conclusion, the orchestra played "God Save the King," which prompted the reviewer for *The Illustrated Sporting and Dramatic News* to assert, "I advised those responsible for the production to have a more telling wind-up."[20]

Aside from jitters and a largely puzzled audience, the songs "Jonah Man" and "The Czar" were hits, which signaled that all was not lost and, after some fine tuning, success was attainable. Most notable in the reviews was a distinct longing for a cake walk, signaling a rare curatorial error on George's part. As reported in *The Sketch*, "one surprising matter was the comparative lack of dancing. I was expecting to see the cake walk in its most intense degree, or some frenzied dancing, but although there were many threats or promises of something of the kind, they came to little."[21] By May 22, the cake walk was reincorporated into the show, with four couples participating, to the delight of the audience; the Dundee *Evening Post* declared, " 'Cake walking' is still 'the thing.' "[22] Partners were chosen at random for the week, and at the end of each week, the winningest couple received a bonus from management. With the added prospect of access to wealthy patrons, the competitive spirit took hold. As things settled, George warmed to the press: "George Walker of this company taught some of the Vanderbilts the steps—and there are signs that it may achieve popularity in society here, for many fashionable ladies have engaged sections of the *In Dahomey* Company to give cake walking exhibitions at their houses."[23] Aida was in her element, and reviewers heaped praise: "Londoners should flock to the Shaftesbury Theatre if only to see the dusky soubrette, Miss Aida Overton Walker, show all the riotous possibilities of the real cake-walk dance, if only to hear a genuine nigger minstrel." Another critic noted, "Very amusing, too, is Miss Aida Overton Walker, a quaint Topsy-like personage, whose antics are an incarnation of irresistible fun." *The Playgoer* remarked, "Teeth gleam, voices ring, eyes beam, and they dance with their whole bodies in an apparent ecstasy of enjoyment, alive to the finger-tips."[24] In all, the show was a feast for the senses and London was hungry for something new and substantial. As predicted, Mme. Patti and several of London's elites began to cake walk in earnest. Members of the cast enjoyed rubbing elbows with the aristocracy, and George was so taken by smart English fashion that he wrote to Lawrence D'Orsay, who was touring in the United States, to get the name of his tailor in England. Shortly after opening, several members of the company fell into the habit of traveling to Ostend, a resort town in Belgium, every Sunday, only to return broke on Monday.[25]

Buckingham Palace

Despite rumors of interest, the royal box at the Shaftesbury remained empty aside from a visit from the king's official theatregoers and the Duke of Connaught. As Bert and George recalled,

> "We had kept up our watch for four or five nights and had concluded that the Duke of Connaught had told King Edward not to attend."
>
> "We thought he had hung up a 'No Good' sign," explained Walker.
>
> "And just about that time," Williams went on, "we received the Royal command to go to Buckingham Palace to help celebrate Prince Eddie's birthday. We were very much pleased," said Williams quickly.
>
> "We were highly pleased," said Walker with a bow. "We appreciated the magnitude of the unprecedented honor."[26]

The command performance took place on June 23, 1903, at a party given by Queen Alexandra for 150 guests in celebration of Prince Edward's ninth birthday. It was an extraordinary opportunity that was exploited for all it was worth, which inspired a transformation in Williams and Walker's billing from the "Real Coons" to the "Royal Comedians." In preparation for the event, the lawn between the lake and the terrace at Buckingham Palace was transformed into a makeshift stage and the scenery was specifically chosen to complement the background of trees. A row of flowers was placed at the edge of the stage in front of the footlights, the wings were decorated with festoons of laurel, and the orchestra was positioned stage left. Jesse Shipp arranged a truncated version of the show and had been troubleshooting on the palace grounds the whole day. At about a quarter to four o'clock, the royal children exited the palace, followed shortly by the king and queen.[27] George was nervous, and recalled, "I pulled myself together and by tellin' myself that as long as I had appeared before New York's 550 I guess I needn't be scared of no King."[28] By the time Bert and George arrived, Jesse had everything in shape, and George remembered, "The sentries at the Palace presented arms when we arrived and we were received in the grand hall by a hundred magnificent servants in scarlet and gold liveries, with knee bre[e]ches and white silk stockings."[29] Labeled the "chief radical" by Bert, Jesse later told him that he might have offended some of the palace staff because he was so busy preparing for the production that he barely bothered to stop and answer their questions. According to Bert, "[Jesse] said that he had not volunteered any information, but that one stout gentleman in a red vest, probably the head butler, had asked if he found anything wrong with the English way of doing things, and he said he had 'let the fellow have it.' He had told him a dozen things that were wrong, from the handling of baggage, on down. . . . To understand Jesse's real worth, one had to know him."[30] Although reduced, the full orchestra and cast totaled more than eighty, minus Abbie Mitchell Cook, who was supposed to have the night off to spend with her infant son. However, around two o'clock, a man rang the bell and told her that her presence was requested at the palace and that a carriage was waiting for her. When she arrived, she was shocked to find her husband, Bert, and Jesse absorbed in a game of craps.[31] When another, smaller game sprang up between two male chorus members during the performance, Jules Hurtig put a stop to it, to which one was reported to have said, with a grin, "We jes' had our game in de royal palace yard."[32]

Bert recalled Jesse's embarrassment during the performance when he learned who he had spouted off to earlier in the day:

> As we peeped, we spoke in hushed whispers. You could hear, all around our stage, "Oh, what a wonderful site!" "Look at the King!" "Isn't the King wonderful?" etc., etc. Suddenly Shipp came up to the peephole where I was and looked through with me. Slowly the procession was approaching. "Lemme see the King," he said grouchily. "There he is," I said. "Where?" "In the front, there, see?" "Oh, My, isn't the King a stunning figure?" this from some of our ladies. "Danged if I see any King in that mob," said Shipp angrily, "Tain't a soul got on a crown nor a royal robe that I can see, where is he?"
>
> I showed him the central figure, now well within our unobstructed view from the peep hole. "That man?" he gasped. "My Gawd, the fat man with the red vest, is the King? That's the man I was roastin' the country to[?] I was looking for a King to *look like a King*!"[33]

Other than Jesse's blunder and a few innocuous liberties taken, the performance was a rousing success. As reported in the Montreal *Gazette*,

They applauded Bert Williams' rendering of the song "Jonah Man," in which his grimaces were genuinely funny, while Walker's "Castle on the [Nile]," with a dancing chorus, set even the royal feet to pattering. The hit of the entertainment, however, was a cake walk, which their Majesties specially demanded. Upon its conclusion the four contesting couples stepped to the front of the stage, while in true cake walk style a cake was held in front of each couple and the couple receiving the most applause was decided to be the winner. The audience quickly grasped the idea and entered into the spirit of the occasion with zest, the King and Queen merrily joining in the applause. The cake was awarded to Lavinia Gatson and Richard [Connors], who, according to the Negroes, really deserved it.[34]

Although there was a policy of no encores because they had to perform again that evening, the king was so taken by Bert's "Jonah Man" that an exception was made. However, it was the cake walk that truly inspired awe among the royals. The dancing was so well-received that the children immediately took to it as if compelled by an outside force. When it was finished, the king was said to have sent Lord Farquhar to enquire as to whether what he witnessed was the "real" cake walk or not. The enthusiasm took George by surprise, who said, "We had heard that we must not expect any demonstration from our royal audience. How different it all proved; I have never performed before more appreciative people. The King seemed especially pleased."[35] At the conclusion of the performance, the curfew bells rang out from the tower of Windsor Castle, and, just as quickly as it all began, it was over.[36] Nonetheless, the English royals made a favorable impression on Bert and George:

> Walker thought that the King was the "real thing." He said that he had a fine jovial face, and that the Queen was perfectly lovely. You expected that Their Majesties would be stiff and icy, but instead they were warm and enthusiastic. "Yes," interposed Williams, "the most Royal acting persons were the servants. The King looks like a good fellow."
> What most strongly impressed Williams was the behavior of the children and the extreme and unfailing gallantry of the little boys towards the little girls. He said he would never forget their manners. He saw a little girl chasing a dog across the

lawn. In doing she passed the Queen. Immediately the children stopped curtsied and then continued the chase. Walker said: "It what a great afternoon for us. I understood this was the first time Their Majesties have ever musical comedians at the palace. I hoped that we entertained and interested Their Majesties as much as they did us."[37]

Shortly after the performance, George sent a letter to the *Rising Son* in Kansas City:

I have had the honor of playing the "King of Dahomey" before his Majesty, the King of England. While he did not wear his royal robes, as I did, and was therefore somewhat at a disadvantage, still he looked every inch a king. He is the real thing. He treated me as one king should another.

The servants conducted us to the beautiful gardens where we gave our show. We were treated greatly. That is the only word for it. We had champagne from the royal cellar and strawberries and cream from the Royal Gardens. The Queen was perfectly lovely. The King was as jolly as he could be and laughed at everything we did. The little Prince and Princesses were as nice as they could be, just like little fairies.

—London, June 26[, 1903][38]

It was also reported that Bert, a Bahamian by birth and subject of the British Crown, experienced some anxiety over whether or not to perform "Evah Darhkey Is a King." However, Bert sang it and made a hit:

Chorus:

Evah dahkey is a king!
Royalty is jes' de ting
Ef yo' social life's a bungle
Jes' yo' go back to yo' jungle
An' remember dat yo' daddy was a King![39]

Despite Bert's anxiety, the king later informed him, possibly over a game of craps, that he enjoyed Jesse's unrestrained criticism and that he thoroughly enjoyed his rendition of "Evah Dahkey Is a King." Much like the "Oh, nothing, only just butting in" incident two years earlier, the sheer novelty of the interaction may have been an isolated and therefore welcome change of protocol for the king, who was quite surprised to hear how Afro-Americans really spoke.[40] George said, "We were so determined to please the royal family that we forgot they were royalties. I did not think the King would like our coon business, but he did. He laughed heartily, and he and the Queen kept their seats to the end of the performance and applauded loudly."[41]

After the royal success at the palace and the king's enthusiastic embrace of the cake walk, the expertise of the cast members was fervently sought after by aristocracy. The demand was so great that the obliging dancers were often too tired to do their nightly performances justice, which prompted a ban on all outside cake-walking instruction. Regardless, one anonymous cast member was quoted as saying, "Order or no order, we jus' go, jus' the same."[42] Aida later divulged that she provided cake-walking lessons to Lady Constance McKenzie, Muriel Wilson, the Duke and Duchess of Connaught, and the Duke and Duchess of Manchester at the London home of Sir Arthur and Lady Paget, whom she met during the Broadway run. She also studied with ballet masters in London.[43]

Following the command performance, Jules Hurtig declared that he "solved the Negro question" and announced plans to export Afro-American companies to Russia and Germany, his home country. Despite George's objection, Hurtig also expected the Williams and Walker aggregation to remain in England for another year. Shortly after, Hurtig returned to New York, as did Will and Abbie Cook, to work on his next production, *The Southerners*, slated to debut at the New York Theatre on May 23, 1904. Ada Guiguesse took her place, and James Vaughn became the company's new conductor.[44] In honor of the show's 150th performance on September 29, 1903, the third act was moved to the opening, and a minuet was added along with a Spanish "dream dance," choreographed by Aida, that also featured Bert as the Fairy Queen. As reported in *The Globe*,

> There was a big house; and the enthusiasm was in proportion. Encore after encore was demanded and conceded. The fresh items include a nigger minuet and a pas seul by one of the "leading ladies"; but, really, no novelties were needed. "In Dahomey" has captured Londoners all along the line. It is Christy Minstrel entertainment in excelsis, with the (comparatively) fair sex well

represented, and an unlimited amount of "action." The American black is even more energetic than the American white. He (or she) is rarely still, and the stolidity of the "Jonah Man" is an agreeable exception. But for that admirable nigger, "melancholy, slow," "In Dahomey" might be too much for the nerves of some of us.[45]

October brought a new infusion of chorus members from the United States in anticipation of the two hundredth performance on November 11. Now the toast of London, Williams and Walker were invited to the Hyde Park Hotel on December 18 when Sir Thomas Lipton was presented with the silver service from the American Yacht Club.[46]

Chance Encounter

In mid-December of 1903, it was reported that Williams and Walker's run at the Shaftesbury was to end on Boxing Day, and, following a much-needed break, they were to begin a ten-week tour of the provinces.[47] The pause also allowed for another influx of chorus members to replace those who wanted to return to the United States. Shortly before *In Dahomey* closed at the Shaftesbury, George befriended William H. Ellis (1864 to 1923), another "oily fellow," as Bert once described George. Among other ventures, Ellis operated a failed cotton plantation that used Black labor in Mexico in the 1890s. Like George, Ellis learned to exploit societal margins to benefit himself and the cause of Black liberation on the frontier between the plantation South and the Mexican haciendas that were prevalent in his native Texas. Part of Ellis's success derived from his racial ambiguity, and he often "passed" as a Mexican or Hawaiian to avoid being Jim Crowed.

When Ellis was in London for the coronation of King Edward VII in August of 1902, he met Ras Makonnen (1852 to 1906), father of the future emperor of Ethiopia, Hon. Haile Selassie (1892 to 1975). Ever the charmer, Ellis secured an invitation to meet King Menelik II (1844 to 1913) of Abyssinia, the last precolonial ruler in Africa. That meeting took place on October 7, 1903, and the following December, Ellis was "passing through" London en route to the United States from Abyssinia. Ellis's goal was to deliver an official letter from the king to the US State Department and President Roosevelt so that a sovereign African nation and, of course, *he* could prosper following the establishment of banks, railroad contracts, and cotton plantations. With a ten-day break in London as he waited for the steamer HMS *Majestic* to set sail on December 23, the fashionable thing to do would have been to see *In Dahomey*.[48] Sensing an opportunity to improve the formula and incorporate "real" Africanness into future productions, George made a connection with Ellis, who could potentially provide access to authentic costumes, artifacts, and photographs to work from as well as a plot based on a real African king. Emboldened by Ellis's lived experience, the next Williams and Walker vehicle was assured to make *In Dahomey* look like the shape-shifting shell game that it ultimately was.[49] However, George's plans would have to wait because he had a tour coming that required a lot of changes to the company and he needed to address his growing dissatisfaction with management.

On the Road in a Foreign Land

After a vacation of more than a month, the newly refreshed and invigorated company made their debut at the Theatre Royal in Hull on February 1, 1904. Next were weeklong engagements in London and Bristol, where some Oxford men saw the show and hosted a stag party for Bert and George.[50] Around that time the company learned that composer and former cast member Will Accooe died at his father's home in New York on April 26.[51] Just thirty years old, he was irreplaceable and one of several losses that would prove devastating to the endurance of the vanguard generation's legacy. While in Edinburgh, Bert and George became Masons in the Lodge Waverley (no. 597). Unlike their brothers in the United States, where discrimination was more of a local custom than an expressed policy or rule, the Scottish Masons readily accepted them. Therefore, George, Bert, and eight others were initiated on May 2, passed on May 16, and raised Master Masons on June 1, 1904.[52]

While in Manchester, Nash sent a letter to Grant Mull in Lawrence to inform him that he would be home in two months.[53] He also wrote a love letter to Lawrence that was published in *The Daily Gazette* on the May 28 titled "A Lawrence Boy's Annual Chat with Home Folks." It was a rare glimpse into his innermost thoughts and feelings during a moment of euphoria:

> I thought perhaps you'd like to have a line or two from me,
> To hear how one of Lawrence's sons has fared across the sea—
> In all my undertakings so much interest you have shown,
> I feel as if I'm duty bound to write a few lines home.

Figure 9.3. The Grand Lodge of Ancient Free and Accepted Masons of Scotland, Lodge Waverley, no. 597. *Source:* Grand Lodge of Ancient Free Masons. Used with permission.

In past years it has been my custom to send a message home in the hope that old and deep memories might be rekindled, quickened and kept alive.

Heretofore my little annual chat with home friends has been couched in humorous and often frivolous language, and I have talked more in the strain of a boy than a man.

This I attribute to the fact that boyish freaks of nature of being more in their formative stage then than now, the frivolous side of life appealed to me more even one year ago than it does now.

Some people get old much quicker than others. By this I mean, age may be often calculated more by experience and observation than by days and years. I am far from being an old man; either from experience or age, but with the process of time I feel a growing tendency coming over me to meditate more on serious matters of life and human experience than I used to do.

A somewhat homesick Nash turned his thoughts toward Lawrence and his plan to institutionalize the success of Williams and Walker:

> Now, dear home friends, I have given you a brief sketch of our travels and experiences on the side of the sea, you may be interested to know what I think of dear old Lawrence, Kansas, after all my travels and experiences in the world.
>
> I have visited many large and beautiful places and have meant thousands of pleasant and happy people. But I have never forgotten dear old Lawrence, Kansas, the place of my birth. Why? Because there are my dear mother and grandmother and many good friends who have known me all my life, and who sympathy and personal interest in my success and welfare in the world have followed me from the day I left home. . . .
>
> Thoughts of early life bind me to Lawrence forever; dear old town and for people will always remain dear to me.
>
> In all parts of the world, whither I have traveled, I always find problems of a manifold nature and hard to solve. In all parts of America we have what is called the colored problem. Men and women are known, not for their worth in their merit, but often by their race and complexion.
>
> Dear friends, I am happy to say such is not true in Lawrence, Kansas.
>
> In all departments of life, colored people are well represented. They take active parts in politics, religion, education and all movements which make for the welfare of all the people. There are colored policemen and colored politicians, who are appointed and supported by white as well as colored people. Lawrence has her colored doctors and lawyers and other professional people. All these things make me proud to be a son of Lawrence.
>
> I hope to come home, perhaps at the end of June to see my dear mother who, is now Mrs. Alice Myers, and by dear grandmother Mrs. Sarah Hayden, and of course the many good friends and acquaintances who always give me a hearty welcome.
>
> You will be pleased to know that my wife tells me that she looks forward with the greatest pleasure to playing in Lawrence, Kansas. My partner, Mr. Bert Williams, who you know so well,

and his wife, Mrs. Lottie Williams, are both looking forward to the time when our show may visit Lawrence, Kansas.

And last but not least, Williams and Walker are now contemplating the erection of the theatre in New York City, which is to be called the Williams and Walker International and Interracial Ethiopian theatre. We believe in the adage: "What man has done can by man be done."

> "Fleecy locks and dark complexion
> Cannot forfeit nature's calm,
> Skin may differ, but affection
> Dwells in white and black the same."
> George W. Walker (Nash)[54]

The expressed adage "What man has done can by man be done," also employed by Black Nationalists like Marcus Garvey (1887 to 1940), may have been a nod to Nash's father's influence. Following a successful stint on Broadway and in London, culminating in a command performance, Nash was brimming with confidence, and he could not help sharing with his hometown. That occasion also marked the first time he expressed his plan to open a theatre that was free of the constraints of Jim Crow and acknowledged his mother's marriage to Frank Myers.

With news of a successful English tour under their belt, Williams and Walker were booked on a national US tour slated to begin in Atlantic City. The cast boarded the RMS *Aurania* in Liverpool, bound for New York, on June 14, 1904.[55] Shortly before their departure, George announced that Williams and Walker planned to part ways with Hurtig and Seamon. No specific reason was ever given, although it was reported that there was friction between the company and the syndicate that put the Shaftesbury deal together as well as from the previous season, in which first-class bookings were few and far between. To boot, neither George nor Bert wanted to return to England with a show that was made for the US market, and management likely wanted them to remain with the current vehicle as long as it remained profitable.[56] Despite George's continued objections, the second company, led by Dan Avery and Charles Hart, was dispatched to England to tour the provinces with several seasoned chorus members from the original cast. That production made its debut in Hull at the Grand Theatre on August 15, 1904. They toured until February 12, 1905, and again with an augmented cast from August 14 until early October 1905, thirty weeks in all. Following disbandment, Avery and Hart appeared at Hammerstein's in Manhattan in early December 1905 as a vaudeville act.[57]

In a ritual that would play out generationally for the foreseeable future, some members of the Williams and Walker company, including Pete Hampton and Laura Bowman, struck out on their own in England. As initiated by members of the Fisk Jubilee Singers some twenty years earlier, when given the opportunity to live and succeed outside of the United States, Afro-Americans often chose to do so. It was a strategically self-determined strategy and an alternative to what was offered by Black Nationalists like George's father: returning to Africa, a place that most Afro-Americans knew little about. Not so for George. He had a major success to his credit that he hoped to leverage for something a little better, although the success and profitability of Williams and Walker hadn't breached the confines of Jim Crow just yet.

Chapter 10

The Royal Strut

1904 to 1905

Triumphant Return

Upon arrival in New York Harbor on June 23, 1904, the impeccably dressed members of the cast waived shining sticks that reflected the noonday sun. As usual, George was "the stunner of the crowd" in his "black and white checked suit, with buttoned flaps on the pockets and enough other 'extras' to bring on a tailors' strike."[1] *The Sun* reported that he proudly displayed his new raiment as "made in London after original designs." Described by George as "a Norfolk front, kinder symbolical of the Southern origin of most of the company, and a Richmond back," he was a sight in his short jacket that was loose in the back with a short belt to take up the slack. The front was plain except for large flaps on all the pockets. In all, he had eleven such suits made.[2] Although beaming, he added a caveat to the glowing accounts of the treatment of the company in England as compared to that of the United States:

> But, we have not returned with any delusions about this not being the best land in the world for a man or a woman of our color to live. There is a color line here, yes, but if a Negro wants a job in this country, he can get it, if he can do the work. He will not be forced to starve to death just because of his color.
>
> Now, we were treated with the greatest kindness and appreciation in England. We were amusing. We were curiosities. We

were freaks, if you choose to put it that way. But everywhere I went, every step of the way, I felt that if I were not in the theatrical profession, if I were not, with the rest of our company, more or less of a novelty, I would be allowed to starve to death before I would ever get a chance to do a lick of work to earn the price of a meal. They are a cold, cold people.

Aida then chimed in with her thoughts on English snobbery and added that the audience wouldn't laugh until "Mrs. So-and-So" laughed, declaring, "It isn't a free country." George closed with his unique perspective that was informed on one hand by his father's philosophy and on the other his unique upbringing in Lawrence. He was aware of the shortcomings of the United States for people of African descent and expressed that it was only a matter of time before equal rights were extended to all:

You let a black man get into an automobile and start off with it over there, [t]he folks on the street will stare and shiver like they were going to throw a fit. I don't know, but I hope that we taught them a little something about the mental capacity of the American Negro. They are used to colored folks from all sorts of outlandish countries. They would come up to us with all sorts of foreign tongues.

"Kee-wee! Polly-woofuzzy-az!" says the first man who was introduced to me over there.

"No friend," says I. "Not that for me. Plain U.S.A. is my talk?"

He fell back and was clean astonished. But after they found we had the goods with us and had some common intelligence we had no trouble at all.

No, this is the colored man's country for a fair chance, just as it is the white man's. We may not know all there is to know, but we know when we are well off.

Despite the "coldness" of British audiences, Williams and Walker's second bite of the apple was successful due to the knowledge gained through their previous experience in 1897; they brought a superior production with the best personnel available and were willing to adapt to their audience. After the company disembarked, a parade of sixteen automobiles ferried the sixty-two members of the cast uptown from the pier with Bert and George in the lead car. Although tired, they held court with "about nine-tenths of the colored fraternity of Greater New York, together with many of their white brethren" and recounted their yearlong adventure at 503 Sixth Avenue.[3]

On July 20, 1904, Nash returned to Lawrence for the first time in two years. Aida did not make the trip; rather, his traveling companion was Green Henri Tapley, his private secretary. Nash brought his new Masonic finery and gifts that included a bolt of suit cloth and fine shaving razors for Grant Mull, one of the town elders who helped him during his youth. Tapley sang a solo at the Warren Street Baptist Church and so impressed the congregation that a full concert was given on July 29. That day, the *Plaindealer* reported that Nash presented Carrie Hughes with a five-dollar check for a year's subscription to the paper along with something extra to help her with expenses, as her young son, Langston, had recently been hospitalized.[4] Excitement was such that *The Daily Gazette* proclaimed, "If ever Nash Walker runs for office in Douglas County he would receive what no other colored man has ever received before, the entire colored vote."[5] While home, Nash sent a letter to Abe Erlanger of Klaw and Erlanger, owners of the New York Theatre, to reassure them that Williams and Walker were ready for a change in management. It went unanswered, so Bert went to their New York office in the Amsterdam Theatre building on Forty-Second Street, where he was advised to wait until the national election was over before making any announcements. After two weeks, Nash left Lawrence and stopped in Kansas City to visit with the cast of Richard and Pringle's Georgia Minstrels and reminisce with old friends before he caught the train east.[6]

As the company rehearsed, the Attucks Music Company began operations at 1255-1257 Broadway, under the management of "Shep" Edmonds. Named after the Black Revolutionary War patriot Crispus Attucks (1723 to 1770), it was the second Black-owned music publisher and hosted a stable of elite writers and composers, including Tom Lemonier, Alex Rogers, J. T. Brymn, Cecil Mack, Jesse Shipp, and Williams and Walker. Central to the company's philosophy was the release high-quality, unmistakably Black music that would help to hasten the end of coon songs through "the perpetuation of Rag and Real Melody and the making of currency." Bert was reported to have said twenty minutes before the venture began, "We know what is worthwhile in popular music, and we intend to stick to superiority."[7]

To further the cause, Williams and Walker, along with Cole and Johnson, became active in the Negro Republican Club in New York located at West Fifty-Third Street, near Eighth Avenue. Understanding that familiarity breeds access, Attucks's music was presented with a new avenue to the mainstream, and by the end of the summer the compositions were heard at elite Black events in cities and towns throughout the country. In May of the following year, Will Cook and Cecil Mack's Gotham music company merged with Attucks to form Gotham-Attucks, "The House of Melody."[8]

Figure 10.1. "Me an' da Minstrel Ban'," words by Alex Rogers, music by James Vaughan, Attucks Music Publishing, New York, 1904. *Source:* Author's collection.

The 1904 to 1905 season with the revised version of *In Dahomey* began in Young's Ocean Pier Music Hall, Atlantic City, on August 15, 1904. Next was Manhattan, then Baltimore, where *The Colored American Magazine* noted that "Mr. George Walker is the Beau Brummel of Ethiopian swelldom, and without a rival in his particular line of work."[9] Several new songs were added including "When the Moon Shines on the Moonshine" and a new feature for Bert, "I May Be Crazy, but I Ain't No Fool," which according to one reviewer failed to surpass "Jonah Man."[10] Other additions included new vehicles for George: "He Ain't Got No Mamie," "My Dear Luzon," and "Me an' da Minstrel Ban'," a nostalgic callback to the midday parades on Massachusetts Street when he carried banners for visiting minstrel shows. Understandably, almost all new material was published through the Attucks Music Company.[11] Sylvester Russell saw the show on September 3 and proclaimed, "[I] found it to be very much to my liking," taking credit for its success: "I am fully prepared to say that this organization has reached perfection only by changes which I have suggested, and by an indirect regard for what I had chosen to say about past performances." He also praised George's growing prowess, both on and offstage:

> George W. Walker seems to have developed with time in his artistic element as a kid gloved comedian. On this occasion he dressed at all times with good taste. His English dress suit and white pointed cut vest, and his English silk hat and overcoat were something a little too smart for this country. He showed more comedy in his dialogues with Williams than ever before and his song "Me and The Minstrel Band," with a minstrel parade chorus march was a very novel feature. "Dear Luzon" was another song which admitted the words "I've been to London on the Strand," which he sang smilingly.[12]

Although Russell was unhappy that Aida's wheelbarrow scene had been cut, he enjoyed her rendition of "Why Adam Sinned" and "A Rich Coon's Babe," performed in a pleated Swiss dress, bordered with yellow satin, as well as her "Spanish green" dress in the Spanish dance. Russell astutely noted that she had no interactions with Bert or George onstage, calling her a "lonesome little thing," rather than "a troublesome little thing" as she was described in the program. He also acknowledged the company's growing influence on the Black theatregoing public: "The fact that all the stars in the company wore diamonds, seen from the naked eye, and all of the stockholders in the outside were busier than at any other theatre; the gallery rush being greater and the seats all being sold out and without an extra word of encouragement from the New York newspaper critics foretell the rate of speed in which the Negro race will soon be, through foe and flame, advancing."[13]

Next came a swing out west, beginning in St. Louis for three weeks, where the reporter for the *Post-Dispatch* remarked that the Black gallery and White orchestra sections of the theatre competed for dominance in laughter and applause. At the end of the engagement, the company's manager, George W. Harris, reported earnings that exceeded those in London by $5,000.[14] Then came a series of one-night stands that ended in Rockford, Illinois, where the company struggled to secure lodging after they were refused at the Jarvis and Nelson hotels.[15] Next was a weeklong engagement in Chicago that was so popular it was extended twice, and reportedly the famed actor N. C. Goodwin snorted with laughter during the scene where Rareback attempted to extract pay from Shylock for explaining the meaning of the word "apprehend."[16]

Shortly before the final curtain on November 15 in Kansas City, a fight between a White man and Black man in the gallery briefly disrupted the show. Bert and George were onstage, and it was such a commotion that they both stood "spellbound" as jeers like "Fight it out!" came from the gallery. Finally, James Vaughn struck up the orchestra, and the audience settled back down. As was the tradition in Kansas City, a banquet was arranged by Bennie McClure at 915 Baltimore Avenue.[17] Shortly after came Lawrence for matinee and evening performances, where balcony seats were sold out by ten o'clock on the day of the performance. The company arrived in the morning, and Nash held court on Massachusetts Street as he doled out extravagant gifts, one of which was a Colt 1903 hammerless, nine-shot, semiautomatic pistol, which he presented to Officer Jim Monroe. Following the evening performance, a ball was given at Everett Hall.[18]

Next was Topeka, where the *Daily Capital* trumpeted George's Kansas roots: "George W. Walker, the smaller of the two, and the one who always appears on the stage as the colored swell, is from Lawrence, and many a citizen of the university town tells of the times when Walker shined his shoes. Since then the colored boy has been known to pay $25 a day for hotel accommodations."[19] Along with the rags-to-riches story, the *Topeka State Journal* reported that local audiences could expect a substantial hike in ticket prices, from twenty-five cents to one dollar and fifty cents as compared to other venues on the tour. Regardless, people were so anxious to get tickets that more than a hundred waited all night on the sidewalk, and some nearly came to blows. Aida was reportedly "in bad voice," so her feature piece, "Why Adam Sinned," was given to an unnamed understudy who did not do it justice.[20] They then moved west, culminating in a two-week engagement at San Francisco's Grand Opera House. The *Call* reported, "Not a seat lacked its human upholstery, and everybody was there. Some spots looked like a chessboard, with black to win, for darktown is very proud of its Williams and Walker."[21] The engagement was extended another week. Following a Christmas Eve performance in Sacramento, the tour continued through other California towns led them to Portland, Oregon, and several other stops in the Pacific Northwest, ending in Spokane, Washington. While they were in Spokane, soprano Minnie Brown (1879 to 1936) was added to the cast.[22]

The company began February of 1905 in Manitoba, Canada, followed by a stint in the Twin Cities, including the Bijou in Minneapolis, where despite one of the coldest winters in memory, demand for tickets was high.[23] Upon their arrival, George was interviewed by H. G. Davis of the *Minneapolis Journal*, and his sense of cultural sovereignty could not be contained:

> We want to build a theatre for colored players, and to preserve that old folk song and traditions of the southern darkeys. In connection with it I would also establish a school for training the actors and particularly to train their voices. You know every darkey has a peculiar sweetness in his voice. It's in his throat when he's born. I want to keep it there. When the voice is cultivated that softness is often lost, and I would have colored singers trained to hold that peculiar quality. Then, of course, there'd be a dramatic school for serious work.[24]

During their residency in the Twin Cities, George sent a letter to Hurtig and Seamon to formally terminate their contract and, at the request of Klaw and Erlanger, simultaneously made an overture to Lew Dockstader for the coming season.[25] Dockstader was a well-established minstrel man who wanted to permanently transition into management and had some success with Williams and Walker's "When Miss Maria Johnson Marries Me" in 1896.[26] George later said that neither he nor Bert thought Dockstader was up to the task, but Klaw and Erlanger's assurances were "as good as gold," and they believed that if Dockstader faltered, the former would step in to ensure their success. As before, George banked on the idea that a change in management would open the gates to first-class bookings and, by extension, profits. As investors, neither Will McConnell, George Lederer Hurtig and Seamon, nor Klaw and Erlanger were interested in challenging social norms, especially if it jeopardized their return on a proven moneymaker.[27] However, Klaw and Erlanger controlled a nationwide syndicate of first-class theatres, which included the New York Theatre, where *In Dahomey* had a successful, although short, run on Broadway. With the Shubert circuit being the only other option, George decided to wager it all. The next vehicle was to be first class in every way, and he wanted the theatres to match.[28]

While the Williams and Walker company was engaged in Minneapolis, Richard Connors, a popular tenor who often sang "When the Moon Shines on the Moonshine," was shot by James "Ike" Rivers, another cast member. The two actors had a rivalry that stemmed from Connors's repeated winning of the cash prizes from the cake walks at London's Shaftesbury Theatre. Matters escalated when they were back in New York. Connors organized a quartet engagement and was given a five-dollar tip that Rivers thought should have been divided among the performers. Other reports mentioned another quarrel over the affection of a female chorus member as well. Finally, on February 17, 1905, Rivers snapped following a disagreement over a quarter that was left on a trunk during a craps game backstage at the Bijou. Ultimately, Rivers shot Connors in the shoulder, and the bullet lodged in his neck. The injury was not expected to be life threatening, but Connors developed pneumonia and died on February 22. His final expenses were covered by Bert and George. Although Rivers claimed self-defense, he was put on trial for murder and acquitted about three months later. He never rejoined the company.[29]

Shortly after the shooting, the company moved to Pittsburgh for a two-week engagement. While in Pittsburgh, George continued his negotiations with Klaw and Erlanger, who still had not warmed to his idea of pursuing first-class bookings. Out of frustration, he sent Erlanger a letter that began with an apology for its length but insisted that it was necessary to convey his thoughts. He reminded Erlanger of the previous letter that he sent from Lawrence and how Bert was treated when he called on them, the company's drawing power, Klaw and Erlanger's history of supporting Black companies, his hope for a productive discussion in New York, and their next vehicle: "We shall have a new production, which promises to be not only a revelation but a revolution in Musical Comedy Plays. We have spent, and we are still spending, all the time, thought and money we can muster on this new production. Our hearts and souls are fixed on Broadway and we are depending solely on our good friend Mr. Abe Erlanger to put us there!"[30]

As a show of seriousness, George enclosed a copy of his six-month notice to Hurtig and Seamon. He also reiterated the potential of the new show and appealed to Erlanger's business sense, essentially begging for access. Although George's power was growing in the business, the letter expressed precisely how precarious his position was. His aspirations were at the mercy of benevolently ignorant and culturally superfluous gatekeepers who asserted that no matter how good the company was, it would remain second class. As George continued to engage with management in vain, he made the most of his connection with William Ellis to produce a more realistic depiction of Africa and the diaspora. However, despite financial and commercial success, he was still hemorrhaging money as fast as he made it. The grandeur of the new production required a lot of seed money and access to first-class houses to generate more operating cash and leverage. Even so, when Klaw and Erlanger made their agreement with Williams and Walker, they did so despite objections from several theatre managers in their circuit who refused to accommodate a successful Black show for two weeks out of fear of losing patronage during the other fifty. Nevertheless, George was poised to begin a period of unrivaled expansion of his organization to match his unparalleled aspiration.

Following Pittsburgh, the tour continued to Philadelphia and then to Boston for two weeks, where *The Herald* reported, "George W. Walker was highly amusing in his work, and his funny little laugh, his ludicrous explanations to his friend Shylock, his nimble dancing and clever all-round comedy work made him a prime favorite with all. In the last scene his wonderful display of diamonds took the breath away from many of the auditors, so dazzling was the effect of the glittering sash across his massive shirt front."[31]

Upon closing in Boston, they played in several cities in New York and small towns in Pennsylvania. When they reached Harrisburg, the lack of accommodations forced most of the cast to lodge at the theatre. Likewise, when they moved to Pottsville, there were not enough hotel rooms to match the demand in the small mining town, so Bert, George, and their spouses slept at the home of the theatre's manager. The town was especially grateful for their visit and made assurances that the scarcity of accommodations was not a Jim Crow flimflam. In a show of respect for the hospitality and as a tune-up for season's end, an intercompany baseball game was played at Dolan's Park in Yorkville. Two sets of nine (Giants and Skeeters) were formed among the men, and the women chose a side to root for along with the townies. The Giants, with Bert batting fifth, crushed the Skeeters 24 to 9.[32] Following several other stops in Pennsylvania, the company returned to

Manhattan for two weeks, then extended to a third. During that engagement, Bert scored massively with "Nobody," a new hard-luck collaboration with Alex Rogers.[33] Intended to replace "I May Be Crazy, but I ain't no Fool," which unsuccessfully replaced "Jonah Man," "Nobody" would soon become the most popular hit of his career.

While they were in Manhattan, a baseball game was organized between the Williams and Walker company and The Smart Set at Olympic Field at 136th Street and Fifth Avenue on May 19, 1905. Reportedly, The Smart Set were clad in tuxedos, while Williams and Walker were in full dress suits, and heavyweight champion Jack Johnson was the umpire. Twelve hundred people crowded onto the grounds, and the game nearly ended in a brawl. Bert insisted that the score was 16 to 4 in favor of Williams and Walker, and said, "They claim a tie, because they rung in all their heavy hitters out of the batting order in the last inning. But we beat 'em at that." Manager Moore of The Smart Set insisted on a 14-to-14 draw, claiming his team "tied 'em, and then they wouldn't play an extra inning." When asked to clarify in his official capacity as umpire, Jack Johnson said, "Ah won't be mixed up in this heah thing. Ah ain't no fool." A playoff was scheduled, but none was reported.[34] On June 8, the final day of the season, George played host to a small, rowdy delegation from Lawrence that threw a "box party" every time he appeared onstage, and they sent him a bouquet of flowers during the final act.[35]

The end of the 1904 to 1905 season was a welcome event for the "Royal Comedians." The company broke records for attendance and profits on what George saw as a victory lap before the main event. The season had been a grueling one that made a small fortune for Hurtig and Seamon, approaching $75,000. Other accounts reported profits between $15,000 and $40,000, of which Bert and George were said to have gotten a third or as much as half.[36] Management saw it as a goose that laid golden eggs and likely wanted it to be repeated for the foreseeable future. However, George had something else in mind that was more ambitious than any Black production to date. Reports had begun to circulate in the West about a forthcoming lavish comic opera, which reinvigorated the fight for first-class houses and continued to ruffle feathers.[37] Following a meeting in the offices of Klaw and Erlanger with Lew Dockstader and James K. Hackett, where they continued to vouch for Dockstader's character and talent as a manager whose assets were reported to be in the millions, George finally severed ties with Hurtig and Seamon and, against his better judgement, signed with

Dockstader.[38] It was a risky move, but, with few options, George felt that it was necessary to achieve his vision.

Abyssinian Summer

Abyssinia, George's chosen vehicle for permanent entry to the first-class theatre world, was inspired in part by tales of King Menelik II and his court from William H. Ellis, whom George met in London more than a year earlier.[39] With the prospect of realistic scenery and costumes, it was up to Jesse Shipp to tie it all together. George told the *Pittsburgh Daily Post*,

> Our selection of Abyssinia as the scene of our play was not by chance, but rather after considerable study on the matter. The aim was to have an African piece in which it would be entirely proper to have all colored actors play the parts and at the same time get away from the stereotyped coon show which has the familiar Southern setting and the plantation Negroes. It is safe to say that King Menelik the native ruler of Abyssinia, is about the only full-blooded African ruler occupying an important throne, and his recent participation in the St. Louis exposition and the treaty with the United States have brought him into prominence with the civilized world. Hence our choice.
>
> I know Mr. Ellis, who acted as the United States representative in the signing of the treaty. I spent many hours getting ideas from him of the native costumes, architecture, customs, music and minor details as well as many photographs from which several of the scenes are taken. We also made a trip from New York to Chicago to see a curio dealer who makes annual trips to that country in the pursuit of his business to get information on the subject.[40]

Now that George had access to genuine African culture and a company that rivaled any in the country, expectations for *Abyssinia* were high. The show's solidarity with a living Black head of state who was fighting to maintain independence from European oppression made it one of the most anticipated offerings of the coming season. However, the break from Hurtig and Seamon did not go smoothly, because the former managers attempted to renew the existing contract unilaterally to force Williams and Walker to remain under their control until September 1908. The matter was brought before the United States Circuit Court on July 5, 1905, and the judge determined that the agreement was that of a partnership and not "master and servant," meaning that Williams and Walker were free to leave.[41] Lew Dockstader, a self-proclaimed "man of nerve," declared in an interview shortly after the lawsuit, "Last year Williams and Walker cleared nearly $50,000 and while I am not a man to count my chickens until they are hatched, I figure on clearing $75,000 with that show this year. Only a few days after I signed Williams and Walker[,] I was offered $35,000 for my contract, but I wouldn't have taken $100,000. You see I have them for a term of years."[42]

An unfortunate byproduct of the public row with Hurtig and Seamon was the disclosure of Bert and George's income, at twenty thousand for the year before royalties from sheet music, recently brought under their control since the merger of the Attucks and Gotham music companies.[43] The news made national headlines, prompting *The Buffalo Enquirer* to quip, "I see Williams and Walker, the colored comedians, cleared up $40,000 last year. It pays to take the cake." *The Philadelphia Inquirer* asserted, "Evidently the color line is not drawn on the stage." The *Buffalo Evening News* went as far as to present a graph of Williams and Walker's salary and compared it with that of the chief justice of the Supreme Court, bank presidents, insurance kingpins, and cabinet members.[44] Bert and George's conspicuous lifestyle and profitability brought an ugly truth to the lips of popular sentiment: Why should a pair of "Coons" get such an opportunity before *every* White person? Such a notion was unthinkable for some, and it remained a point of contention from that point on. It was one thing to be a success under cover of "Cooness," but their ostentatiousness was as unforgivable as their Blackness, especially following George's abandonment of a wildly successful show for an unproven one. From the outside, it made little business sense. From the inside, it was a logical step toward real and lasting equity for Afro-American art.

During the summer of 1905, George's crowning achievement was the Williams and Walker Glee Club, a response to the loss of Rivers and Connor. As an extension of the Williams and Walker Quartet, the Glee Club allowed the most talented of the company's male singers to earn extra merit-based income, kept them in top form, and gave them an opportunity to master new material for the coming season. Because they were under contract, they could not be poached by another organization, and money disputes,

Figure 10.2. "Williams and Walker Glee Club." Top: Green Henri Tapley, J. Mantell Thomas, Arthur H. Payne, Charles Moore, J. Lubrie Hill, Modeste Bel Guillaume, Frank B. Williams. Middle: unknown, James Escort Lightfoot, W. C. Elkins, unknown, unknown. Bottom: unknown, Theodore Pankey, Rex C. Sterling. Source: *The Colored American Magazine* 9, no. 5 (November 1905): 655. Beinecke Rare Book and Manuscript Library.

as between Rivers and Connors, were less likely because all bookings were controlled by George. Under the direction of William C. Elkins, the Williams and Walker Glee Club made its debut at an Elks benefit in Boston on May 23, 1905, and was booked throughout the summer. On the cutting edge, it was something like an updated, more sophisticated version of a jubilee quartet; they specialized in everything from plantation songs to modern ragtime and Western classical music.[45] Like their jubilee predecessors, they hoped to inspire and uplift their audiences in an inoffensive, professional, and uniquely Afro-American way. As characterized by George in the *Boston Evening Transcript* shortly after the announcement of the ensemble, "The entire membership of this company is made up of men and women of good character, their purpose being not merely the acquisition of money and fame, but also their development along artistic, personal and moral lines. To this end they are constantly studying."[46]

Next George made trips to Philadelphia and Baltimore to find suitable sopranos for the coming season. He also prepared for the arrival of his mother and grandmother for a three-week visit, which included the celebration of his thirty-third birthday and a vacation so lavish, they'd agree to relocate to New York permanently.[47] George and family made their way to Boston with the Glee Club, and he kept a close eye on his new creation. By all accounts, they succeeded, and sang with an infectious sense of joy, prompting *The Globe* to label them "one of the sights of the city for tourists." On the morning of July 28, they called on Dr. and Mrs. Booker T. Washington at their summer home. They were accompanied by Charles Alexander (1868 to 1923), Boston-based writer and editor of the new *Alexander's Magazine*. The summer culminated in New York with the Glee Club's performance of J. Rosamond Johnson's new Negro anthem, "Lift Every Voice and Sing," at the Annual Session of the National Negro Business League.[48]

Unfortunately, George failed to convince his mother and grandmother to relocate to New York, and they returned to Lawrence.[49] Never one to sit idle, he announced plans for his "Ethiopian Theatre" in New York, where Black plays could be produced under Black control. Once established, he called for duplicate spaces in Boston, Chicago, and Philadelphia where the Afro-American experience could be codified for the production of plays, sheet music, recordings, and, eventually, the new medium of film. In the meantime, George, Aida, and her family moved into a house at 122 West Twenty-Sixth Street, next to Aida's mother's dressmaker shop. Thus ended the most profitable season for Williams and Walker to date, and Abe Levy reportedly deposited $16,000 of George's savings in Watkins Bank in Lawrence.[50]

Part Three
The Struggle

Chapter 11

The Abyss

1905 to 1907

Give Us the Strength to Lift As We Climb

The production of *Abyssinia* was purposefully large, so large that it could not fit in the small, modestly priced theatres where the Williams and Walker company traditionally presented their shows on multiple one-night stands, including the Bowersock in Lawrence. With a projected cast of one hundred and sporting three train cars for scenery and costumes as well as live donkeys, camels, and lions, it was George's best attempt to end the debate over first-class access for the company's productions. To bring the production to life, an unprecedented $30,000 budget was approved for the vehicle, which boasted a weekly payroll of $2,700, unheard of for a Black offering.[1] By mid-August 1905, new cast members, paid twenty dollars a week plus expenses, began arriving for work and expected to be paid. Unfortunately, funding failed to materialize.

During the first week of September, George was spotted with Bert, Sam Lucas, Ed Goggins, and Ernest Hogan at the Nail Brothers Hotel living the high life.[2] Despite the appearance of leisure, he was confronted with a mountain of problems to overcome, from a lack of financial support to outright obstruction by Dockstader. As described in *The Freeman*,

> George Walker, of Williams and Walker, had an actor once in his cast that was doing just a little dramatic stunt. The manager came up to Mr. Walker cold turkey and asked him to cut the

man and part out of the show. Mr. Walker explained that he had engaged the man for the season and could not discharge him without a reason. The manager said, "Send the man home; I will send him his salary every week." Mr. Walker said no; that the man had rare ability and was doing his part better than anyone in the cast; also that it was up to Williams and Walker to show the public that the Negro could do something else besides make a fool of himself and his race. Mr. Walker won his point after a bitter contest. But this just goes to show what the managers of Negro shows think of the Negro as an actor.[3]

With less than half of the promised $30,000 in hand, Dockstader insisted on cutting the cast from a hundred to sixty, so George refused to take the production on the road. The reported excuse for the shortfall was the failure of Klaw and Erlanger to secure bookings in first-class houses. Instead, they chose to book smaller, $1.50 houses, as Williams and Walker had utilized for the three previous seasons. George repeatedly visited Klaw and Erlanger's office for answers but he was stonewalled.[4] Additionally, Dockstader secured bookings for his own minstrel troupe but not *Abyssinia*. Infuriated, George publicly declared that he was under the weather, but during the first week of September, he secretly traveled to Cleveland to confront Dockstader in person and return his $10,000 signing bonus.[5] The potentially fatal delay of the production forced Bert and George to seek a vaudeville engagement at the Rialto Theatre to fund rehearsals out of their own pockets, netting $11,200 over eight weeks. Despite their best effort, they were out of cash at the end of the month.[6] With no other option, George sent an angry letter to Klaw and Erlanger on October 6, 1905:

Gentlemen;—

It is with sincere regret that I have to inform you that for the present, the Williams and Walker company has been dismissed. After Mr. Dockstader failed to carry out his contract, I endeavored in every possible manner to protect the organization, but have concluded, it will be better business policy for Mr. Williams and myself to go to work and earn the money to return to Mr. Dockstader all he has invested and then to pay for, and produce our own show.

Mr. Dockstader's contention at this time, that we wanted too much show and Company, comes with very bad grace. He was and has been fully informed since last May, when he made the contract of all our intentions, both as to production and Company. He saw the Company in rehearsal and expressed himself as satisfied and pleased in every way. It was not until the middle of September and the show had been in rehearsal for six weeks, that he found any fault or made any objections. We thought then and still think that he was unreasonable and from the fact that we have learned that he has been offering the show for sale for some time, it would indicate that his objections were not real, but simply to cover his inability to go on with his contract.

We earnestly desire your confidence and will guarantee that when we are in a position to produce "Abyssinia" it will be a show worthy of your best endeavors, to book. It will excel anything ever before attempted and will not only have great merit as a performance, but great box-office possibilities.

Yours very respectfully,

George W. Walker[7]

Unfortunately, a solution was not forthcoming because George insisted that management live up to their end of the agreement as far as cast size, payroll, and booking were concerned. With little recourse, George authorized the article "'Abyssinia' Postponed" in *The Colored American Magazine* to clear the air.[8] Long after the fact, Sylvester Russell extolled George's efforts, but at the time he said little:

> Mr. Walker's executive ability was known only to the manager with whom he had had dealings, and they inwardly disliked him because he was bold and fearless enough to stand up for what the services of Williams and Walker were worth. He rarely ever received encouragement, not even from his partner, who wilted at Walker's exorbitant demands as the price for their services . . . Mr. Walker's business instinct was of a kind that would not accept anything that was forced upon him. He had the great propensity of combining show talent with his business ability.[9]

To stay afloat, the company was split into three entities: Williams and Walker, Aida's Abyssinian Maidens/Girls, and the Glee Club. Eventually, most found work in vaudeville while the management issues were ironed out. Meanwhile, Avery and Hart made a triumphant return to the United States during the second week of November 1905, and the second company disbanded.[10] During the downtime, Aida published a carefully worded article titled "Colored Men and Women on the Stage" in *The Colored American Magazine*, possibly in response to a discussion with Sylvester Russell, to address some of the systemic problems that impeded Black artists. Among other issues, she tackled the underestimation of the potential of what some saw as an improper way of life. She then moved on to emphatically state her belief in the potential power of the Afro-American actor as a cultural ambassador in the future. Then came the most important component of her argument for the respect of Afro-American culture, and she expressed the need to study it from a standpoint of love, admiration, and candor. Finally, she addressed the need for intelligent and capable young people to ensure the future of the philosophy that she, her husband, and several of their contemporaries were only just beginning to implement. On October 23, 1905, Aida and her Eight Abyssinia Girls debuted at Hurtig and Seamon's Theatre in Harlem, followed by Yonkers and New Haven.[11]

After rehearsing at the Gotham Attucks building on Twenty-Eighth Street, Bert and George were engaged by Oscar Hammerstein to appear at the Victoria Theatre for an indefinite run. However, rumors of discord between the two partners began to spread among the thespian community. Some of Williams and Walker's Black contemporaries were angry at the injustice and the potential setback of the natural progress for Black art, while others were infuriated by George's impetuousness because they believed he was pushing for too much, too soon.[12] Eventually, the full context of George's war with management became known, and retractions were made, the most prominent being from Sylvester Russell: "George Walker has been commended in the highest terms for the way he handled the late complications concerning the Williams and Walker company, and also the good treatment of the members who rehearsed in New York, and Williams and Walker will have no trouble in recalling them."[13] A week later, he refined his point even further: "If there is any plea that managers in the West and Southwest would not play Williams and Walker on account of color, the plea is out of date and New York managers have a very weak disease, if the syndicate could not break the ice instead of curling their tails at the New

York end."¹⁴ George was in uncharted waters, and the frustration must have been overwhelming at times, but he persevered, kept the company together, and eventually prevailed.

"Nobody"

As Williams and Walker transitioned into vaudeville and endeavored to salvage the season, Bert's "Nobody," a masterstroke of character study, became a smash hit and drove his popularity to unprecedented heights:

Verse:

When life seems full of clouds and rain
And I am full of nothin' and pain
Who soothes my thumpin', bumpin' brain?
Nobody

Verse:

When winter comes with snow and sleet
And me with hunger and cold feet
Who says, "Here's twenty-five cents, go ahead and get somethin' to eat"?
Nobody

Chorus:

I ain't never done nothin' to nobody
I ain't never done nothin' to nobody, no time
So until I get somethin' from somebody sometime
I'll never do nothin' for nobody, no time

Verse:

When summer comes all cool and clear and my friends see me drawing near
Who says "Come in, have some beer"?
Nobody

Verse:

When I was in that railroad wreck
And thought I'd cashed in my last check
Who took the engine off my neck?
Not a soul.[15]

"Nobody" made waves at the end of the previous season, and by the following October it was heard on stages all over the country. Likewise, recordings of Bert's original rendition were the rage on wax cylinder, available coast to coast via Columbia Records, and its sheet music sales were essential to the early success of Gotham-Attucks.[16] As Bert's signature song, it remained with him for the rest of his life, but at the moment he was contained in vaudeville. As an extension of Ernest Hogan's success with "All Coons," there was great potential for wealth generation from record sales. To that point, only White performers could earn royalties from their recordings, but with some strategy and a critical mass of supremely talented Black artists, the future looked promising. Solidarity and a steady output over time was the key.

As the end of the year approached, hope waned in the Black press for an offering from Williams and Walker outside of vaudeville:

> When Mr. Dockstader had failed—miserably failed—to successfully book "Abyssinia" in first-class houses, as he had promised to do so, Williams and Walker, happily, would not agree to stage their stupendous production in any other kind of houses. Mr. Dockstader on every hand was unable, it seems, to carry out the contract he had signed. Before they would appear at a disadvantage, Williams and Walker decided for the present they would not appear at all. This is proper, and for their stand, they have the gratitude of the Afro-American people and the applause of the theatre public.[17]

For those who wanted to stifle the company's access to top-priced, top-paying venues, it was simply a waiting game. All things being equal, the theatre syndicate decided that booking a Black production into their first-class theatres would hurt their overall business. George understood that intimately, as he expressed nearly two years later in Lawrence: "Not many people really hate us. It's a matter of money, mostly—an economic question. Down here at Wiedemann's, Negroes are not served at all. That isn't because Mr. Wiedemann hates black people, but because it would hurt his business to serve both races. It's an economic question to him. So it is almost everywhere—a question of business."[18] Understandably, the managers of first-class theatres were deathly afraid of losing their livelihood. As profitable as Williams and Walker's shows were, it took a near-superhuman effort to maintain it. According to George,

> We have got to be stricter even than white shows. Think what it would mean to our aspirations to be a great show if it began to be whispered about that there was anything immoral, even in the least degree, about our show. "A lot of dirty niggers!," everybody would cry, and we couldn't get over the effects of it in a thousand years. We not only want to keep our company and our show decent, but we have simply got to do it or get out of business.[19]

Despite their troubles, Bert and George met with success in vaudeville at Hammerstein's doing a burlesque of the bedchamber scene from *Othello*, with Bert playing Desdemona, featuring the song "Pretty Desdemone."[20] On opening night, George ran into Alice Rohe (1876 to 1957), a hometown girl from Lawrence who had become a successful journalist. She wrote about the encounter in the article "Rediscovery of George Walker":

> "The last time I saw him," I reflected, "he was shining father's shoes for the sum of a nickel back in Lawrence, then, and now," I gasped, as I caught a flash of diamonds from a heavily studded cane and a huge diamond finger ring of a smiling personage just coming off the stage, "he could buy all of Lawrence, Kan., with a good slice of Leavenworth County thrown in."
>
> "But then," I thought consolingly, "I had discovered George W. Walker."
>
> "I'm willing to forget it all if you are." I volunteered, apologetically, as we gave the hand of friendship.
>
> "Forget what?" smiled the diamond-studded Mr. Walker.
>
> "Oh, Kansas and the reminisces of our childhood." I explained.
>
> "Do your worst!" dared he of the broad smile. "I'm proud of coming from Kansas."

"Yes, we all are," I interrupted. "It's considered a feat, isn't it? It's a good place to come from."[21]

Taken aback by Nash's splendor, Rohe waxed nostalgic, and he invited her to his home:

"Come and see!" was the invitation.

And I went. Yes, went into a gorgeous house—a whole house, if you please—in West Twenty-sixth Street, that would make our most esteemed citizens of the Sunflower State sit up and gasp with envy.

Think of it! Here was a parlor with Marie Antoinette cabinets full of bric-a-brac; here was a library with the works of Guy de Maupassant, Maeterlinck, Isben, Thackeray, Dickens, and, shades of Kansans, let me describe Mr. Walker's boudoir. It's all done in pale blue satin, with a beautiful pale blue silk bedspread with lace over it; pale blue scarfs, and, oh! such loads of heavy silver toilet articles on the dresser.

It was all too splendid, almost as grand as the loads and loads of Silver and cut glass on the big buffet just off the library.

And, talk about clothes! Well, you should see the swell outfits of this Beau Brummel comedian. And jewels—but Mr. Walker didn't want to talk about clothes or jewelry. After his valet had exhibited a few wonderful tailored aerations, just for the sake of Kansas, Mr. Walker preferred talking about the building of a new theatre for the purpose of helping young colored men and women to a chance on the stage.

Nash also shared some of his correspondences with Dr. Booker T. Washington and thoroughly impressed Rohe with his knowledge and insight into the so-called race problem:

"I make lots of money," said Mr. Walker, "but I spend it. Why, I have to lay aside more money, just to give away in a day, now, than I saw in the whole year when I was doing the five cent-shine that back in Kansas."

"How did I succeed? Well, Mr. Williams and I both believe that, to please an audience, we must give the real Negro character. Few Negroes will burlesque their own race. In fact, we don't have to be burlesqued if we stick to nature. That's where the average darkey performer loses out. We know that when we try to act like white folks the public won't want us. There are enough bad white actors now."

A bit notorious, the Beau Brummel of the "Cullud" race may have lived up to his name on this occasion. However, he was smart enough to not bring his indiscretions to his home, where extended family and friends were ever-present. That was, in part, what the Hotel Marshall was for.

The engagement at Hammerstein's was so successful that George renegotiated the contract from $1,000 a week to $1,700 and a percentage of the door to buy Dockstader out of his signing bonus at a rate of $750 a week. The lucrative contract also provided an opportunity to employ a sizable supporting cast and incorporate new material from *Abyssinia*.[22] While backstage at Hammerstein's, George gave an interview that was published in an article titled "Negro on Stage Can't Be Serious":

> Talk to me about the infusion of white blood for the betterment of the negro race. I do not believe in it. I tell you the black man's future lies in his faculties—physical and mental—as a negro. I think the white race [has] not realized the latent possibilities and us.
>
> Our civilization is a little beyond its infancy when you come to think of it. Why a few hundred years ago we were savages. Given time and advantages, which have brought the white people into their present stage, we shall be a wonderful people. If you don't believe me, wait and see.

The interviewer took note of the diamond cigarette case George drew from his pocket, which he lit with a diamond match.

> I'd just like to have you take in a few further facts while we're on the subject. There can't be any dispute as to our musical ability. This, too is undeveloped. Ragtime is just part of the chaos, out of which real geniuses will someday be evolved.
>
> We shall have great Negro masters of music in the generation to come. We shall have great poets too, for our race is a poetic one. But all these things will take time. Our poets must stick to Negro dialect to make themselves heard, or to sell their

wares, and our composers must write ragtime for the same reason, until the white man's serious consideration has been earned.

That, after all is the desideratum—to get the serious acceptance of our efforts. Why I was talking a few days ago to a young Negro playwright who is anxious to do a comedy drama for Williams and myself. He had a good, and I think, quite an original idea, but there was a number of love scenes in the piece—that wouldn't do of course. Why not? Well, can you fancy a love scene between two colored people that would not bring a laugh? The colored man's love affairs are like his ragtime and his dialect poems. No matter how carefully written they must not be otherwise than amusing. Mind I am not saying that generally we have as yet earned the right for serious consideration, and I know that we must wait for it and work for it.

George's valet entered the dressing room:

"Will yo' wear yo' white flannel suit, sah, or de afternoon frock coat?"

"Lay out my cutaway frock and that lavender tie."

Bert entered the room:

"George is at it again, I see. Go'ge I allus did say one thing."

"What's that?"

"I allus didn't think dat ef we ever goes broke in this business, yo can make a fortune for both of us as a preacher."[23]

While engaged at Hammerstein's, Bert and George cleared about $2,000 a week each and were second in earnings to Lillian Russell. Simultaneously, W. C. Kelly, a monologist from Virginia, refused to appear on a bill if Williams and Walker were on top, stating that Manhattan sported a "mawkish sentiment in favor of the blacks." Fortunately, Oscar Hammerstein sided with Williams and Walker and removed Kelly from the show.[24] George laughed it off with Frank Mallory, who published a quote in the *The Freeman*:

> The man is foolish. The day is passed for that sort of thing. Both white men and black have a right to earn a living in whatever manner they find most congenial, providing they injure no one else. We do not obtrude ourselves on white performers, and they need have nothing to do with us if that is their desire, but if vaudeville performers are going to draw the color line, either

they or we will have to give up the work, for there is hardly a vaudeville show in which colored performers do not appear.

I do not think I will be thought conceited if I point to the fact that Williams and Walker are pretty well established, while Mr. Kelly's fame is still somewhat in retirement, as it were. Of course, if he is looking for a little advertisement, he will probably get it at our expense, but it is pretty small work at best.

We are Negroes, doing a Negro specialty, which, with all due regard to their ability, no white man can do, we are not interfering with anyone else's work and, with all due regard to Mr. Kelly, we are paid more money in a week for our work, than he gets in three months for his. The man is lacking in brains, that's what's the matter with him.[25]

By the time Williams and Walker closed at Hammerstein's, George had had enough of Klaw and Erlanger's antics and fired off an angry, three-page missive on *Abyssinia*-themed letterhead by the cartoonist Herbert Everett Amos:

Dear Sir:—

Since it became evident that Mr. Lew Dockstader was not able to carry out his part of the contract as manager for Williams and Walker in our New Production "Abyssinia," I have called at your office on several occasions in the hopes that we might discuss plans and perhaps devise some means by which certain difficulties could be bridged over so that Williams and Walker's show might go out in spite of discrepancies which arose between us and Mr. Dockstader.

Now that Williams and Walker have managed to pull through some of the difficulties in which we were placed by Mr. Dockstader, I think it is my duty to write you this letter and ask you to carefully consider its contents.

I would say, but for the fact that you personally advised us to sign with Mr. Lew Dockstader, we never would have thought of him as a man capable of managing Williams and Walker. First, because he being a minstrel man, we had not the slightest idea that he had sufficient prestige to get such booking as we think we are entitled to and can get if in the hands of men of money and influence. We know Messrs. Klaw and Erlanger and when you advised us to sign with Mr. Dockstader, the day Messrs. Dockstader, Hackett, Williams and Walker came to your office; to Williams and Walker, your advice meant that your great power and influence was backing Mr. Dockstader. Williams and Walker had had business dealings with you and to us, your word was as good as gold.

I am aware of the fact that sentiment and hard cold business do not go hand in hand; but men must have confidence in each other's word and while Williams and Walker may have failed to act on strict business lines, when we failed to have a guarantee from you that, if Mr. Dockstader failed you would see us through, we did place in implicit faith in the thought that as Mr. Erlanger had stood by us in the past, he would do so in the future. I wish also to emphasize this one fact: notwithstanding Mr. Dockstader's conduct has been exceedingly unbusiness like and in some instances shaky. Williams and Walker still have confidence in Mr. Erlanger, hence we wish you to know our thoughts and some of the great inconveniences which Mr. Dockstader has put us.

When Mr. Dockstader had failed to carry out his part of the contract, my partner and I took counsel together, and I proceeded at once to Cleveland, Ohio, where Mr. Dockstader was playing; employed a lawyer and entered into agreements to reimburse the money he had laid out on our show. This was all done in good faith and to show Mr. Dockstader at Williams and Walker believe in strict honesty and all business transactions.

We organized and built the show according to an agreement between Williams and Walker and Lew Dockstader. We carried out our part of the agreement to the letter and when Mr. Dockstader failed, we at once agreed to reimburse him the money he had laid out. Very much to our surprise, since we have been at work, Mr. Dockstader's lawyer comes forward with claims which we were not morally bound to pay.

Does it seem incredible that Mr. Dockstader should ask Williams and Walker to pay rent for an office in which he transacted his own private business in building up his own minstrel show? Mr. Wilson rendered personal service to Mr. Dockstader when he attended rehearsals of the Williams and Walker show and now we have been charged for Mr. Wilson's service.

We are all men and must fight our own battles: this I know to be a hard fact. The fact that one man induces men to do business together is no argument that that man acts as a guardian for either side. But when I consider all the facts in the case, I think you ought to know what this introduction has cost Williams and Walker. This affair has cost us upward of $15,000 in cash; a season's work together with the worry which Mr. Dockstader's lawyer is causing us. Put yourself in our position: I would ask: how would these facts strike you?

Not to draw upon your time add too great length, I would say, in closing: I have been wondering if an evil genius has been at work to change your former friendly attitude towards Williams and Walker is why I have not been able to see you when I have called at your office? Prior to the arrangement to do business with Mr. Dockstader, I used to gain admittance to your office with ease. I cannot find any explanation for this seeming change of attitude.

I have known of cases where, when white and colored men failed to do business together, in order to present the bright side of their case, White men would misrepresent facts about colored men. I do not say that Williams and Walker's side of the case, between them and Dockstader, has been misrepresented: but I do think as you have doubtless heard the other side, you should know all the facts in the whole case.

Here are a few more facts which may further interest you. During the past summer Williams and Walker were literally besieged by newspapermen, time and again, wanted to know if Klaw and Erlanger were in any way interested in the new show, or if they had advised us to sign with Dockstader? We never divulged one word which would lead to anyone to even imagine that Messrs. Klaw and Erlanger had ever made a single suggestion to Williams and Walker. We did this because we thought it was wisdom to do so.

Now Sir, may I ask: Since it was through your advice that we were landed in the difficulties we find ourselves: Can you not now make some suggestions which may enable us to regain some of the ground we have lost? We are still free from complications which might stand in the way of our doing business with anyone we may wish.

Thanking you for all past favors and hoping to have a reply from you, I am, Sir,

Very Respectfully,

George W. Walker

For Williams and Walker[26]

Neither overstated nor aggressive, George's anger was unmistakable and may have been the first time that Erlanger was taken to task by a Black person. Although a reply was issued, it has not survived. After the fact, Dockstader claimed that without his consent, Williams and Walker issued contracts in his name and he bore no responsibility for them. In response to their ongoing struggles with securing legitimate bookings, George attempted to purchase the four-year-old Circle Theatre, a vaudeville house at 1825 Broadway in Manhattan that had been relegated to burlesque, but the acquisition never materialized.[27]

As *Abyssinia* continued to flounder, Bert and George moved their act to Proctor's 23rd and then 58th Street theatres to headline while Aida and her Abyssinian Maidens went to the Colonial and then to the Orpheum to test new material. Still trying to right the ship, George sent another letter to Abe Erlanger on November 30 and asked for a meeting to iron out the problems and salvage the season. Erlanger replied and expressed a desire to meet with George on December 12.[28]

Throughout December, Bert and George bounced from theatre to theatre with a growing supporting cast and earned $2,000 at Amphion Theatre during Christmas week.[29] During that engagement, Williams and Walker entered into an agreement with Melville B. Raymond for a reduced version of *Abyssinia*, slated to begin touring in February of 1906. As ill-advised as it looked, George knew that was likely the only way to save the company. Once their vaudeville engagements ended in early January, they focused on *Abyssinia* full time in anticipation of an abbreviated season.[30]

Emancipation

The year 1906 began with a new manager and a newfound sense of optimism that *Abyssinia* could be taken out in short order. George kept as many people working as he could during the shutdown, and most returned. He also sang lead on a recorded duet of "Pretty Desdamone" with Bert. It was his best effort to date and showed some real growth, complete with side banter, chuckles, and vibrato over Bert's counterpoint. It was available sometime around March 12, 1906, and was his final recording.[31] George also published an article titled "The Colored Performers on the American Stage" in the January 13, 1906, issue of *The Freeman*. In it, he extolled the unique talents of Black people and the need for solidarity as well the need for proper training for younger performers. He also called for a new Black institution to protect Black entertainers as an extension of his failed attempt to buy the Circle Theatre in Manhattan:

> We who live in New York City have no place where we can go to give and receive information and encouragement. We drift about the city and blunder upon each other here in there, by mere chance. Our meetings are so haphazard that when we do meet, we never or rarely ever exchange views on the subject of our standing.
>
> At the present there is a great need for theatrical club in New York City which should focus on the artistic interests of colored performers throughout this country and Europe, for the time has come when many colored professionals are finding work in foreign fields. There has been much talk about such an institution or headquarters, as I hear mention, but thus far there has been nothing but talk! No definite steps have been taken to establish a home in New York City for colored professionals. . . .
>
> First of all, we need [some place where] all professional colored people can meet and exchange views and feel perfectly at home. We need a bureau of general and particular information about colored professionals. A place where facts about all colored shows on tour can be had daily and weekly. In case any show should wish to send to New York for an actor or actress, information could be sent direct to the colored theatrical club

which would always be in touch with colored performers and much time and expense would thus be saved.[32]

On February 5, 1906, it was announced that *Abyssinia* would open at the Shubert's Majestic Theatre on the February 19. However, the company's excitement was tempered by news of Paul Laurence Dunbar's death from consumption. The loss of the first Negro poet laureate reverberated for the rest of George's life.[33] In the meantime, he circumvented the first-class-theatre embargo by working with the Shuberts. Midnight rehearsals began in earnest on the Majestic stage that went until six or seven o'clock in the morning until the opening. Despite their efforts, the opening was pushed back to February 20 for a proper dress rehearsal and photos.[34] The cast had been reduced to fewer than sixty, and the live animals were removed, except the donkey George rode in the first act. Jesse Shipp's plot did not disappoint and provided ample opportunity for specialized acts and banter between Bert and George. The opening scene was set in a marketplace in Borema Springs, Addis Ababa, the capital of Abyssinia, with a mountain pass and waterfall in the background, for the male chorus's offering "Ode to King Menelik." Erastus Johnson (George) rode in on a donkey, while Jasmine "Jas" Jenkins (Bert) trailed behind on foot, sported an automobile horn, and delineated why he should be on the animal at length.

As the story went, Erastus, a Kansan, won $15,000 in the Louisiana lottery and invited his friend, Jas, and a few other townsmen to travel to Europe to help spend the loot. When they reached Paris, Rastus learned of Abyssinia and, having never been there, decided to go and see it for himself. Rastus believed that if he dressed like a king, the locals would treat him like one and allow him to buy a kingdom of his own. Once landed, Jas bought seemingly every frivolous thing in sight with Rastus's money, from a camel to an extravagant "vaas" that he unwittingly stole. Little did they know that all of Abyssinia was in pursuit of an unidentified and dangerous bandit. Rastus's ostentatious spending and his kingly attire, which resembled the bandit's own costume, quickly drew suspicion. In the third scene, Jas was put on trial in the court of King Menelik, where he tried to explain to the king that when he bargained for the "vaas" he wasn't trying to steal it. However, when the dealer insisted on immediate payment, Jas discovered that he was short and tried to explain. Then the merchant broke the "vaas" over his head, and a melee ensued to subdue the would-be bandits and bring them to the court of the king. According to Bert, that scene was an audience favorite: "It's pretty nearly like the real thing. Sometimes it gets too realistic. It is a common thing for some of us to lose patches of hide in that scene. Once I had my nose squished flat by the rough and tumble getting too natural."[35]

Menelik, a just king, sent for the merchant to verify Jas's story. If true, he'd go free, but if found to be untrue, his right hand was to be severed at the wrist. The decision was to be announced by the striking of a gong; three bells meant the loss of his hand, and four bells meant an acquittal. The throne room was vacated by all except Jas, Rastus, and a guard. Jas sat on the council table and pretended to read a book while Rastus protested that Jas had once again gotten them into trouble; that he had no business wanting a "vaas" in the first place; that he didn't have anything for it after he got it; and that, even if he did want it, he should have paid for it like an honorable gentleman. Jas sullenly replied that he had spent all his money on a camel and that it was *his* hand in question:

> Now, you went and done it! I brung you over here to Abyssinia where you can get some culture and you go walking through all this culture, looking like some vulture. I even take you swimming, half-hoping you gonna drown, but the water takes one look at you and it begins to frown and it backs up to your—knees! What you gonna do? Huh? You know the punishment for what you done! They gonna cut off your hand. What you gonna look like with one hand and a nub, huh?
>
> I'll put a hook on it.[36]

Rastus then left Jas at his lowest of low, which inspired him to sing his latest hard-luck ballad, "Here It Comes Again." During the third verse, he began to address his present difficulties and the potential loss of his right hand, when the first stroke of the gong was heard offstage. As Jas was frozen with fear, Bert's pantomime skills were on full display. Then, another stroke of the gong. As his fear intensified into the comically absurd, the third gong sounded. Almost immediately, Jas straightened his spine and fearsomely stared out at the audience until the fourth gong sounded. Now exonerated, he relaxed, and his body settled back into its familiar stoop while a smile of sheer joy enveloped his face. He collapsed, grasped his right hand with the left, and affectionately shook it to thunderous applause from the audience. He then rose to his feet and, with the aid of the trap drummer, broke into his lumbering signature dance, during which his spine creaked whenever he bent backward. Often, "Nobody" was reprised as an

Figure 11.1a–b. Publicity photographs of George Walker and chorus in the stage production *Abyssinia*, as published in an unknown magazine. *Source:* Billy Rose Theatre Division, New York Public Library. Public domain.

encore because most audiences would not let Bert leave the stage without performing it. Nevertheless, the show had to continue, and he'd eventually shuffle off to the wings, not to be seen again until the final act.³⁷

Opening night was packed with a surprising amount of White people, which surprised reviewers because *Abyssinia* lacked the inaugural novelty of *In Dahomey*. Franklin Fyles, who referred to George as "Coon Walker," declared, "The producers seem to have said to themselves, 'Now we'll show these white folks that we can do things on the stage just like they can;' but who cares if they can? And a majority of the audience is sorry that they do. For there is barely a trace of Negroism in the play."³⁸

Despite missing the point entirely, most critics understood what it took to put it all together. *The New York Times* noted, "The piece is far in advance of their last vehicle, 'In Dahomey,' in costumes, scenery, and effects, while the work of the singers, especially in the chorus, surpasses all their previous efforts."³⁹ Aida's Abyssinian Maidens were well-received, and George scored with "It's Hard to Find a King Like Me," dressed as a tribal king, as well as with "Rastus Johnson U.S.A.," which he sung with the chorus. Acton Davies of the New York *Sun* was displeased with the conspicuous presence of Black patrons who were angered by their exclusion from the orchestra section of the theatre. Not to be outdone, a bum-rush was effected between acts, and in short order the lobby and foyer were all filled with Black bodies ready to take the orchestra. According to Davies,

> [D]roves of negroes invaded the beautiful restaurant and café next door, in search of liquid refreshment. It was a rather extraordinary spectacle and the Majestic's clientele did not seem to appreciate it any more than they did the play. "Abyssinia" is a hopeless proposition from any point of view. Williams and Walker are uncommonly clever comedians, of that there is no question, but their new play has no wit, no situations, no tunes and absolutely no fun in it. Walker and all the other members of the company, except Williams, who used his familiar burnt cork make-up, seemed possessed of the one desire to act and look as much like whites as possible. The result was, that the women in the troupe, made up with rouge and powder, presented a ghostly appearance and the entire absence of any Senegambian flavor to the performance ruined it from a commercial point of view. . . . It is safe to say that it will be a long time before a theater of the Majestic's standing will try such an experiment

again. In their old line of work, Williams and Walker were exceptionally funny men, but they ought to remember the old proverb about "trying to gild the lily," for it works both ways.[40]

Exacerbating the frustration of White critics was the enthusiasm of the Black patrons who cheered rowdily for Bert after he finished singing "Here It Comes Again" and continued to do so for five minutes after the curtain fell.[41] Ironically, White critics failed to see the hypocrisy of their assertions that an appropriate amount of "Negroism" was lacking in the show while there was entirely too much "Negroness" in the theatre. To that end, the reviewer from *The Philadelphia Enquirer* surmised, "Williams was the sole spot of humor in the whole conglomeration, largely because he remained the comic 'nigger.' Audiences do not care for the colored man as a serious item on the stage. They like the comic 'coon' but won't stand for the idea of Senegambian dignity. For this reason 'Abyssinia' is doomed and its projectors mourn."[42]

Sylvester Russell saw the show twice during its third and fourth weeks at the Majestic and, according to him, suffered two indignities. First, he "receive[ed] the indiscretion of a 'jolly' from Bert A. Williams, who made the critic look like a doormat." Second, "George Walker wrote to Alan Dale [of the *Evening World*] thanking him for what? While the black critic-editor had to pose as nobody." After blasting them further, Russell intimated, "Williams and Walker are not really rich men yet and much will depend upon their future unaffected behavior."[43] Likely at the insistence of *The Freeman*'s editor, George L. Knox (1884 to 1926), he revisited the simmering tension that he brought to the surface and declared, "The friction between Williams and Walker and the critic will be at an end, as far as the critic is concerned." However, his revisitation of the subject matter likely exacerbated tension with Williams and Walker.[44]

Despite bad reviews, advance-ticket sales for the final two weeks were strong, and several congratulatory telegrams were published in *The Freeman*.[45] By design, when *Abyssinia* began to tour late in the season, first-class houses were not available. With second- and third-class houses as the only option, a slew of one-night stands between residencies was the only choice. While in Washington, DC, the company played a baseball game against the team from Howard University at American League Park on May 1 at four o'clock, with Jack Johnson as umpire again. According to reports, the game was exciting, and both teams hit the ball well, but the thespians were hampered by eleven unforced errors that allowed Howard to pad their score.[46] While engaged in

Pittsburgh, they played a nail-biter against the Olympia Baseball Club at Bedford Basin Park that required an extra inning before being called a tie at 7 to 7.[47] A few weeks later, they accepted another challenge to a ballgame with a local team, the Canadians, on June 21. George pitched for the first time, and the final score was 21 to 19 in favor of Williams and Walker.[48]

Windy City Breakdown

While the season ended in late May for other companies, Williams and Walker moved to the Great Northern in Chicago for a six-week residence to make up for the shortfall. As in New York, White critics were entertained but continued to demand more "Negroism" and less *Negroness*.[49] One stormy matinee day, an old German man knocked on the stage door and asked for a Bert or George. The stage manager got his name and asked him to wait while he relayed the information to the dressing room, and said, "There's an old man outside in the hall who says he knows you; his name is Herman." Bert and George instantly took notice and rushed past the stage manager to find the man who saved them from starvation during the winter of 1896.

They escorted him back to the dressing room as giddy as the young men they once were. Now that the tables had turned, Bert and George were able to help Herman, who was struggling. They took him shopping for a new suit of clothes and went with him to his flat to meet his wife and children, who also received gifts from them.[50]

As the show toured during that short season, they were haunted by the specter of Thomas Dixon's *The Clansman*, a controversial and poorly produced play that promoted the lost cause of the Confederacy to inspire White people to reclaim the "Old South."[51] Understandably, Bert and George refrained from comment for months, but a reporter from *The Inter Ocean* got under George's skin as he was preparing to don his kingly attire between scenes:

> Why, that play, as I have read of it, emphasizes the supported demand of negroes for so-called social equality. Social equality. Why, the negroes don't ask [for] social equality. How could they get social equality when the white man himself doesn't get it? You know there are thousands of white men in this city [whom] you wouldn't receive on the ground[s] of social equality. What the negroes ask is commercial equality, and only when they show

they are entitled to it. When we have accomplished what we aim at as serious minded citizens we don't want to be discriminated against just because we are negroes. The time is coming when we will not be discriminated against and the question of social equality will adjust itself.

"The Clansman" does not present the negro problem. It is the white man's problem. It is Mr. Dixon's problem. We haven't any problem. What is "The Clansman," to be classed as removing the question of prejudice? Judged from what the unbiased critics in the papers have said, it is an aggregation of poor actors. If he was sincere in his efforts to get a first-class performance, even of a prejudiced play, would he not have gotten the best to be had in this country? I wouldn't call that play "The Clansman," I would call it "The Skinsman."

Why, they tell me that they've got one scene where a negro is trying to keep a white girl in a room. Why, is it necessary for an author to depict the worst there is in the negro, to hold it up before the public in order to make his play a success? We've got criminals; we know it. But why should the negro criminal be held up as a type of his race any more than a white criminal?[52]

Bert chimed in:

I don't live in a state where they've annulled the fifteenth amendment yet, and don't expect to. But they've got pretty near it in some places, but even there I don't believe they can change us. If immigration and five years' residence is enough to make an American citizen with full rights as any Polander, Russian, or Hungarian can get, I want to know what rights are residents 250 years in this country, even with the period of slavery included an amendment to the fundamental law adopted by the entire American people for our benefit, confers?

George had nearly completed his transformation into the king of Abyssinia and offered his thoughts on what Negroes wanted:

What we ask on the part of the white is more faith in the sincerity of the colored people. You have in this country societies for the prevention of cruelty to animals that will start the machinery of the law to going if they hear of a case of a horse being abused. But do they ever raise their voices when colored men and women are maltreated, as they are almost daily? If God is that unjust, we are going to have a mighty hard time in the hereafter. There is plenty of bad among us, and we want to get rid of it as soon as possible. But we can't do it anymore than the white man can.

Do you ever hear of any Southern people complain of the negroes during the war when they went away from their homes and left their women and children in charge of the old black mammies in the old black Joes? Didn't they keep them as faithfully as they could ask? This trouble all happened after the war, and the white men themselves were responsible for a good deal of it.

Accompanying the article was a pen-and-ink drawing that highlighted the dichotomy of the perceived personalities of the two stars. George spoke with a frankness that sounded a lot like his father and was less willing to suffer fools than his partner, particularly when it came to well-meaning apologists for White supremacy. In the drawing, Bert was depicted as overweight, insecure, and slumping in stereotypical (acceptable) fashion, while George was depicted as vain, ungrateful, materialistic, and disrespectful when asked to explain his perspective as a person of double consciousness to a person of privileged, single consciousness.

As potentially controversial as the *Clansman* interview was, it paled in comparison to George's greatest blunder. On June 23, 1906, reports indicated that Aida had severed ties with the company and was replaced by an understudy due to George's infidelity with a chorus member named Hattie Hopkins-Chenault. She had joined the cast in 1902 and played Varinoe alongside her husband, Lawrence, who joined early in the season.[53] As reported, George and Hattie were so late for the evening's performance on June 20 that the second act was put on first to bide time. According to the *Chicago Conservator*, "After a time, Mr. Walker, blowing and puffing from over haste in locomotion to reach the stage, came in, closely followed by the beautiful 'Varinoe' of the stage. Mr. Walker and his belated coworker in the big show could give no satisfactory explanation of their whereabouts during the twilight moments, and Mr. Walker's pretty little wife began to philosophize."[54] Aida completed the performance without incident but refused to speak to George, packed her trunk, and left for New York, "through with

Figure 11.2. Accompanying illustration for "What Williams and Walker Think of the Clansman." *Source: CIO,* June 24, 1906, 34.

both her handsome hubby and his big show."[55] That evening, the female chorus met and decided that Hopkins and her husband had to go. Sylvester Russell implied there was more to the incident: "A[i]da Overton Walker deserves great credit if the reports are true that she made mincemeat of a sweet singer of the Sunny South with auburn hair, who by the way, has been getting too tricky for her own good of late and liable to be exposed. If George Walker doesn't look wise, his family affairs will place him in the down and out skiddo class to stay."[56]

Aida's departure ended the run at the Great Northern as well as the truncated season. George said nothing to the press, which fueled further speculation. He had cultivated his Colored Beau Brummel persona for nearly a decade, so it was generally assumed that infidelity was a way of life for him, but that was his only documented case. Aida reportedly began divorce proceedings, made overtures to vaudeville booking agents as a solo act, and attempted to replace the Memphis Students on an upcoming European tour with her Abyssinian Maidens under the direction of Will Dixon. Meanwhile, George lingered in Chicago for a few days, visited some friends, and likely did some soul searching.[57] In August, he created a stir with the manifesto "The Real 'Coon' on the American Stage" in *The Theatre* magazine, his first account of the company's origin and his professional philosophy: "I have no hesitation in stating that the departure from what was popularly known as the American 'darky' ragtime limitations to native African characteristics has

Figure 11.3. Aida featured prominently in George's article "The Real 'Coon' on the American Stage." Source: *The Theatre*, August 1906, 224–26.

The Real "Coon" on the American Stage
By GEORGE W. WALKER

White, N. Y.
GEORGE W. WALKER

White, N. Y.
BERT A. WILLIAMS

THE stage has always fascinated me. To stand before the footlights and entertain large audiences has ever been the dream of my life. When but a lad, I joined a company of amateur colored minstrels in my native town, Lawrence, Kansas. There were thirteen of us, but I cannot say that we had bad luck. We gave annual performances, and were always well patronized, and our net receipts from the box were usually gratifying. Negro minstrels, organized and put on the road by white men, soon after the emancipation of the Southern slaves, were very successful throughout the Northern and Western States, but hardly anyone was optimistic enough in those early days of the black man on the American stage to believe that he would ever rise above being a mere minstrel man. I started out with the idea that it was possible for the black performer to do better. My associates shared my views to some extent, but to most of them the future offered little encouragement, and the longer I remained at home the more impossible it seemed for me ever to realize my ambition. So I left Lawrence and went West to California. I did not make the trip in a single leap, but made my way from Lawrence to San Francisco by easy stages.

In those days—about 18 years ago—the West was not so up-to-date as it is now. The Westerners were good-hearted, but a bit rough and ready. I had to rough it, and rough it I did. But I got there, and that was the main thing.

There were many quack doctors doing business in the West. They traveled from one town to another in wagons, and gave shows in order to get large crowds of people together, so as to sell medicine. When a boy, I was quite an entertainer. I could sing and dance, and was good at face-making, beating the tambourine, and rattling the bones. I was not lacking in courage, and I did not hesitate to ask the quacks for a job. First one and then the other hired me. When we arrived in a town and our show started I was generally the first to attract attention. I would mount the wagon and commence to sing and dance, make faces, and tell stories, and rattle the bones.

My experience with the quack doctors taught me two good lessons: that white people are always interested in what they call "darky" singing and dancing; and the fact that I could entertain in that way as no white boy could, made me valuable to the quack doctors as an advertising card.

When I reached San Francisco, I left the quacks and went around the theatres and music halls looking for employment. While hanging around one day I saw a gaunt fellow over six feet, of orange hue and about 18 years of age, leaning on a banjo, haggling with a manager—that was Bert A. Williams. He was stage struck, too! We got a job together at seven dollars a week each. That was about fifteen years ago. We have had many ups and downs since those days, but still we hang together.

When we were not working we frequented the playhouses just the same. In those days black-faced white comedians were numerous and very popular. They billed themselves as "coons." Bert and I watched the white "coons," and were often much amused at

White, N. Y.   ADA OVERTON WALKER
One of the most graceful and agile colored dancers on the stage

seeing white men with black cork on their faces trying to imitate black folks. Nothing about these white men's actions was natural, and therefore nothing was as interesting as if black performers had been dancing and singing their own songs in their own way.

There were many more barriers in the way of the black performer in those days than there are now, because, with the exception of the negro minstrels, the black entertainer was little known throughout the Northern and Western States. The opposition on account of racial and color prejudices and the white comedians who "blacked up" stood in the way of the natural black performer, and petty jealousies common among professional people also greatly retarded the artistic progress of the Afro-American.

How to get before the public and prove what ability we might possess was a hard problem for Williams and Walker to solve. We thought that as there seemed to be a great demand for black faces on the stage, we would do all we could to get what we felt belonged to us by the laws of nature. We finally decided that as white men with black faces were billing themselves "coons," Williams and Walker would do well to bill themselves as the "Two Real Coons," and so we did. Our bills attracted the attention of managers, and gradually we made our way in.

After playing for a pretty good run at the Midway Theatre, in San Francisco, our eyes were turned toward the East, and our helped greatly to increase the value of the black performer on the American stage."⁵⁸ To boot, Aida was highlighted with the largest photograph of the three principal performers of the company, in part for her growing importance and likely to smooth over George's recent indiscretion. He closed with a bit of optimism: "There is an artistic side to the black race, and if it could be properly developed on the stage, I believe the theatre-going public would profit much by it. . . . The love, the humor, and the pathos of the black race in this country afford a field for wide study, and I am sure the stage is the place where the character of the African race can be studied from a real artistic point of view, with special advantages to all lovers of music and theatrical art."⁵⁹

The article proved very popular and was reprinted in part in the *Lawrence Daily Journal*, *The Daily Gazette*, and *The Colored American Magazine*, where George was complimented in the September 1906 issue: "Walker is without peer as an actor among his own and there are very few challenges arising out of the pale crowd of comedians which he could not dispose of easily. He is an enormous favorite with intelligent lovers of rich comedy and is an enviable opposite to Williams the happiest of funmakers."⁶⁰ Although compromises were made, *Abyssinia* was innovative, entertaining, and in demand. However, the problem of access to first-class theatres remained unsolved, and the situation further deteriorated because management, again, acted more like gatekeepers than openers. Moreover, as big as George's professional problems were, his marriage was in serious jeopardy. Aida was essential to Williams and Walker's success, and the coming season would prove that beyond the shadow of a doubt.

New Season, Same Trouble

Abyssinia was carried over, and the 1906 to 1907 season began at the Grand Theatre, New York, on August 18 for a two-week engagement, followed by the Majestic for another fortnight. George somehow convinced Aida to remain with the company, likely through a series of compromises that allowed her to continue her artistic growth and personal independence. She incorporated new dancing specialties and additional songs with "The Island of By-and-By" and "Build a Nest for Birdie," and they were featured as a couple in "I'll Keep a Warm Spot in My Heart for You."⁶¹ However, at this point, her marriage to George may have been more for appearances and business than love.

Figure 11.4. "I'll Keep a Warm Spot in My Heart for You," words and music by Bob Cole, J. Rosamond Johnson and James Weldon Johnson, Jos. W. Stern & Co., New York, 1906. *Source:* Author's collection.

Although the show remained as popular as ever, Melville Raymond disappeared in the middle of August and stopped issuing payroll checks. On September 12, George filed an injunction against Raymond, who had embezzled $1,900 to fund his effort to beat out Klaw and Erlanger for a management contract of the Hippodrome in Baltimore. Raymond had also taken charge of Cole and Johnson's *Shoo-Fly Regiment*, which left him overextended, so he stole from Williams and Walker to stave off bankruptcy. Their business manager, Jack Shoemaker, had been paying the company's share of receipts to Raymond's receiver until the first week of September, when the receiver advised him to stop. By the following pay night, Shoemaker was forced to borrow from the manager of the Majestic Theatre to make payroll, on top of an $1,800 deficit that also required a loan to meet. To make matters worse, Raymond had scheduled four weeks of one-night stands and had secretly relocated to Baltimore while his office in New York was besieged with employees and managers of various companies that were stranded or failed to launch. A restraining order was granted, and theatrical screen printer James D. Barton was appointed receiver for Williams and Walker, with a bond fixed at $10,000 and authorization to terminate the production if he deemed necessary. As a result, George was forced to cancel the first two of four weeks of one-night stands that were scheduled to begin on September 18 in Pittston, Pennsylvania, and struck a hasty deal with Hurtig and Seamon to spend a week at the Yorkville Theatre and another at the Metropolis, during the last two weeks of September.[62]

Following the Hurtig and Seamon stint, *Abyssinia* got another late start, which meant there were no first-class venues available, and any engagements made at lower-class theatres meant bumping another production. Nevertheless, the tour began at the twenty-five-to-seventy-five-cent Masonic Theatre in Louisville for a week on October 1, then moved to the Park in Indianapolis, a ten-to-fifty-cent house.[63] With low revenues from packed houses, a profitable season looked unlikely for the second consecutive season. Despite it all, George was proud of his most ambitious vehicle and looked to the future:

> My greatest ambition is to get money enough together to build a theater, if possible to build one in New York, one in Philadelphia and one in Boston. Chicago is so far the only city in the United States that can boast of a Negro theatre [the Pekin]—one where the actors, musicians, management and, in fact, everyone connected with the enterprise, are colored men. My idea is to erect theaters in which we can train Negroes to realize that a colored person has parts worthy of serious noticed by himself and by others. There is no reason why we should be

forced to do these old time nigger acts. It's all rot. This slapstick banana-handkerchief-bladder and flower-in-the-face act, with which Negro acting is associated. It ought to die out, and I think Williams & Walker have helped kill it. It's a long way from a corner medicine show in Lawrence, Kan., to being a star in a production such as "Abyssinia," but that the distance can be covered by perseverance and energy.[64]

Now that Aida was growing in influence, she, too, offered her opinion on the present state of things:

You haven't the faintest conception of the difficulties which must be overcome, of the prejudices which must be left slumbering, of the things we must avoid whenever we write or sing a piece of music, put on a play or a sketch, walk out in the street or land in a new town.

No white actor can understand these things, much less appreciate them. Every little thing we do must be thought out and arranged by Negroes, because they alone know how easy it is for a colored show to offend a white audience.

Let me to give you an example: in all the ten years that I have appeared and helped to produce a great many plays of musical nature there has never been even the remotest suspicion of a love story in any of them.

During those same ten years I do not think there has ever been a single white company which has produced any kind of musical play in which a love story was not the central notion.

Now, why is this? It is not an accident or because we do not want to put on plays as beautiful and as artistic in every way as do the white actors, but because there is a popular prejudice against love scenes enacted by negroes. This is just one of the 10,000 things we must think of every time we make a step. The public does not appreciate our limitations, or, rather at the limitations which other persons have made for us.[65]

As frustration mounted, the Walkers grew more frank in their criticism of the limiting factors of the American social order for Black people. Meanwhile, vaudeville managers including David Belasco attempted to sign

Bert as a solo act. In response, George made an uncharacteristically somber and conciliatory statement without a trace of his usual bravado:

> We try to give a show that will not offend. The Southern "nigger" can see it and laugh, and the Northern "darky" can be well amused. There has been much written recently concerning the inferiority of the colored race. I believe God is just, and though there may be an inferior race, there is still the possibility of superior individuals in that race. A black pigment, so small that thousands can hang to a needle's point, should not cause undue prejudice against a race.
>
> In our shows we try to present the comedy of the primitive races of the oriental world connected with the modern American "darkey."
>
> Mr. Bert Williams and Lottie Williams, his wife, and myself and Aida Overton Walker, my wife, have been together eight years, use the same dressing rooms and take pride in producing an entertainment which will be a credit to our race. I believe that it is fair and I feel gratified in the reception accorded us in America and in England.[66]

Upon closing in Indianapolis, they traveled to Kansas City for a week beginning October 14, 1906. While close to home, a "more prosperous than ever" Nash visited Lawrence to begin building the home for his mother and grandmother and tapped his friend John W. Clark (1871 to 1930) to oversee the project. It was Nash's first time home since his uncle Sanford died in May, and the company soon followed for their first visit since 1904. Around forty-five mostly Black people stood in line for hours, waiting for Woodward's store to open, and $300 worth of tickets were sold in an hour.[67] Nash was excited to be home and told the *Gazette*, "We would not come to Kansas at all if it were not for Lawrence the dearest own place in the whole country. We are just as glad to get back home as any of you folks are to see us, and the stop here is one bright spot in our long season's hard work."[68] So many people came to the performance that fifty to seventy-five people spilled out into the foyer, and, as usual, the Black contingent was especially enthusiastic. In Topeka, ticket sales were strong, but only for the sub-seventy-five-cent seats, and attendance was uncharacteristically sparse. This was due, at least in part, to the management decision to restrict the seating of Black patrons in the orchestra section, but also some White patrons were put off by the ambitious production, wanting a more traditional, minstrel-style show. Following Topeka were several one-nighters ending in a two-week engagement in St. Louis.[69]

On November 15, the earnings for the season were published, and they showed a slim profit of $3,867, despite playing in third-class houses. Although lower ticket prices benefited their Black fans, no discount could make up for the lack of available seats in Jim Crow theatres. Following a $383 loss in December, Bert and George fired their lawyer, Franklin Bien, and hired David Gerber, of the Dittenhoefer, Gerber and James law firm, to sever ties with Raymond.[70] Nevertheless, the tour continued east, with the last stop in Brooklyn. On March 7, 1907, the receiver for the company showed a loss of $1,035 and, along with it, George's leverage for first-class bookings. Shortly before the season ended, they were billed as "a dollar-and-a-half attraction at popular prices" in Baltimore.[71]

In early May, the Williams and Walker nine trounced the Elks at Vare Park, Philadelphia, and played the local Giants in Atlantic City just before the end of the season. For the second year, they had worked twice as hard to get half as far, and the company was exhausted. With that, they unceremoniously retired *Abyssinia* in favor of *Bandanna Land*, a more conventional offering, and disbanded for the summer.[72]

Chapter 12

"Bon Bon Buddy"

1907 to 1908

Turning the Corner

In early March of 1907, an anecdote about some popular Black thespians appeared in *The Freeman*:

> At the St. James building [at 1133 Broadway, Ernest Hogan] was telling some friends how Williams and Walker, Cole and Johnson and himself had met by accident in the café, and an argument started at once as to what they would drink. Cole and Johnson wanted a couple of bottles of champagne and Williams and Walker wanted a sherry. After listening [for] a while, Hogan jumped up and said, "Oh, let's have two bottles of ink."
> Williams, seeing the point, immediately said: "Yes, and bring a blotter on the side."[1]

Although a jovial meeting, it was one of the final occasions when all five stars would be in the same room together. As for Bert and George, changes had to be made to recover from *Abyssinia* and as usual, that began with management. There was a rumor about a deal with a firm run by Foraker and Tillman for the coming season, but the Shuberts were the only firm left with access to first-class houses.[2] Rumors of the change were met with dismay and skepticism, especially in large-market cities like Pittsburgh, where the *Post-Gazette* asserted,

> Either the New York or telegraph is indulging in its customary malice toward the Shuberts or else it is printing a damaging truth. That paper said last week that the Shuberts had signed Williams and Walker, the negro comedians, and would send them out over their circuit of theatres. Williams and Walker in the Belasco theatre, for instance, would about settle the hash of the "independents" in Pittsburgh. The story is hardly true. The Shuberts are far too wise to attempt such a risk with the clientele they are building up in Pittsburgh. If the story is not true it ought to be flatly denied, however.[3]

A similar sentiment was expressed in the *Mansfield News-Journal*: "Eve[r] since Williams and Walker returned from London they have nursed an almost uncontrollable ambition to play in the 'two dollar' houses. . . . Now, it appears, that the Shuberts will enter into a contract to take them over, raising the standard of the company to the height demanded by two dollar audiences and giving the team of colored entertainers a chance to see what they can do in the way of entertaining 'our best people.' "[4]

As far as most first-class theatre owners and critics in the United States were concerned, George and the Shuberts were exacerbating a problem for which there was no solution. Moreover, the situation was further complicated when Klaw and Erlanger and the Shuberts merged into a trust as the United States Amusement Company. After a week of negotiations at the close of the 1906 to 1907 season, the details of the agreement were finalized, in which Williams and Walker were guaranteed booking in two-dollar houses, and the day-to-day management fell to F. Ray Comstock. Unbeknownst to George, the agreement called for the Shuberts to switch their houses to vaudeville, which forced him into a deal with Stair and Havlin, managers of Cole and Johnson and operators of a second-class circuit. Through it all, George remained positive, and likely a little nostalgic, given the subject matter of the new show. In a letter to an unnamed friend that was published in Lawrence, he expressed a longing to retire there in the cottage that he was constructing for his mother and grandmother.[5]

With eyes on the next season, Bert and George opened their summer vaudeville season at the Chestnut Street Opera House in Philadelphia, a Klaw and Erlanger theatre, on May 20, 1907, at $2,500 a week.[6] Although thrown together, *On the Road to Bandanna Land* was at the top of the bill and promoted as "vaudeville's most expensive show." It may have been inspired by the "Road to Gatorville" sketch from act 2, scene 2 of *In Dahomey*. It was a hit, and, according to *The Pittsburgh Gazette Times*, Williams and Walker had "wisely gone back to being real negroes again."[7] George M. Young of *Variety* was one of the first to review the new act:

> The opening is a rather talky dialogue with little merit. A couple of songs by Williams gives Walker the chance to change to one of his familiar "dandy coon" make-ups. . . . His "get-up" is a work of art and colors, and he gives an exhibition of "strutting" that brought rounds of approval. A quartet of girls are used in the finish of the "strut," Walker driving them about the stage with ribbons and flourishing a whip. The stage picture is attractive and novel. As a finale Williams appears in dresses, representing a wench on parade and presents a ludicrous picture. There is nothing apparent to suggest that much trouble was taken to arrange the skit, but it was no doubt thrown together to furnish twenty minutes of fun, and in this it succeeds. And it is well-liked.[8]

The "rounds of approval" for George's new offering was probably inspired by the introduction of his first smash hit song, "Bon Bon Buddy." They moved to the Grand, where they continued to refine the act and please audiences.[9]

Along with Williams and Walker's return to success, Lester Walton, former private secretary for Ernest Hogan, emerged as a friendly critical voice at the *New York Age* in September of 1906. In the June 27, 1907, edition, Walton congratulated Bert and George for having weathered the *Abyssinia* debacle: "Williams and Walker did something never before accomplished by another theatrical company: go into the hands of a receiver and come out in the end with a large sum to its credit."[10]

On July 3, 1907, the relationship between Williams and Walker and Melville B. Raymond formally ended. Unlike their comrades Cole and Johnson, who lost money with Raymond, the receiver reported the company's business exceeded $20,000 monthly during the past season and $30,000 net profits for the shortened 1905 to 1906 season.[11] Although Sylvester Russell wanted *Abyssinia* to continue, George ended the two-year struggle and summarily moved on. Philosophically, he had come full circle and openly pondered the personal cost of his journey and the trappings of stardom in Jim Crow America:

> You don't know the agony of good clothes. Why, I envy the street laborer that can lay on the sidewalk and rest. I am supposed

to be a fashion plate, for the edification of my own race, but it's tough to be a stilted example of something that you know you are not.

What a delight it would be to get into my old Kansas clothes and go fishing. I long to be a plebian, for they are happier. I walk down Broadway and my own race look at me in envy, but if they only knew the discomfort of my royal raiment they would be satisfied to be as they are, it's awful to wear a collar on a hot day like this, but I have to do it, merely because I am a model of the "dickty" coon, and my bread and butter depends on my living up to this model.

If I strike a happy medium in dress, whereby I can be distinctive, and yet comfortable, in pure white linen for instance, I am supposed to be assuming the part of a black Chesterfield, and to many I become amusing. I am between the devil and the deep sea. I can't dress as a laborer, and I can't wear decent dress, because of criticism.

I used to think how great fame would be, especially for the colored man, but when you attain it, you find your attainment is merely an empty idealism. How I long for the old days in Kansas, and the real comforts that went with [a] poverty-stricken childhood, but I am a black man, who is carrying the black man's burden. It's so hard, because there is an equalizer in nature that makes things truly equal, but often I am dissatisfied. Those boys down on the Natchez Levee are now my ideal. Think of the comfort they enjoy. Rolling cotton on the Bob E. Lee, amid laughter and fun. Tired at night, they go home to Mandy or Priscilla, eat the evening meal, and retire early, so as to be up early to enjoy [another day's] work and fun. To them I am George Walker, the black Chesterfield; but in reality, I am merely a human being, who is striving and hoping that his work will meet the approval of men. I can't help being what I am, for I am a fatalist in belief as much as Omar Khayyam was. I am ignorant, from my own point of view, because there are professors holding chairs at Yale and Harvard, who can tell me the exact date that Cervantes was born, and why Cleopatra loved Marc Anthony, but I also know that the stilted little brain of Prof. Bugg knows its own power and confesses it to himself.

Therefore, I who am ignorant from the world's point of view, take an inventory of myself. I find that the Almighty gave me a superb physical strength, and the courage to fight an unequal battle, so I take advantage of my stock in trade. People may call me the various names that go with a Black man's heritage, and I must grin and bear it. There is no come[-]back, and I am glad there is not. I have the strength of my own ancestor, the gorilla, if Darwin is to be believed; but of what use is that strength when pride is broken[,] and judgment says to be wary of superior numbers. I've studied reincarnation and have seen the fact that what dominates me, might have once been dominated by me, and I am satisfied to take my medicine in an inverse ratio. The white man that lives out in the tropics will soon produce a race of dark, suntanned people. Running wild, against the cool winds, soon gets the lips chapped and thick in their progeny. The hair curls, because the sun absorbs the oil of the hair; and after a thousand years the white man presents to his own progeny, a race that has been kiln dried by an African sun, and yet are white inside.

Dear old Bobby Burns said, "A man is a man for a' that," and I hope so. It gets tiresome being the underdog all the time, but how can you help it, if we live under an inexorable fate? So, take me, good clothes and glittering teeth. I am what I am, because I can't help it.[12]

George's efforts to parlay the company's profitability into a permanent place in first-class theatres had taken its toll. He remained in limbo, with no access to the privileges of Whiteness and unable to return to the anonymity of earlier days. There was too much momentum to stop, and with a large cast and staff depending on him, quitting was not an option. However, before he could move on, he needed a rest, and there was only one place where he felt safe enough to recuperate, Lawrence.

Big Show in Lawrence

Following Pittsburgh, Nash refused three weeklong vaudeville engagements at $2,000 per week and made his way to Lawrence with Aida and her best friend, Maggie Davis, future wife of Jesse Shipp and longtime member of the chorus, to see the new family home.[13] They arrived on June 12 at noon to the usual fanfare, pomp, and circumstance: "There he comes! Get out of the way! I can't see him through you. Well, ain't he swell though? Say, they say those togs was made in London. Huh, I know the time when that fellow never had no London togs, he felt swell then if someone gave him a second-hand suit and a pair of old patent leathers. Shut up, I tell you, he ain't deaf. Gee-ee, just look at him."[14]

Figure 12.1. Nash Walker in his "Bon Bon Buddy" raiment. *Source: TSJ*, December 5, 1908, 7.

Nash was sporting his new, form-fitting, ice-cream-white suit à la "Bon Bon Buddy," sandals, and fine hosiery that inspired a trend among the men of Lawrence.[15] Despite the finery and excitement, Nash was in Lawrence to keep a low profile for ten days, recuperate from the stress of the previous two seasons, and put the finishing touches on "Abyssinio," the new house located at 401 Indiana Street. It was fitted with the finest modern accoutrements including a bathroom on the second floor with heavy porcelain appliances and custom furnishings from the Grand Rapids Furniture Company. The parlor featured a suite of solid mahogany, upholstered in heavy green and gold tapestry cloth, and also included a large rug and magnificent piano as well as two beautiful gray squares of Arabian needlework. The legs of the bespoke furniture sported a French, curved pattern as well. The dining room was fitted with solid, quarter-sawn, golden oak paneling, and the table and chairs were finished with a lighter stain. The basement housed the furnace and laundry along with extra storage space. The kitchen was small yet conveniently arranged, and the stairway was outfitted with smooth, dull brown oak. Valued at $5,000, the thoroughly modern home was fitted with gas and electric lights throughout for entertaining guests of the highest order. In the evenings, locals caught glimpses of Nash in a dark house suit as he tinkered and adjusted screens, lounged in the backyard, and ate oranges while seated on Mission furniture on the porch with friends.[16]

Feeling a little sentimental, Nash visited his old loafing spots during the day and chatted with the bootblacks on Massachusetts Street.[17] Aida's ability to speak French and Italian coupled with her frank honesty caused a bit of a stir. Described in the *Daily World* as "a vivacious little woman" with "something of the elasticity of her steps in her speech," she left an impression:

> Making herself quite at ease, she speaks with a broad inflection that savors of high life "across the pond." Her diamonds, of which she wears a profusion, are large and lustrous, the most conspicuous being the ear-rings—two great horse-shoe hoops of gold studded thick, each with ten or a dozen large stones.
>
> "We like to come here" said she, "because this is Mr. Walker's old home. We try to play here every year, but are terribly handicapped for want of room for our production. We can never get all our scenery on, and our people are cramped in the ensemble scenes."

Figure 12.2. "Abyssinio," 401 Indiana Street, Lawrence, Kansas, as it appeared in 2018. *Source:* Photo by the author.

"Nash" complained of the same thing, in a mild way. "I wish somebody would build a fine, new theater here," said he. "What is needed is a play-house that will seat more people, have a larger stage easier to reach, and be on the ground floor. I don't know how large it should be, but we could easily fill a house containing two thousand people in this town."[18]

On June 22, the night before they caught a train to Chicago to meet up with Bert to begin rehearsals, a party was given at the new house, and some fifty people crammed in, and supper was served at one o'clock in the morning.[19] Nash's grandmother, Sarah, likely did not participate in much of the celebration because she was suffering from dropsy—late-stage heart failure.

Bandanna Land

Although lavish, Williams and Walker's latest production, *Bandanna Land*, steered clear of the nationalism of the previous two vehicles, but the old spirit was still there, in a domestic sense. Further, the stateside theme gave voice to the newly mobile, technologically savvy Afro-American, who knew more about the reality of Black life in the American South, North, and West than Africa, a place they had been culturally separated from for hundreds of years. Unlike the previous vehicles, *Bandanna Land* attempted to address a fundamental hindrance to Black progress, the collective lack of wealth from land ownership. The title was inspired by stories from George's grandmother Sarah and her customary bandanna head covering, which was also a hallmark of minstrelsy. Kansas played a role in the development of the plot, and Nash went a step further and included the real names of Lawrencians in the play.[20] Moreover, he added Topeka-born Junius Mordecai (J. Mord.) Allen (1875 to 1953), a boilermaker and poet, as a dialect lyricist to replace the late Paul Laurence Dunbar. Allen had recently published *Rhymes, Tales and Rhymed Tales*, and Nash believed him to be a logical successor.[21]

Before rehearsals began, George gave an effervescent and optimistic speech to the company. Will Cook and Will Vodery drilled the thirty new chorus members with their usual flair. As soon as the opening numbers were secure, the remaining thirty were brought in to complete the musical numbers as Jesse Shipp completed the book with help from Alex Rogers.[22] On August 22, the company moved its base of operations to the Whitehead House, Asbury Park, New Jersey, where Bert and Lottie had registered two weeks earlier. Simultaneously, George's grandmother took a turn for the worse. She had been bedridden since the beginning of the month and asked for him, so he returned to Lawrence and stayed until August 25. By the time he returned, he still had not memorized the seven thousand words of dialogue for their debut in Red Bank, New Jersey, on August 30.

Sarah Hayden died on September 7, 1907, at home with Alice by her side. She was eighty-four years old, and her homegoing took place on September 15 at two o'clock at Warren Street Baptist Church before internment at Oak Hill Cemetery in Lawrence.[23] Although she never saw *Bandanna Land*, she was the inspiration that gave a new significance to the vehicle and likely strengthened George's resolve. While shrouded in farce, *Bandanna Land* brought the reality of double consciousness, personified on the stage, into the single consciousness of White America like never before. With a budget of $28,000 and a projected cast of sixty, it was nearly as extravagant as *Abyssinia*. As George told the *Lawrence Daily World*,

> "Bandanna Land" is to be written especially for the company, and will attempt to depict faithfully, and at the same time render as nearly classical as may be, the music and life of the Sunny South. Old familiar ballads will be taken largely as themes, and the various talents of the members of the company will be matched as nearly as may be with songs and dialogue to show them to advantage.
>
> We shall not be contented merely to present Southern Negro songs and characters. We are going to try to elevate that music, without losing any of its original charm, and show the wonderful possibilities that we believe are in it. In short, we are going to try to make the sweet, catchy songs of our ancestors as nearly classical as is possible.[24]

In keeping with the formula, the Southern setting was conspicuously free of White people, but still there was no love scene. Although George and Aida would eventually test the boundary of that prohibition, it remained a severe handicap. Also, in keeping with first-class tradition, Aida and Abbie Mitchell Cook appeared in specially curated features with no comedy. All told, the show required two sixty-foot baggage cars to transport the scenery designed by Carns, New York.[25]

As the plot went, old Zachariah Skunkton, a wealthy planter, had a trusty servant named Bowser who had a son whom he named Skunkton in honor of his beloved master. That so pleased the planter that he secretly placed $25,000 in a bank for the child to receive when he reached twenty-one. At that time, Skunkton Bowser (Bert) was a minstrel show roustabout and knew nothing until his childhood buddy, Bud Jenkins (George), told him of the fortune awaiting him in Georgia. In the first act—set in a Dixie dooryard with real chickens in a coop and in a smokehouse in North Georgia—the two down-on-their-luck roustabouts made their entrance. Between sections of banter, "Corn Song (Mandy Lou)," "Kinky," "Tain't Gwine to Be No Rain," "Exhortation," and "Until Then" were featured songs.

The second act took place at the Mount Zion Baptist Church fair fundraiser for brethren in foreign lands and sported elaborate scenery. There, Skunkton learned of his inheritance, and Bud promptly appointed himself guardian over Skunkton and his money. Further complicating matters was Mose Blackston (Jesse Shipp), a lawyer for the Trust Syndicate Co-operative Realty Company, who hatched a scheme to buy a large piece of property and establish a pleasure park for Colored folks, which Bud named "Bandanna Land" in memory of his grandmother's antebellum home. By that time, Bud was dressed to kill and loaded down with diamonds, while Skunkton dressed as usual and was drunk on applejack. In that scene, the leading ladies appeared: Lottie as an old maid of 1692; Abbie Mitchell Cook, who sang "Red, Red Rose"; and Aida, who sang "It's Hard to Love Somebody . . . ," accompanied by five male chorus members. Other featured songs were "Minuet," "When I Was Sweet Sixteen," "Just the Same," "Somewhere," and "Late Hours." George closed the second act with his hit song "Bon Bon Buddy." In the third act, the syndicate bought Amos Simmons's farm, and when a railroad company purchased half of it from them for $10,000, they built Bandanna Land. With the aid of unlimited gin, they made so much noise at their Negro jubilee that the railroad company agreed to buy the park at an exorbitant rate.

Still unable to secure first-class booking, *Bandanna Land* made its premier at the West End Casino, Asbury Park, New Jersey, on August 29, 1907. They traveled west through various towns playing one-night stands, until a weeklong engagement in Kansas City, where the West Side Social Club held a dance for about three hundred people in honor of the company at Vineyard Hall. While close to home, Nash made a quick trip to Lawrence to see his mother and to give his grandmother's grave a marble marker. Following additional dates in Kansas, the company made it to Lawrence, where a large contingent of Black folks lined up before sunrise to secure tickets, which were sold out before the end of the day.[26]

Figure 12.3. Still from act 2 of *Bandanna Land*. Source: *Leslie's Illustrated Weekly Newspaper*, April 23, 1908, 399.

Although bittersweet, Nash's fourth visit to Lawrence that year brought the same level of excitement as always. That night, the Bowersock took in a record $777 and was stuffed to capacity with an estimated eight hundred attending, many of whom stood through the entire performance. Nash and company did not disappoint, and his "Bon Bon Buddy" was recalled more than a dozen times. Following the performance there was a reception.[27] The *Journal* said,

> Nash Walker is growing fast. He has always been good when he made this town but Williams has had the advantage and reputation. People have thought that while Nash was good Williams was better. This year they were as evenly matched as a team could be. Each is strong in his particular part and probably neither could do the part of the other. They supplemented each other splendidly. Walker has grown wonderfully in the past few years. He has a naturalness that is becoming and a genius that is of a high order.[28]

Thus far, the White press had savored Williams and Walker's return to "real" Coonness, and some could barely contain their excitement. Even the critic for the *Lawrence Daily Journal* referred to the company's previous international offerings as "unnatural."[29] *The Topeka State Journal* declared, "This is said to be the best show in which these colored comedians ever appeared, physically because it is directly characteristic of the colored man. It is a Negro musical comedy—all that this implies—humor, comedy, songs and music."[30] *Variety* summed it up with an affirmation of Bert and George's skill at maneuvering the minefield of fickle White expectations: "If the purpose of Bandanna Land is to compromise upon 'picturesque' as between grotesque and serious, it works out splendidly."[31]

Now with the most visible platform for any Black woman in the United States, Aida introduced new dance sequences, beginning with "A Dream of the Orient," in Akron, in early October of 1907:

> In it [she] portrays the grace and stealth of the panther and the sinuous winding of a serpent. She steals on like the rattler, about to charm the jungle bird, warily and cautiously. Then she glides lightly around it and darts in at the prey. The dance is eerie and uncanny at first, then doleful, finally becoming spritely, until it ends in a climax of motion that is like the hurling, swirling

activity of a Soudan dervish. Miss Walker invented it herself, and some say it is far superior to the fire dance that made such a hit a few years ago.[32]

Despite a warm reception from critics, the show languished in small theatres, in which compromises and workarounds were constant. Lester Walton of the *New York Age* took Williams and Walker's management to task for failing to live up to their end of the contract: "In conformity with their contract Williams and Walker put together a show of the Broadway variety. They are, I understand, raising the price of admissions in the popular price houses; but what I want to see is that the Shubert, Comstock, et al., live up to their contract and give Williams and Walker the very best booking possible, as they meritoriously deserve."[33] Regardless, Williams and Walker's momentum began to return. George drove audiences wild with "Bon Bon Buddy" in a manner that had previously been Bert's exclusive domain. According to D. E. Tobias,

> Dress is Walker's stock in trade. It is a part of his method of making business. Walker believes in the modern American idea that the most successful businessmen in the country are the men who know how to advertise their business to advantage. Walker contends that clothes help to advertise his theatrical business. Many critics who have criticized Walker adversely on account of his flashy stage costumes and brilliant street clothes have helped to keep him before the public. Critics who have given Walker credit for his costumes and street dress have helped to keep him before the public. Williams and Walker have made a much closer study of the public than the public has made of them. The secret of their success is due to the fact that they are close students of the public and endeavor to keep the public thinking about and wanting to see them.[34]

In a similar fashion to his previous hit "Me an' da Minstrel Ban," George was able to channel his childhood experience as a busker, barker, and his grandmother's "Chocolate Drop" in "Bon Bon Buddy":

Verse I:

When I was a tiny pick
Say just 'bout so years old

The folks nick named me "Buddy"
That is so I have been told
I spend most of my younger days with gran'mom and
    gran'pop
And gran'ma used to always call me "Granny's chocolate drop"
Now "Chocolate drop" and "Buddy" seemed to stick to me
    somehow
Then someone added "Bon Bon"
So here's what they call me now

Chorus:

Bon Bon Buddy the chocolate drop
Dat's me
Bon Bon Buddy is all that I want to be
I've gained no fame but I ain't 'shame
I'm satisfied with my nick name
Bon Bon Buddy the chocolate drop
Dat's me

Verse II:

I think sometimes to myself
You was a lucky boy
To get a nice nick name
And then be grand'ma's pride and joy
There was one boy in our town, they called him ugly Will
There was another one I know they called him stubborn Phil
Then there was one called Dummy Smith
And one called Baby Blue
And they all used to tell me
Bud it's pretty soft for you[35]

    Of particular interest to many theatregoers was a special diamond set into a gold cap that was affixed to George's right incisor. Although most audience members did not notice it, some people in the first few rows were puzzled by the faint gleam coming from his famously white teeth.[36]
    An early highlight of the season was a five-week residency in Chicago that gave the company time to relax a bit. Despite a financial panic and a war in vaudeville, the city was electrified with enthusiasm, so much so

Figure 12.4. "Bon Bon Buddy, the Chocolate Drop," Words by Alex Rogers, music by Will Marion Cook, Gotham-Attucks Music Co., New York, 1907. *Source:* Author's collection.

that the *Chicago Tribune* suggested that the Great Northern be renovated to the size of the Auditorium to accommodate the scores of people who were turned away each night:

Mr. Walker wears the usual gorgeous raiment and is as skillful in his dancing and cake walking as ever, and wheedles Williams around just as neatly and likably as before. Mrs. Walker has a dance in the last act which is of elaborate character and which shows her in all her wonderful grace and neediness. It is a joy to watch her. Alex Rogers does a piece of character work as Amos that is in all respects masterly. There is not a look, movement, or vocal inflection that is not true to the life. All the other principles are just what they should be, and the performance is a true pleasure from start to finish.[37]

After closing in Chicago, the company had weeklong engagements in several cities before arriving in Pittsburgh for Christmas.[38] At the beginning of the engagement, George gave an interview with the *Pittsburgh Press* on the familiar subject of his fashion sense:

Riding on the streetcar the other day, two gentlemen, whose audible remarks I could not fail to hear, were arguing as to who I was.

One said to the other, "Who is that swell darky standing there? It must be Joe Gans [the boxer] or a race horse coon. Look at his face. Look at that flash on his hand. Gee whiz he is a swell darky."

And his friend said, "Why that's George Walker, of Williams & Walker. If you don't believe me, go over and ask him. I'll bet it's him."

The first almost immediately addressed me with the question, "Are you George Walker?" And I answered him, "Yes."

I should explain that it is not unusual for a white man to ask a darkey what would seem to be as rather personal questions, and I was not surprised at his next question, for I could see that he was interested.

"May I ask, why do you wear such flashy clothes and that large diamond ring?" And I told him that in many cases white people would not believe I was George Walker, if I did not wear them. The general public expect to see me as a flashy sort of a darkey and I do not disappoint them as far as appearance goes.

I do not wear these fancy clothes and diamonds alone because I can afford them, but wear them as a matter of business as well as personal pride or vanity, as you might call it. I admire nice clothes and I like to take pride in the wearing of them; but I do hope I don't create a false or haughty impression on anyone who sees me or with whom I come in contact.

My clothes are all created or built from my own ideas, by the best tailors in New York City. Why, I have stood from two or three hours more than once for the fitting of one suit, so that when it was finished it would fit perfectly.

Here we were all getting off the car and I was invited to have a drink by these gentlemen, so we repaired to a nearby café, where one of them said he had never drank with the nigger before; but would make this an exception.

"I thank you very much for the kind invitation," said I, "but I can only drink with you as a man and not an exception. This being agreeable, I offer the following:

> Right is right, if a man is a man,
> If human feeling is just the same,
> If you believe in that to the highest degree,
> It is a pleasure, I'll assure you, to drink with thee."[39]

Never one to squander a teachable moment, George took great risk in letting those men know that it was *he* who would have to make an exception to drink with them and that was something he had no desire to do. Although akin to other situations among White gentry, White men on the street were far less likely to see the humor in such a comment and could have responded with violence for which they were not likely to be held accountable.

Bandanna Land opened at the Shubert-owned Majestic Theatre in Manhattan on February 3, 1908. In honor of their opening on Broadway, Aida and George introduced their version of the wildly popular "Merry Widow" waltz at the close of the second act. Lester Walton gushed about the production and believed that George and Aida outdid their White counterparts who had been interpreting the dance since 1907:

> I forgot that I was on hand as a critic, and found myself enjoying the show as much as some of the fellow members of my race who insisted in making their presence known as well as themselves obnoxious to those seated near them by their unsuppressed laughter and merriment. . . . If you go to the New Amsterdam Theatre

and see the two principles dance the "Merry Widow Waltz" and then attend the Majestic Theatre and see Aida Overton Walker and her husband dance the same waltz, if you are fair, you will say that the colored performers have Miss [Ethel] Jackson and her partner "skinned a mile" (pardon slang).[40]

Although nearly every successful show in New York had jumped on the "Merry Widow" bandwagon, Franklin Fyles of the *Washington Post* described the difference between George and Aida's version of the waltz and that of the growing list of others:

> So why not the Negroes? This scene is in a moonlit garden, no less romantic than the Marsovian widow's in Paris. The sensuous strains are heard. Then an octoroon, gorgeous in mauve shaded like an orchid, dances into view. Presently, [George] Walker appears on a marble terrace. His extravagance of dress has reached its limits. His corseted figure is perfectly fitted with black evening clothes of the latest cut, but a lining of rose-colored satin shows as the tails flap. And his waistcoat is of [gold cloth]. Naturally, the black-and-tan lady is fascinated. She gives him a sort of Viennese high sign. He comes toward her with grace and elegance that would give credit to any of the fifty-seven varieties of Danilo. Then he seizes her by the neck and, gazing into each other's eyes, they swing through the slow waltz. But when they reappear, instead of repeating the Viennese languor of the original, they rag it. The waltz becomes the syncopated cake walk, and thus one more variation is added to the "Merry Widow" epidemic.[41]

At the close of the second act on opening night in New York, Bert and George were given ten encores and returned until they were too exhausted to dance. Despite being labeled a "failure" by the *Standard Union*, the show was so well-received that the final curtain fell well after eleven o'clock that night.[42] Although Bert's new ballad, "Late Hours," scored well, it did not get the same reception as "Nobody." However, his new pantomime routine that was based on a mentally ill man whom he observed in a Lincoln, Nebraska, hospital in October of 1906 was so masterful that he was called upon to repeat it for the rest of his life.[43] As a testament to their success on opening night, George received a letter from Robert Motts (1861 to

Figure 12.5a and 12.5b. "The Merry Widow Waltz Performed by Negroes, Mrs. Ada Overton Walker and Mr. George Walker in the Famous Dance," *The Sketch*, April 1, 1908. *Source:* Author's collection.

1911), who requested an immediate infusion of female chorus members for the Black-owned Pekin Theatre in Chicago.[44]

Bandanna Land had the trajectory to be the biggest hit from Williams and Walker to date. Producer F. Ray Comstock was "exhibiting a smile almost as large as the boyish promoter himself" as he stood in the box office every night watching people crowd into the theatre.[45] Shortly after the opening, Booker T. Washington tried to see a few minutes of the show anonymously before making his way to his hotel but caused such a stir when he took his seat that Bert and George stopped the show and sent an aide to find the source of the commotion. Once it was determined that Dr. Washington was in the house, they offered him a box, but he declined and later said, "I greatly appreciated the heartiness and sincerity of their welcome." By the third week on Broadway, cast members brought their trunks and personal effects to the theatre in expectation of an extended run.[46]

On February 13, 1908, the multiracial Thirteen Club gave a dinner at the Harlem Casino Café, where they pondered "Is Race Prejudice a Form of Superstition?" with no Afro-American representation. Incensed by the omission, George fired off a missive that was published in the Lawrence *Daily Gazette*, *New-York Tribune*, the New York *Evening Post*, and *New York American* so the club could not deny its existence or their choice to discuss racism without including any representation from the group of people who were the major sufferers from it: "Gentlemen, please explain how it came to pass, that your learned society failed to invite a representative of my race to speak at your dinner. Is it possible that you have members who are seeking to emancipate themselves from superstition, and yet they failed to be broad enough to ask a man of African blood in his veins to be present and take part in your deliberations."[47] Clearly out of frustration, George had become less apologetic for pointing out certain inaccuracies and inequities of life as a high-functioning, second-class citizen. However, he knew better than anyone that a meeting of "model minorities" had more of a performative goal in mind than bringing actual change. So, to save them time, he systematically dismantled the topic to bring the omitted aspects of the issue to light.

In late February of 1908, Meyer "Bim the Button Man" Bimberg (1862 to 1908) announced plans to erect a theatre for Williams and Walker on the south side of Sixth Avenue at Forty-Third Street: "I have bought the plot and have plans drawn[.] The report is true and the theatre will be built. There is a great chance for a New York playhouse for colored folk, and it will make money."[48] How George met Bim the Button Man and developed the idea is unknown. When F. Ray Comstock was asked to verify the rumor, he reportedly did so with a wink. As there was no other option, it was to be a Jim Crow theatre, with the gallery reserved for Whites and the balcony for Blacks. Nevertheless, as an independent Black-owned theatre, it would have been free to engage anyone at a price determined by the management and not a syndicate controlled by fear of reprisal from racist patrons.[49] In anticipation of the deal, George entered into negotiations with Albert Pickering of the Tivoli Theatre in Cape Town, South Africa, to bring in a chorus of singing Zulu warriors of the Sheba tribe, under the leadership of Chief Atwanaguambu. With the memory of the Dahomey Village still in mind, George planned to acclimate the men to the climate and the rigors of Black life in the United States in a traditional kraal (village) on Long Island during the coming summer in anticipation of regular work in the fall. Unfortunately, Meyer Bimberg died on March 25, 1908, from tonsillitis, and George's second attempt to buy a theatre faded along with him.[50]

On March 22, George and D. E. Tobias visited an ailing Ernest Hogan at the state sanitorium in Rutland, Massachusetts, where he was attempting to recover from advanced tuberculosis. Although he had been managing his illness for some time, Hogan was unable to perform at the Globe Theatre in Boston during the first week of January in *Oyster Man* and had been in the sanitarium ever since. Looking for relief from his own ailments related to advanced syphilis, Bob Cole had been in regular correspondence with Hogan, who shared his new habit of sleeping outside at night, believing the cold night air was therapeutic. Cole decided to put Hogan's advice to the test at a hotel in Bay City, Michigan, known locally as the "Icehouse," and requested an unheated room. That night, the temperature dropped to twenty degrees below zero. Despite a large stockpile of blankets, the following morning, Cole discovered that one of his ears was frozen. He was so dejected by his experiment that he reportedly fined two of his cast members for mentioning it.[51] It was an ominous sign of things to come.

As *Bandanna Land* surpassed all previous vehicles in popularity, it drew elite White patronage, including the Vanderbilts, Huntingtons, and opera star Mme. Luisa Tetrazzini, accompanied by theatre owner and producer Oscar Hammerstein, former New York Governor P. B. S. Pinchback, and famed tenor Enrico Caruso.[52] Surely the most satisfying high-profile patron of the Broadway run was Abraham Erlanger, whose presence in one of the Majestic's boxes underscored George's belief that a Black production could find, repeat, and sustain success on "The Great White Way." Williams and Walker's popularity among White thespians was no secret, but some of the admiration from White colleagues contained notions of their implied supremacy. Eventually, a special, discount matinee was scheduled on March 28 for White performers who wanted to see the show but couldn't because they too were working during the performances.[53]

On March 31, 1908, Williams and Walker celebrated their seventh week at the Majestic and their sixteenth year of partnership. To mark the occasion, a poll was taken among the cast members and theatregoers to determine what songs from past productions should be reprised in place of the third act. The night of the show, Bert and George entered wearing linen dusters and tall hats. Then, twirling light bamboo canes, they began the refrain of an unnamed song from *Policy Players* and did some buck dancing. Next came Aida's "Why Adam Sinned," followed by Bert's rendition of "A Ghost of a Coon" and George's revival of "The Leader of the Ball." The celebration closed with solos from J. F. Mores and J. Leubrie Hill as well as a rendition of "Dora Dean" by Bert, George, and the chorus. Too ill to attend, Ernest Hogan sent a congratulatory telegram: "Sixteen years ago, I tried to open your eyes to the great future of the Negro actor. I am glad you have taken advantage of [my] advice, because no other Negro artists can claim such a glorious record you have all to be proud of. The credit is yours and you have sixteen more of very hard work before you. May God give you strength and perpetuate the great work you have done. God bless you both.—Ernest Hogan."[54] Bert and George were showered with violets and roses from the gallery, and the augmented show was so popular that it was repeated on April 2. Shortly after, the company celebrated their seventy-fifth performance at the Majestic. The company earned $10,000 by the fifth week of the run, and more than ninety-three thousand people saw the show.[55]

Toward the end of their unprecedented four-month run at the Majestic, George presented to Aida a string of forty pearls valued at $325 each, in honor of their tenth wedding anniversary. Aida was ecstatic—that is, until a few days later, when she removed it from her satchel and placed it on her dressing room table for a few minutes. When she stood to report to makeup for the first act, she noticed it "wriggle like a snake," and "in a bound[,] she cleared the door of her dressing room and ran screaming across the stage." Trying to understand the situation, George picked the pearls up off the floor, placed them on the table, and waited for signs of unnatural life. Just as before, "the rope of pearls began to crawl and wriggle, and one side of the door easing went out with George Walker in his indescribable flight." Without a satisfactory explanation for what had just occurred, no one from the company would venture into that dressing room for the rest of the night. Eventually George convinced a stage doorman to capture the jewel snake. Once done, George put it in a box and tied it with rope and wire before securing it in a trunk. The next day, he and Aida returned the necklace to the jeweler on Broadway. So full of anxiety to relieve themselves of the piece, they accepted the first offer from the store's manager and left with a $6,300 check and a loss of $6,700. Later, the jeweler explained that Aida's dressing room table was directly over a radiator, and as the heat warmed up the wire that the pearls were strung on, it expanded, and that made the pearls appear as though they were moving on their own. The movement was exacerbated by periodic gusts of cold air from the stage that caused further movement from contraction. The necklace was later resold to one of the richest brides in the country before she sailed to her new castle home in Europe.[56]

Shortly after the hundredth performance of *Bandanna Land* on April 16, 1908, which included engraved brass hand mirrors as a door prize, it closed on Broadway and moved across the river to Brooklyn, then to houses in Connecticut. Fitted with new uniforms, the baseball team played a four-inning game against a pickup team from Dublin, Connecticut, in Bartlett's lot in front of two hundred people, and tied 6 to 6. Then, the company moved to Cincinnati and Philadelphia, where the highest-priced tickets were sold for one dollar, although it was a first-class house. Bert was relieved because he could visit Lottie, who permanently left the company a few weeks before the Broadway run due to an undisclosed illness. While in town, the baseball team played a game at Union Park on May 15 before the company returned to Brooklyn for the final week of the season. The company was initially booked throughout New England for weeklong engagements and in popular-priced vaudeville houses in Washington, DC; Baltimore; and Atlantic City, but they were canceled. The baseball team played another match against the Colored Vaudevillians at the Bronx Oval at 166th Street and Boulevard Avenue. The Vaudevillians prevailed 7 to 6, but the game was so hotly contested that on the following Tuesday when Bert and Bob Slater, manager for the Vaudevillians, met unexpectedly at the Gotham Attucks office, each agreed to put up a hundred-dollar wager on a rematch, which likely never happened.[57]

At season's end, George organized a vaudeville act called "Williams and Walker's Bon Bon Buddies" that included George Williams, Henry Troy, Andrew A. Copeland, and Jennie and Muriel Ringgold. The new act made its first appearance at Young's Pier, Atlantic City, on Decoration Day in the hopes of refining it for a possible four-week tour of Cuba. Harrison Stewart was also sent into vaudeville with a company of ten, and the Glee Club went to Keith's in Boston and Philadelphia for two weeks at each theatre. At the end of the Glee Club's engagement, they were replaced by Eugene King (d. 1911) and Leo Bailey (ca. 1889 to 1955), "The Williams and Walker Fresh Kids," formerly of Sissieretta Jones's company. They were likely intended to be the next Avery and Hart and began working with older Williams and Walker material.[58] Bert and George entered a vaudeville contract with Percy G. Williams and performed the skit "The Guardian and the Heir." Their schedule, arranged by Lykens and Levy, included their first appearance in Harlem in three years. Their large salaries prompted *The Nashville Globe* to declare, "At $2,000 per week. My! 'Real Coons' come high in the East!"[59] Although vaudeville theatres were third-rate or discount houses, Bert and George made a killing because the act was mostly older material reworked for the throngs who could not or would not go to see them in first- or second-class houses. Had they been content with vaudeville and smaller houses with fewer actors, their take would have been exponentially more than what they usually earned.

Amid rumors of a possible return to London in July of 1908, the close of the season marked some changes in the company, most notably the exit of Ada Guiguesse; her husband, Sterling Rex; and multi-instrumentalist and composer Joe Jordan. Abbie Mitchell Cook was permanently replaced by Minnie Brown, who took on the part of Angelina Diggs, formerly played by Ada Guiguesse, who replaced Lottie Williams.[60] Back in New York, Aida organized a gala benefit for the White Rose Industrial Association Home for Colored Working Girls at Grand Central Palace on June 3 that netted $500. It was largely a revue of the current Williams and Walker material, and the officer's list was a who's who of Black society in New York, including Jack and Grace Nail, Lillian Marshall, and, ironically, Hattie McIntosh, who was caught in a compromising position with George in Chicago nearly two years earlier.[61]

Ernest Hogan had recently relocated to a New Jersey health resort, where he lived in a four-room cottage with his mother, and a gala benefit was organized for him at the West End Theatre on June 21 that took in $600. Several White stars offered to appear, including George Cohan, Lew Fields, Sam Bernard, Eva Tanguay, and Edna Wallace Hopper. However, that aggregation paled in comparison to Hogan's Black colleagues, who came in droves to show their respect: Williams and Walker; Cole and Johnson; S. H. Dudley; John Rucker; "Jolly" John Larkins; Bobby and May Kemp; Joe and Sadie Britain; Tom Brown, Hogan's first partner; George Cooper;

Bill "Bojangles" Robinson; and others. According to Lester Walton, Bert and George took the house by storm and "George Walker, in a neat white suit, almost floated on air." Aida sang "Bill Simmons' Sister" in a beautiful gown before a quartet composed of Bert, George, Bob Cole, and Rosamond Johnson sang the first line of Henry Wadsworth Longfellow's "I Stood on the Bridge at Midnight," and it was "a howling success."[62] In recognition of Hogan's declining health, the outpouring of support and affection from colleagues and fans highlighted his importance and ultimately his irreplaceability within the Black thespian elite. With him off the road, there was one less successful Black company to further the cause of Black artistic liberty and cultural sovereignty. Despite the bleak forecast, the 1907 to 1908 season was the company's most successful yet, and the absence of Black talent in vaudeville left a void for Avery and Hart to become the highest paid Black act on the circuit during the following season.[63]

Chapter 13

Who's Leavin' Who?

1908 to 1909

Feelin' Froggish

Amid more struggle over booking suitable venues for the company, Nash left Manhattan for Lawrence on July 7, 1908, to spend his thirty-sixth birthday with his mother before her summer vacation in Colorado. Aida went to Lakewood, New Jersey, likely to visit family and recuperate from the seasonal grind.[1] Shortly before he departed, he fulfilled one of his lifelong goals with the establishment of the Frogs at his home at 52 West 133rd Street. Named in honor of Aristophanes's play and Aesop's fable, the newly established Afro-American fraternal organization of elite thespians, businessmen, and musicians was poised to facilitate great things within the American cultural sphere. Although George had promoted the idea for a few years, its philosophical tie to the ancient "father of comedy" came from founding members Bob Cole and Lester Walton:

> The "Frogs" have been formed for social, historical and library purposes with a view to promoting social intercourse between the representative members of the Negro theatrical profession and to those connected directly or indirectly with art, literature, music, scientific and liberal professions and the patrons of arts; for the creation of a library relating to especially to the history of the Negro, and the record of all worthy achievements and the

collection and preservation of all folklore, whether that of song or terpsichorean originality, of pictures and bills of the plays in which the Negro has participated.²

To mark the occasion and establish a tradition, the first annual Frolic of the Frogs was scheduled for August 17, 1908, at the Manhattan Casino, at Eighth Avenue and 155th Street.³ However, the founders had to argue the validity of their name and mission in the state supreme court because the presiding judge, Justice John W. Goff, misunderstood the link between their stated purpose and name: "The accomplishment, or even the effort to accomplish this scheme of aesthetic magnificence is to be highly commended. But the corporate name selected is so incongruous that I hesitate to cement the connection between the sublime and the ridiculous."⁴

Undeterred, the Frogs met at Reisenweber's Cafe, on Fifty-Eighth Street and Eighth Avenue in Columbus Circle, on the day of the unfortunate ruling. They pooled their money and gave it to the Nail and Parker real estate firm to acquire a ten-room, $14,000 clubhouse, or "Frog Pond," at 111 West 132nd Street. Simultaneously, *The New York Age* and other New York papers made a case for the Frogs, calling Goff out by name. On August 11, Justice Goff sent a letter to Lester Walton to express his surprise that anyone would think his ruling was outside the rule of law, which only strengthened the resolve of the Frogs and sympathetic members of the press.⁵

While Nash was recuperating in Lawrence, Shipp and Cook drilled the chorus on the stage of the Majestic Theatre beginning July 15, for the opening in Atlantic City on August 3, 1908. As the Williams and Walker company was usually the last to close and the first to open, the coming season was projected to be even more successful than the previous, opening the possibility of another, second company and profits that would allow Williams and Walker to finally buy a theatre of their own outright.⁶

While on Massachusetts Street in Lawrence on the morning of July 13, 1908, Nash was asked about retirement, and he told the *Daily Journal*, "I would hate to be idle. I want a play that will get at the real heart of the people more and I am going to have it. That's what I want to do before I retire." Later that morning he made his way to Topeka, likely to visit with J. Mord. Allen, who was visiting his parents. Nash believed that Allen was the best dialect writer available and that his talent was essential to fulfil his desire of producing the kind of play he spoke about in the *Journal*.⁷

On his thirty-sixth birthday, Nash published the essay "The Fly in the Ointment" in the Lawrence *Daily World*, lamenting the lack of a grand theatre in his hometown:

But why, oh why is there always a fly in the ointment? Why must a thing be almost what you would have it be? Is Tantalus never to be blessed with a flood? Don't you guess what I mean? I am talking about Lawrence's theatre. I am vexed because when I talk to my professional friends, I must use much care in boosting my hometown. Because when I give tongue to my pride in Lawrence, I am usually reminded of its playhouse—and I do not like to feel that my feathers must fall peacock-like. Sarcasms about Lawrence make me, temporarily, an "undesirable citizen."

> If they only had a theatre at my home,
> Gee. But 'twould be a joy to me to come
> And bring our troupe to make a show.
> And tell them, "Yes, my home, you know,"
> If they only had a theatre at my home.
> If they only had a theatre at my home.
> For one, I'll help to boost a Bowersock boom.
> More—if 'twill help, I'll not refuse to come and once more shine his shoes
> If he'll only build a theatre at my home.
> George W. Walker
> "Nash"[8]

That evening, there was a party at his mother's home, and Nash sang "Bon Bon Buddy," which took on a special meaning considering the almost autobiographical nature of the song and that it was sung among people who had known him since childhood as well as J. Mord. Allen. The following day, he left for New York to prepare for the coming season, slated to begin with *Bandanna Land* and end with a new vehicle, *Near the Nile*. His patience worn thin, George's new mantra was "Either first-class houses or tents."[9]

Bandanna Land opened on August 3, 1908, at the Savoy, a first-class house in Atlantic City. The production's cast was banqueted every night by the local Black population. Next was Baltimore for another week, where the company played a baseball game against the Annapolis Grays at the Bartlett-Hayward Athletic Association's grounds. There was supposed to be an engagement at the Belasco, a restricted theatre in Washington, DC, but, wisely, it was canceled, and the company moved to the Grand, in New York, for two weeks, where Bert introduced a new smash hit song, "Right Church, but the Wrong Pew." George offered "Any Old Place in Yankee Land Is Good Enough for Me" at the end of the first act, and Aida scored with "The Sheath Gown in Darktown." At the start of the second week, Aida debuted her "Vision of Salome" dance, and shortly after, George introduced a new white suit for "Bon Bon Buddy."[10]

The first Frolic of the Frogs was the gala event of the season and included attendees from the South and West who were on their way to the Negro Business League meeting in Baltimore. Female patrons were given green pendants with "Frogs" spelled out in large white letters. It was the largest reported crowd for an event at the Casino, and they took full advantage of an ideal summer night. As reported by Frog Lester Walton,

> It was about 10:15 Monday evening when the white citizens began to wonder what was doing in the Bronx. About that time the "L" trains and the Eighth Avenue service line became exclusive property of the colored population, and every car bound for the casino suggested that there was considerable "Jim Crowing" being done. We, as a race, are not averse to being in cars together, especially on such meetings as last Monday, but we don't like the idea of thinking we have to do certain things just because we are colored, and in this land of the brave and the free.[11]

From then until two o'clock in the morning, a line of attendees waited to make their entrance. There was supposed to be a short program from the female chorus of the Williams and Walker and Cole and Johnson companies, but after three o'clock people continued to pour in, and the performance was scrapped. Lester Walton further observed that "it was way past dawn, and the sun was already doing duty. That many of the men went directly to work in their Sunday best goes without saying."[12] It is likely that a pair of photographs of the founding members of the organization were made that night. Seen in their tuxedos and matching sashes, the Frogs were the epitome of style, and their mission was clear. However, like Bob Cole, George had begun to show signs of mental and physical instability. In one of the two published photographs, one can see J. Rosamond Johnson steadying George's left leg as he slumped in his chair with a vacant look on his face, and in the other photograph a compensating George looks to have forced his smile. Shortly after the Frolic, applications for membership poured in, but new membership was closed, possibly due to George's condition and the demands of the coming season.[13]

Figure 13.1. The Frogs I. *Top, left to right:* Bob Cole, Lester Walton, Sam Corker Jr., Bert Williams, James Reese Europe, Alex Rogers; *bottom*: Tom Brown, J. Rosamond Johnson, George Walker, Jesse Shipp, Cecil Mack. *Source: The New York Age*, December 24, 1908, 12.

A Vision of Salome on the Road to Dayton

At the start of the 1908 to 1909 season, there were at least seven dancer-actresses presenting their version of Salome's dance in New York, including Eva Tanguay, Isadora Duncan, Gertrude Hoffman, La Sylph, and Vera Olcott. Although it had worn out its welcome among critics, it continued to be very popular with audiences, and Aida naturally decided to present her own interpretation following the removal of the "Merry Widow Waltz" from the show. Due to the disbandment of Ernest Hogan's *Oyster Man* company, Muriel Ringgold resigned and took over Aida's speaking parts, so she was free to leave the entrapment of "comedienne" and become the artist that she truly was.[14] To not offend White sensibilities with Black sexuality, Aida was clad in a skintight, flesh-colored bodysuit with only her head, hands, and feet exposed as she danced to Joe Jordan's music. At the rise of

Figure 13.2. The Frogs II. *Source:* Photo by White Studio ©Photographs and Prints Division, Schomburg Center for Research in Black Culture, New York Public Library. Used with permission.

the curtain, Salome reviewed the banquet hall, where the music possessed her, culminating with the presentation of the head of John the Baptist.[15] According to Lester Walton, "Miss Walker should be congratulated on her desire to make 'Salome' a cleaner dance and void of suggestiveness, but in doing so she gives a version that is mild in comparison with Gertrude Hoffman, La Sylph and others; for some of these dancers at times remind one of a burlesque show—yet they say this is the original interpretation of 'Salome.' "[16]

Performing in artistic handcuffs, Aida's performance inspired some anxiety in Walton, because he knew that most White critics would judge her conservative offering without considering the context. However, her strength was in her originality and, without a touch of lewdness, Aida's "Vision of Salome" was a subdued yet artistic triumph.[17] Not to be outdone, Bert introduced his interpretation of the dance with a watermelon substituted for the head of John the Baptist at the Hyperion Theatre in New Haven.

Next came several one-nighters, ending in Fall River, where the company baseball team played the local police department on the afternoon of their performance. As reported in *The Fall River Daily Globe*, "Spokesman Perry says the police would shock the community with the beating they have corked up for the colored artists." Although Jesse Shipp Jr. (1881 to 1922) struck out eleven, the thespians lost 7 to 6, once again due to unforced errors. In Boston, they fell to the Washington Athletic Club 8 to 3 in front of a thousand spectators but defeated the Hotel Touraine team 11 to 10 in an exciting game on the American League grounds.[18]

For the four-week residency at the Shubert-managed Orpheum in Boston, George was assured that premium seats were to be offered at $1.50, but, upon their arrival, some of the best seats in the house were going for one dollar. Because the show was doing well, he agreed to let it stand if a correction was made at the next Shubert-controlled house. Nevertheless, he relayed his frustration to Lester Walton, who wrote,

> As George Walker admits, it is, indeed, a difficult task to convince the white managers that a colored show should play to first-class prices, despite the fact that Williams and Walker are considered one of the strongest drawing cards in the show business. Then, after the managers are convinced, they do not act accordingly.
>
> With the large and expensive show Williams and Walker are carrying it is utterly impossible for them to make the money to which they are entitled unless they play to first-class prices. As they are getting a first-class musical show they should get value received for the goods they are producing.[19]

During the run, Bert jokingly informed the local press that he and George had radical plans for the coming season, including starting a new kind of show where they both played in whiteface, Bert appearing as a Dutchman and George as an Irishman.[20] Early in the residency, the *Globe* noted, "'Bon Bon Buddy,' sung by George W. Walker is whistled and hummed by nearly every auditor as they go home." When *Bandanna Land* entered its fourth week, the theatre was still at or near capacity every night.[21] Underneath it all, the show's success was marred by growing signs of George's deteriorating health. Effie King Wilson (1888 to 1944), one of the "Bon Bon Buddy" girls, noticed that George began singing in a "thick-lipped manner, drowning out the lyrics." Believing it was an improvised gag, the chorus all smiled until they learned that something was very wrong. Although George's uncharacteristic behavior presented as a stroke, the truth was far less socially acceptable: he was suffering from late-stage syphilis, both common and incurable at the time. Often terminal, the disease would wreak havoc on the Black thespian community in the coming years with devastating results. In the meantime, the situation was kept private and the company operated as normal.²²

October 1, 1908, marked the private celebration of Bert and George's partnership with a field day. An intercompany baseball game was played between the Right Church team, captained by Bert, who trounced the Buddies, captained by George (nonparticipating), by a score of 17 to 6. A fifty-yard dash, potato race, fat woman's race, standing and running broad jump, and other events took place with two-dollar prizes for the winners. The next night, the company reprised their sixteenth anniversary performance, and all female attendees were given a door prize, likely leftover hand mirrors from their Broadway run. Following the performance, the stage was cleared, and a long table was set up for a banquet, courtesy of Bert and George. Their final week in Boston saw a return of the "Merry Widow" waltz as a feature for George and Aida, possibly because it was familiar, she could lead, and it was nonspeaking.²³

After Boston, George fell into a deep depression. Bert took charge of physically and emotionally preparing him for each performance, which worked for a time—with diminishing returns. However, when left alone, George became despondent, and it sometimes took the combined effort of Bert and Jack Shoemaker to bring him out of his sorrow. Nevertheless, the tour made its way to several Eastern cities before a weeklong residence in Brooklyn.²⁴ While the company was in New York, acro-dancer Sherman

Figure 13.3. "The Last Williams and Walker Company—'Bandannaland'—Field Day, Boston, Oct. 1, 1908." *Source:* Tom Fletcher, *100 Years of the Negro in Show Business* (Burdge, 1954), 234.

Coates (1872 to 1912) of the Watermelon Trust was sought out as a possible understudy for George. It was an unprecedented move for the company and another sign of George's eroding ability to maintain the Herculean effort that he had sustained for nearly two decades. To most of the White public, Bert *was* the show and George was simply a setup man, but Bert required unconditional trust in his partner to be successful in front of a variegated audience night after night. The dynamic interplay that Bert and George had developed since 1892 could not be duplicated with just one of the two partners and a stand-in. In any event, Coates was not added to the cast, and neither was Dan Avery nor Leo Bailey, who scored with "Bon Bon Buddy" in vaudeville that season and was described by Lester Walton as "George Walker, No. 2."[25] As far as Bert was concerned, it was George or nothing: "From the day we became partners we were never separated, he never had any difficulty of opinion, and no harsh or unkind words ever were passed between us. When George became ill, I knew I could never even think of securing anyone to take his place."[26] Bert's expressed loyalty aside, it is also possible that George's ego did not allow the reality of his illness to dictate what he was going to do and when. Moreover, who had the ability and cunning to maintain the business operations in his absence? Reportedly Bert, Aida, and Jack Shoemaker suggested the inevitability of institutionalizing him, but he refused, believing he could finish the season. To complicate matters, Aida's mother, Pauline, was ailing as well.[27]

Despite George's declining health, the reviews indicated that the show was as popular as ever. The company's engagement in Brooklyn seems to have gone off without a hitch, and the theatre was filled nearly to capacity every night. Although it was known only by a select few, George was confined to his hotel room when not on stage and was in no condition to speak to press or management. Next, the company played several one-dollar houses beginning in Trenton, culminating in Pittsburgh, where they performed for a week. The local Black population enthusiastically crowded the balcony, but the gallery was sparse on opening night, so management allowed Black access to the lower balcony.[28] It was a small victory, but many of the Black patrons felt that Bert and George should have spoken up on their behalf. As lamented in *The Freeman*, "this, it will be seen, is indeed a plaintive tale, and seemingly bodes ill for the future of the team through no direct fault of their own. The white people simply will not tolerate the black brother in their midst on the lower floor of these $1.50 houses even if the colored people were able or inclined to separate themselves from that amount to see a show."[29]

Following the Pittsburgh engagement, they moved to Toledo for a week and St. Louis for three weeks, under strenuous protest from Dan Fishell, the resident manager. However, the first week was a record setter.[30] By the beginning of their third and final week, the *Post-Dispatch* boasted that the night of November 29 was their twenty-second performance at capacity, but *The Freeman* reported that the show was "several thousand dollars to the bad on the season," likely due to the amount of one-nighters in dollar houses and George's loosening control. Next came more one-nighters in Missouri and Kansas, ending in Lawrence.[31] In a piece titled "Hi Nash," the *Daily Journal* declared, "It is a pleasure to welcome such a man back to Lawrence. He has done a man's work in the world and done it in a man's way. Here's to you, Nash, and may you always be happy, may you always be very happy."[32] The *Daily World* also published a respectful salutation for Nash's homecoming:

> Nash Walker, with his happy smile and many diamonds, was in Lawrence today for his annual visit and will show at the opera house tonight. Nash was pleased to see everyone and said that he wouldn't miss his annual visit to Lawrence for all the rest of the dates during the year put together. Quite the delegation of his friends were down to the train to greet him and he will have a busy time of it during his short stay in Lawrence.[33]

Although enthusiasm was high, attendance did not measure up to previous engagements, likely because few Black patrons could not afford the higher, $1.50 ticket price. Topeka followed, where the audience "fought for admission."[34] *The Topeka State Journal* recalled, "The house was filled to capacity. The doors were opened at 7 o'clock. A dozen officers were stationed at the gallery alone, but the crowd surged in so fast that the doors were broken from their hinges. And when it comes to noise and applause whether called for or not, you have to give it to a colored audience. Williams and Walker pleased the crowd, and the white people never restrained their applause. Curtain calls were numerous."[35] The tour then moved through the Midwest, spending Christmas and New Year's week at the Shubert in Kansas City. The unusual booking inspired the *Kansas City Globe* to question the upgrade: "Williams and Walker [are] at Shubert next week for [the] first time. Many people [are] surprised at this peculiar innovation. The audiences will be quite dark. Wonder why they didn't go as usual to the Grand, perhaps [the] proper place for what is called a 'nigger show.' "[36]

Nash and Aida may have spent Christmas with his mother in Lawrence, but no mention was made in the local papers. Alice had not seen her son since they performed in Lawrence, about two weeks prior, and surely recognized his declining health more clearly than others who were with him daily. She decided to join the tour for the coming engagement in Chicago, perhaps to help him deal with his advancing illness.

On Christmas Eve, several editorials from Black actors were published in *The New York Age* including a reprint of Aida's "Opportunities the Stage Offers Intelligent and Talented Women" and a retrospective from George titled "Bert and Me and Them," possibly with the help of Veronica Adams in Chicago:

> Our payroll is about $2,300 a week. Do you know what that means? Take your pencils and figure out how many families could be supported comfortably on that. Then look at all the talent, the many-sided talent, we are employing and encouraging. Add to this what we contribute to maintain understanding of the race in the estimation of the lighter majority. Now, do you see us in the light of a race institution? That is what we aspire to be, and if we ever attain our ambition I earnestly hope and honestly believe that our children, that are to be, will say a good word in there day for "Bert and me and them."[37]

The turn of the year to 1909 brought the company back to the Great Northern in Chicago, where they settled in for a five-week run. Bert was especially happy because he could see Lottie, who was confined to her bed in Provident Hospital. As usual, the show was well-received, and with a lot of help George compensated for his deteriorating mental and physical health. According to the *Chicago Tribune*, "the smiling Walker still makes much of his 'Bon Bon Buddy, the Chocolate Drop,' calling the full company to his assistance in a well built up finale."[38] Constance Skinner of the *Chicago American* remarked that when she saw the show on opening night, it was "crowded to the roof," with some obnoxiously enthusiastic Black patrons in attendance: "It was an audience composed largely of the sort of people who clap noisily every time their favorite [character] opens his mouth. They make so much noise themselves that neither they nor anyone else can hear half the lines."[39] Skinner also noted that the scenery looked worn and that George's part had been reduced to feeding Bert's dialogue and singing "Bon Bon Buddy." The stars were onstage together for less time than in the past, and, more importantly, George's performance of "Bon Bon Buddy" utilized the entire cast. The dash and go was gone, and, for the first time, a bit of dust had settled on the act. Skinner knew something was wrong. Likewise, *The New York Age* noted that members of the company had stopped sending progress reports of the tour several weeks earlier, likely due to a gag order.[40]

As if on cue, under the moniker of "America's Greatest Colored Stage Critic," a noticeably agitated Sylvester Russell, who had yet to see the play, took aim at George, Lester Walton, and the Frogs: "Everything is classed. The effect to actors is somewhat confusing and their hunger is not appeased by theorist critics which new[ly] developed newspapers with stage pages have brought into play. The establishment of an exclusive actors' club by certain well-to-do actors and the installation of a young dramatic editor in their ranks who is not in their class financially, but there to do their bidding, is but an effort to control the press."[41] Likening the group to a "pleasure society," Russell believed the guiding principles of the Frogs were just a veneer that covered a less attractive reality that lacked substance underneath. He then questioned George's ambition to secure a lasting presence in first-class theatres, believing that it had distorted his perception of the larger picture for Black people who were outside of his circle of elites:

> If Mr. Walker, who is at the head of this movement, insists on fostering the issue in advance of general sentiment and universal approval, he will not only establish a feeling between theatre patrons of the two races, which would cause many of the best element of each race to stay away from the show rather than be subject to a feeling of consort by humiliation, but would ultimately weaken the patronage of the big colored shows. As far as the name of "first-class theatre" is concerned, the difference is so small as to be unworthy of a fostered contest by Mr. Walker just for the benefit of the vanity of Williams and Walker to establish a personal precedent.

As far as Russell was concerned, his thinking was in line with Booker T. Washington. It was too much, too fast, and therefore self-serving, given the mixed results.

On Monday, January 11, 1909, George, Aida, and their mothers had a midnight supper at Lett's Hotel to celebrate Alice's fifty-second birthday.[42] Shortly after, Veronica Adams published an interview with George titled "The Dramatic Stage as an Upbuilder of the Race" in *The Inter Ocean*. It contains a refined version of the ideas he had expressed in the earlier "Bert and Me and Them" that turned out to be his final public statement on Black cultural sovereignty: "We want our folks, the Negroes to like us. Over and above the money and the prestige is a love for the race. We feel that [to] a degree we represent the race, and every hair's breath [sic] of achievement we make is to its credit. For first last and all the time we are Negroes. We know it, the race knows it, and the public knows it and we want them to keep knowing it."[43] By the third week in Chicago, George was singing "Down Among the Sugar Cane," a new song that was supposed to carry over to the next production, *Near the Nile*.[44] Bert also introduced "Drinking" in place of "Late Hours," which scored a hit among Black patrons. *The Chicago Eagle* reported, "Last Saturday night, where the balcony wore a variegated aspect, the comedian got the laughter started and after he had kept them going for ten minutes one dusky belle called out from the balcony, 'Oh, yo' Mistah Williams, if yo' don't stop dat monkey business I'se gwine roll right down outen dis gallery on somebody's haid.' "[45]

Although they continued to score big, the company was struggling. On January 21, *The New York Age* reported that several cast members including Bert, Alex Rogers, and L. H. Saulsbury were ill with throat trouble. Jesse Shipp was said to be absent from several performances due to rheumatism, Mazie Bush was recovering from appendicitis surgery, and Maggie Davis had been out ill as well. There was no mention of George other than that he was slated to lead the grand march at the Actor's Ball at the Colosseum on January 28 and that he and Bert were going to make an appearance at an "Old Fashioned Party" at the Chateau. By the final week of the engagement, public demand for the show was so high that the *Broad Ax* joked about the theatre removing the orchestra pit to make room for fifty more seats. On February 2, Alice returned to Lawrence.[46] That night, millionaire John Borden bought out the entire theatre for $5,000 so the company could make a "command performance" at his home at 89 Bellevue Place at Lake Shore Drive for fifty guests including the Spanish noble Ricardo Soriano and his wife, María Italia Blair Mitchell. When supper concluded at ten o'clock, an aggregation of thirty-five actors and twenty orchestra members performed in the ballroom. According to the *Chicago Tribune*, "the first intimation the Borden neighbors had of anything out of the ordinary was when the colored girls merrily tripped out of the machines and dived under the canopy across the sidewalk. . . . From the time the curtain arose the action was quick. Dusky damsels from the Williams and Walker show did some buck and wing dancing and singing and delighted everyone present."[47]

The hastily built stage rocked to and fro as Aida sang "Kinky," assisted by several "Kinky Girls," and Bert brought the house down with "Nobody." Bert and George filled much of the time with stock material, and George's "Bon Bon Buddy" made a hit with María Italia Blair Mitchell.[48] Sylvester Russell summed the situation up as only he could: "Williams and Walker's appearance before the King was for honors; for the Vanderbilts it was for money, but for Mrs. Borden, of Chicago it came by force."[49] Following the pomp, circumstance, and pageantry, the company closed on February 6 with a show that was almost entirely new, save George's ever-shrinking contribution. The next stop for the company was at the Park Theatre, Indianapolis, for three nights. Pauline was so ill that Aida took her back to Manhattan and Susie Simmons took Aida's place. As such, Aida's specialty numbers, "Maori" and "A Sheath Gown in Darktown," were cut, and the show was now noticeably shorter.[50] Aida's absence also called upon Bert and Green Tapley to take on more responsibility for George's care. For the first time in many years, Williams and Walker had no answer for the challenges in front of them, and the company began to unravel.

The return to Indianapolis also allowed Sylvester Russell to revisit old grudges and the truth as he saw it: an educated guess based on limited information and inference. When combined with his arrogance, he often went too far, but he could be counted on to deliver the straight dope as he wagged his paternalistic finger at George:

> George Walker must not again attempt to foster the issue nor assume that he has won the future victory which his new managers will later assure him, but he must let them, alone, have the credit. The contention of the Shuberts for the placing of Williams & Walker was only a part of the fight in war with Klaw & Erlanger leading toward their dethronement. It will be time enough for Williams & Walker to play all first-class theatres after the Shuberts win the fight, and it will then be one or perhaps two seasons before either Williams & Walker, Cole & Johnson, or, perhaps, Ernest Hogan, will be ready.[51]

Although he was correct, Russell's ignorance of the seriousness of the situation was apparent. Neither Bob Cole, Ernest Hogan, nor George Walker had two years to wait.

On February 12, 1909, the Grand Dress Ball was announced for the Bermuda Club at Convention Hall in Kansas City to be held on March 29. It was to be led by Bert in his first appearance without George since

1892.⁵² Between Indianapolis and the Dayton engagements, the company took a short hiatus while Bert rushed George back to Manhattan to see a doctor. By that time, he was hoarse, regularly forgot his lines, and his coordination was all but gone. More importantly, he had grown disturbingly reliant on Bert for his emotional stability. As reported in the *Dayton Herald*, "while in New York he visited a throat specialist, who informed him that he would have to discontinue singing, as his throat was in a bad condition. As he does a great deal of singing throughout the play, this preyed upon Walker's mind, who frequently remarked to Bert Williams that he feared he was a drawback to him."⁵³

George's anxiety may have been exacerbated by his decades-old insecurity about his voice, the likely reason why he never recorded after "Pretty Desdemone" in 1906. Also, he may have followed the lead of his friend and former musical director H. T. Burleigh, who disliked the fidelity of early recordings.⁵⁴ By that time, he was no longer involved with the day-to-day operations of the company, the closest thing he had to an offspring. Nevertheless, the company opened at the National Theatre, Dayton, for three days on February 15, 1909. When Bert, George, and Jack Shoemaker visited the theatre, the treasurer noticed George's "peculiar actions" and that he was never without the company of Bert or Jack.⁵⁵ Despite his condition, George made it through the first two nights, but on the third night he visibly struggled to remember his lines and had to be prompted by Bert. As a matter of course, audiences were in the habit of waiting for Bert, not George, so the redacted show dragged uncharacteristically. George's primary responsibility was to facilitate the fast pace of the show, and without that the formula lost its appeal.

After the performance George was a "nervous wreck." He desperately wanted to finish the season, but the reality was unavoidable; his mind and body had failed him. That night, the decision was made to place George in a sanitarium due to "incipient insanity." Bert escorted him back to Manhattan, and a telegram was sent to his mother that told her to expect him soon.⁵⁶ The next day, *The New York Age* announced that George had temporarily retired and Aida was to assume his trademark "Bon Bon Buddy" feature:

> Owing to overwork, George W. Walker of the Williams and Walker company, contemplates taking a lay-off within a few weeks, and will probably enjoy a vacation of two or three months at Mount Clemens, Michigan. His attending physician states that after a much-needed rest he will be able to attend the rehearsals of Williams and Walker's new show in the summer.

It is probable that he will leave the "Bandanna Land" company at Louisville, Kentucky, at the end of next week's engagement.

Aida Overton Walker has been in New York city for several days, having arrived here the latter part of last week from Indianapolis, accompanied by her mother, Mme. Pauline Reed, who is wardrobe mistress of the "Bandanna Land" company. Mme. Reed has been ill for several days, and it was thought that a vacation in New York would do her good. While here Miss Walker has been having a costume made for the "Bon Bon Buddy" song which she will sing when George W. Walker leaves the company for a vacation of several months.[57]

Simultaneously, a letter from Tapley was published in several Lawrence newspapers:

Dayton, Ohio, February 17, 1909.

Editor of the Journal,

Lawrence, Kansas,

Dear Sir:—I thought it might be news that Mr. Walker will be in Lawrence about the 24th. His nervous system is in a rather bad way and his physician has prescribed three weeks of absolute rest. Rest and Lawrence seem to be synonymous with him, wherefore the prodigal son. But—and this is one main excuse for this letter—the doctors say that his friends in Lawrence must not kill any fatted calves. Not till he gets well. Just now his resting can't be made too soothing and the best thing his friends can do for him will be to contribute to his solitude.

Of course, when he gets well—but Lawrence ought to know "Nash" by now. Hoping your paper will make the prescribed rest fortissimo,

I am, yours truly,

G. H. Tapley,

Secretary to Williams and Walker.[58]

The company laid off in Dayton and then moved to Louisville for a week at the Masonic Theatre, slated to begin on February 22, 1909. The news of George's illness prompted a lot of speculation in New York. *The Freeman* tried to quell the rumor mill by distancing the company's recent time in Indianapolis from any discord: "It is being rumored that George Walker of Williams and Walker is suffering from overwork. It may be so, but his work on the stage in Indianapolis, so far as the audience knew, showed no trace of it. Walker was right there, good and proper, the Beau Brummell of the stage, doing the neatest turns known to the art."[59] In fact, the report may have glossed over the truth because of the editor Knox's friendship with George. On the same day, Sylvester Russell published a not-so-thinly-veiled poem about George and Aida:

> Big headed know it all,
> Golly how he kin dance;
> Wifey's ragtime thrills the hall,
> Cuter than Clarice Vance[60]

When reached for comment, Bert was widely quoted as saying,

> George has been acting in a peculiar manner for some time. It has been necessary for me to repeat his cues for him, and even at times whisper his lines, as he will completely forget them. Before leaving New York[,] a throat specialist told George that he would have to discontinue singing, as his throat is in bad condition. This has preyed upon his mind, as he believed that he was losing his prestige as a comedian. George was a studious actor. He studied his part, his audiences and himself. He tried at all times to remain a high-class comedian. He'll be alright soon.[61]

Unfortunately, Bert's reference to George in the past tense further fueled rumors about the demise of Williams and Walker and the formation of a super company composed of S. H. Dudley (1872 to 1940), Cole and Johnson, Williams and Walker, and Ernest Hogan. Will Cook tried to quash the rumors and asserted that George could be found at his home resting, but when reporters called, George and Aida had already departed for the Louisville engagement.[62] The next day, Alice also tried to quell rumors in Lawrence: "I'm expecting Nash on any train. He wired me that he would be in this evening [February 24]. The report that the show has broken up is entirely false. His wife, Aida Overton Walker, will sing 'Bon Bon Buddy,' and one of the men of the company will take his part in the rest of the play until Nash is better. He is just worn out and needs rest, that is all there is to it."[63] *The Jeffersonian Gazette* and other Lawrence papers also tempered the rumors by adding a note of caution: "Lawrence is Walker's home, and if there is any truth in the statement, his friends here know nothing about it, or if they do know anything they are not putting it out for publication. Walker has hundreds of friends here, who will hope that the report is unfounded, and that he will continue to delight his hundreds of friends, as he has done in years past."[64]

Figure 13.4. "Aida Overton Walker in Male Attire Singing 'Bon Bon Buddy.'" Source: *New York Age*, March 18, 1909, 6.

Figure 13.5. "Miss Walker as Salome." *Source: New York Age*, August 8, 1912, 6.

To make up for his gaffe, Bert told a reporter from *Billboard* that George's "crisis" was temporary and had passed before he left for Lawrence, where he was expected to rest to prevent a second, possibly more severe attack.[65] Through it all, attendance records were broken in Louisville, where Alex Rogers performed George's speaking parts in the first act and Jesse Shipp handled the second. Aida's "Bon Bon Buddy" provided a unique contrast with her Salome feature, and she was recalled ten times. According to Chappie, Bert's valet, "when she dressed up like George and sang 'Bon Bon Buddy, the Chocolate Drop,' she almost made you forget her husband."[66] Nash was due in Lawrence to wait for space at the St. Joseph Sanitarium in Mount Clemens, Michigan, possibly recommended by the Shubert brothers, who sent their father, David, to the nearby Madea Hotel and Mineral Baths for treatment in early 1909. Also, Bert vacationed there with Al and Mamie Anderson in July of 1897.[67] For Bert, it was heartbreaking, and his initial response signaled precisely what was to come. Chappie recalled, "The night [George] left the show he came up to Bert and said: 'Well, Bert, I'm going to leave you.' Williams almost cried, turned around and said: 'No, you're not. I'm going to leave you.' Then he shuffled on the stage and went into his act. It was the most pathetic thing I ever saw."[68] With the weight of the world on his shoulders, George put on a brave face and watched Jesse, Alex, and Aida perform his role from a reserved seat.

Return of the Favorite Son

On the morning of February 25, 1909, at a quarter past six o'clock, Nash and Tapley boarded the Union Pacific train to Lawrence for what was reported at the time to be a three-week rest in anticipation of a full recovery.[69] The following day, the *Lawrence Daily World* published a statement from Nash:

> It's great to get back in Kansas and this fresh air again. I feel better already. There's nothing the matter with me except that I am worn out and need a rest. The papers have made a lot of bugaboo over it, but I'll be alright again in a few weeks.
>
> No, there'll be no duck hunting or anything like that for me. I want to rest, just sleep and loaf, sleep and loaf and visit with my friends until I am in good shape again. I want to see all my old friends again and will do lots of visiting before I go back to work.
>
> I've got to join the company again at the end of three weeks at Philadelphia. You know we're under Shubert management now. For the next three weeks we are to play at theatres owned by the Shubert people, so they could not kick on the contract, if I was not able to appear.
>
> Mr. Comstock, knowing how badly I needed rest, very kindly gave me the opportunity to slip back to my old Kansas home and rest up. And you can just know I am going to do it before I have to get into the ropes again in Philadelphia.[70]

Although the situation was much more severe than he let on, it was vitally important to continue the ruse so that the small gains he made would not be summarily scattered to the wind. Tapley continued to deflect rumors in a telegram to *The Freeman*: "It is true that Mr. Walker's health is in an impaired condition. This is the result of overworked nerves, and his physician has prescribed a three weeks' rest, which he is going to take. He wants it understood that there is nothing alarming in Mr. Walker's condition."[71] Langston Hughes recalled that his mother, Carrie, had supper at "Abyssinio," where they "ate from plates with gold edging," during that trip.[72] While the company opened in Cincinnati, he did his best to be the "Nash" of old and was seen riding about town in the best Stanhope coach available, wearing a checked suit with pearl waistcoat buttons, dove-colored spats, and gray derby. *The Kansas City Times* described the scene:

> The bootblacks forget their patrons to run to the windows to see him drive-by, while the gong in the Eldridge house rings in vain, for the bellboys and porters are all engaged in watching for the comedian. Nash's secretary, who is not given to somber clothing, accompanies the actor on his drives. The bootblacks hardly dare to hope to rise to "Nash's" dignity. They'd be mighty glad to be his secretary. While Nash is resting here, about all the secretary has to do is to hold the horse while his employer stops in at the stores and offices along Massachusetts Street to see the men whose shoes he used to shine.[73]

On one of his outings, Nash spoke with a reporter at the *Daily World* about staging a comeback via a revival of *Corinda* (*Clorindy*), to be staged by Spiro and Martin's Black Serenaders at the Hill Opera House in Petaluma, California, in mid-July of 1909. He still owned the rights to the production, and it was a logical move to generate income. However, other than the name, the production was more of a traditional minstrel show that bore no remembrance to the original. Although intended to be a ten-week tour, it closed after a few engagements in northern California.[74]

As reports on the company trickled in, the news was bittersweet. It was still a big draw without him, but the members of the theatrical press who never cared for George were quick to dismiss his fundamental importance to Williams and Walker's success: "the absence of Walker is no serious handicap to the show, which amuses in its usual way."[75] Likewise, Aida's new responsibilities inspired "Dorothy," the writer for *The Freeman*'s "Women and Their Interests" column, to take a jab at George in a piece titled "Women and Overwork":

> One so seldom fears of a woman giving up any position on account of overwork. It seems that her capacity for work is immeasurable. When she becomes tired she works anyway. When a man begins to feel badly he generally puts out the fashionable report that he is overworked and goes in for repairs. George Walker, the famous comedian, is overworked, and his wife, Aida Overton, takes his part (new lines to suit her having been written) and a new costume for the "Bon Bon Buddy" song. Isn't this one point of proof[?] Mrs. Walker has worked just as hard, we are sure, as her husband, but she is overworked and she goes on taking up his work and responsibilities.[76]

As with George, Aida's contribution to the company had yet to reach its full potential, and she did not receive recognition for all that she did. However, the truth was far more nuanced, as would become painfully apparent during the following, final season of the Williams and Walker Company.

As Nash convalesced, his outings continued to be a spectacle, and the town fathers hurried through the city primary business so they could get a glimpse of him when he was downtown on March 4, 1909.[77] When he made his way to the various newsrooms in town, he tried to project optimism, vitality, and action:

> He has a regular routine mapped out for himself which he follows rigidly. He arises quite early and takes a two mile walk out in the country. Then he comes back[,] opens his mail and attends to business. There is a good deal of this too, and Nash has his private secretary with him. Every day Nash receives a detailed account of his company, what business they have been doing and other valuable information about them. Then he spends the rest of the day riding about town or just taking life easy.[78]

When the company opened in Philadelphia on March 8, Aida was a hit. The *Enquirer* declared, "Success was the more complete in that her appearance was unexpected to the large audience, unaware of Walker's serious illness." Although George knew better than anyone that his hope of rejoining the cast in Philadelphia was unrealistic, he had to say something to counteract reports that he had been "placed in a New York sanitarium, in a demented condition."[79]

As he convalesced during the spring of 1909, Nash may have renewed his relationship with his father. A report from the *Colorado Statesman* suggested that the younger Walker was scheduled to give the address "The Negro as I Find Him" at the twenty-fourth anniversary of the Colorado African Colonization Company at Shorter African Methodist Episcopal Church on March 11, 1909, in Denver. Whether it was a mistake, speculative boasting, or simply wishful thinking, he did not attend. On that day, he and Tapley were in Topeka as the guests of Mr. and Mrs. J. M. Wright.[80] Shortly before they left Lawrence for Manhattan, Tapley sang at the meeting of the Colored Literary Society of Lawrence on March 14 and put on a recital at Alice's home. That day, Nash received a heartbreaking letter that stated Bert was "lost without his side partner," and that the company wished him well. The following evening, Nash and Tapley left Lawrence, touting a return to the cast in Brooklyn.[81]

Once *Bandanna Land* made it back to New York, critics began to note that, despite the show's continued popularity, George's absence could not be ignored. As Lester Walton reported, "in several of the scenes where George Walker has been particularly effective there was a pathetic suggestiveness that made you long for the other member of the team. The two comedians have worked so long and so successfully together it would be unnatural for the public to look for one without the other—at least at this time."[82] The *Brooklyn Citizen*: "George has been ill for some weeks now, and it is pretty safe to say that every member of the company will be glad when he returns. He was always just surfeited with exhilarating spirits of the infectious kind, which affected every member of the colored organization, and which sent the show along with the snap and vim that it lacks now."[83]

The day Nash left Lawrence, he told the *Daily World*, "I feel much better. This touch of Kansas air has done wonders for me, and mother has made a well man out of me." However, the reporter saw through the facade and did not share his optimism: "In spite of all his confidence however[,] Walker did not look any too strong and his friends here will watch the reports with interest to see how he bears up under the strain of his work."[84] He was now fighting two battles, one to maintain control of his business and livelihood and another with his own deteriorating mind and body. Fortunately, most in the press continued to support the idea that his retirement was only temporary, despite overwhelming evidence to the contrary. George and Tapley made it to New York on March 20 and, after he telegrammed his mother, immediately saw to the company's business, which had changed significantly during their absence.[85] Theatrical agents and managers circled like buzzards and waited for season's end. *The New York Age* reported: "Vaudeville managers are already making Bert Williams' life a serious one. Both of the large booking houses are desirous of knowing when 'Bandanna Land' will close, as they are making the well-known comedian flattering offers that are in four figures. One of the strangest incidents occurred a few days ago when a theatrical manager asked him if he wanted to star in a white show. We would not like to see such an arrangement."[86]

Privately, everyone in the business knew that George was finished, and it was only a matter of time until he could no longer agitate and leverage Bert's loyalty and star power to transcend the Jim Crow prescription. Bert was vulnerable for the first time since Williams and Walker entered the scene, and there was no answer for what was likely to come. Without George's steadying hand, the company's season ended as he prepared to enter Homeland Sanitorium, a twenty-bed facility in Lakewood, New Jersey. Because Aida had ties to that town, it is possible that she made the arrangements when she was in New York shortly after her mother took ill. If George did check into Homeland early on, it is likely that he moved to St. James Hall in the Pines Hospital, another private sanitorium in Lakewood, shortly after. That facility was run by Mother M. Virginia, formerly of the Sisters of St. Joseph, who ran the sanatorium in Mount Clemens, Michigan.[87]

On April 3, 1909, *Bandanna Land* closed for the season at the Yorkville Theatre, Manhattan. George was not present, but he wrote a letter that was read aloud to the company, expressing his regrets and his hope for a prosperous summer. When Bert was asked to speak, he said that his one wish was to open the next season with his partner by his side. Citing the loss of Gussie L. Davis (1863 to 1899), one of the first successful ragtime composers, to a "nervous breakdown [that] proved fatal," Juli Jones of *The Freeman* offered perspective on George's prognosis and inevitable loss. Inadvertently, it provided a rare glimpse into the private conversations in theatrical and journalistic circles about George's morality and lifestyle:

> Mr. Walker's case makes the old saying true, "There's Beautiful flowers and trees growing on many sleeping volcanoes." Mr. Walker hid his troubles under a sweet smile, but mother nature took her course, and Mr. Walker has taken advantage of the beginning and will conquer his slight attack easily. For he is a young man, when you look over the field of colored actors that have broken down from overwork in trying to raise the Negro

to a higher position in their chosen profession, yet to be seriously criticized by their friends, saying that [sexual] dissipation was the cause, without one ounce of truth to verify their talk.[88]

It was a harbinger of things to come as well as the major reason that the accomplishments of the vanguard generation of Black actors who were born after emancipation was so fleeting. Nevertheless, Aida put on a brave face and prepared to take several chorus members into vaudeville.[89]

Exit Ernest Hogan

Although initial reports from the beginning of the season sounded optimistic, Ernest Hogan's tuberculosis progressed rapidly, and he was moved to a farm in New Jersey and his family was summoned in early August of 1908. By December, he relocated to the Bronx with his mother and niece and was reportedly continuing to write and compose.[90] By early March he was on the decline: "Ernest Hogan had a bad spell last week at his home, 1002 Brook Ave., New York City. Poor Ernest is bad off, and there is no need of trying to keep it covered. His friends who wish to see him alive had better visit him as his condition is now real serious."[91] *The New York Age* reported that he rallied for a short time but took a turn for the worse in mid-April. It is likely that George visited him when he made his return to New York, but no mention was made in the press. Conscious to the end and almost as though he were waiting for the close of the season so his closest friends could attend his funeral, Ernest Hogan died on the morning of Thursday, May 20, 1909. Bert, Alex Rogers, Charles Hart, Bob Cole, and Rosamond Johnson were pallbearers at the New York funeral service at the Church of St. Benedict, the Moor. For them, he was like an older brother who was free with his advice and always willing to collaborate as they collectively found their way. His remains were sent to Bowling Green, Kentucky, for burial in the Crowdus family plot.

George remained in Lakewood and could not attend Hogan's service. As he struggled to keep the company together, he planned to work on lyrics with J. Mord. Allen over the summer months while Aida and Bert worked independently, she with Williams and Walker cast members and he as a solo act for the first time.[92] Unfortunately, George's absence allowed a longstanding philosophical rift between Aida and Bert to metastasize into a cancer within the Williams and Walker organization during the spring and summer of 1909. Unlike Aida, Bert was willing to accept a lot of money in exchange for the destruction of the company and near total isolation that came with White control, what *they* saw as "integration." Aida's power flowed largely through George, and without him she was likely seen as just another replaceable contract player by management. Bert was now the only partner of sound mind and body and was inundated with new powers and responsibilities that he never wanted or knew how to handle. It was George's ship, and without him, it was rudderless and sinking. One by one, longtime cast members began to leave.

Chapter 14

You Never Miss the Water . . .

1909 to 1911

The Frogs met during the first week of May 1909 to plan the second Frolic at the Manhattan Casino. It is unknown whether George was present, although he made weekly visits to Manhattan throughout the summer to generate income through the Williams and Walker brand. As such, Jesse and Cordelia Mitchell had an act called *The Creole Black Prince* and presented "Bon Bon Buddy" for a short time. Williams and Walker's *Chocolate Drops with King and Bailey* had been a strong draw since its inception and had steady work in vaudeville in Canada and the West on the Sullivan and Considine circuit; it was planned to continue on the Morris circuit in the coming season. The Glee Club was engaged as well, while Cecil Mack converted part of the second act of *Bandanna Land* into a vaudeville turn called *The Lime Kiln Club*, which debuted during the first week of June.[1]

Aida began the offseason with rehearsals in preparation for an extended summer of vaudeville, beginning with a benefit for the St. Philip's Parish Home at the Grand Central Palace, Manhattan. Next, she took her "Eight Bandanna Girls" on the road and performed the sensational dance "Africque—the Kara Kara."[2] As things continued to slip farther from George's grasp, he tried in vain to address some issues with Jack Shoemaker that resulted from a bidding war between the William Morris and Victor United booking agencies to engage Bert as a solo act in vaudeville. Eventually Bert signed with the Keith-Proctor group and opened at Keith's Boston on May 9, 1909, as the headliner at $1,000 a week for seven weeks.[3] Despite the windfall, Bert was anxious and depressed and initially refused to perform

"Nobody," but his valet, Chappie, snuck the score into the conductor's papers. As Chappie recalled, "Well, when they heard 'Nobody,' the crowd went wild, and Bert had a cinch after that. He was mighty grateful, all right."[4] Just before he opened in New York, Bert disclosed to *Variety* that he alone would lead the company in the following season and that he didn't expect to work with George again for at least a year, emphasizing, "When my old pal is alright, we will be together again." He then performed at Hammerstein's, Pittsburgh, Detroit, and then returned to Manhattan, just before the Frolic.[5]

The second Frolic of the Frogs took place on the evening of June 14, 1909, at the Manhattan Casino. Blessed with good weather, attendance was high and bested the previous year "by an eyelash." Although Lester Walton left early, dancing went on until well after dawn. Bert was unable to attend because he was working at Shea's Theatre, Buffalo, and George was not present either. Shortly thereafter, he was moved from Lakehurst, New Jersey, to the St. Joseph Sanitarium in Mount Clemens, Michigan, which ultimately separated him from what remained of the Williams and Walker company. With his demise clearly in sight, management opted to simply wait him out. They already had Bert, the only *thing* of value to them.[6]

The Big Smokescreen

Shipp and Rogers delayed working on the script for the new show until June when "one of New York's most famous physicians settled the matter" on George's fitness to perform. With George officially out of the cast, J. Mord. Allen was excised from the new production, *Big Smoke*.[7] By then newspapers had compared George's plight to other actors, including John McCullough, William J. Scanlan, and Maurice Barrymore, all of whom struggled with syphilitic madness. Simultaneously, the press for Bert's solo act actively distanced him from George, now referred to as his "former partner." As described in the *Detroit Free Press*, "Bert Williams is the man who made the name of Williams and Walker famous in every city on this continent. He has always been recognized as the brains and talent of the team." However, Bert was not doing well. He drank heavily to compensate for the stress of his isolation and became cross with other Black people. While engaged in Detroit, he got behind the wheel of a car while inebriated and "ran over every living thing inside of a block." He was let off with a ten-dollar fine and immediately returned to New York to begin rehearsals for what was to be the final Williams and Walker show.[8]

Early on, the new show looked like any other Williams and Walker production, minus George, now relegated to a two-season retirement. Rosamond Johnson was tasked with the score, and Aida was expected to assume her usual role with a largely new supporting cast. Sheerly out of desperation, George was rumored to be in talks with Avery and Hart to resume their roles as the head of a second company. However, it was no secret that neither Avery nor Hart enjoyed living in Bert and George's shadow, so a deal never materialized despite their being billed as "Williams and Walker's successors" later that summer.[9] Ever industrious, George tried again to find suitable leads for the second company shortly after his relocation to Mount Clemens. He enlisted the help of Arthur "Strut" Payne (1878 to 1937) to make a special trip to Detroit to visit Harry Fiddler (1872 to 1942) and Byron Shelton (1879 to 1963), who were in *Hotel Laughland* at the Temple Theatre. According to Lester Walton, "Fiddler and Shelton entertained the visitors at dinner, and afterward the quartet took a long walk. The comedian was very talkative, and his condition appeared to be very much improved."[10] Walton's loyalty to George all but invited attacks from Sylvester Russell, who was still largely out of the loop, but the truth had been known for months. George wasn't going to restart his career with a revival of *Clorindy* because his condition hadn't improved, and saying otherwise made Walton more of a press agent than a journalist. Nevertheless, Russell tempered his column with a show of respect for his longtime adversary:

> George W. Walker's illness at this particular hour is of much moment and regret of concern to all, and the anxiety which now rests upon his wife, his partner, his elder family, and especially his associated company, is not well to imagine. Mr. Walker's present malady, although in a light form, calls for long retired rest, as even the mildest cases of mental relaxation must always linger and wait the exactions of a tired brain; so we hope and trust and even pray for his eventual recovery.[11]

Ominously, by the start of rehearsals for the new show on July 15, 1909, Aida had not signed a contract. It is likely that she was negotiating for a full partnership or to act as one in place of George to keep Williams and Walker from becoming a hollow shell. Despite the moderate success of her recent sojourn in vaudeville, rumors of her signing with Hurtig and Seamon as head of a new production of Ernest Hogan's *The Oyster Man* or going abroad to Vienna, Austria, with her Bandanna Girls had begun to spread. Two days later, the news broke: after ten years with the company, she would not return to Williams and Walker. Around July 20, George returned to Manhattan with "Strut" Payne to try to pull things together, but the chasm between Bert and Aida was too large to span. For the first time in his professional life, George Walker's legendary persistence and skill at "arguing" paid no dividends.[12] With the promise of three features, one in each act, in anticipation of her going out with her own company during the following season, Aida signed with Cole and Johnson's *Red Moon* company as their leading lady to perform alongside Abbie Mitchell Cook and Sam Lucas. Immediately after, George was sent to a St. Joseph–affiliated hospital in Far Rockaway, Long Island, with a scheduled return to Lawrence for the month of August, but that never happened.[13]

On July 31, 1909, *Big Smoke* was renamed *Mr. Lode of Koal*, and rehearsals were held at the Bijou Theatre in Manhattan under Jesse Shipp's direction. Jesse did not appear onstage, and with Lottie Grady (1887 to 1970) performing Aida's part, the final Williams and Walker show bore only a slim resemblance to the productions of old. The chorus of forty-six was full of new faces because several of the company's veterans took advantage of their association with Williams and Walker to establish themselves as solo acts.[14] Alex Rogers's character Buggsy was at the heart of the action and set the pace, playing a large role in generating laughs from the audience and providing a foil for Bert's character. The plot followed the model of the company's previous offerings but existed entirely in the realm of fantasy on the mythical island nation of Koal, ruled by King Big Smoke. Chester A. Lode (Bert) had been marooned on the island, just in time to take the place of the real king, who had been kidnapped by some political bandits. Soon after, he was introduced to the populace as the new ruler, while his sponsors subjected him to ingenious and tyrannical persecution. At the close of the first act, Chester was served a luscious sleep-compelling fruit that was reserved exclusively for the king. The second act featured his fruit-enhanced dream, showing him feasting and dancing while introducing the picturesque songs "Dance of the Veiled Mugs," "In Far Off Mandalay," "The Lament," and "The Harbor of Lost Dreams." In the third and final act, the sham ruler awoke, the real King Big Smoke returned, and Chester was condemned to be the janitor in the basement of the palace.

As opening night approached, problems that George normally handled went unaddressed, and Dan Fishell, manager of the Garrick Theatre in St. Louis, tried again to block the engagement. Despite reassurances from management and the record-setting performance there during the previous season, Fishell remained obstinate.[15] Without George in his traditional role and given Bert's deferment to management, who regularly chose convenience

Figure 14.1. *Mr. Lode of Koal Song Album*, Will Rossiter Music Publisher, Chicago, 1909. *Source:* Archeophone Records and estate of Howard Urick.

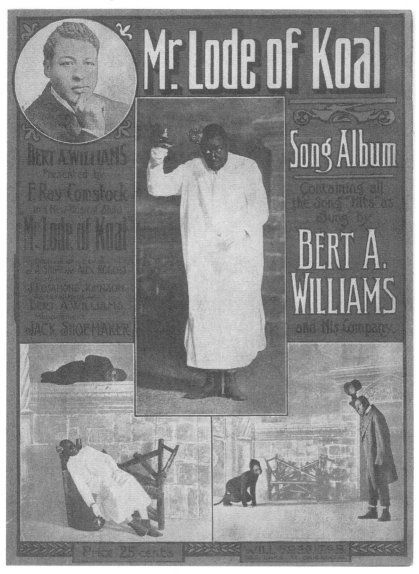

over maintaining the company's integrity, the status quo quickly eroded the gains Williams and Walker had made over the previous decade. Regardless, *Bert and Them* traveled to Toledo and opened at the Casino Theatre for a weeklong engagement on August 29, 1909. Next came the Garrick, where it was well-known that they were neither wanted nor welcome.[16] Regardless, they did well at least in part due to the absence of George. As declared by W. Bob Holland of the *St. Louis Post Dispatch*, "Bert A. Williams appeared at the Garrick last night without his former partner, Walker. The 'big fellow' is as funny as ever, and if the absence of his partner was noticed, it was an agreeable change to many who found Walker's style of humor at times offensive."[17] Subsequently, Bert was billed as "formerly of Williams and Walker" as the company toured throughout the Midwest.[18] Despite boasts of his independence, Bert did not rise to the occasion. Abbie Mitchell Cook recalled,

> When George [took ill] and [Bert] got into this show he was kind of hard. He was heartbroken. He didn't know what he was gonna' do in the show. He didn't know how he was gonna' come out with the show and he was tight, very tight. . . . That's why I think people say he was mean. But he was having a hard time himself. He didn't know how long he was [going to] be in that show. He lived to himself because he didn't have George and shortly his wife. He was by himself. Quite by himself. Only the people he knew very well, maybe you'd see him with.[19]

As the company toured, George was shuffled between West Baden, Mount Clemens, and Lakehurst. Likely confined to a wheelchair, he required round-the-clock assistance from William Moulton (ca. 1885 to 1910), a former cast member from *Bandanna Land* turned caretaker. Next came a gut punch from management and, ostensibly, Bert, who formally severed George's connection with Williams and Walker. On September 17, 1909, a telegram was sent to Lawrence informing Alice to expect Nash on September 23.[20] As reported in the *Daily World*,

> He is almost a physical wreck, being in worse condition than last spring when he was forced to leave the show for a month's stay here. . . .
> Although he will retain a financial interest in the show which made him a fortune, Walker will have no other connection with it and it will be entirely out of his management. Williams, his side partner for so many years, now takes the company and henceforth it will be known as the [Bert] Williams Company.[21]

Upon Nash's return home, a show of solidarity was printed in the *Daily Journal*:

Nash Walker is making a hard fight. He is in bad health just now, but he is putting up one of the biggest fights that any man ever put up to get back his health. Nash has not left the stage, not by any means. He is simply on a year's vacation until he is strong enough to go back, and then he is going to resume his place in Williams and Walker's company which can never be filled by anyone but the inimitable Nash. Lawrence is glad that he is coming home to rest. That is the best place for him, for he is known here and aside from the glory that is attached to his name, the people of Lawrence have a warm place in their hearts for Nash Walker and they are glad that he is coming back here to get well.[22]

Coinciding with the destruction of the company and, by extension, George's access to income, Bert canceled the October 6 engagement at the Bowersock, stating, "It would be like tramping on the grave of my partner."[23] With Chappie's help, Bert kept a very low profile while engaged in nearby Kansas City, much to the disappointment of the locals who were accustomed to throwing balls for the company when they came to town. On opening night, a reporter for *The Kansas City Times* overheard a morose Bert in conversation about George with musician Blind Boone (1864 to 1927), who heaped praise on him: "Poor Walker, I am afraid, will never be in the show business again. Success was too much for him. Whenever anyone tries to flatter me I remember Walker and close my ears to what he says."[24] Bert knew that if he played Lawrence, Nash would have been there and in an even worse state than when he was present, and outvoted at the dissolution of the partnership less than two weeks earlier. With that, he made good on the promise he made six months earlier when George said, "Well Bert, I'm going to leave you," and Bert replied, "No you're not. I'm going to leave *you*."[25] Now former partners, they likely never saw each other again. George was abandoned, flat broke, and now completely dependent on others. If Bert wasn't actively responsible for the destruction of the company, he was far worse, a coward who seemingly did nothing to stop it. In direct response to Bert's remarks in the *Daily Journal*, the *Daily World* issued a statement: "Williams and Walker were together for years and those who knew Nash Walker always believed that he was the one who had made their success possible. While Walker enjoyed the praise that came to him, so far as we can see he was not spoiled by it, but that's the same generous, goodhearted Nash Walker that the people of Lawrence had known since he was a little pickaninny on the streets."[26] During the company's second of three weeks in Chicago, Sylvester Russell reviewed the show and did not hold his tongue: "The mistake that Mr. Williams has made in this new venture is that he has failed to have these people placed in the cast to his own advantage, and to fill the vacancy left by the absence of Mr. and Mrs. Walker. In failing to do this, both his partner, George W. Walker and Mrs. Aida Overton Walker are naturally missed. . . . As the situation now stands, Mr. Williams' supporting cast is miscellaneous and not essential to his success."[27] In Louisville, the audience loved the performance, but the reviewer couldn't help noting a feeling of incompleteness: "There is no doubt but that his absence was missed last night. Williams is funny and droll, but Walker drew out the amusing points to greater advantage to Williams, and therefore, was an added asset to the performances in the past. It is not to be expected that Williams could carry the whole show on his shoulders, yet this is evidently what the management expects him to do in 'Mr. Lode of Koal.' "[28] Shortly after, Bert gave his account of the separation when the company was engaged in Indianapolis: "the big comedian gave it out in a matter of fact way that Mr. Walker and he had separated in the theatrical business for all time, and that it was probable that Mr. Walker would join his wife in the event of heading her own show. Mr. Williams did not say that there had been any upheaval, but that it was simply a business agreement made to benefit both."[29]

Following Indianapolis, the production appeared at the Majestic in Manhattan for five weeks. A widely circulated and somewhat indifferent critique of the show by Franklin Fyles summed up the sentiment of the management structure around Bert at the time: "I'm glad to know that the Bert Williams who outlasts Walker is the shuffling, slouching, naturally comic and artistically accomplished darkey of the two. He gets along just as well without an interlocutor."[30] Despite popular perception, Bert was still a man of double consciousness. However, perception was reality for most White theatre critics and the public, so the situation likely inspired him to further withdraw, even from those who had known him since the beginning. The days of balls, smokers, and dances were over. After a successful Manhattan residency, the engagement ended quietly, and the company continued to tour before landing in Philadelphia for two weeks. At the end of that engagement, William Elkins, longtime cast member and choral director, left, as did music director James Vaughn, Hattie Hopkins, Charles "Bass" Foster, Ed Tolliver, and recent additions Siren and Navarro.[31] The company was nearing collapse. When the reduced aggregation attempted to move to Syracuse, deep snowdrifts delayed them at the Broad Street Station for most of their travel day. As a result, they arrived late, and the second act ended at eleven thirty at night. The inexperienced cast was exhausted, and many grew disheartened with Bert's lack of leadership as they played short dates around the Northeast, closing out the season in Brooklyn earlier than ever on March 5, 1910. Bert addressed the cast and told them that he hoped to see everyone back when the company reopened with a new show in the coming season after some issues with management were addressed. Yet Bert had been secretly holding a contract for more than a week that would have taken him abroad over the Moss-Stoll circuit for $1,000 a week for four weeks, with options to extend another sixteen. Similar offers poured in when George took ill, but he opted to stay with the company, likely because he was still under contract with the Shuberts until 1912.[32] Nevertheless, management ensured that the company was in a shambles. Although the show was entertaining for most White theatregoers, the *Colorado Statesman* intimated, "This has not been a successful season, not because the company wasn't first class, but so many people miss George Walker, the best straight [man] ever seen on the stage, white or black."[33]

In recognition of Bert's failure to sustain the troupe, *The Freeman*'s Uncle Rad Kees made an ominous prediction:

> That Walker was the brains of this famous team goes without question, and unless you have come in direct contact with the various phases of the Negro theatrical you can have no conception of the great responsibility placed upon such a person. Yet I dare say, through it all, there is not one person who can conscientiously say that Walker was ever other than a gentleman, and those of you who have had any such experience at all in this line will agree with me that to be a businessman and a gentleman in the theatrical business is almost an impossibility. Mr. Walker was one of the few colored stars who was constantly trying to open new and greater fields for the colored performer—always hiring and holding as many together as was in his power, giving each a fair opportunity of showing what he could do, and always having a smile, a pleasant word and good advice for all, giving at all times a bit of cheer where the heart seemed sad, and ever ready to intercede and demand wherever there was a possibility of advancement; but the man wasn't iron, and evidently had many troubles of his own, some of which he will, no doubt, carry to his grave.

That the theatrical world has missed Ernest Hogan, so does it also miss George Walker, and I will miss Bob Cole when he has passed into history. Each has fought a noble battle, and while they are unquestionably an honor to their profession, they are certainly accredited to their race.[34]

With that, what was the most powerful and profitable Black theatre company in the world was no more.

Aida's *Red Moon*

Cole and Johnson's *Red Moon* company opened the season with Aida at the Plainfield (NJ) Theatre on the August 26, 1909, then traveled throughout the Midwest until they reached the Globe Theatre in Chicago, where they stayed for two weeks beginning November 14. After the disbandment of the Williams and Walker company, George was "all out of money, position and health" and eventually made his way from New York to Mount Clemens with William Moulton on October 13, 1909.[35] During her Chicago residency, Aida briefly visited with George as he journeyed back to Lawrence with an excessive amount of clothes in tow. A laughable claim was made that he weighed 176 pounds, and according to the *Detroit Informer*, "aside from a noticeable nervousness, 'George' looks better than he ever did."[36] After meeting with Aida in Chicago, Nash and Moulton made it to Lawrence on November 30. Reporters inquired about rumors that their beloved Nash, no longer speaking for himself or tooling about town in a carriage, was a "physical wreck." Admitting only that he was "a little sick," Moulton proclaimed,

> Just in bluffing the public a little. You see Mr. Walker had to get a good rest, and enjoy life a little and this is the easiest way to get it. We have been at Mt. Clemens having a good time and Mr. Walker is in fine condition.
>
> We came in last night to see Mr. Walker's mother and to spend a short time with his old friends. I think we shall be here six or eight weeks and then we will go East. Mr. Walker will be back on the stage next season with Williams. There is nothing to the story that there has been a split up in the firm.[37]

Shortly after the company was dissolved, Alice indicated that she planned to sell her home so that she could relocate to New York and care for her son, but that never happened. Likewise, Langston Hughes claimed to have witnessed Nash give a concert of phonograph recordings at his aunt's church, St. Luke African Methodist Episcopal (AME) Church at the corner of East Ninth and New York Street, for the mortgage fund, but reports indicate that it was actually Alice and Moulton who gave the concert in early January of 1910.[38] On January 8, the team of (Lawrence) Deas (1878 to 1951), (Harry) Reed, and (Ella) Deas (b. 1884)—vaudeville analogues to George, Bert, and Aida—were slated to reprise *Bandanna Land* in the coming season. On January 15, Nash, Alice, and Moulton arrived in Topeka to meet with the team and view their performance from a box at the Novelty Theatre.[39] Likely through Alice or Moulton, George made his final public statement: "I was tired of laying around Lawrence, doing nothing and just run up here to Topeka for a look at the sights. I am going to take a good rest and expect to be in perfect condition again by next fall when I will re-join my company."[40]

Deas, Reed, and Deas were expected to begin rehearsals in October after closing in Oshkosh, but the venture never materialized. Thus, George's third and final attempt to continue the Williams and Walker name failed.[41] His final public appearance was on January 21, 1910, when he attended a performance of S. H. Dudley's The Smart Set in *His Honor, the Barber* at the Bowersock:

> The choruses in the show were extremely well gotten up, everyone in the show last night did his best to make good, for there in a box in full evening dress sat Nash Walker, the king of them all on the stage, and his mother and secretary. It was to the box where Nash sat, the envy of them all that the whole show played. The rest of the house was incidental. To the members of the Smart Set company it was evident that Nash was the big part of the audience.[42]

There was a reception for the cast after the show that Nash did not attend, but he was the likely topic of conversation because few, if any, had seen him since the first Frolic of the Frogs in August of 1908, when he began presenting signs of illness. Loyal to the end and still claiming that George was improving, Lester Walton published a letter from Moulton a few days later:

To the Dramatic Editor of *The Age*,

It will undoubtedly interest you and the readers of the theatrical material in the New York Age to know that George W. Walker is still at home with his mother in Lawrence, Kansas and is taking what he calls the rest cure.

His condition is improving daily, and it is hoped that by October he will have fully recovered from his illness and will be able to return to the stage where we all know his presence is greatly missed.

Very truly yours,

W. C. Moulton

Secretary to Mr. Walker.[43]

Shortly before the Williams and Walker company was dissolved, Walton visited F. Ray Comstock's office in the Shubert building for an update on George's condition and the situation of the most popular Black theatre company in the country. According to Walton, Comstock feigned ignorance:

I have not heard from Mr. Walker for months, and I don't know his true condition. I am certainly glad to learn, however, that he is improved, for besides realizing that this stage sustains quite a loss by his temporary retirement, I have a high regard for him personally.

As to whether Mr. Walker contemplates appearing next season with his wife, Aida Overton Walker, I must say it is news to me. On the subject as to whether I have another year's contract with him I have nothing to say.[44]

It is unknown whether Comstock understood the situation and was feeding Walton a lie to protect his stake in securing Bert as a solo act or not. He expressed no desire to close *Mr. Lode of Koal*, although that is what happened in short order. Regardless, with Walton's access to Bert and George when they were in town, he likely knew the truth but never published it.

Within six months of Nash Walker's final appearance at the Bowersock, the decision was made to send him to the State Hospital in Central Islip, Long Island, for end-of-life care. On May 11, Green Henri Tapley made an emergency trip to Lawrence because William Moulton returned to Manhattan, where he died from complications of scarlet fever on June 19, 1910.[45] The following day, Tapley resumed his role as caretaker and brought George to Chicago to see a few friends before they made their way to New York. Sylvester Russell reported that George's friends were horrified by what they saw: "Mr. Walker was unable to recognize his most intimate friends and his mind is now a blank and his form of insanity is a hopeless case of mental decay, said by doctors to be incurable."[46]

For those who had been kept in the dark about the severity of the situation, the undeniable truth about Black theatre's greatest champion was devastating, and it inspired Russell to give a heartfelt summation of George's importance to the vanguard generation: "Mr. Walker was not only the greatest fashion plate of his race in dress and characteristics, but his superiority in his class was always underestimated, owing to the fact that his power to coach his partner to a blunt hilarious episode of laughter robbed him of his own reward in the final climax."[47] George's next stop was Manhattan to see Aida for a few days before continuing to Central Islip, the end of the line.[48]

At the close of the season, Aida expected to begin preparing for her own production with Bob Cole, and rumors spread that several former members of the Williams and Walker company would join her. However, on Independence Day, Cole and Johnson had a private meeting with their management Stair and Havlin at the English House, a Black-owned hotel at 145 North Street in Catskill. Without Aida's input, they decided that Cole and Johnson would temporarily retire from the stage due to management's inability to secure bookings in houses that charged more than one dollar for the best seats and the growing instability of the circuit. Although undisclosed at the time, Bob Cole had begun his own decline, the likely reason for their retirement. The disbandment to the Cole and Johnson company left only one final option for Aida: S. H. Dudley's The Smart Set under the management of Barton and Wiswell. Again, she secured a specialty feature in each act and maintained creative control. As a principal member of The Smart Set, Aida and Dudley were rumored to combine forces to become the Dudley and Walker company. However, it was a lateral move at best, and she was still playing in smaller, discount houses that were not suitable for the grand productions that she had grown accustomed to working in.[49]

Integration's Folly

In mid-May 1910, the announcement came that Bert would not return to the road with his own company and planned to be the sole Black member of the Ziegfeld Follies of 1910 in *Jardin de Paris* as the Caretaker. On June 13, Bert was slated to begin a two-week-long engagement in Atlantic City before moving to Hammerstein's Victoria Theatre for two weeks at more than $1,000 per week as a solo act.[50] Shortly thereafter, rehearsals for the Follies began. One of the first scenes they tried out was a burlesque of the impending matchup between champion Jack Johnson and Jim Jeffries, with Bert playing Johnson.

Under the direction of syndicate chief Abe Erlanger, George's old nemesis, Bert unintentionally positioned himself for a crime of opportunity. Reportedly, Bert rehearsed well with Harry Watson, who played Jeffries. One day, Erlanger decided to demonstrate the kind of realism that he wanted, laced up a pair of gloves, and caught Bert square on the jaw. A little dazed, Bert recovered and began to playfully but repeatedly tap Erlanger on the top of his head with one hand while protecting his head from Erlanger's relentless advance with the other. Unknown to Erlanger and everyone else, Bert had studied with "The Old Master," Joe Gans (1874 to 1910), since November of 1899, and despite the self-deprecating nature of his stage persona, he was, at times, a man of action. The unprovoked aggression continued until Bert reached his limit. Surely, the years of denial, gatekeeping, stonewalling, and sabotage flashed before his mind as he uncurled a right hook that found Erlanger square on his chin. As portrayed in "The Greatest Comedian on the American Stage," "Mr. Erlanger fell to the floor in a more or less comatose condition and rolled halfway across the stage. He struggled to his feet, a little groggy and considerably chagrined, and, turning to [Harry] Watson, said, 'There, that's the way I want it done.'"[51]

In short order, Bert summarily laid waste to the man who told his former partner that a Black show would never be accepted on Broadway and then sabotaged the greatest Black production to date to make it true. There were no reprisals for his action that day. In the grand scheme of things, it was a miniscule victory. The Williams and Walker Company was gone. As the beta test for assimilation, disguised as integration, Bert's acquiescence ensured the destruction of a hard-won and established Black institution to enrich a White one, thus signaling the end of an unprecedented era of achievement. Moreover, Bert's new status did not help his moroseness, and he continued to drink heavily. Chappie recalled, "About a week after the show opened, Bert fell asleep on a subway one night on his way to the theatre and didn't wake up until he reached the Battery."[52]

As George faded further into memory, syphilis's association with sexual promiscuity allowed the morally prudish free rein to speculate. As he was considered the "Beau Brummell of the Negro race," several extramarital affairs were rumored to be the source of his impending demise. One unsubstantiated account claimed that Jeanette Foster, the "Bon Bon Buddy Gibson Girl" and the "Chocolate Drop Venus," was one of his lovers.[53] Another, far more famous rumored liaison was with Eva Tanguay, the "I Don't Care Girl," championed by vaudevillian George Jessell and others. Tanguay, a White woman, shared a vaudeville booking with Williams and Walker at Percy G. Williams's theatre in early June of 1908, but there is no surviving proof of a romance between George and Tanguay, although there is circumstantial evidence for an affair between Tanguay and Bert.[54]

Speculation aside, the "cloudy and unsettled" state of Black theatre was a clear and present source of anxiety. In 1907, there were five large touring shows employing hundreds of Black actors, support staff, and technicians. By 1910, only two remained. Further, with Bert Williams assimilated into the Follies, no Black people could see him perform, which further fueled the rumor mill. Eventually, Sylvester Russell changed his mind and defended George's brand of diplomacy in an argument with Lawrence Deas and Theodore Pankey in front of the Pekin Theatre in Chicago—it was management, not George, who decided to renege on contracts and freeze the company out for months, necessitating multiple management changes followed by further contract breaches by management. White managers coveted the income generated by the Williams and Walker company but did not want to see the company and its members build wealth and institutions that served Black cultural interests. Although Jim Crow was the law of the land, it was neither just nor right, and Black people were well within their rights to expose its unconstitutionality.[55]

Although most reports indicated that George's condition was improving quickly and a new production, *The Land of Monkeys*, was slated to debut in September 1910, one honest article from Denver stated that his condition was critical and there was "no hope for him."[56] Meanwhile, Bob Cole began to spiral as well. Following a public mental breakdown at Ninety-Eighth and Columbus Street, he was taken to Bellevue Hospital on October 11. The following day, he was moved to a private sanitarium located at Woodcliff-on-Hudson, New Jersey, and then to the Manhattan State Hospital, Ward Island. J. Rosamond Johnson insisted that his partner would only be out for a few weeks, but the situation was far more serious.[57] In a rare moment of stark honesty, Lester Walton published a piece titled "The Passing of the Triumvirate": "With what is now regarded as the temporary retirement of Bob Cole, the enforced and indefinite absence of George Walker and the death of Ernest Hogan, the stage is minus what was generally considered the business brains of the colored profession."[58] With no good news on the horizon, the coming season was greeted with a stoic yet diminished resolve. However, Aida found creative success with S. H. Dudley in *His Honor, the Barber*. Written by Edwin Hanford, it featured music and lyrics by James T. Brymn, Smith, and Burris. The plot centered on Raspberry Snow (Dudley), a soldier of fortune who aspired to shave President William Howard Taft's face. It was peppered with humorous situations between dancing specialties from Aida. In the first act, she sang "Golly, Ain't I Wicked" in a child's dress à la "Pickaninny Days" with several chorus members. Ford Dabney's "Porto Rico," a dance number similar to her "Salome," was featured at the close of the second act, and she opened the third with her new signature piece, "That's Why They Call Me Shine," in drag as a tribute to George and a follow-up to "Bon Bon Buddy." Cecil Mack's lyrics elegantly celebrated Black beauty undercover and created a hit that (minus the introduction) lasted for several decades.[59]

Chorus:

'Cause my hair is curly
'Cause my teeth are pearly
Just because I always wear a smile
Like to dress up in the latest style
'Cause I'm glad I'm living
Take troubles smiling, never whine
Just because my color's shady
Slightly different maybe,
That's why they call me Shine

A more refined dancer than George, Aida shed his signature ice-cream-white suit in favor of chocolate brown and did her best to keep him in the minds of all who saw her perform.

His Honor, the Barber opened at the Colonial Theatre in Annapolis on September 3, 1910, and toured the East until the week of October 2, 1910, when Aida was summoned to the bedside of her mother, whose

Figure 14.2. "That's Why They Call Me Shine," words by R. C. McPherson, music by Ford Dabney, Gotham Attucks Music Co., New York, 1910. *Source:* Author's collection.

condition had worsened. Pauline Reed died on October 14, and her funeral was held two days later in the home she shared with George and Aida at 52 West 133rd Street. She was just forty-nine years old. Aida rejoined the company in Newark during the following week. Lester Walton expressed a profound sense of hopelessness and exclaimed, "To what, am I (The Colored Stage)—a once promising and forcing profession in the race coming to?"[60]

In early November 1910, George suffered a "serious backset," and Alice made her way to Central Islip on December 6 to hold vigil by his bedside. Having just lost her mother, Aida prepared to lose George as well and hired a private nurse at fifty dollars a week for palliative care. Nevertheless, she performed throughout the Midwest and reached Cincinnati in early January of 1911 when the news came: George William "Nash" Walker was dead.[61]

"See That His Grave's Kept Green"

George succumbed to paresis on January 6, 1911, at seven o'clock in the evening at the State Hospital in Central Islip, according to reports, "deranged by prosperity." It was a thinly veiled association with drapetomania, the antebellum-era condition intended to explain why enslaved Africans would choose to escape enslavement, in opposition to their perceived "natural" inclinations.[62] The fact that he lived so long was a testament to his inner strength and a lifetime of physical fitness. At the time, Aida and Bert were working, so Alice was the only loved one present. According to the *Chicago Defender*, Bert took the news especially hard: "Bert A. Williams, now traveling with a white company, has no doubt labored under a great burden of sorrow since the day his partner was declared hopelessly insane and that death at Brooklyn, New York, he broke down and wept bitterly supported by the embrace of his faithful friend and valet in his dressing room. It is authentically reported that he was unable to go on in the scene in the last act of the show."[63]

On January 9, 1911, at eleven o'clock in the morning, a large wake was held in Manhattan at J. C. Thomas's funeral home at 89 West 134th Street. Aida's pastor, Reverend Hutchins C. Bishop of St. Philip's Protestant Episcopal Church, officiated. "Strut" Payne sang George's favorite hymn, "I Need Thee Every Hour," accompanied by Rosamond Johnson on the organ. Under police protection, the body lay in state until the following Tuesday so that an estimated thirty thousand people could pay their respects. That afternoon, a memorial concert was given by James Reese Europe's (1881 to 1919) New Amsterdam Orchestra that hosted a who's who of the Afro-American theatrical world, including Bert and Aida, who immediately returned to the road after its conclusion.[64] Shortly thereafter, Lester Walton published a bit of prose from J. Mord. Allen and himself in *The New York Age*:

Figure 14.3. Possibly the last surviving photograph of Williams and Walker, circa late summer 1908. *Source:* Author's collection.

To George Walker—(Written for *The New York Age*)

    I.   Good-bye, George, God bless you
          For the unpaid good you've done.
          At last you've fought the losing fight,
          And fought and lost. Alone?
          No! Not alone. For you know now

           That thousand-voiced prayer
           Has pleaded to the God for you,
           To pity and to spare.

II.   Good-bye, George. We'll miss you.
      We have hoped our willful need
      Of you, and what exalted you
      Would cry to God and plead.
      Have hoped—in spite of doctors—
      That, up above the blue,
      God would ordained a miracle,
      'Twere so well spent on you.

III. But, now, dear George, it's curtain,
      And never a curtain-call.
      Still, open hand, and hopeful word
      And upward lift—aye, all
      That made you—Great man as were—
      A brother to the least,
      Shall keep your memory alive
      While life is in our breast.

IV. Good-bye, George. We'll mourn you.
      Who knew you, love you best.
      Since God is just, it's certain
      You have gone to blissful rest.
      I'll never fear the reckoning
      When *my* Account is due,
      If God knows half the good of me,
      That I, George, know of you.
      —J. Mord. Allen
      Topeka, Kansas

Bye-Bye for a Little While (Dedicated to George W. Walker)

    The new go has sounded,
    The angels are calling.
    Yes: I am ready and go;

Away with these trials,
Away with these strains,
There, Oh There, where the angels
Are calling, I am ready to go.

"Dust to dust," he hath said,
To whom I reverently bow.
The day of birth is the start of trials,
The date of death is the start of relief.
The ancients have taught.
So humbly and submissively I am ready to roam;
There on yonder, where trials don't exist;
There on yonder, where peace is eternal,
Efforts, trials and endeavors that in this world go amiss,
I no longer need worry nor bother of this.
Peace of mind and rest to my soul.
On and on there, Gondor is my last journey home.
A heave, a strain, a sigh, no more pain, just gone.
Peace to you all.
May we all meet in peace, and with the angels roam.
—A Friend [Lester Walton].[65]

Following the wake in Manhattan, Alice accompanied the remains and two wagon loads of flowers to Chicago. The floral arrangements included offerings from the Colored Vaudeville Benevolent Association, the Clef Club (the Black musical association led by James Reese Europe), the Masonic order, The Smart Set Company, and one from Bert inscribed "Dear Old Pal." After the body was transferred from LaSalle to Polk Street Station, Green Henri Tapley joined Alice. Others present were several former members of the Williams and Walker company, now under contract at the Pekin Theatre, including Jesse and Maggie Shipp; Mr. and Mrs. William Elkins; Jerry Mills; Charles Gilpin (1878 to 1930); Hattie McIntosh; Mr. and Mrs. Sam Davis; Sylvester Russell; and George Williams. At the station, a small ceremony was held, where the custom $800 purple plush, copper-lined mahogany casket banked with floral designs and silver handles, encased in a cedar box, was opened. According to Russell, "the corpse did not look natural, his cheeks and temples were sunken and showed signs of many days of suffering." Jesse was overcome at the sight of his friend's emaciated corpse, dressed in his best, now ill-fitting evening suit and Masonic regalia.[66]

At six o'clock in the evening, Alice and Tapley, who was pale with grief, boarded the Santa Fe railroad and accompanied the remains to Lawrence for burial with so many flowers from the New York and Chicago stops that a separate train car was required.[67] They arrived in Lawrence on January 12, and the remains were taken to Lescher and Power undertaking rooms. Joe Howard, composer of "Hello My Baby" and boyhood friend of Nash, happened to be engaged at the Bowersock. That evening, he gave a heartfelt tribute on stage and declared, "This is the proudest and happiest day of my life" as he discussed the debt he owed for the help he received after running away from home during his childhood.[68]

After the public viewing, the remains were taken to "Abyssinio" and then to the Warren Street Baptist Church, where a funeral was held on Sunday, January 15, 1911, at two o'clock. The chapel overflowed and the sweet smell of the wreaths filled the air. The spectacle wasn't lost on young Langston Hughes, who remembered, "I got my hand slapped for pointing at the flowers, because it was not polite for a child to point."[69] Reverend G. N. Jackson preached the sermon from Acts 13:36, in reference to King David, "After he had served his own generation by the will of God, he fell asleep," accompanied by Gieg's "Ase's Death" and "Beethoven's Funeral March" played by Theodore C. Copeland. "Nearer My God to Thee" followed, and after prayers "The Gospel Train," one of Nash's favorite hymns, was sung before "Sleep On, Sleep On," rendered by Marie Overstreet.[70] Finally, Sylvester Russell's poem "See That His Grave's Kept Green" was read by Ruth Bradley:

> See that his grave's kept green,
>   As to the west return, and sigh;
> We chant farewell, though silently,
>   And bow with tear-dimmed eye.
> See that his grave's kept green;
>   Rejoice, be glad, and do not weep;
> Prevent the wind's breath soft and still—
>   That he in peace may sleep.
>
> See that his grave's kept green,
>   As he retires from the show,
> George Walker, the genius of his day—
>   And "Nash" of long ago.

> See that his grave's kept green:
>   For there, his soul looks from the sky;
> The fairest angel ever seen—
>   Now bids the world goodbye.[71]

The funeral train to Oak Hill Cemetery was one of the longest ever seen in Lawrence. Under the care of the Masons of the Western Star Lodge, no. 1, Nash Walker was laid to rest close to his uncle Sanford and grandmother Sarah. Alice was inconsolable at the gravesite and relied heavily on Tapley, who also bore the burden of presenting her with a wreath from the Chicago delegation of the Negro Business League before he placed another from managers Motts, Corker, Klein, and Brennon at the gravesite.[72]

As people anguished over what would happen next, Lester Walton attempted to make sense of the void created by George Walker's absence:

> Of all institutions and influences, the stage is one of the greatest civilizers of today; and George W. Walker has played an important part in the process of civilizing the white public with regard to what the American Negro of modern times really is. In years to come, when some of us today and those of tomorrow look backward on his life and work; when we as a race become imbued with a higher regard for our history and the doings of those who have gone before; when the Negro will have learned that it is not for the white man to first manifest high appreciation of the history of his race, then the loss of George W. Walker will be more fully realized, and he will be reviewed and held as one of the great men of his time and of his people.[73]

Likewise, the *Plaindealer* expressed an all-too-familiar lament that would plague every Black institution and culturally based movement that challenged the status quo of White supremacy and the desire for Black cultural sovereignty:

> We have sounded a note of warning to our young people to look out for the future and be ready to fill the places of others in all walks of life. Too few of them are making preparations along this line. If a colored man establishes a business—large or small and dies or retires, it is seldom if ever another of his race can

be found to continue anything that has been well established. This is a serious problem for the colored race to solve and it is high time that our leaders give the matter serious consideration.

The passing of the famous team, Williams and Walker, simply because no one can fill the latter's place will be the fate of other high-class covered theatrical stars. Cole and Johnson, another high-class team has gone the way because there is no one to take the place of Bob Cole, the greatest tramp impersonator that ever appeared before the footlights. Others will follow.

We say the Negro is being trained wrong. He needs business training to cope with the progressive life of the white American.

George Walker [ful]filled his mission, did well and passed to the great beyond just as he reached the place to accomplish more and greater things for the race. Who is left to take his place?[74]

Following the deaths of Pauline and George and Bert's solo foray into a White company, Aida remained with The Smart Set. Now free from the burden of financing palliative care for two people, she was asked if she was interested in joining a White company. Her answer was an indictment of Bert's attempt to assimilate:

> Yes, but I don't want to leave my race. The race has only too few strong characters on the stage today, and while I am but a small ripple on the great ocean of Dramatic Art, I may do some good. I may inspire some racial confidence, and unless circumstances force me to the white race I shall never go. I am sorry that Mr. Williams left us. We are not strong enough to spare him to the white race, you see. I fear that if those of us who have been pioneers leave the race, we will have to start all over again, as Williams and Walker started many years ago. I am a race woman, and I am always sorry to see the white race take our genius from us.[75]

Aida's frank honesty was not a surprise, but it had to sting. In less than six months, Bert went from a beloved member of the Black actors' fraternity to a fly in the ointment. Only Chappie remained with him as the sole reminder of what once was one of the most powerful theatre companies in the country. Although well compensated, Bert was socially isolated, and his drinking would take its toll in the coming years as he kept a conspicuously low profile.

As welcome as Aida's declaration was, Sylvester Russell wanted her to reconcile and reunite with Bert and Jesse Shipp. However, that was not likely given how things transpired when George was ill and the way the company was dissolved.[76] Nevertheless, Russell pleaded for another young leader on par with George that he knew wasn't coming: "Among the flowers of youth was George W. Walker, the Negro stage Napoléon of his day. The one man who boldly stood up in his exalted position and made it possible for the Negro thespian of his time, but in whom we did not really discover until he had passed away. . . . But the ship is deserted now; the captain is gone and the crew is scattered."[77] After years of lambasting his every move, Russell finally admitted that George wanted the best, sought the best, and expected the best from everything he did and everyone he worked with, including management. He was a once-in-a-generation talent, and, in the blink of an eye, he was gone. All that was left was to mourn him and try again.

When Aida's season closed on May 20, 1911, she prepared to appear with several chorus members in dancing and musical specialties over the United circuit as well as at Hammerstein's Victoria Theatre and Percy Williams's houses. With the help of some elite belles and beaux of Washington, DC, and her many friends in the profession, she organized a vaudeville benefit at the Howard Theatre on May 30 and 31 to raise funds for a granite memorial for George. In conjunction, Aida commissioned Henry Ossawa Tanner (1859 to 1937) to paint a portrait of him that was expected to hang in the Carnegie Library at Howard University.[78] Bob Cole was committed at Manhattan Hospital, Ward's Island, and could not attend. Bert had not seen many of his former colleagues since he joined the Follies a year earlier and was expected to appear, but his contract prevented it. As a consolation, Bert spent a day with George's mother on April 6, 1911, when he was engaged in Leavenworth, Kansas; it was the last time he set foot in Lawrence.[79]

Although the first night went well, bad weather hampered the benefit's success on the second night, and it netted only $250.[80] For reasons unknown, George's grave went unmarked for nearly a decade, which sparked an editor's note in *The Topeka Plaindealer* in December of 1918: "While in Lawrence a few days ago some friends of the late Nash Walker said that it was a disgrace to the professional people and the race at large that the grave of such a distinguished comedian as Nash Walker should go unmarked. We are of the same opinion and think some effort should be made to erect a tombstone to mark the spot where the remains of this noted celebrit[y] now lie."[81]

Chapter 15

... 'Til the Well Runs Dry

The Irreplicable Bob Cole

On July 29, 1911, seven months after George's death, Bob Cole checked himself out of the hospital on Ward's Island and entered a sanitarium in Amityville, Long Island. After demonstrating that he was "rational and quiet," Cole returned to the English House in Catskill with his mother to continue his recovery. However, shortly before going to press on the evening of August 2, 1911, *The New York Age* received word that Bob Cole was dead. His friends recalled that on the day before he was in good spirits and played several of his compositions for fellow guests. Following supper with his mother at four thirty, someone came into the parlor and said something to the effect, "Bob Cole? I thought you were dead!" Likely triggered by the stranger's realization, Cole told his mother that he was going for a short walk with some friends, and excused himself. When they reached Catskill Creek about two blocks away, Cole remarked that the water looked inviting, waded in fully dressed, swam for a few minutes, and disappeared below the surface for a time, reappeared, yelled out, and then went under. At first, his companions thought he was playing a joke, but he drowned. As they pulled his lifeless body from the creek, someone ran back to inform his mother, who had parted with her son just fifteen minutes earlier. Having seen the effect syphilis had on George and others, Bob Cole took matters into his own hands and ended his life.[1]

In less than three years, Ernest Hogan, George Walker, Robert Motts (manager of the Pekin), and Bob Cole passed from the scene. Along with them went the vanguard generation's hope of establishing a critical mass of Afro-American cultural sovereignty. As a historical scholar, composer, musician, singer, playwright, comedian, and stage manager, Cole was far and away the most talented of the group. He labored night and day on his art in the hope of advancing the status of Afro-Americans and their access to personal liberty. When pressed on the source of his drive and philosophy, he told the *Canadian Courier*, "You ask me how it feels to be a Negro. When I consider the above facts and regard the Great Plan of Nature designed by the Great Ruler of the Universe, I must answer, like the coal digger answered me: I've been one so long it kinder feels natural, and I've got so used to it now I wouldn't be anything else.' "[2] He was buried at Woodlawn Cemetery in the Bronx.

Aida's Final "Shine"

Since joining the Follies in 1910, Bert played in houses that George could only dream of presenting Williams and Walker vehicles in. However, they were all Jim Crow houses, which meant near total isolation. Bert continually found solace in the bottle as he worked in cities far from Lottie, who was often too ill to travel. During the 1910 season, she tried to join him on tour but fell down the staircase at the Grand Central Palace in Chicago and was confined to her bed for several days. A similar incident happened during the previous season as well, which exacerbated Bert's stress.[3]

Believing that he was helping and protecting his investment, Joe Shoemaker made a public case for Bert to be granted "Honorary Whiteness" when "White Is as White Does" appeared in *The New York Age* during the summer of 1912. Citing that Bert was "white at heart" because of his ability to make polite conversation with Southern White women and his fondness for Emerson, Shoemaker declared "That's being white because it's doing right." Shoemaker further asserted that when George became too ill to perform, both he and Bert provided for him, including his funeral expenses, to prove that "people will agree that this is white treatment."[4]

Understandably, Aida was infuriated and attempted to set the record straight with the op-ed "Respect Memory of the Dead" a week later: "It would be well if he practiced what he preached, and the only way left [for] Mr. Shoemaker to show Mr. Williams' WHITENESS is by showing that he has done his duty to his partner, I think it's a poor way of impressing the readers of *The Age* of Mr. Williams' finer points as a man."[5] She continued with the assertion that, regardless of his racial status, Bert's paying of George's funeral expenses was "an act of friendship" and that "Mr. Walker was also [Shoemaker's] employer in the past, and at that time, the duties of his position, being of a confidential nature, were not intended for publication." She closed with

> Mr. Walker was a man at all times. A good provider for his family. Cared tenderly for his parents in their declining years. Gave the best years of his life striving to make it possible for others in his profession. It is due to Mr. Walker's efforts that I enjoy my present position; that Mr. Williams enjoys his present position, and many others. He was a true partner to his partner to the end. Died at peace with God and man. Let him rest!

Shoemaker's ploy forced Aida's hand, and, when coupled with her own worsening health from Bright's (kidney) disease, the consequence of her loyalty to George proved catastrophic for her career. In conjunction, the 1912 to 1913 season was a wash because vaudeville managers collectively refused to book Black acts. According to Eubie Blake, it was retaliation for Jack Johnson's marriage to a White woman named Etta Terry Duryea. Moreover, Bert's financially successful method of assimilation became the benchmark for Black stardom for the rest of the twentieth century and beyond.[6]

In a show of solidarity that was never reciprocated, Aida helped Bert stage a testimonial for Sam Lucas at Young's Casino in Manhattan on January 28, 1913. She appeared sparingly after that, taking what Lester Walton described as "a much needed rest."[7] Walton then brokered a temporary truce between Bert and Aida to share the stage during the Frogs' big minstrel show at the Manhattan Casino on August 11, 1913, which marked Bert's first appearance with Black actors since the close of *Mr. Lode of Koal*. To prevent any false hope, Walton emphasized, "The possibility of seeing Mr. Williams under similar conditions will be remote."[8]

Aida's "Shine" act in male attire was still a big draw, as she worked sporadically in vaudeville. Although a highly respected performer who spent lavishly on her show, she never attained the success that she envisioned or deserved during the remaining three years of her life. Her final public row with Bert saw to that. As an unapologetically Black woman and widow of a pariah who was tolerated only because he brought in money, the power structure within the industry wanted little to do with her. As her health continued to fail, her ability and willingness to fight followed suit.[9]

During the week of November 3, 1913, Aida organized an all-star event and performed mostly new material at the Pekin Theatre in Chicago. Declared a "knockout" by Sylvester Russell, it was extended a week. Some believed that it might have been the spark to revive the struggling theatre, which had been mostly dark since the death of its owner and producer Robert Motts, seven months after George and just a few days before Bob Cole. Despite the popularity of the event, the group did not tour after their second week, likely due to Aida's absence. Following the Pekin engagement, she returned to Manhattan accompanied by her nurse, Mary Johnson.[10] On July 16, 1914, Aida staged her final offering, the *Tango Picnic*, at the Manhattan Casino. The engagement was a success, and it was repeated at Hammerstein's during the first week of August on a bill that included Mae West (1893 to 1980).[11]

Following the *Tango Picnic*, Aida slowed her activity and lost her appetite. Resigned to her fate, she took to her bed on September 28, 1914. From that moment on she was surrounded by her best friend, Maggie Davis-Shipp, and Mary Johnson, who had been with her constantly for the previous year or so and may have provided palliative care for Pauline and George. On October 11, Aida was asked if there was anyone she wanted to see, and she replied, "Only Mamma, and she's waiting for me." At ten after six that evening, Aida Overton Walker died from Bright's disease (congestion of the kidneys). It is unknown whether her death was caused by syphilis, contracted from George, or if her kidney problems were inherited.[12]

At the time of her death, Aida was still known as one of the finest dancers in the United States, regardless of color, but her talent could not supplant the impudence of her unapologetic racial solidarity. She did not leave a will, but her former castmates Bert, Lottie, and Jesse Shipp thought that Mary Johnson should have been her rightful heir. However, her paternal uncle John W. Overton, whom the *Chicago Defender* indicated was "not friendly" with his niece, estimated the value of her estate at $250 and may have laid claim to it. Upwards of twenty-five carriages, filled with fifty-one floral arrangements, followed the hearse to Cypress Hills Cemetery in Brooklyn, where she was buried beside her mother and grandmother. Despite the outpouring of love, sadness, and testimonials, her grave remained unmarked for more than a century.[13]

As with George, Ernest Hogan, Bob Cole, and several others, Aida's loss was unfathomable. With no one to properly replace the best of the vanguard generation of Black celebrities of the early twentieth century, their legacy quickly disintegrated. Gatekeeping by the White establishment ensured that the void was filled by lesser versions who followed Bert's example or by White imitators, now without burnt cork. In George and Aida's case, it was Irene (1893 to 1969) and Vernon (1887 to 1918) Castle who danced their way to worldwide fame by popularizing sanitized versions of Black dances

Figure 15.1. "Castle Lame Duck Waltz," by James Reese Europe and Ford T. Dabney, Jos. W. Stern & Co., New York, 1913. *Source:* Author's collection.

while accompanied by James Reese Europe's New Amsterdam Orchestra. Such treatment propagated the convenient (for White people) idea that White people were the sole origin and destination of American popular culture.

The following is a brief account of some of the institutions and people associated with George Walker who operated beyond his lifetime.

Gotham Attucks

As the second Black-owned publishing company, its founders proved that profits made from Afro-American cultural products could remain with their creators. However, with so much money at stake, control of its destiny was short-lived. Beginning in January 1907, a long and costly battle over "He's a Cousin of Mine" between Gotham Attucks and the Harris-Morris publishing company, a White firm, lasted for more than a year. Then "Shep" Edmonds sold his interest for $55,000; Will Cook took charge of the company and established a Chicago office with Noah D. Thompson as manager in early 1909.[14] Bert's association with the firm ended after *Mr. Lode of Koal*, and without the Williams and Walker company promoting songs on the road, the company languished. Its operators resorted to issuing free copies of older songs in several newspapers that summer to generate new customers.[15] Their measures were unsuccessful, and the firm was sold to Ferdinand E. Mierisch. In 1911 "The House of Melody" closed its doors and passed into obscurity. When "Nobody" was republished in 1932, all association with Gotham Attucks was removed from the sheet music cover, replaced with "when performing this composition kindly give all program credits to Edward B. Marks Music Corporation." Subsequent reprints of "That's Why They Call Me Shine" followed suit. Jack Mills acquired the catalog in August of 1933, and the name was never revived.[16]

W-H-C Theatre

George Walker had not been successful using conventional methods to establish a theatre, but former Williams and Walker affiliates Black Carl and George Archer successfully opened the Palace Hall Theatre at Fifty-First Street and Seventh Avenue, a first-class vaudeville theatre in Manhattan, on October 3, 1909. Although their venture did not last, it was a solid proof of concept.[17] Two years later, the Frogs and the newly formed Johnson Amusement Company, located at 247 West Forty-Sixth Street, attempted to raise $165,000 to establish a Black-owned theatre in Harlem on 138th Street between Fifth and Lenox Avenue. It was intended to be a first-class structure, designed to house a theatre and conference rooms, measuring eighty by ninety feet, with 1,200 to 1,400 seats, a first-floor balcony, and thirty-two boxes, a first for Manhattan. By the time of the announcement, a $25,000 deposit had already been given to the Runkle Construction Company.[18]

It was intended as a public venture, and five investors put up the initial $50,000 to form the basis of shares in the theatre, which were offered to investors at ten dollars a share, guaranteeing a 6 percent return in the first year and an increase each year thereafter. The public was engaged to determine the name of the theatre, and on March 1, 1912, the board unanimously agreed on the Walker-Hogan-Cole (W-H-C) Theatre. With capital still lagging from investment-weary Afro-Americans, the announcement inspired new interest from as far as Mississippi, Colorado, and Cuba. George's mother, Alice, brimmed with excitement and published a letter of thanks in *The New York Age* saying in part, "It is a great way to pay equal tribute to the memory of these dear young men, each of whom spent his short life uplifting the moral standard of the stage work of our people." Ground was broken on Monday, March 11, but work was hampered by inclement weather and institutional impediments until May.[19] In early June, the company announced that the foundation was complete and the cornerstone was soon to follow in July. Shortly after, all activity ceased. On July 20, a lien was placed on the Johnson Amusement Company for $1,039.50, likely due to nonpayment for the foundation work. The W-H-C Theatre was never mentioned after the August 1, 1912, issue of *The New York Age*, and the concept was abandoned.[20]

Bert Williams

In the wake of George's death and Bert's estrangement from Aida, Bert's crossover stardom came at high cost. He had little to no contact with other Black people except in the offseason, especially after the closure of the Hotel Marshall in September of 1913.[21] The void was filled somewhat by Matheny's Cafe at 135th Street and Seventh Avenue in Harlem, where he could steal a few honest moments. That was the only atmosphere in which he showed his remaining devotion to George, as Tom Fletcher remembered: "One thing that would make Bert Williams lose his ready smile was an unfavorable mention of his late partner, George Walker. He said he had never loved anyone, including his parents, as he did George, and for anyone to say anything bad about George would bring out his lowest level of feelings."[22] When Bert finished the 1913 season, he severed ties with the Follies, although he remained under contract with Klaw and Erlanger. Shortly thereafter, he became the first Black film star, appearing in the silent film *Lime Kiln Club Field Day*. Produced in

1913 by the Biograph Film Company for Klaw and Erlanger with alumni of the Williams and Walker company, it was an adaptation of Cecil Mack's vaudeville offering from the second act of *Bandanna Land*. Although never released, it may have been Bert's most important film because it was as close as anyone would ever get to seeing the Williams and Walker cast on film, and it featured a cake walk and an onscreen kiss between Bert and costar Odessa Warren Grey. Next came *The Natural Born Gambler* in 1916, where he performed his famous pantomimed poker routine, and the much-less-successful *Fish*, where Bert played a mischievous child.[23]

As time moved on, some Black people's admiration and respect for Bert pivoted to anger and resentment. Sylvester Russell offered a possible explanation for his behavior that also served as an indictment: "He was born in Nassau in the West Indies. Nor is he, heart and soul, with the colored race except by force of condition."[24] Bert knew that he was capable of real artistry but chose to be a servant in paradise as the lovable loser in White companies.[25] Serving an entirely new purpose with the same act, he was eventually surpassed in popularity by former Williams and Walker chorus member Charles Gilpin, who found stardom in the 1919 production of *Abraham Lincoln* and played the starring role of Brutus Jones in *Emperor Jones* in 1920, both dramatic roles. Those productions allowed Gilpin to be one of the first Black actors to gain access to real dramatic material beyond *Uncle Tom's Cabin* and the minstrel constraints that still compelled Bert to perform in blackface for condescension-laced laughter.

In an effort to return to his artistic home, an ailing Bert joined the Black cast of *Under the Bamboo Tree* in late 1921. Unfortunately, he developed pneumonia soon after, and, rather than seek treatment, he continued to work, because without him the show would have likely folded. The company opened at the Garrick in Detroit for a week on February 26, 1922. Bert was unable to continue beyond opening night. During the first act on the second night, he suffered through a high fever and began to sweat profusely through his cork. Like his first time in blackface, he wiped away the sweat, revealing streaks in his makeup, only this time, he wasn't petrified with fear. It wasn't until he was replaced by an understudy that the audience understood that he was deathly ill. He was immediately sent back to New York for a blood transfusion, but it was too late. As feared, the show promptly closed after the performance, and Bert died at home on the morning of March 4, 1922, at the age of forty-seven. Lottie, too, had been ailing since *Bandanna Land*, and she suffered through multiple surgeries through the years and eventually passed away on the afternoon of March 17, 1929, at the age of sixty-three.[26]

Jerry Nashville Walker

After the establishment of the Colorado African Colonization Company in 1902, Nashville Walker listed himself in Denver city directories as a solicitor or clerk rather than servant or house man as in years past.[27] The depth of his contribution to *In Dahomey* remains unknown, but it was surely more than a coincidence.

On January 19, 1911, just a few weeks after George's death, Nashville Walker sent his proposal to Monrovia to officially begin repatriating Afro-Americans to Liberia. The following April, he received a letter from President Arthur Barclay (1854 to 1938) confirming the establishment of a fifty-thousand-acre land grant. Although he claimed to have transported twenty thousand people to Liberia, the true total remains unknown, but the remainder of his life was devoted to getting Black people out of the United States. He never made the trip himself, and at the age of seventy-five, Jerry Nashville Walker died impoverished at his home at 2240 Larimer Street in Denver on November 9, 1922. He was buried in Riverside Cemetery in Denver, in an unmarked grave.[28]

Alice Myers

Following her son's death, Alice Myers took in laundry and boarders because she could no longer afford the yearly taxes for her home, "Abyssinio." Citing desertion in July of 1910, she also filed for divorce from Frank Myers in May of 1912. In November of that year, the Warren Street Baptist Church completed a remodel in which several improvements were made to the limestone structure as well as a dozen memorial windows, one of which was dedicated to Nash Walker. Alice continued to be a member and regularly sang solos. Times were as hard as when she had escaped bondage, and it was later said that she searched the yard in vain for a stash of money that Nash had supposedly hidden somewhere. By mid-May 1913, she was forced to leave "Abyssinio," and it was listed for sale by J. W. Shaw, who owned a local lumberyard. It was still on the market when Alice's youngest brother, Will Hayden, died suddenly of a pulmonary hemorrhage on the morning of September 10, 1913, and was buried at Oak Hill, just feet away from Nash, Sanford, and Sarah in an unmarked grave. By that time, Alice was suffering from heart trouble. Nevertheless, she continued to take in laundry and boarders, babysat, and received some financial support from Aida until her death in 1914.[29]

After losing her home, Alice moved often between crowded rooming houses, first at 915 Louisiana Street until 1915, at 836 Ohio Street until 1917, and then at 1327 New Jersey Street for a few years. Through it all, she tried to keep up appearances, and when performers who knew Nash came to town, she often visited with them.[30] By 1926, she was unable to work and became dependent on local charities, destined for "the poor farm." After hearing of her "destitute circumstances," lyricist and composer Noble Sissle (1889 to 1975), of the famed vaudeville team Sissle and Blake, with the help of Bill "Bojangles" Robinson (1878 to 1949), organized a series of fundraisers for her, the first of which netted $200. On June 22, Bojangles, with help from Flournoy Miller (1885 to 1971) of the comedy team Miller and Lyles, educator William H. Davis (1848 to 1938), and Mrs. Sadie Warren-Davis (1868 to 1946), wife of the New York *Amsterdam News* editor "Easy Ed" Warren and mother of former Williams and Walker chorus member and costar of *Lime Club Kiln Field Day* Odessa Warren, organized another benefit at the Alhambra Theatre. Bojangles paid for Alice's transportation to Manhattan for the event, and she was accompanied by his mother-in-law. At the midway point, he introduced her to the audience, and a basket was passed through the theatre, which netted more than $300. Less expenses, the event raised $1,731, with the possibility of an additional $235 if granted an exemption from the war tax. For Alice's return trip through Chicago for the next event, Bojangles provided a Pullman drawing room for her and covered all expenses.[31]

Following the benefit shows, Robinson oversaw the purchase of a home at 1133 New York Street in Lawrence for Alice, during the summer of 1926. Likely for financial reasons, she sold the house to Lawrence Johnson in May of 1928 but continued to live in it until May of 1930. In response to her continued financial and physical decline, another benefit was organized in Lawrence with a production of a musical comedy titled *Foiled*, taken from the popular musical *The Hurry-Up Bride*, at the Orpheum theatre on the evening of June 3, 1930. Organized by an unnamed Black charity in Kansas City, Kansas, and the YMCA, the event was likely to help cover her moving expenses to a home for the destitute at 1400 Seventeenth Street in Kansas City, Missouri, where she died on March 22, 1933, from heart failure at the age of seventy-six. She was interred under a walnut tree in an unmarked grave on March 27 at Maple Hill Cemetery, Kansas City, Kansas.[32]

Figure 15.2. Bill "Bojangles" Robinson and Alice Myers in front of a home that he purchased for her in Lawrence in early September 1926. *Source: Pittsburgh Courier,* September 25, 1926, 9.

The Frogs

The first meeting of the Frogs after George's funeral was on the evening of January 22, 1911, at the club's aerial bungalow at 15 West 137th Street. That evening, they set June 26 as the date for the Frolic of 1911 at the Manhattan Casino. Also, they decided to move their headquarters to a property at 111 West 132nd Street that had been purchased for $12,000 in May of 1910. For unknown reasons, the move to the new "pond" was not completed until June of 1913, just in time for that year's Frolic. It was a ten-room, two-bath, red-brick house, complete with electric lights, gas, and other conveniences. The basement housed the grill, kitchen, and buffet; the parlor contained the library and art; the music rooms were on the first floor; the billiard, pool, and poster rooms on the second floor; and on the third floor were the executive offices and sleeping rooms. Despite their elite status, the Frogs were almost immediately supplanted by the Clef Club, established on April 11, 1910, by Frog James Reese Europe. Ironically, the Clef Club's first concert was at that year's Frolic. Europe also organized and conducted a wildly successful performance at Carnegie Hall on May 2, 1912. In keeping with the mission of the Frogs, the Clef Club provided stable income for hundreds of Black performers for several years and fostered artistic development on a scale that George could only imagine.[33]

Following the Frolic of 1913 and a short minstrel tour, the Frogs' activity slowed significantly. Instead of their traditional dance, they decided to host Prof. Sterrett's Circus on June 29, 1914, at the Manhattan Casino for eight thousand patrons. Shortly after, Frog and former Williams and Walker cast member Sam Corker Jr. died suddenly after falling from a ladder on August 17, 1914. The following September, the Frogs' collection from actors, authors, and composers, totaling more than eight hundred pieces, was loaned to the National Exhibition and Amusement Company by Isaac Hines, proprietor of the Professional Club, an upscale bar at 23 West 134th Street. Although diminished, they added a pool to the pond in May of 1917 and opened a satellite office in Richmond, Virginia.[34]

In July of 1926, the Frogs announced the purchase of a small theatre at 46 West 135th Street, near Lenox Avenue in Harlem, to be operated by and for the Black community. Slated to open that fall, it was to be a 299-seat playhouse with all the modern amenities. In keeping with the group's 1908 bylaws, it was not intended to be a commercial venture, but no other mention was made after the announcement. On May 18, 1927, they hosted a Creole gumbo feed in honor of J. Rosamond Johnson at the Footlights Club at 115 West 131st Street to celebrate his coming trip to Europe following release of *God's Trombones*. There was a dozen or more speeches and toasts from the aging former theatrical elite that sparked rumors of the Frogs staging a "comeback."[35] Although well-attended, the final event was emblematic of a bygone era, which gave credence to Sylvester Russell's criticism of the Frogs as being more of an elitist social club than a cultural institution. If the contrary was the case, Lester Walton did not see fit to print it in *The New York Age*, the only newspaper to catalog the activities of the club until the founding members were no longer relevant. However, as of 2025, the Pittsburgh, Chicago, and possibly Savannah chapters still thrive.

Sylvester Russell

Throughout a career of nearly thirty years at *The Freeman*, *Chicago Defender*, *Pittsburgh Courier*, and the self-published *Star*, Sylvester Russell never minced words, which sometimes led to physical altercations. As noted by Jack L. Cooper (1888 to 1970), "He would write of your act or acting as he saw it and then hide from you when he saw you coming as he was small of stature and not very strong physically."[36] Most notably, Russell was assaulted by S. H. Dudley in 1911, following his published irritation with the actor's son's singing during a performance at the Globe Theatre in Chicago. Two years later, trap drummer Charles Gilliam assaulted him following a bad review in 1913 when he performed with Aida at the Pekin. Although he was the best-known Black critic in the country, he had few friends, and he died alone and impoverished from heart disease in his Chicago flat on October 8, 1930, three weeks after Alex Rogers.[37]

Black Theatre After Williams and Walker

Following the disbandment of Williams and Walker, Black people were summarily evicted from Broadway until Sissle and Blake's *Shuffle Along* in 1921, which opened the year before Bert's death. According to Eubie Blake, James Reese Europe wanted to head up a new Black show with Sissle and Blake and make a return to Broadway after World War I. Europe's death in 1919 prevented that, but the seed was planted. Originally titled *Who's Stealin'*, it was a combination of two shows starring the comedians Miller and Lyles, direct descendants of Bert and George's comedic style.[38]

Despite its developmental difficulties, when it finally opened in New York, *Shuffle Along* caused a sensation that was similar to Bert and George's impact at Koster and Bial's twenty-five years earlier. Although the show featured "Love Will Find a Way," an ode to Black love, and other innovative songs, many of the same impediments that Williams and Walker encountered were still in play. Without a critical mass of Black shows to serve as a proof of concept, Sissle and Blake were unable to repeat their success, while White producers seized control and staged several revues that, much like the process of assimilating ragtime via sheet music, took advantage of Black talent in ways that removed the fundamental characteristics of Black creative processes. As a quiet and potent method to remove evidence of Black contribution, the act of privately coveting yet publicly distaining Black people and cultural products has established an inequitable tradition that has yet to be discredited and abandoned. That uniquely American tradition, brought on by the legacy of our original birth defect, gives credence and substance to Aida's prophetic statement when she learned of the death of her friend and early dance partner Grace Halliday: "One thing about your work is that it lives after you, but ours dies with us; when we die it is all past."[39]

Despite his expungement, George "Nash" Walker's mark on the theatrical world was felt and appreciated long after his death by those who knew and respected him. As expressed by Romeo L. Dougherty (1885 to 1944), Aida's former publicity manager, fifteen years after George's death, "until the coming of Walker both colored and white America had almost accepted the idea of associating the colored artist with a buffoonery from which nothing could divorce him, but Walker surrounded himself with an array of brilliant colored writers and producers when opportunity beckoned and proved to America that Negroes, when given the chance, could produce something which could appeal not only to America but to Europe as well."[40]

The vanguard generation demonstrated the potential of double consciousness and, unfortunately, its price. Nevertheless, theirs is a history of precedent, the manifestation of their ancestors' wildest dreams: the first to leave the recipe for the essence of what it means to be Black in the post-emancipation United States. George knew it, wanted us to know it and to keep knowing it. Therefore, *we* must put in the work to learn our ancestors' stories and speak their names. If not us, someone else will, still.

Appendix
Williams and Walker Engagements

1893—Martin and Selig's Colored Minstrels (California Tour)

Gibbon's Hall, San Jose, September 19; San Louis Obispo Opera House, October 12; School House, New Jerusalem, October 20; Foresters Hall, Redondo, October 26; unknown theatre, Compton, October 30; Academy of Music, Redlands, November 3; Pomona Opera House, November 6; and Hanford Opera House, November 23.

1894 to 1898—Dahomey Village, San Francisco, January to May, 1894; Jack Cremorne's Midway Plaisance, San Francisco, circa December 1893 to November 1895; Orpheum, Los Angeles, November 18 to December 28, 1895; Imperial and Oxford, Chicago, week of March 15, 1896; Lyceum, week of April 13, 1896; Chicago Opera House, week of May 25, 1896; Wonderland, Detroit, week of July 19, 1896; West Baden (IN) Opera House, August 18 and 21, 1896—Willis, Clark, Roof Garden Vaudeville Company; Ferris Wheel Park, Chicago, two weeks beginning August 30, 1896; *Gold Bug*, Manhattan Casino, September 22, 1896; Columbia, Brooklyn, week of September 28, 1896—Eugene Sandow's *Olympia* in *Two Coons in Town*; Hollis, Boston, week of October 5, 1896, in Peter Daily's *A Good Thing*; Musee, McKeesport, PA, week of October 12, 1896; Koster and Bial's, Manhattan, October 25 to November 21, 1896; Proctor's 23rd Street, week of November 23, 1896; Koster and Bial's, November 30, 1896, to January 16, 1897; Proctor's 23rd Street, week of January 17, 1897; Koster and Bial's, week of January 24, 1897; Hyde and Behman's, Brooklyn, two weeks beginning January 31, 1897; Koster and Bial's, Manhattan, four weeks beginning February 14, 1897; (simultaneously week of March 7) Hyde and Behman's, Brooklyn, two weeks beginning March 7, 1897; Bijou, Philadelphia, week of March 14; Keith's, week of April 4, 1897; Empire, London, April 19 to May 16, 1897; Koster and Bial's, Manhattan, May 30 to June 29, 1897; Keith's, Brooklyn, week of August 8, 1897; Koster and Bial's, Manhattan, week of August 16, 1897; Hammerstein's Olympia Roof Garden, two weeks beginning August 22, 1897; Proctor's 23rd Street, week of September 12, 1897; Hyde and Behman's, Brooklyn, week of September 19, 1897—Hyde's Comedians in *The Upper Ten and Lower Five of Blackville*; whereabouts unknown September 26 to October 2, 1897; Proctor's 23rd Street, Manhattan, week of October 3, 1897; Auditorium Music Hall and Palm Garden, Baltimore, week of October 10, 1897; Kernan's Lyceum, District of Columbia, week of October 17, 1897; East End, Pittsburgh, October 28 to 31, 1897; Fountain, Cincinnati, week of November 1, 1897; Park, Indianapolis, week of November 8, 1897; Buckingham, Louisville, week of November 14, 1897; Olympic, Chicago, week of November 21, 1897; Haymarket, week of November 29, 1897; Chicago Opera House, week of December 6, 1897; whereabouts unknown December 13 to 16, 1897; Proctor's 23rd Street, Manhattan, week of December 19, 1897; Hyde and Behman's, Brooklyn, week of January 3, 1898; Gayety, two weeks beginning January 9, 1898; Gilmore's Auditorium, Philadelphia, week of January 23, 1898; Grand, District of Columbia, week of January 31, 1898; Auditorium Music Hall, Baltimore, week of February 7, 1898; Avenue, Pittsburg, week of February 14, 1898; Fountain, Cincinnati, week of February 20, 1898; Hopkins Grand, St. Louis, week of February 27, 1898; Olympic, Chicago, week of March 6, 1898; Haymarket, week of March 13, 1898; Chicago Opera House, week of March 20, 1898; whereabouts unknown March 27 to April 9, 1898; Orpheum, San Francisco, two weeks beginning April 10, 1898; Orpheum, Sacramento, week of April 24, 1898; Orpheum, Los Angeles, week of May 1, 1898.

Summer Vaudeville—Pleasure Palace, Brooklyn, week of May 15, 1898; Olympic, Chicago week of May 22, 1898, in *The Uptemper Ten of Coontown*; Chicago Opera House, week of June 6, 1898; Hopkins, two weeks beginning June 12, 1898; Forest Park Highlands, St. Louis, two weeks beginning June 26, 1898; Masonic Temple Roof Garden, Chicago, week of July 10, 1898; whereabouts unknown July 17 to 23, 1898; Proctor's Pleasure Palace, Manhattan, three weeks beginning July 24, 1898; and Keith's, Brooklyn, week of August 14, 1898.

1898 to 1899—*Senegambian Carnival, Clorindy or Origin of the Cake Walk, A Lucky Coon*

Principal Cast—Bert Williams, Phineas "Dollar Bill" Burnall; George Walker, Archie "Silver King" Getup; Joe Hodges, Wise Ike; Ed Mallory, Mose Puffs; Frank Mallory, George Toots; Ed Goggin, the purser; Charles Davis, the pilot; Ed Harris, Policeman Graball; William C. Elkins, Elder Wayback; James Jackson, Lazy Joseph; Mamie Emmerson, Miss Marie Belford; Lola Launchmere, Aunt Lucinda; Mazie Brooks, Miss Susanna; Lottie Thompson, Miss Prim; Ada Overton, Miss Fitzwell; Grace Halliday, Miss Redfin.

Featured Cast—Black Carl, magician; Henry Williams, the king of all flatfoot dancers; Clarence Duval (Lord Bonnie), the leader of the cake walk, Charles Moore; Carrie Carter; Henry Thomas, phenomenal basso; Ollie Burgoyne; Louis Henry Saulisbury; Jesse Shipp, stage manager; and Harry T. Burleigh, musical director (left the company in January of 1899).

Boston Theatre, week of September 5, 1898; Casino Roof Garden, Manhattan, September 11, 1898; Chestnut Street, Philadelphia, week of September 12, 1898; Grand, Cincinnati, week of September 18, 1898; Star, Buffalo, week of September 25, 1898 (canceled); People's, Philadelphia, week of October 2, 1898; Academy, Washington, DC, week of October 9, 1898; stranded week of October 16, 1898; Proctor's 23rd Street, Manhattan, week of October 23, 1898; Hyde and Behman's (sans company), Brooklyn, week of October 30, 1898; Koster and Bial's, Manhattan, three weeks beginning November 6, 1898; Park, Brooklyn, week of December 11, 1898; Bon Ton, Jersey City, week of December 19, 1898; Hyperion, New Haven, CT, December 27, 1898; Parson's, Hartford, December 28, 1898; Poli's, Waterbury, December 31, 1898; Dewey, Manhattan, week of January 2, 1899; Hurtig and Seamon's Harlem Music Hall, January 8, 1899; Olympic, Providence, RI, week of January 9, 1899; Gayety, Brooklyn, week of January 16, 1899; Gilmore's Auditorium, Philadelphia, January 23, 1899; Howard Athenaeum, Boston, week of January 29, 1899; Hurtig and Seamon's Harlem Music Hall, week of February 6, 1899; Dewey, Manhattan, week of February 13, 1899; Duquesne, Pittsburgh, week of February 19, 1899; Park, Dayton, February 27 to March 1, 1899; Fountain Square, Cincinnati, week of March 5, 1899; Great Northern, Chicago, two weeks beginning March 12, 1899; Academy, Chicago, March 26, 1899; Alhambra, Chicago, week of April 3, 1899; Columbia, St. Louis, week of April 9, 1899; Imperial, St.

Louis, week of April 16, 1899; Sheah's, Buffalo, week of April 24, 1899; Gilmore's Auditorium, Philadelphia, two weeks beginning April 30, 1899; Academy of Music, DC, May 7 to 13, 1899; Dewey, Manhattan, week of May 14, 1899.

Summer Vaudeville—Auditorium Pier, Atlantic City, week of August 28, 1899.

1899 to 1900—*The Policy Players*

Principal Cast—Bert Williams, Dusty Cheapman; George Walker, Happy Hotstuff; Mazie Brooks, Mrs. Readymoney, a seamstress in the Astorbilt Family; Lola Launchmere, Mrs. Tubly, a wash lady; Ada Overton, Kioka, and Grace Halliday, Kama (a pair of Honolulu belles); Lottie Thompson, Miss Gushington, of other times; Mamie Emmerson, Canon Nador Lizie, a hard proposition; Ollie Burgoyne, Capricious Young, but more than seven at that; Maggie Davis, Estelle Puglsly, Mattie Evans, and Effie Wilson, nurses; Euginia Wadsworth and Daisy Harris, pastry cooks; Elorence Ellsworth, Ruby; Anna Cooke, Pearle; Madge Warren, Rosa; Odessa Warren, Lily; and Maude Thompson Jones, Violet (Up-to-date-Girls); Mattie Wilkes, Cadenzo Animato, a prima donna out of a job; Joe Hodges, Diamond Joe, pres., mgr., and chief clerk of the Liberal Investment Company; Frank Mallory, Dandy Jack Rugby, a footman, also dream interpreter; Ed Mallory, Clarence Whipley, a coachman; and Fred Douglass, Canon Nader, an awful tough man.

Featured Cast—Reese Brothers and Fred Douglas, the world's champion gun manipulators; the great George Catlin, the only colored Chinese impersonator; Trixie Wade, comedienne; Sam and Ida Kelly, sketch artists; Prof. Fox, bird and animal imitation; the Williams and Walker quartet, William C. Elkins (director and first bass), Edwin S. Thomas (second bass), Frank B. Williams (first tenor), and William Orme (second tenor); Ed Harris, impersonator; Richard Connors, singing comedian; Will Marion Cook, musical director; Jesse Shipp, stage manager; Sam Tuck, manager.

Hoyt's, South Norwalk, CT, September 23, 1899; Parson's, Hartford, September 26, 1899; Hyperion, New Haven, September 27, 1899; Lyceum, New London, September 28, 1899; Academy of Music, Fall River, MA, September 30, 1899; Harmanus Lyceum, Albany, NY, week of October 1, 1899; Hurtig and Seamon's Music Hall, Manhattan, week of October 8,

1899; Star, week of October 16, 1899; Gilmore's Auditorium, Philadelphia, week of October 23, 1899; Bijou, Brooklyn, week of October 29, 1899; Holliday Street, Baltimore, week of November 6, 1899; New Grand, DC, week of November 13, 1899; Bijou, Philadelphia, week of November 20, 1899; Avenue, Louisville, week of November 26, 1899; Walnut Street, Cincinnati, December 3, 1899; Columbia, Cincinnati, week of December 4; whereabouts unknown December 10 to 16, 1899; Lyceum, Detroit, week of December 17, 1899; Great Northern, Chicago, week of December 24, 1899; Columbia, St. Louis, week of December 31, 1899; Orpheum, Kansas City, week of January 7, 1900; Crawford Grand, Leavenworth, January 14, 1900; Bowersock, Lawrence, January 15, 1900; Crawford, Topeka, January 16, 1900; Funke, Atchison, January 17, 1900; Lyceum, St. Joseph, MO, January 18, 1900; Funke, Lincoln, NE, January 19 to 20, 1900; Creighton-Orpheum, Omaha, week of January 21, 1900; Dohany, Council Bluffs, IA, January 28, 1900; Grand, Des Moines, January 29 to 30, 1900; whereabouts unknown January 31 to February 3; Burtis, Davenport, February 4, 1900; Grand, Bloomington, IN, February 6, 1900; whereabouts unknown February 7 to 8; Powers Grand, Decatur, February 9, 1900; unknown theatre, Terre Haute, February 10, 1900; Park, Indianapolis, February 12 to 14, 1900; Walker, Champaign, IL, February 16, 1900; Great Northern, Chicago, two weeks beginning February 18, 1900; Altoona (PA) Opera House, March 3, 1900; possibly Providence, RI, March 4 to 10, 1900; Grand, Boston, week of March 11, 1900; Bijou, Brooklyn, week of March 19, 1900; Gilmore's Auditorium, Philadelphia, week of March 26, 1900; Koster and Bial's, Manhattan, two weeks beginning April 2, 1900; whereabouts unknown April 15 to 21, 1900; Hurtig and Seamon's Harlem Music Hall, week of April 22, 1900; Hoyt's, Norwalk, CT, April 30, 1900; Delavan, Meridian, May 1, 1900; Hyperion, New Haven, May 2, 1900; Lyceum, New London, May 3, 1900; Star, Manhattan, week of May 6, 1900.

Summer Vaudeville—Shea's Garden, Buffalo, (four-person act) week of June 10, 1900; Keith's, Boston, week of July 23, 1900; Keith's, Brooklyn, week of July 29, 1900; Point of the Pines, Boston, week of July 29, 1900, in *The Golf Links* (featuring members of the Williams and Walker and Cole and Johnson companies); Proctor's 23rd Street, Manhattan, week of August 5, 1900, in *The Wedding of King Booloolum and Queen Razzerina, a Zulu Specialty*; home of Adolph and Martha Asmus, Jersey City, in a burlesque of *Romeo and Juliet*, August 10, 1900; Proctor's Fifth Avenue, Manhattan, week of August 20, 1900.

1900 to 1901—*Sons of Ham*

Principal Cast—Bert Williams, Tobias Wormwood; George Walker, Harty Laughter; Fred Douglass, Willie Wataboy; Arthur Reese, Aniesta Babdola; Ollie Reese, Jenarusha Hassambad; Frank Sutton, Frank; Henry Winfried, Henry; James Burress, James; George Pickett, Joe Jenkins; Richard Connors, Joshua Pipes; Anna E. Cook, Dinah Patterson; Clara Freeman, Patsy Patterson; Pauline Freeman, Fluffy; Mamie Emmerson, Jane; Jennie Shepard, Tillie; Odessa Warren, Polly; Fannie Winfried, Mollie; May Rector, Tuffy; Florence Ellsworth, Samantha Johnson; Nelly Wells, Sou; Lavina Jones, Lize; Marie Williams, Daphne; Alice Mackay-Accooe, Mariah; G. W. Washington, Ben Jenkins; Jesse Shipp, Prof. Switchen; Green Henri Tapley, Jeneriska Hassambad; Pete Hampton, Uncle Hampton Flam; Nellie Glenn, Lou; Lottie Williams, Gabby Slangtry, a booking agent; Ada Overton, Caroline Jenkins; Will Marion Cook, musical director; Jesse Shipp, stage manager; and Sam Tuck, manager.

Featured Cast—"Black" Carl Dante; Stella Wiley; George Harris; James McDonald; W. H. Chappelle; Fred W. Simpson; John C. Pittman; Arthur Coates; Shepard N. Edmonds; Will Murray; Charles Moore; Maggie Davis; Abbie Cook; Estella Ware; Billy Miller; Blanche Arlington; Midget Price; Lillian Perrin; Marie Locals; Eugenia Wright; Bertha Ellis; Sydney Perrin; Leslie Triplett; Henry Skuder; Russell Brandon; Jas. Jackson; Freeman sisters, singers and acrobatic dancers; famous Golden Gate Quartet—Sutton, Coates, Winfred and Coates, comedians, vocalists, and buck dancers; Pittman and Simpson, novel musical artists; Edmonds and Murray, comedians and eccentric dancers; Fred Douglass and Reese brothers, champion baton jugglers and gymnasts; Miss Eddie Mitchell, the phenomenal soprano vocalist; and George Catlin, the only Colored Chinese impersonator.

Act I: Scene 1—The home of Ham, Swampville, Tennessee; Scene 2—Footpath between Riske College and Crystal Spring; Scene 3—Riske College.

Act II: Scene 1—Interior of Ham's home; Scene 2—Exterior of town hall, Swampville, Tennessee.

People's, Mount Vernon, NY, September 17, 1900; Delavan, Meriden, CT, September 18 to 21, 1900; Lyceum, New London, September 24, 1900; Broadway, Norwich, September 25, 1900; Parsons's, Hartford, September

26, 1900; Court Square, Springfield, MA, September 27, 1900; Auditorium, Philadelphia, week of October 1, 1900; Bijou, Brooklyn, week of October 8, 1900; Star, Manhattan, week of October 14, 1900; Hurtig and Seamon's Harlem Music Hall, Manhattan, October 21 to 27, 1900; Gayety, Brooklyn, October 28, 1900; Poli's, Waterbury, CT, October 31, 1900; Grand, New Haven, November 1 to 3, 1900; whereabouts unknown November 4 to 14, 1900; Baker, Rochester, November 15 to 17, 1900; Bijou, Pittsburgh, week of November 18, 1900 (canceled due to smallpox)—Canton; Chillicothe, OH, November 29, 1900; Lexington, November 30 to December 1, 1900; Walnut, Cincinnati, December 9, 1900, and Kansas City; (tour resumed) Wysor Grand, Muncie, IN, December 25 to 26, 1900; Mattoon (IL) Theatre, December 29, 1900; Grand, St. Louis, week of December 30, 1900; Alhambra, Milwaukee, WS, January 6 to 11, 1901; Alhambra, Wauwatosa, WI, January 12, 1901; Great Northern, Chicago, week of January 13, 1901; Orpheum, Kansas City, week of January 20, 1901; Orpheum, Omaha, NE, week of January 27, 1901; Funke, Lincoln, February 4 to 6, 1901; Crawford, Topeka, February 7, 1901; Lyceum, St. Joseph, MO, February 8 to 9, 1901; Crawford, Leavenworth, February 10, 1901; Bowersock, Lawrence, February 11, 1901; Hegarty's, Moberly, MO, February 12, 1901; whereabouts unknown February 13 to 16, 1901, possibly Des Moines, IA; Burtis, Davenport, February 17, 1901; Tonganoxie (KS) Opera House, February 18, 1901; Powers Grand, Decatur, IN, February 20, 1901; Grand, Bloomington, February 22, 1901; Academy, Chicago, week of February 24, 1901; Brooklyn Music Hall, March 3 to 6, 1901; Lyceum, Perrysburg, OH, March 7 to 9, 1901; Heuck's, Cincinnati, week of March 10, 1901; whereabouts unknown March 17 to 26, 1901; Altoona (PA) Opera House, March 27, 1901; Grand, Harrisburg, March 28, 1901; Fulton, Lancaster, March 29, 1901; Hurtig and Seamon's Music Hall, Manhattan, week of March 31, 1901; Auditorium, Philadelphia, week of April 7, 1901; Empire, Newark, NJ, April 14 to 21, 1901; Gayety, Brooklyn, April 22, 1901; Eleventh Avenue, Altoona, PA, April 27; Grand, Manhattan, week of April 28, 1901; Park, Boston, two weeks beginning May 6, 1901.

Summer Vaudeville—Keith's, Boston, two weeks beginning May 26, 1901; Keith's, Brooklyn, two weeks beginning June 9, 1901; Keith's, Philadelphia, June 24, 1901; Woolworth Roof Garden, Lancaster, two weeks beginning July 15, 1901, in *The Golf Links*; Auditorium Pier, Atlantic City, week of August 5, 1901; Steel Pier, Atlantic City, August 22, 1901; Brighton Beach Music Hall, Brooklyn, week of September 1, 1901.

1901 to 1902—*Sons of Ham*

Added George Denis; Alberta Ormes; Louis H. Salisbury; Leon Williams; Walter Robinson; Frank B. Williams; the Pugsley Sisters; Sat Dixon; Nattie Bowman; and Sally Thorpe following the close of John W. Isham's *King Rastus* company in early May of 1901. Between August and September 1901, Annie Ross Williams and Lloyd G. Gibbs were added.

People's, Mount Vernon, NY, September 16, 1901; Park City, Bridgeport, CT, September 17, 1901; whereabouts unknown September 18 to 19, 1901; Poli's, Naugatuck/Waterbury, September 20, 1901; whereabouts unknown September 21 to 23, 1901; Lyceum, New London, September 24, 1901; Court Square, Springfield, MA, September 26, 1901; Parson's, Hartford, CT, September 28, 1901; Bijou, Brooklyn, week of September 30, 1901; Auditorium, Philadelphia, week of October 7, 1901; Hurtig and Seamon's Harlem Music Hall, two weeks beginning October 13, 1901; Gayety, Brooklyn, October 28, 1901; People's, Philadelphia, week of November 4, 1901; Empire, Montclair, NJ, week of November 11, 1901; Academy of Music, Atlantic City, November 18, 1901; Mishler's Academy of Music, Reading, PA, November 19, 1901; whereabouts unknown November 20 to 21, 1901; Lyric, Allentown, November 22, 1901; Fulton, Lancaster, November 23, 1901; whereabouts unknown November 24 to 26, 1901; Grand, Akron, OH, November 27, 1901; Valentine, Toledo, OH, November 28, 1901; Faurot, Lima, November 30, 1901; unknown theatre, Bowling Green, KY, December 1, 1901; Victoria, Dayton, OH, December 2 to 4, 1901; whereabouts unknown December 5 to 6, 1901; Lexington (KY) Opera House, December 7, 1901; Heuck's, Cincinnati, week of December 8, 1901; Great Northern, Chicago, week of December 15, 1901; Avenue, Louisville, week of December 22, 1901; Grand, St. Louis, week of December 29, 1901; Grand, Kansas City, week of January 5, 1902; Crawford, Topeka, January 13, 1902; Bowersock, Lawrence, January 14, 1902; whereabouts unknown January 15 to 16, 1902; Grand, Bloomington, ID, January 17, 1902; Grand, Decatur, IL, January 18, 1902; Alhambra, Chicago, week of January 19, 1902; Academy, Chicago, week of January 26, 1902; Lyceum, Detroit, week of February 2, 1902; whereabouts unknown week of February 9, 1902; Teck, Buffalo, February 16, 1902; unknown theatre, Syracuse, February 17 to 19, 1902; Baker, Rochester, February 20 to 22, 1902; Lyceum, Buffalo, week of February 24, 1902; Grand, Manhattan, week of March 3, 1902; National, Philadelphia, week of March 10, 1902; Bijou, Brooklyn, week of March 16, 1902; Boyd's, Omaha, NE, March 30 to April 2, 1902;

California, San Francisco, CA, April 6 to 20, 1902; Yosemite, Stockton, April 21, 1902; Clunie, Sacramento, April 22, 1902; Marquam, Portland, OR, April 24 to 26, 1902; Grand, Seattle, WA, April 27 to 30, 1902; Vancouver (BC) Opera House, May 2, 1902; Tacoma (WA) Theatre, May 3, 1902; Spokane Theatre, May 5 to 6, 1902; Union, Missoula, MT, May 8, 1902; Helena, May 9, 1902; Anaconda-Margaret, Butte, May 10, 1902; Sutton's Broadway, Butte, May 11 to 13, 1902; Grand, Ogden, UT, May 15, 1902; Salt Lake Theatre, May 16 to 17, 1902; Park, Grand Junction, May 19, 1902; Wheeler, Aspen, CO, May 20, 1902; Elk's, Leadville, May 21, 1902; Grand, Pueblo, May 22, 1902; Tabor Grand, Denver, CO, week of May 25, 1902; Great Northern, Chicago, June 8 to 21, 1902.

Summer Vaudeville—Woolworth Roof Garden, Lancaster, PA, week of June 30, 1902, in *The Golf Links* (featuring members of the Williams and Walker and Cole and Johnson companies); Brighton Beach Music Hall, Brooklyn, two weeks beginning July 27 in *The Zulu Babes*.

1902 to 1903—*In Dahomey*

Principal Cast—Bert Williams, Shylock Homestead; George Walker, Rareback Pinkerton; Jesse Shipp, Hustling Charlie; Alex Rogers, George Reeder; J. Leubrie Hill, Dr. Straight; James Lightfoot, Hamilton Lightfoot; George Catlin, Me-Sing, a Chinese cook; Richard Connors, Leathers; George Pickett, Officer Still; Theodore Pankey, Messenger Rush, but not often; James Hill, Bill Primrose; Hattie McIntosh, Cecilia Lightfoot; Lottie Williams, Mrs. Stringer; Aida Overton Walker, Rosetta Lightfoot.

Featured Cast—Bessie Vaughn; Ida Day; "Tiny Jones"; Charles Moore, Kate Jones; Mazie Bush; Jesse Ellis; Maggie Davis; Hattie Hopkins; Hattie McIntosh; Renie Morris; Daisy Tapley; Ella Anderson, Lizzie Avery; Levinia Rogers; Jim Vaughn; William C. Elkins; Walter Richardson; Will Accooe; Chip Ruff; John Leubrie Hill; Green Henri Tapley; Henry Troy; Marshall Craig; Theodore Pankey; Harry Stafford; and Charles L. Saulsbury.

Act I: Scene 1—Public square in Boston.

Act II: Scene 1—Exterior of Lightfoot's home, Gatorville, Florida; Scene 2—Road, one and a half miles from Gatorville; Scene 3—Interior of the Lightfoot home.

Act III: Scene 1—Swamp in Dahomey; Scene 2—Garden of the caboceer (governor of the Providence). Execution tower in the distance.

Grand Opera House, Stamford, CT, September 8, 1902; Hyperion, New Haven, September 10, 1902; whereabouts unknown September 11 to 14, 1902; Lyceum, New London, September 15, 1902; Hartford Opera House, September 16 to 17, 1902; Court Square, Holyoke, MA, September 19, 1902; Worcester, MA, September 20, 1902; Music Hall, Boston, week of September 22, 1902; Auditorium, Philadelphia, week of September 29, 1902; Grand, Brooklyn, week of October 6, 1902; Folly, Brooklyn, Week of October 13, 1902; Grand, Manhattan, week of October 20, 1902; Taylor, Trenton, NJ, October 27, 1902; Academy of Music, Reading, PA, October 28, 1902; Fulton, Lancaster, October 29, 1902; Grand, Harrisburg, October 30, 1902; Altoona Opera House, October 31, 1902; Empire, Pittsburgh, week of November 3, 1902; Lyceum, Cleveland, OH, week of November 10, 1902; Colonial, Akron, November 17, 1902; Schultz, Zanesville, November 18, 1902; Lexington, KY, November 22, 1902; Avenue, Louisville, week of November 24, 1902; Heuck's, Cincinnati, November 30, 1902; Grand, Columbus, December 8 to 10, 1902; Wysor Grand, Muncie, IN, December 11, 1902; Temple, Fort Wayne, December 12, 1902; Great Northern, Chicago, week of December 14, 1902; Grand, Bloomington, IN, December 22, 1902; Grand, Jacksonville, IL, December 24, 1902; Grand, Decatur, December 26, 1902; Temple, Alton, December 27, 1902; Grand, St. Louis, MO, week of December 28, 1902; Grand, Kansas City, week of January 4, 1903; Leavenworth Opera House, January 11, 1903; Bowersock, Lawrence, January 12, 1903; Grand, Topeka, January 13, 1903; Lyceum, St. Joseph, MO, January 14 to 15, 1903; Oliver, Lincoln, January 16 to 17, 1903; Boyd's, Omaha, NE, January 18 to 21, 1903; Grand, Des Moines, IA, January 22 to 24, 1903; layoff from January 25 to 30, 1903; Grand, St. Paul, MN, week of January 31, 1903; Bijou, Minneapolis, week of February 8, 1903; New York Theatre (Broadway), February 18 to April 4, 1903; Shaftesbury, London, May 18 to December 26, 1903; command performance, Buckingham Palace, London, June 23, 1903.

Synopsis as of September 29, 1903:

Prologue: Garden of caboceer's palace, Dahomey.

Act I: Public square, Boston.

Act II: Scene 1—Exterior of Lightfoot's home, Gatorville, FL; Scene 2—A road one and a half miles from Gatorville; Scene 3—Interior of Lightfoot's home.

Royal, Hull, week of February 1, 1904; Alexandra, London, week of February 8, 1904; Prince of Wales's residence, London, week of February 16, 1904; Marlborough, London, week of February 22, 1904; Kennington, London, week of March 6, 1904; King's Grand, London, week of March 14, 1904; Prince's, Bristol, week of March 21, 1904; Crown, London, two weeks beginning March 28, 1904; Theatre Royal, Newcastle, week of April 11, 1904; Lyceum, Sheffield, week of April 18, 1904; Royal Court, Liverpool, week of April 25, 1904; Lyceum, Edinburgh, Scotland, week of May 2, 1904; Prince's, Manchester, two weeks beginning May 9, 1904; Borough, Stratford, week of May 23, 1904.

1904 to 1905—*In Dahomey*

Addition of George Hammond, Je-Je; Adolph Henderson, Messenger Rush; and John Edwards, James. Chorus: Ruby Taylor; Marguerite Ward; and Minnie Brown.

Young's Ocean Pier, Atlantic City, two weeks beginning August 15, 1904; Grand, Manhattan, week of August 27, 1904; Lyric, Baltimore, week of September 12, 1904; Grand, St. Louis, three weeks beginning September 18, 1904; Temple, Alton, IL, October 9, 1904; Grand, Decatur, October 10, 1904; Grand, Bloomington, ID, October 12, 1904; Myers Grand, Janesville, WI, October 14, 1904; Rockford, IL, October 15, 1904; Great Northern, Chicago, three weeks beginning October 16, 1904; Grand, Peoria, November 6 to 8, 1904; Burtis, Davenport, IA, November 9, 1904; Keokuk Opera House, IA, November 10, 1904; Burlington, Des Moines, November 11, 1904; Grand, Kansas City, week of November 13, 1904; Bowersock, Lawrence, November 21, 1904; Crawford, Topeka, November 22, 1904; Oliver, Lincoln, NE, November 23, 1904; Boyd's, Omaha, November 24 to 26, 1904; Tabor Grand, Denver, November 27, 1904; Grand, San Francisco, three weeks beginning December 4, 1904; Barton, Fresno, December 25, 1904; Yosemite, Stockton, December 26, 1904; Clunie, Sacramento, December 27, 1904; Macdonough, Oakland, December 29 to 30, 1904; Marquam, Portland, OR, January 4, 1905; Tacoma (WA) Theatre, January 6 to 7, 1905; Grand, Seattle, January 8 to 11, 1905; Victoria (BC) Theatre, January 12 to 13, 1905; Beck's,

Bellingham, WA, January 14, 1905; Pullman Auditorium, January 18, 1905; Spokane Theatre, January 20 to 22, 1905; Union, Missoula, MT, January 24, 1905; Helena, January 25, 1905; Broadway, Butte, January 26 to 27, 1905; Fargo, ND, January 30, 1905; Winnipeg (MB) Theatre, February 1 to 2, 1905; Lyceum, Duluth, MN, February 4, 1905; Grand, St. Paul, week of February 5, 1905; Bijou, Minneapolis, week of February 12, 1905; Gayety, Pittsburgh, two weeks beginning February 19, 1905; Ye Park, Philadelphia, two weeks beginning March 5, 1905; Globe, Boston, two weeks beginning March 20, 1905; National, Rochester, April 3 to 5, 1905; possibly Harlem Opera House, April 6 to 9, 1905; West End, Manhattan, week of April 10, 1905; Majestic, Brooklyn, two weeks beginning April 17, 1905; Lyric, Allentown, PA, May 1, 1905; State Street, Trenton, NJ, May 2, 1905; Savoy, Atlantic City, May 4, 1905; Fulton, Lancaster, PA, May 5, 1905; Lyceum, Harrisburg, May 6, 1905; Academy, Pottsville, May 8, 1905; Nesbitt, Wilkes-Barre, May 9, 1905; Lyceum, Scranton, May 11, 1905; unknown theatre, Troy, NY May 12, 1905; unknown theatre, Schenectady, May 13, 1905; Grand, Manhattan, three weeks beginning May 15, 1905.

Summer Vaudeville—Williams and Walker Glee Club—Proctor's 23rd Street, Manhattan, week of July 2, 1905, with Williams and Walker; Keith's, Philadelphia, week of July 10, 1905; Keith's, Brooklyn, week of July 17, 1905; and Keith's, Boston, two weeks beginning July 24, 1905.

1905 to 1906—*Abyssinia*

*The Williams and Walker Company divided into several small aggregations for vaudeville engagements.

Aida Overton Walker and Her Abyssinian Maidens—Maggie Davis; Jessie Ellis; Katherine Jones; Wilhelmina Martin; Ida Day; Lavinia Gaston; and Bessie Vaughn.

Doic, Yonkers, NY, week of October 16, 1905; New York Theatre, week of October 22, 1905; Bijou, New Haven, CT, week of October 30, 1905; Proctor's 23rd Street, Manhattan, two weeks beginning November 5, 1905; Colonial, week of November 20, 1905; Orpheum, Brooklyn, week of November 26, 1905; Imperial, Brooklyn, two weeks beginning December 4, 1905.

Williams and Walker Glee Club—William C. Elkins; J. L. Hill; Green Henri Tapley; Sterling C. Rex; Charles Henry Young; Charles Henry Moore;

Charles Lincoln; Theodore Pankey; James Escort Lightfoot; J. Mantell Thomas; Adolph Manuel Henderson; Arthur H. Payne; Lloyd G. Gibbs; Lewis Henry Saulisbury; and Modeste Bel Guilleume.

Grand, Philadelphia, week of October 9, 1905; whereabouts unknown October 15 to 22, 1905; Shea's, Buffalo, week of October 23, 1905; Temple, Detroit, week of November 6, 1905; Victoria, Manhattan, November 13 to 18, 1905; Hurtig and Seamon's Harlem Music Hall, week of November 19, 1905; Madison Square Garden Concert Hall, November 27, 1905; Hyde and Behman's, Brooklyn, week of November 27, 1905; Grand, Brooklyn, week of December 3, 1905; Imperial, Brooklyn, week of December 10, 1905; possibly Alhambra, Manhattan, December 18, 1905, to January 6, 1906; Keeny's, Newark, NJ, week of January 7, 1906.

Williams and Walker—Hammerstein's Victoria, Manhattan, three weeks beginning October 29, 1905; Proctor's 23rd Street, week of November 19, 1905; Proctor's 58th Street, week of November 27, 1905; Colonial, week of December 3, 1905; Alhambra, week of December 11, 1905; Orpheum, Brooklyn, week of December 17, 1905; Amphion, Brooklyn, week of December 24, 1905; Imperial, week of January 1, 1906.

Williams and Walker's Dixie Serenaders—Sheedy's, Fall River, MA, week of January 7, 1906.

Abyssinia

Principal Cast—Bert Williams, Jasmine Jenkins; George Walker, Rastus Johnson; James Vaughn, musical director; Jesse A. Shipp, stage manager / The Affa Negus Tegulet; Alex Rogers, Shambal Ballaso; Charles H. Moore, Elder Fowler; Charles L. Moore, Omreeka; R. Henri Strange, King Menelik II; James Lightfoot, Zamish; Craig C. Williams, James; William C. Elkins, Hadji; George Catlin, Wong Foo; Williams Foster, Serma; Hattie McIntosh, Aunt Callie Parker; Aida Overton Walker, choreographer/Miriam; Ada Guiguesse, Nettie; Lavinia Rogers, Lucinda; Lottie Williams, Miss Primly; Hattie (Hopkins) Chenault, Varinoe; Aline Harris, Daphne; Maggie Davis, Serena; and Katie Jones, Allamo.

Featured Cast—Green Henri Tapley; Sterling Rex; Arthur H. Payne; L. H. Saulsbury; Laurence Chenault; M. Bel Guillaume; J. Mantel Thomas; Lloyd G. Gibbs; Adolph Henderson; Charles Gilpin; W. H. Chapelle; Frank

Williams; William Rarker; Charles Young; Robert Young; Charles H. Hall; Charles H. Forster; James H. Lilliard; James Roberts; Charles Randall; Louis Johnson; James Nelson; Sirean W. Barnett; Tom J. Sadler; D. C. Scott; Rudolph Haverman; Daisy Tapley; Bessie Payne; Marion Adams Harris; Alice Royal; Minnie Brown; Jessie Ellis; Bessie Brady; Evelyn Brady; Lizzie Pugsley; Marian Bolden; Anita Bush; Lena Mitchell; Hattie Christian; Wilimina Martin; Ethel Du Pas; Jennie Ringgold; Kathlyn Jones; Florence DeMoss; India Allen; Annie Ross; Adrian Hawkins; Willie Barnes; Blanch Arlington; Bessie and Patsy Brody; Harry Stafford, electrician; and Preston Clark, property man.

Majestic, Manhattan (Broadway), February 20 to March 17, 1906; Savoy, Atlantic City, March 19 to 21, 1906; Fulton, Lancaster, PA, March 22, 1906; Lyceum, Harrisburg, March 23 to 24, 1906; Lyric, Allentown, March 26, 1906; Academy, Reading, March 27, 1906; York, March 28, 1906; Academy, Fall River, MA, March 31, 1906; Newport (RI) Opera House, April 1, 1906; Globe, Boston, week of April 2, 1906; Ye Park, Philadelphia, two weeks beginning April 9, 1906; West End, Manhattan, April 23, 1906; off April 24 to 29, 1906; Convention Hall, DC, April 30 to May 2, 1906; Folly, Brooklyn, week of May 7, 1906; Bijou, Pittsburgh, two weeks beginning May 14, 1906; Great Northern, Chicago, six weeks beginning May 27 (ended July 7), 1906.

1906 to 1907—*Abyssinia*

Grand, Manhattan, two weeks beginning August 18, 1906; Majestic, Manhattan (Broadway), two weeks beginning September 3, 1906; Yorkville, IL, September 16, 1906; Metropolis, Manhattan, week of September 23, 1906; Masonic, Louisville, KY, week of October 1, 1906; Park, Indianapolis, October 8 to 10, 1906; Grand, Terre Haute, October 11 to 12, 1906; Temple Theatre, Alton, IL, October 13, 1906; Grand, Kansas City, week of October 14, 1906; Bowersock, Lawrence, October 22, 1906; Oliver, Lincoln, NE, October 23 to 24, 1906; Krug, Omaha, October 25 to 27, 1906; Grand, Topeka, KS, October 28, 1906; Tootle, St. Joseph, MO, October 29 to 30, 1906; La Belle, Pittsburgh, KS, October 31, 1906; Baldwin, Springfield, MO, November 1, 1906; Sedalia, November 3, 1906; Grand, St. Louis, two weeks beginning November 4, 1906; Great Northern, Chicago, two weeks beginning November 18, 1906; Lyceum, Detroit, two weeks beginning December 2, 1906; Racine (WI) Theatre, December 16,

1906; possibly Orpheum, Rockford, IL, December 17, 1906; Joliet Theatre, December 18, 1906; Grand, Bloomington, ID, December 19, 1906; Chatterton (IL) Opera House, Springfield, December 20, 1906; Powers' Grand, Decatur, December 21, 1906; whereabouts unknown December 22 to 24, 1906; Heuck's, Cincinnati, week of December 25, 1906; National, Dayton, December 31, 1906, to January 2, 1907; Bijou, Pittsburgh, week of January 7, 1907; Palm, Cleveland, week of January 14, 1907; Grand, Canton, January 21, 1907; Park, Youngstown, January 22, 1907; Grand, Steubenville, January 23, 1907; Colonial, Akron, January 24, 1907; Hamilton, Jefferson, January 26, 1907; Lyceum, Toledo, week of January 27, 1907; unknown theatre, Grand Rapids, January 28 to February 7, 1907; Athenaeum, Jackson, MI, February 8, 1907; possibly Hamilton, Canada, February 9 to 17, 1907; Folly, Brooklyn, week of February 18, 1907; West End, Manhattan, two weeks beginning February 24, 1907, Academy, Jersey City, March 14 to 16, 1907; Globe, Boston, two weeks beginning March 18, 1907; Ye Park, Philadelphia; Lynn (MA) Theatre, April 1, 1907; Court the Franklin, Fall River, April 3, 1907; Parsons, Hartford, CT, April 4, 1907; Square, Springfield, MA, April 5, 1907; Harmanus Bleeker Hall, Albany, NY, April 6, 1907; Majestic, Utica, April 9, 1907; Lyceum, Scranton, PA, April 11, 1907; Lyceum, Harrisburg, April 12, 1907; Fulton, Lancaster, April 13, 1907; Ye Park, Philadelphia, two weeks beginning April 15, 1907; Blaney's, Baltimore, week of April 28, 1907; Savoy, Atlantic City, week of May 6, 1907.

Summer Vaudeville—Chestnut Street, Philadelphia, two weeks beginning May 13, 1907, and Grand, Pittsburgh, week of June 2.

1907 to 1908—*Bandanna Land*

Principal Cast—Bert A. Williams, Skunkton Bowser; George Walker, Bud "Bon Bon Buddy" Jenkins; Alex Rogers, Amos Simmons, who owns the property that all the fuss is about; Bertha Clark, Cynthia, a niece of Amos; Hattie McIntosh, Sylvie Simmons, Amos's wife; Aida Overton Walker, Dina Simmons, Amos's daughter; Charles H. Moore, Pete Simmons, Amos's brother; (Dina's schoolmates:) Maggie Davis, Julia Smothers; Bessie Vaughn, Sue Higgens; Ida Day, Babe Brown; Marguerite Ward, Sis Black; Katie Jones, Becky White; Lottie Williams, Angelina Diggs, teacher in the country school and president of the "Every Little Bit Helps Society"; R. Henri Strange, Fountain Lewis, owner of the Carrolton Hotel Barber Shop; Mord

Alan, Si Springer, janitor of the G.U.O.O.F. Hall; James E. Lightfoot, Mr. Wilson, large shareholder in the corporation; Sterling Rex, Mr. Jones, large shareholder in the corporation; John Leubrie Hill, Bill Turner, chairman of the corporation meeting; Lloyd G. Gibbs, Deacon Sparks; George Catlin, Jack Dimery (Uncle Apple Jack); James M. Thomas, (board of trustees of the T.S.C.R. Co.) Sid Morgan; Matt Housley, Neil Carter; H. B. Guillaume, Dick Beel; Angelo Housley, Bill Hayden; Charles Hall, Jim Strode; Arthur Payne, Mr. White; L. H. Saulsbury, Abe Milum; J. P. Reed, Mr. Black; G. Henri Tapley, Tom Brown; Frank H. Williams, Mr. Green; W. H. "Chappie" Chapelle, Sleepy Jim Harper; Henry Troy, Mr. Collins, sec. of the corporation; J. A. Shipp, Mose Blackstone, a lawyer and founder of the T.S.C.R.; Lavinia Rogers, Sadie Tompkins; Henry Troy, Fred Lewis, Fountain Lewis's nephew; members of the entertainment, finance and decoration committees by the Misses. Guiguesse, Clough, Jordan, Bluford, Ellis, Payne, Fowler, Young, Martin, M. Brown, L. Brown, and Banks.

West End Casino, Asbury Park, NJ, August 29, 1907; Frick Lyceum, Red Bank, August 30, 1907; West End Theatre, Long Branch, August 31 to September 1, 1907; New Plainfield Theatre, September 3, 1907; Grand, Wilmington, DE, September 4, 1907; Lyceum, Scranton, PA, September 9, 1907; Nesbit, Wilkes-Barre, September 10, 1907; Collingwood, Poughkeepsie, NY, September 12, 1907; Bands, Troy, September 13, 1907; Majestic, Utica, September 14, 1907; National, Rochester, September 16 to 18, 1907; Weiting, Syracuse, September 19 to 21, 1907; unknown theatre, Cleveland, week of September 22, 1907; Colonial, Akron, October 1, 1907; Ceramic, Liverpool, OH, October 2, 1907; Weller Theatre, Zanesville, OH, week of October 3, 1907; Walker, Champaign, IL, October 10, 1907; Wabash, Decatur, October 11, 1907; Empire, Quincy, October 12, 1907; Grand, Kansas City, week of October 13, 1907; Crawford Grand, Leavenworth, October 20, 1907; Tootle, St. Joseph, MO, October 21 to 22, 1907; Crawford Grand, Topeka, KS, October 23, 1907; Bowersock, Lawrence, October 24, 1907; Sedalia Theatre, October 26, 1907; Grand, St. Louis, two weeks beginning October 27, 1907; Great Northern, Chicago, three weeks beginning November 10, 1907; Majestic, Grand Rapids, MI, December 2, 1907; Lyceum, Detroit, week of December 3, 1907; Masonic, Louisville, week of December 9, 1907; Walnut, Cincinnati, week of December 15, 1907; Bijou, Pittsburgh, week of December 22, 1907; Lyceum, Perrysburg, OH, December 29, 1907, to January 1, 1908; New Powers, Grand Rapids, January 2 to 4, 1908; Lyceum, Detroit, week of January 5, 1908; Lyceum, Windsor, ON, Canada, week of

January 12, 1908; Ye Park, Philadelphia, two weeks beginning January 19, 1908; Majestic, Manhattan (Broadway), twelve weeks beginning February 3, 1908; Majestic, Brooklyn, week of April 20, 1908; Poli's, Waterbury, CT, April 27, 1908; Hyperion, New Haven, April 28, 1908; Parsons, Hartford, April 29 to 30, 1908; Poli's New Theatre, Meriden, May 2, 1908; Nixon's Apollo, Atlantic City, week of May 4, 1908; Academy of Music, Pittsburgh, week of May 11, 1908; Folly, Brooklyn, week of May 18, 1908.

Summer Vaudeville—Colonial, Manhattan week of June 1, 1908, in *The Guardian and the Heir*; Orpheum, Brooklyn, week of June 8, 1908; and Alhambra, Manhattan, week of June 15.

Williams and Walker's Glee Club, Keith's, Boston, two weeks beginning May 25, and Keith's Philadelphia, two weeks beginning June 15.

Williams and Walker's Chocolate Drops—Youngs Pier, Atlantic City, week of May 25, 1907.

Aida Overton Walker's Vaudeville Entertainment and Dance, a benefit for the White Rose Industrial Association Home for Colored Working Girls, Grand Central Palace, Manhattan, June 3, 1908.

1908 to 1909—*Bandanna Land*

Savoy, Atlantic City, week of August 3, 1908; Academy of Music, Baltimore, week of August 10, 1908; Grand, Manhattan, two weeks beginning August 17, 1908; Hyperion, New Haven, CT, August 31, 1908; Broadway, Norwich, September 1, 1908; Lyceum, New London, September 2, 1908; Academy, Fall River, MA, September 4, 1908; Orpheum, Boston, four weeks beginning September 5, 1908; Providence (RI) Opera House, October 5 to 7, 1908; Court Square, Springfield, MA, October 8, 1908; Hyperion, New Haven, CT, October 9, 1908; unknown theatre, Bridgeport, October 10 to 11, 1908; Majestic, Jersey City, week of October 12, 1908; Grand, Brooklyn, week of October 19, 1908; Taylor, Trenton, NJ, October 26, 1908; Majestic, Harrisburg, PA, October 27, 1908; Mishler, Altoona, October 28, 1908; Cambria, Jonestown, October 29, 1908; White's, McKeesport, October 31, 1908; Duquesne, Pittsburgh, November 2 to 7, 1908; Lyceum, Toledo, OH, week of November 8, 1908; Garrick, St. Louis, MO, three weeks beginning November 15, 1908; Temple, Alton, IL, December 6, 1908; Columbia, MO,

December 7, 1908; Sedalia (KS) Theatre, December 8, 1908; Bowersock, Lawrence, December 9, 1908; Grand, Topeka, December 10, 1908; Atchison Theatre, December 11, 1908; Orpheum, Leavenworth, December 12, 1908; Oliver, Lincoln, NE, December 14, 1908; New Grand, Sioux City, IA, December 15 to 16, 1908; Boyd, Omaha, NE, December 17 to 19, 1908; Shubert, Kansas City, week of December 21, 1908; Great Northern, Chicago, four weeks beginning January 4, 1909; Park, Indianapolis, February 8 to 10, 1909; National, Dayton, February 15 to 17, 1909; (without George) Masonic, Louisville, week of February 22, 1909; Walnut, Cincinnati, week of February 28, 1909; Grand, Philadelphia, week of March 8, 1909; Metropolis, Manhattan, week of March 14, 1909; Majestic, Brooklyn, week of March 22, 1909; Yorkville, Manhattan, week of March 28, 1909.

Williams and Walker's Chocolate Drops with King and Bailey—Lincoln Square, Manhattan, probably week of September 7, 1908; Empire, Berkshire, MA, week of September 14, 1908; Hurtig and Seamon's Harlem Music Hall, week of October 18, 1908; unknown theatre, October 19 to December 13, 1908; Orpheum, Reading, PA, week of December 14, 1908; possibly Lyric, Newark, NJ, week of December 21, 1908; Columbia, Brooklyn, week of December 27, 1908; Alhambra, Manhattan, week of January 24, 1909; Orpheum, Boston, week of February 1, 1909; Fulton, Brooklyn, week of February 8, 1909; Bijou, Winnipeg, MB, Canada, two weeks beginning March 1, 1909; Unique, Minneapolis, week of March 22, 1909; Washington, Spokane, WA, week of April 4, 1909; Orpheum, Vancouver, BC, Canada, two weeks beginning April 11, 1909; Grand, Tacoma, WA, week of April 26, 1909; Grand, Portland, OR, week of May 3, 1909; National, San Francisco, week of May 16, 1909; Bell, Oakland, week of May 23, 1909; Wigwam, San Francisco, week of June 1, 1909; whereabouts unknown June 7 to 13, 1909; Los Angeles Theatre, week of June 14, 1909; Majestic, Denver, week of June 28, 1909; whereabouts unknown July 4 to 18, 1909; Unique, Des Moines, week of July 19, 1909; Capital Beach, Lincoln, week of July 26, 1909.

1909 to 1910—*Mr. Lode of Koal*

Cast—Bert Williams, Chester A. Lode; Alex Rogers, Buggsy; J. Leubrie Hill, Buttram; Charles Moore, Weedhead; Clarence Redd, Third Lieutenant; J. M. Thomas, Second Lieutenant; Sterling Rex, First Lieutenant; Henry Troy, Cap; James Lightfoot, Saig; Matt Housley, Blootch; Thomas Brown,

Gimlet; Lottie Grady, Mysteria; Siren Navarro, Gluten and Whirlina; Charles McKenzie, Singlink; Hattie McIntosh, Woozy; Hattie Hopkins, Hoola; Lavinia Rogers, Rubeena; Georgia Gomez, Kinklets; Maggie Davis, Diano; Ida Day, Discretia; Ada Banks, A. Saylor; Bessie Brady, What; Jesse Ellis, Osee; Katie Jones, Giddina; and Anita Bush, Ho.

Chorus—William C. Elkins, William Chappelle, Lloyd Gibbs, Arthur Payne, L. H. Saulsbury, Chester Hawkes, Charles Foster, W. H. Holland, R. M. Cooper, G. Henri Tapley, Walter Hilliard, Edward Tolliver, Florence Brown, Inez Clough, Ada Guiguesse, Minnie Brown, Josephine DeVance, Mamie A. Payne, Bessie Vaughn, Effie King, May York, Enice Lewis, and Bessie Thomas.

Executive Staff—Jack Shoemaker, manager; Clarence D. Parker, business manager; Jesse Shipp, stage manager; William C. Elkins, chorus director; William Spedick, trap drummer; Harry S. Stafford, master mechanic; Robert R. Craig, master of properties; D. F. Reder, electrician; J. A. Shipp Jr., master of transportation; and Lizzie De Massey, wardrobe mistress.

Casino, Toledo, OH, week of August 30, 1909; Garrick, St. Louis, two weeks beginning September 5, 1909; Burtis, Davenport, IA, September 16, 1909; Auditorium, Des Moines, September 17 to 18, 1909; Shubert, Kansas City, week of September 19, 1909; Burwood, Omaha, September 26 to 29, 1909; Oliver, Lincoln, September 30, 1909; Tootle, St. Joseph, MO, October 2, 1909; Great Northern, Chicago, three weeks beginning October 3, 1909; Bowersock, Lawrence, October 6, 1909 (canceled); Joliet (IL) Theatre, October 24, 1909; Masonic, Louisville, October 25 to 27, 1909; Park, Indianapolis, October 28 to 30, 1909; Majestic, Manhattan (Broadway), five weeks beginning November 1, 1909; Providence (RI) Opera House, December 6 to 8, 1909; Hartford (CT) Opera House, December 10 to 11, 1909; Grand, Philadelphia, two weeks beginning December 13, 1909; Bastable, Syracuse, December 27 to 29, 1909; Cook, Rochester, December 30, 1909, to January 1, 1910; Lyceum, Pittsburgh, week of January 3, 1910; unknown theatre, Columbus, January 10 to 12, 1910; whereabouts unknown January 13 to 15, 1910; Lyceum, Cleveland, week of January 16, 1910; Globe, Boston, two weeks beginning January 24, 1910; unknown theatre, Albany, February 7 to 9, 1910; Savoy, Atlantic City, February 10 to 12, 1910; National, Philadelphia, week of February 13, 1910; Amphion, Brooklyn, week of February 20, 1910; Court, Brooklyn, week of February 27, 1910.

Williams and Walker's Chocolate Drops with King and Bailey—Mozart, Elmira, NY, week of September 13, 1909; Family, Lancaster, PA, week of September 20, 1909; Auditorium, York, NY, week of July 27, 1909; whereabouts unknown October 3 to 10, 1909; Keeny's Fulton Street, Brooklyn, week of October 11, 1909; whereabouts unknown October 17 to November 20, 1909; American Music Hall (formerly Orpheum), Boston, week of November 21, 1909; Fulton, Brooklyn, week of November 29, 1909; New Lyceum, DC, week of December 6, 1909; New Monumental, Baltimore, week of December 13, 1909; Trocadero, Philadelphia, week of December 20, 1909; American Music Hall, Newark, week of December 27, 1909; whereabouts unknown January 2 to 16, 1910; Miner's, Newark, week of January 17, 1910; Casino, Brooklyn, week of January 24, 1910; Empire, Brooklyn, week of January 31, 1910; whereabouts unknown February 6 to 20, 1910; Orpheum, Cincinnati, week of February 21, 1910; whereabouts unknown February 27 to March 13, 1910; Crystal, Milwaukee, week of March 14, 1910; whereabouts unknown March 20 to April 24, 1910; Miles, Minneapolis, week of April 25, 1910; Grand, Fargo, ND, week of May 2, 1910; Majestic, La Crosse, WI, week of May 9, 1910; whereabouts unknown May 15 to July 24, 1910; American Music Hall, New York, week of July 25, 1910.

Second Company

1900 to 1901—*A Lucky Coon / The Policy Players*

Ben Hunn, Dusty Cheapman; Walter Dixon, Happy Hotstuff; Carl "The Prince" Dante; Stella Wiley; Blanche Arlington; Midget Price; Fanny Wise; Lillian Perrin; Marie Locals; Eugenia Wright; Bertha Ellis; Sidney and Lillian Perrin; Charles Foster; Leslie Triplet; Henry Skuder; Clarence Logan; Russell Brandow; James Jackson; Mamie Emerson; Bob Armstrong; Simpson Pitman; and Bailey and Fletcher.

Stillman Music Hall, Bridgewater, October 16, 1900; Gaiety, Scranton, October 22 to 24, 1900; Baker, Rochester, October 30 to 31, 1900; toured New York State in November 1900; whereabouts unknown December 1900 to February 1901; Brooklyn Music Hall, week of March 4, 1901; American, Patterson, week of April 1, 1901.

1902—*Sons of Ham*

Dan Avery, Hearty Laughter; Charles Hart, Tobias Wormwood; Clara Freeman, Kioka; Louis Love; Alberta Ormes; Allie Brown, slack-wire performer; Estella Pugsley Hart; Griffith Wilson; Norris Smith; John Edwards; Annie Ross; Sam Cousens; Norris Smith; Pete Washington; and Anna Cook.
Young's Ocean Pier, Atlantic City, October 2 to 4, 1901; Lyceum, New London, week of October 13, 1901; Empire, Holyoke, October 27 to 29, 1901; Greenfield (MA) Playhouse, October 31, 1901; Grand, Springfield, November 4, 1901; Jacques, Meridian, November 6, 1901; Poli's, Waterbury, November 7, 1901; whereabouts unknown November 8 to 26, 1901; Bloomsburg (PA), November 27, 1901; Danville Opera House, November 28, 1901; Empire, DC, week of December 1, 1901; Grand, Wilmington, December 10, 1901; whereabouts unknown December 11 to 21, 1901; Grand, New Haven, December 22 to 24, 1901.

1904—*In Dahomey*

Prologue: Noris Smith, Fanny Wise, Pete Washington, and Charles White.

Cast: Dan Avery, Rareback Pinkerton; Charles Hart, Shylock Homestead; Pete Hampton*, Hamilton Lightfoot; Fred Douglass*, Dr. Straight; Walter Dixon, Hustling Charlie; Leon Williams, George Reeder; Walter Richardson, Henry Stanfield; Pete Washington*, Mose Lightfoot; Norris Smith, Harry; Theodore Wilson, Leather; Dan Washington, Officer Still; Jack Brown, Messenger Rush; Charles White, a waiter; William Garland, Clarence; Lizzie Avery*, Flossie; Tiny Jones*, Lucille; Fanny Wise, Pansy; Nettie Goff, Lieutenant Martha; Laura Bowman, Cecilin; Stella Hart, Mr. Stringer; Pauline Freeman*, Rosetta Lightfoot; Len Williams, Flockaday, manager; and Norris Smith.

*Original cast member

Grand, Hull, England week of August 15, 1904; Lyceum, Sheffield, week of August 29, 1904; Empire, Oldham, week of September 5, 1904; Grand, Fulham, week of September 12, 1904; Ealing, London, week of September 19, 1904; Marlborough, London, week of September 26, 1904; Theatre Royal Portsmouth, week of October 3, 1904; whereabouts unknown October 10 to 16, 1904; Coronet, London, week of October 17, 1904; whereabouts unknown October 23 to 30, 1904; Theatre Royal, Dublin, week of October 31, 1904; Theatre Royal, Belfast, week of November 7, 1904; Queen's, Manchester, week of November 14, 1904; Grand, Birmingham, week of November 28, 1904; Theatre Royal, Bradford, Ireland, week of December 5, 1904; whereabouts unknown December 11 to 18, 1904; Theatre Royal, Stockton, week of December 19, 1904; Grand, Newcastle, week of January 2, 1905; whereabouts unknown January 8 to 22, 1905; Dalston, London, week of January 23, 1905; Grand, Swansea, Wales, week of January 30, 1905; Lyceum, Newport, week of February 6, 1905.

(Avery and Hart only) Pavilion, Newcastle, week of March 6, 1905; Alhambra, London, week of March 27, 1905.

With augmented cast—Theatre Royal, London, week of August 14, 1905; whereabouts unknown August 28 to September 3, 1905; Avenue, Newcastle, week of September 4, 1905; Royal, Leicester, week of September 11, 1905; Grand, Isle of Man, week of September 28, 1905.

Notes

Chapter 1

1. George Walker, "The Dramatic Stage as an Upbuilder of the Race," interview by Veronica Adams, *The Inter Ocean* (hereafter cited as *CIO*), January 17, 1909, 28. See also George W. Walker, "Bert and Me and Them," *The New York Age* (hereafter cited as *NYA*), December 24, 1908, 12.

2. "The Great Names He Knew Live On," *New York Herald Tribune*, September 8, 1935, 2. Much of this section originally appeared in Daniel Atkinson, "George 'Nash' Walker: The Unsung Favorite Son of Lawrence, Kansas," in *Embattled Lawrence*, vol. 2, *The Enduring Struggle for Freedom*, ed. Dennis Domer (Watkins Museum of History, 2022), 126–37.

3. Richard Cordley, *A History of Lawrence, Kansas: From the First Settlement to the Close of the Rebellion* (E. F. Caldwell / Lawrence Journal Press, 1895), 183–84.

4. The surviving slave schedules, probate records, and research provided by Tom A. Rafiner in *Caught Between Three Fires: Cass County, Mo., Chaos, and Order No. 11, 1860–1865* (pub. by author, 2010) indicate that an enslaved man named Spencer Hayden lived and worked on a farm that was owned by Jarvis Hayden (d. 1852) in Cass County that was very close to the farm where Sarah lived. Further, the 1905 City of Lawrence Directory (Lawrence Public Library) lists Sarah Hayden as the widow of Spencer. Spencer's place of birth was listed in the 1911 census: Lawrence Ward 1, Douglas, Kansas, ED 0064, 1910, roll T624_438, p. 4A, Family History Library (FHL) microfilm 1374451. A record of Alice's fifty-second birthday was published in *The Broad Ax*, January 16, 1909, 2.

5. Sarah Hayden's obituary in the *Lawrence Daily Journal* (hereafter cited as *LDJ*), September 12, 1907, 1. See also William Hayden's obituary in *The Jeffersonian Gazette* (Lawrence, KS; hereafter cited as *LJG*), September 10, 1913, 1; 1865 Kansas state census, microfilm roll KS18653, line 19 (Kansas State Historical Society, Topeka, KS); Debby Lowery and Judy Sweets, *African-Americans in the 1865 Kansas State Census (Douglas County)* (pub. by authors, 2006).

6. The 1870 census lists the Walker children as Anna, b. 1844; Jerry, b. 1847; Catve, b. 1850; Nancy, b. 1852; Grandison, b. 1863; and Hannah, b. 1864. 1870 census, Township 17, Range 6, Talladega, Alabama, roll M593_41, p. 446B, FHL microfilm 545540.

7. See *Rocky Mountain News*, September 25, 1916, 25. Nashville Walker claimed that he served in the Tenth Alabama Infantry Regiment as an officer's servant; the Ninth Maryland Regiment for three months in 1863, before his mother secured his release; the Fifth Massachusetts Cavalry Regiment for nine months under Colonel Cowdrey; and the Second New York Cavalry Regiment until the end of the war as body servant to Colonel Morgan H. Chrysler. For an example of Nashville Walker's high status in the community, see "Not So," *LDJ*, August 3, 1871, 3; and *Republican Journal*, January 11, 1876, 3. Nashville Walker was named as one of the directors of the Eagle Baseball Club in Lawrence.

8. See "Nash Walker Is Here," *LDJ*, July 13, 1908, 1.

9. *Lawrence Daily World* (hereafter cited as *LDW*), June 10, 1907, 2.

10. 1880 census, Lawrence, Kansas, ED 067, roll 380, p. 66D; 1885 Kansas Territory census, roll KS1885_40, line 17 (Kansas State Historical Society, Topeka, KS); *City of Lawrence Directories, 1873–74, 1879, 1883, 1888, and 1890–91*, Lawrence Public Library; *The Colorado Daily Chieftain*, June 10, 1881, and May 23, 1902.

11. "A Lawrence Boy's Annual Chat with Home Folks," *Lawrence Daily Gazette* (hereafter cited as *LDG*), May 28, 1904, 2.

12. *Western Home Journal*, May 29, 1884, 3.

13. "Black Moses Seen in Denver Negro," *Rocky Mountain News*, September 17, 1916, 25.

14. Editorials, *Denver Post*, May 29, 1907, 12.

15. Population information published in *Western Home Journal*, July 5, 1877, 8; "A Good Show and a Big House," *LDJ*, February 12, 1901, 4; and "Walker a Kansan," *Topeka State Journal* (hereafter cited as *TSJ*), January 11, 1902, 11.

16. "More or Less Personal," *Lincoln Nebraska State Journal*, January 26, 1900, 4; and an untitled obituary in *The Atchison Daily Globe*, January 7, 1911, 5. See also "Bon Bon Buddy (The Chocolate Drop)," lyrics by Alex Rogers, music by Will Marion Cook (Gotham-Attucks, 1907). The song was George Walker's biggest hit, and a callback to his childhood in Lawrence.

17. *LDJ*, July 26, 1902, 4.

18. *Atchison Daily Globe*, April 18, 1906, 5; "Abe Levy in Atchison," *LDG*, April 24, 1906, 3.

19. City directory, Denver, CO, 1879. See also "Anniversary of the Colorado Colonization Society," *Colorado Statesman*, March 20, 1909, 5; "Nash Walker, Pioneer Citizen and Local Celebrity, Dies," *Colorado Statesman*, November 18, 1922, 5.

20. "Nash Walker Here," *Lawrence Weekly World* (hereafter cited as *LWW*), May 19, 1898, 5. See also Langston Hughes, *The Big Sea* (Alfred A. Knopf, 1940), 22–23.

21. "Williams and Walker Back for Visit Home," *LDW*, December 8, 1908, 6.

22. "William Allen White Tells New York About 'Nash' Walker," *LDW*, March 16, 1908, 1.

23. "Ere in Our Life," *LDG*, July 30, 1917, 3.

24. See Edwin Rice, *Monarchs of Minstrelsy: From Daddy Rice to Date* (Kenny Publishing, 1911), 7–11; William J. Mahar, *Behind the Burnt Cork Mask: Early Blackface Minstrelsy and Antebellum American Popular Culture* (University of Illinois Press, 1999); Eric Lott, *Love and Theft: Blackface Minstrelsy and the American Working Class* (Oxford University Press, 1993).

25. "A Minstrel 40 Years Ago," *Kansas City Star*, December 15, 1920, 6. While on tour with Hyde's Minstrels in 1898, George reacquainted himself with James McIntyre by telling him, "Well, I'm that kid that was blown across the street."

26. Angela Y. Davis, "I Used to Be Your Sweet Mama: Ideology, Sexuality, and Domesticity," in *Blues Legacies and Black Feminism: Gertrude "Ma" Rainey, Bessie Smith, and Billie Holiday*, by Davis (Random House, 1999).

27. For examples of ads and reviews, see *LDJ*, July 2, 1873, 3; November 30, 1876, 2; May 15, 1879, 4; August 22, 1883, 4; October 21, 1885, 4; March 30, 1887, 3; and August 14, 1890, 4.

28. *LDG*, September 30, 1891, 4.

29. "Uncle Tom's Cabin," *LDJ*, March 3, 1892, 4; *The Kansas Daily Tribune*, May 21, 1879, 4. The Hyers Sisters performed in Lawrence on October 17, 1883, in *The Blackville Twins* and October 2, 1891, in *The Darkies Dream*. Of chief importance were their appearances on December 18, 1877; November 3, 1886; and May 1, 1890, in *Out of Bondage* with Sam Lucas. Along with his work with the Hyers Sisters, Lucas performed in Lawrence in the cast of *Underground Railroad*, presented on May 21, 1879.

30. *LDJ*, January 18, 1900, 4; "Is Coming Home," *LDW*, June 10, 1907, 2.

31. *LJG*, July 24, 1902, 1; "All About Eva Brown," *LDW*, May 4, 1908, 2.

32. "Bert Williams Doesn't Gamble 'No Mo,'" *Washington (DC) Times*, August 9, 1908, 2.

33. Brent M. S. Campney, *This Is Not Dixie: Racist Violence in Kansas, 1861–1927* (University of Illinois Press, 2015), 81–82.

34. "Defends His Race to the Thirteen Club," *LDJ*, July 25, 1908, 3.

35. *Western Recorder* (Lawrence, KS), May 31, 1883, 3; *LDJ*, May 14, 1887, 3; *LDJ*, December 29, 1898, 3; Hughes, *The Big Sea*, 24.

36. *Evening Tribune*, May 14, 1889, 3; *LDJ*, September 10, 1889; "Had a Pleasant Visit," *LDJ*, July 26, 1902, 4; "To the Good People of Lawrence," *LDW*, July 28, 1902, 3; *Daily Record*, September 12, 1889, 4. See also *Evening Tribune*, March 25, 1889, 1; March 26, 1889, 4; May 20, 1889, 3; May 22, 1889, 3. On March 24, 1889, Nash's uncle Will Hayden, a fellow delinquent with an unsavory

reputation, was stabbed repeatedly in front of Zook's by "tough" Ed Nelson, who also served on the rockpile as he awaited trial.

37. "Ball and Banquet in Honor of Williams and Walker," *Rising Son* (Kansas City, MO), January 16, 1903, 1.

38. See *LJG*, January 18, 1911, 3. Although Howard's autobiography makes no mention of Nash Walker, Howard gave "a touching tribute" in Lawrence shortly after Nash's burial in 1911.

39. George W. Walker, "The Real 'Coon' on the American Stage," *The Theatre*, August 1906, 224–25.

40. "Williams and Walker," *The Freeman* (Indianapolis; hereafter cited as *INF*), October 6, 1906, 7.

41. *LJG*, July 24, 1902, 1.

42. *TSJ*, January 11, 1902, 11.

43. George claimed to have been a bellhop at the Great Northern Hotel during the World's Columbian Exposition of 1893 (see *INF*, October 6, 1906, 7). However, this does not match his later assertion that he met Bert Williams in San Francisco on March 31, 1892 (see *NYA*, March 19, 1908, 6; *Morning Telegraph*, September 25, 1902, 12). Complicating things is another, conflated origin story, ascribed to George, that claimed he met Bert Williams while working as a scene shifter for amateur night on May 30, 1889, in Chicago. However, Williams would have been fifteen at the time and was living with his parents in Riverside, California ("How Williams and Walker Met," *Pittsburgh Daily Post*, May 27, 1906, 22).

44. See "Moore Laughed at the Amateurs," *Chicago Tribune*, May 13, 1888, 9; "S.R.O. Sign Was Out," *LDJ*, January 16, 1900, 4.

45. "Lawrence, KAS," *Times-Observer* (Topeka), December 5, 1891, 1; "City News in Brief," *LDJ*, December 7, 1891, 4, and December 8, 1891, 4.

Chapter 2

Coined by W. E. B. Du Bois in his seminal text *Souls of Black Folk* (A. C. McClurg, 1903), "double consciousness" denotes the burden of Afro-American existence of knowing better but doing what is necessary to attain a certain measure of success while preserving dignity, as in Paul Laurence Dunbar's "We Wear the Mask" from *Lyrics of Lowly Life* (Dodd, Mead, 1896), 167.

1. *LDJ*, July 8, 1891, 4; *LDJ*, July 9, 1891, 4; *LJG*, July 22, 1891, 4; *INF*, January 14, 1911, 7.

2. George W. Walker, "The Real 'Coon' on the American Stage," *The Theatre*, August 1906, 224–25.

3. Walker, "Real 'Coon.'"

4. Oral history of Abbie Mitchell, Philip Sterling research materials on Bert Williams (*T-Mss 1991-026), Schomburg Center for Research in Black Culture,

New York Public Library; "The Discovery of George (Nash) Walker, of Williams and Walker . . . ," *INF*, October 6, 1906, 7. See also Herbert Asbury, *The Barbary Coast: An Informal History of the San Francisco Underworld* (Garden City Publishing), 1933.

    5. "Bert Williams: Boy – Gentlemen – Comedian," *Chicago Record-Herald*, September 25, 1910, 7.

    6. "Former Riversider Has Made Good as Comedian," *Riverside Daily Press*, August 27, 1910, 7.

    7. Bert Williams, "The Comic Side of Trouble," *The American Magazine* 85 (January–June 1918): 34.

    8. Affirmed by the sixteenth anniversary celebration of the partnership of Williams and Walker on March 31, 1908, and George's later recollection that Bert was about eighteen when they met. See also *NYA*, March 19, 1908, 6; *The Morning Telegraph*, September 25, 1902, 12; *San Francisco Call*, April 20, 1902, 24. In 1902, the partners indicated that it was the tenth anniversary of the pair's debut on the Midway in 1892.

    9. Williams, "Comic Side." There are no student records of Bert Williams at Leland Stanford University.

    10. "Notes of Plays and Players," *Chicago Tribune*, January 17, 1909, 45.

    11. "Bert Williams Tells of Walker," *INF*, January 14, 1911, 5.

    12. Walker, "Real 'Coon,' " 224–25.

    13. George W. Walker, "Bert and Me and Them," *NYA*, December 24, 1908, 12.

    14. "Bert Williams Tells of Walker," 5. If their meeting was in 1893 rather than 1892, there may be truth to George's claim that he worked at the Great Northern Hotel in Chicago during the Columbian Exposition.

    15. "Mission San Jose," *Oakland Enquirer*, September 27, 1893, 2; "Williams Tells," 7; "How Williams and Walker Met," *Pittsburgh Daily Post*, May 27, 1906, 22; *NYA*, March 19, 1908, 6, April 2, 1908, 6; *The New York Times* (hereafter cited as *NYT*), March 29, 1908, 49.

    16. "Ada Overton Walker," James Weldon Johnson and Grace Nail Johnson papers, MSS 49, box 67, folder 280, Yale Collection of American Literature, Beinecke Rare Book and Manuscript Library.

    17. *San Francisco Examiner*, April 11, 1896, 8; *INF*, January 21, 1911, 6; *NYA*, March 11, 1922, 6; *Riverside Daily Press*, August 27, 1910, 7.

    18. Untitled review, *Hanford Semi-Weekly Journal*, November 28, 1893, 5. Although later press releases claim their stranding was in Bakersfield, it appears to have been in Hanford, some eighty-five miles north.

    19. *TSJ*, January 11, 1902, 11; *Daily Morning Journal and Courier* (New Haven, CT), September 8, 1902, 5; untitled review, *Hanford Semi-Weekly Journal*, November 28, 1893, 5.

    20. Misha Berson, *The San Francisco Stage: From Golden Spike to Great Earthquake, 1869–1906*, San Francisco Performing Arts Library and Museum Series, no.

2 (San Francisco Performing Arts Library and Museum, 1989). See also *Indianapolis Journal*, May 29, 1904, 4.

21. Walker, "Bert and Me and Them," 12; "Williams and Walker's Success," *Pittsburgh Daily Post*, March 5, 1905, 26. See also *Pittsburgh Press*, November 16, 1900, 9.

22. See Robert C. Toll, *On with the Show! The First Century of Show Business in America* (Oxford University Press, 1976), 265–93; Bernard Sobel, *A Pictorial History of Vaudeville* (Bonanza Books, 1961); George Jessel, *Elegy in Manhattan* (Holt, Rinehart and Winston, 1961).

23. Walker, "Bert and Me and Them," 4.

24. Walker, "Real 'Coon,'" 224, 226.

25. Christopher Robert Reed, *"All the World Is Here!": The Black Presence at White City* (Indiana University Press, 2000), 43; Robert W. Rydell, *All the World's a Fair : Visions of Empire at American International Expositions, 1876–1916* (University of Chicago Press, 1984), 136–38.

26. See Contract between Xavier Pené and World's Columbian Exposition, July 15, 1892, carton 283, dossier 1887, Archives nationales d'outre-mer, Généralités.

27. See "Refuse a Fair Day: Negro Delegates Denounce the Jubilee at the Exposition," *Chicago Daily Tribune*, June 28, 1893, 8; "Fred Douglass Is Angry," *Chicago Daily Tribune*, December 6, 1893, 6.

28. Dunbar, *Lyrics of Lowly Life*, 167.

29. *San Francisco Chronicle*, May 3, 1893, 1.

30. *Chicago Daily Tribune*, May 4, 1893, 1; *CIO*, May 5, 1893, 2, and "Hard to Get In," May 26, 1893, 5.

31. See *Chicago Daily Tribune*, September 20, 1893, 4, and September 21, 1893, 3.

32. "Dahomey Village Coming," *San Francisco Chronicle*, September 24, 1893, 9.

33. Monroe N. Work, "The Origin of 'Ragtime' Music," *Negro Year Book: An Annual Encyclopedia of the Negro, 1925–1926* (A.M.E. Sunday School Union, 1926), 343.

34. *CIO*, August 6, 1893, 7; *Chicago Tribune*, August 26, 1893, 3; Reed, *"All the World,"* 71.

35. The income and exposure generated by jubilee ensembles were essential to the stability of burgeoning historically Black colleges and universities. However, the political compromises made for White consumption tainted the legacy of the tradition, which relegated it to the institutions they served. Jubilee was quickly supplanted by other Afro-American expressive forms that drew more from the genuine folk culture, although the caveat of White acceptance has remained in perpetuity.

36. Edward A. Berlin, *Reflections and Research on Ragtime*, ISAM monograph 24 (Institute for Studies in American Music, Conservatory of Music, Brooklyn College of the City of New York, 1987), 1; Reid Badger, *The Great American Fair:*

The World's Columbian Exposition & American Culture (Nelson Hall, 1979), 120; *St. Louis Globe-Democrat*, March 26, 1893, 11. The Texas Medley Quartet also included James "Ike" Rivers, a future cast member of the Williams and Walker Company.

37. "City Gives 'Jazz' to Musical World," *Chicago Defender*, October 29, 1932, 7.
38. Walker, "Bert and Me and Them," 12.
39. Walker, 12.
40. Eubie Blake and Eileen Southern, "Conversation with Eubie Blake: A Legend in His Own Lifetime," *The Black Perspective in Music* 1, no. 1 (1973): 55. For more on the social conditions surrounding ragtime and jazz, see composer Ed Bland's (1926 to 1913) 1959 short film *The Cry of Jazz*, Unheard Music Series (Music Video Distributors, 2004), 4:23–5:08 and 7:56–9:11.
41. *San Francisco Chronicle*, January 11, 1894, 4, and March 16, 1894, 5; *Morning Call*, January 17, 1894, 3.
42. *San Francisco Chronicle*, May 26, 1894, 4; *Morning Call*, May 28, 1894, 10.
43. Walker, "Real 'Coon,'" 224–25.
44. See *Times-Picayune* (New Orleans), May 21, 1894, 3; *San Francisco Chronicle*, August 1, 1894, 5; *The Herald* (Los Angeles), August 5, 1894, 16.
45. *San Francisco Call*, April 20, 1902, 24.
46. "Williams and Walker," *INF*, March 12, 1910, 5–6.
47. Mabel Rowland, *Bert Williams: Son of Laughter: A Symposium of Tribute to the Man and to His Work* (English Crafters, 1923), 19–20.
48. Rowland, *Bert Williams*, 27.
49. Walker, "Real 'Coon,'" 224–25.
50. "Cake-Walks and Culture," *The World* (New York), January 23, 1898, 33.
51. "Harrison Stewart," *NYA*, July 9, 1908, 6.

Chapter 3

1. *The Herald* (Los Angeles), November 18, 1895, 4; quotation from "Amusements," *Los Angeles Times*, November 24, 1895, 1. See also *New York Clipper*, December 7, 1895, 630, and December 14, 1895, 646; "Bert Williams Tells of Walker," *INF*, January 14, 1911, 5.
2. "At the Theatres," *Los Angeles Times*, April 24, 1898, 41.
3. "Orpheum," *The Herald* (Los Angeles), November 25, 1895, 5. See also *The Herald*, November 26, 1895, 4. *Buck* refers to a percussive, proto-tap style, while *wing* refers to a loosely percussive swaying of the limbs that was a precursor to popular dances in the twentieth century like the Charleston, funky chicken, and Blood/Crip walk, among others. A refined combination of buck and wing formed the basis for the cake walk, the first Afro-American-inspired dance craze, at the close of the nineteenth century, which Williams and Walker would soon come to personify. See also Tom Fletcher, *100 Years of the Negro in Show Business: The Tom*

Fletcher Story (Burdge, 1954), 230. Fletcher also claimed that in the early days of Williams and Walker, both men wore burnt cork, although there is no evidence to support that.

4. *Los Angeles Times*, December 1, 1895, 16.

5. Fletcher, *100 Years*, 229.

6. "Orpheum," *The Herald* (Los Angeles), December 26, 1895, 4.

7. Untitled caption, *The Herald*, December 15, 1895, 14. See also *The Herald*, December 17, 1895, 4.

8. "Orpheum," *Los Angeles Times*, December 24, 1895, 6.

9. Fletcher, *100 Years*, 108–9; "Mah Angeline and Dora Deane," *San Francisco Examiner*, May 19, 1896, 9.

10. *Golden Reunion in Ragtime*, featuring Eubie Blake, Joe Jordan, and Charles Thompson, side B, track 4, Stereoddities, 1962.

11. Bernard L. Peterson Jr., *Profiles of African American Stage Performers and Theatre People, 1816–1960* (Greenwood Press, 2001).

12. "The Value of the Critic Press Agent to the Actor or Actress," *Colorado Statesman*, February 25, 1911, 12. See also George W. Walker, "Bert and Me and Them," *NYA*, December 24, 1908, 12.

13. "Who Purloined 'Mah Angeline?,'" *San Francisco Call*, May 18, 1896, 12.

14. *San Francisco Call*, June 2, 1898, 8; *San Francisco Chronicle*, June 2, 1898, 7; Broder v. Zeno Mauvais Music Co., 88 F. 74 (C.C.N.D. Cal. 1898).

15. George W. Walker, "Bert and Me and Them," *NYA*, December 24, 1908, 12.

16. Eric Ledell Smith, *Bert Williams: A Biography of the Pioneer Black Comedian* (McFarland, 1992), 16–17.

17. "Death of George W. Walker," *NYA*, January 12, 1911, 6.

18. "Bert Williams Tells of Walker," 5. See also *San Pedro Daily Pilot*, March 6, 1922, 2; Mabel Rowland, *Bert Williams: Son of Laughter: A Symposium of Tribute to the Man and to His Work* (English Crafters, 1923), 156; Ann Charters, *Nobody: The Story of Bert Williams* (Macmillan, 1970), 25–26. Charters incorrectly asserted the incident took place in Texas, but Williams and Walker never performed in the South.

19. Charters, *Nobody*, 25–26. See also *San Pedro Daily Pilot*, March 6, 1922, 2; *1897 Chicago Blue Book* (Chicago Directory Company, 1896), 822; "Bert Williams Tells of Walker," 5.

20. Sylvester Russell, "A Quiet Evening with Jesse Shipp," *INF*, September 16, 1905, 5. See also "Jesse A. Shipp," *Variety*, May 8, 1934, 62.

21. *Chicago Tribune*, February 27, 1896, 5. See also *Evansville Courier and Press*, September 8, 1901, 7. Some historians believe that Isham was Afro-American, but critic Phil H. Brown asserted that he was a "Hebrew."

22. James W. Johnson, *Black Manhattan* (Da Capo Press, 1991), 95.

23. *Chicago Tribune*, March 1, 1896, 32; *Evansville Courier and Press*, September 8, 1901, 7.

24. Rowland, *Bert Williams*, 34.

25. Walker, "Bert and Me and Them," 12.

26. See Jeanne Klein, "The Cake Walk Photo Girl and Other Footnotes in African American Musical Theatre," *Theatre Survey* 60, no. 1 (2019): 67–90, https://doi.org/10.1017/S0040557418000509; Rowland, *Bert Williams*, 34; Jayna Brown, *Babylon Girls: Black Women Performers and the Shaping of the Modern* (Duke University Press, 2008), 150–51; "Baby, Will You Always Love Me True?," words by Billy Johnson, music by Bob Cole, Broder and Schlam, New York / San Francisco, 1897, Dr. H. T. Sampson, Jr. Collection, Jackson State University Library.

27. Rowland, *Bert Williams*, 73–75.

28. *CIO*, March 15, 1896, 37; *Evening Express* (Los Angeles), March 20, 1896, 5; *Chicago Chronicle*, March 15, 1896, 19, and April 15, 1896, 6; *Chicago Tribune*, May 26, 1896, 5; *Detroit Free Press*, July 19, 1896, 2.

29. Eileen Southern, *The Music of Black Americans: A History*, 2nd ed. (W. W. Norton, 1983), 92.

30. "Theatrical Notes," *The Times* (District of Columbia), January 30, 1898, 14.

31. Bert Williams, "The Comic Side of Trouble," *American Magazine* 85 (January–June 1918): 60.

32. Fletcher, *100 Years*, 242–43.

33. "From Melodrama to Opera," *Kansas City Times*, September 24, 1909, 16.

34. Reprinted in "Williams and Walker," *Coffeyville Herald*, March 21, 1908, 1.

35. Their future manager Lew Dockstader scored with "When Miss Maria Johnson Marries Me," words and music by Williams and Walker (Spaulding and Gray, New York, 1896).

36. *Courier-Journal* (Louisville, KY), April 13, 1896, 5, and November 28, 1899, 7; *Saturday Evening Mail* (Terre Haute, IN), August 1, 1896, 1; *TSJ*, January 11, 1902, 11.

37. Walker, "Bert and Me and Them," 12.

38. *West Baden Springs Journal*, August 18, 1896, 1, and August 25, 1896, 1; *CIO*, September 8, 1896, 8; *Chicago Chronicle*, September 10, 1896, 6; Williams, "Comic Side," 60.

39. "Pursuit of Merriment," *NYT*, September 22, 1896, 5; *Variety*, March 17, 1922, 14; *The Sun* (New York), September 13, 1896, 3; *NYT*, September 20, 1896, 11; Walker, "Bert and Me and Them," 12.

40. "The Start of Williams and Walker," *Philadelphia Inquirer*, March 7, 1909, 2. See also *Morning Telegraph*, July 26, 1902, page unknown. Theatre critic Acton Davies also claimed that Truly Shattuck gave a similar account to him and subsequently claimed responsibility for Williams and Walker's rediscovery.

41. "Start of Williams and Walker," 2. Trevathan likely pirated Haitian-born guitarist Louise "Mama Lou" Rogers's (d. 1918) compositions "Ta-ra-ra Boom-de-ay," "Hot Time in the Old Town Tonight," "Bully of the Town," and others in St. Louis.

42. "Start of Williams and Walker," 2.

43. "George Lederer Interview," *Variety*, March 17, 1922, 14.
44. *The Sun* (New York), September 13, 1896, 3; *New York Journal*, September 24, 1896, 7; "Start of Williams and Walker," 2.
45. "Bert Williams Tells of Walker," 5; Walker, "Bert and Me and Them," 12; "George Lederer Interview," 14.
46. "The Columbia," *Brooklyn Daily Eagle*, September 29, 1896, 7.
47. Williams, "Comic Side," 60; "Bert Williams Tells of Walker," 5; *TSJ*, January 11, 1902, 11.
48. *Boston Globe*, October 4, 1896, 18; *Boston Post*, October 10, 1896, 5.
49. "Bert Williams Tells of Walker," 5. According to Bert, "Montgomery & Stone had been booked for the Musee, Pittsburg. They refused to fill the engagement and we took their place."
50. See *The Pittsburgh Press*, May 23, 1909, 6; *Pittsburgh Daily Post*, May 17, 1906, 7.

Chapter 4

1. Untitled caption in "The Stage," *Washington (DC) Times*, January 30, 1898, 14.
2. Untitled article, Ernest Hogan folder, Helen Armstead-Johnson miscellaneous theatre collections, Schomberg Center for Research in Black Culture, New York Public Library.
3. Tom Fletcher, *100 Years of the Negro in Show Business: The Tom Fletcher Story* (Burdge, 1954), 137.
4. Fletcher, *100 Years*, 138. See also "Helped to Make Ragtime Popular," *Democrat and Chronicle* (Rochester, NY), June 10, 1907, 10. Hogan denied inventing ragtime and suggested that it was part of the culture à la "time immemorial."
5. See *INF*, August 24, 1901, 6.
6. George W. Walker, "The Real 'Coon' on the American Stage," *The Theatre*, August 1906, 224–25.
7. See Lawrence W. Levine, *Black Culture and Black Consciousness: Afro-American Folk Thought from Slavery to Freedom* (Oxford University Press, 2007), 16; Marshall Stearns and Jean Stearns, *Jazz Dance: The Story of American Vernacular Dance* (Da Capo Press, 1994), 122–24.
8. "To Cakewalk Successfully One Must Be Light-Hearted," *Indianapolis News*, March 28, 1903, 16.
9. For example, see *St. Louis Post-Dispatch*, April 3, 1898, 20; "Grotesque," *San Francisco Call*, June 16, 1899, 6; *The Gazette* (York, PA), May 26, 1903, 5; *Middlesex County Times* (London), February 4, 1905, 6.
10. *Boston Traveler*, May 13, 1909, quoted in Stearns and Stearns, *Jazz Dance*, 117, 86.

11. Iver Bernstein, *The New York City Draft Riots: Their Significance for American Society and Politics in the Age of the Civil War*, ACLS Humanities EBook (Oxford University Press, 1990), 17–42.

12. *Afro-American Ledger*, January 29, 1910, page unknown. The Nail family was a major contributor to what would become the Harlem Renaissance. John "Jack" E. Nail, who often passed as a White real estate investor, bought up small sections of uptown neighborhoods. The ruse worked, and when Black renters began to move into previously all-White buildings, it inspired White flight out of the area.

13. *NYT*, October 25, 1896, 27; *Pittsburgh Daily Post*, May 17, 1906, 7; George W. Walker, "Bert and Me and Them," *NYA*, December 24, 1908, 12; "Bert Williams Tells of Walker," *INF*, January 14, 1911, 5.

14. "The Fall of the Vaudeville Kings," *CIO*, January 17, 1904, 40.

15. Quoted in Mabel Rowland, *Bert Williams: Son of Laughter: A Symposium of Tribute to the Man and to His Work* (English Crafters, 1923), 34.

16. Walker, "Bert and Me and Them," 12. See also *Buffalo Review*, April 22, 1899, 5.

17. Quoted in Rowland, *Bert Williams*, 21–22.

18. "The New Jokes of the Week," *New York Journal*, November 1, 1896, 14.

19. Quoted in Rowland, *Bert Williams*, 34–35.

20. Untitled review, *The Sun* (New York), December 3, 1896, 7.

21. "Music and the Stage," *NYA*, July 18, 1912, 6.

22. "Theatre News," *Brooklyn Daily Eagle*, February 7, 1897, 24.

23. *LDW*, February 16, 1897, 3; *The Standard* (London), February 20, 1897, 16.

24. It is possible that the inspiration to wear a monocle came from Billy Clifford, whom George shared billing with at the Orpheum in Los Angeles.

25. *The Sun* (New York), December 14, 1896, 5, and January 17, 1897, 12; *Brooklyn Daily Eagle*, March 7, 1897, 18, March 15, 1897, 8, and March 16, 1897, 7; "Bert Williams Tells of Walker," 5.

26. *INF*, February 8, 1902, 1; *Board of Trade: Commercial and Statistical Department and Successors: Inwards Passenger Lists, 1897*, class BT26, piece 102, 1897, National Archives, Kew, UK; *Morning Post* (London), April 21, 1897, 4; *The Era* (London), April 24, 1897, 18; *Los Angeles Times*, May 9, 1897, 21.

27. Bert Williams, "The Comic Side of Trouble," *The American Magazine* 85 (January–June 1918): 60.

28. Untitled caption, *Los Angeles Times*, August 22, 1897, 15.

29. Guisard, "Comedian Asserts Colored Players Must Yield to Prejudice," *San Francisco Call*, April 20, 1902, 24.

30. "Gossip of the Stage and Players," *Los Angeles Times*, June 20, 1897, 22. See also "Cake Walks and Culture," *The World* (New York), January 23, 1898, 33. Bert mentioned that he and George had visited "London, Paris and all the continental cities."

31. Untitled caption, *The Era* (London), May 29, 1897, 13.

32. *Passenger Lists of Vessels Arriving at New York, 1820–97*, microfilm 237, line 3; p. 24; *New York Journal and Advertiser*, May 30, 1897, 53.

33. "A Lawrence Boy," *LWW*, July 15, 1897, 7.

34. *LDJ*, August 9, 1897, 4; "Darkest Vaudeville," *Leslie's Weekly*, July 22, 1897, 52. The 1900 census shows Alice Myers living with her husband, Frank Myers, and her mother, Sarah Hayden, at 319 R1 East El Paso Avenue in Cripple Creek, CO. Census of Cripple Creek, Teller, Colorado, ED 0128, 1900, p. 19, FHL microfilm 1240130.

35. Stearns and Stearns, *Jazz Dance*, 86; Nadine George-Graves, *Royalty of Negro Vaudeville: The Whitman Sisters and the Negotiation of Race, Gender, and Class in African-American Theatre, 1900–1940* (St. Martin's Press, 2000), 16. Although delayed by their father's objection, the four Whitman sisters would eventually make good and establish a lasting presence on the American stage.

36. "The Cake Walk as It Is Done by Genuine Negroes," *American Woman's Home Journal* (New York), August 22, 1897, 12. See also "The Stage," James Weldon Johnson and Grace Nail Johnson papers, JWJ MSS 49, box 137, folder 1148, Yale Collection of American Literature, Beinecke Rare Book and Manuscript Library.

37. *The Sun* (New York), December 3, 1896, 7. The sixth and unnumbered (ninth) image of the Franz Huld series of cake-walk postcards may have depicted a comical situation described in the review: "the first fellow takes both women, one on each arm, and, leaving the other man grimacing vengefully, starts on a second tour of grace." See also *Brooklyn Times Union*, October 3, 1896, 8. Wiley was performing at the Empire in Brooklyn with Black Patti's Troubadours early in the month; and *Brooklyn Times Union*, September 22, 1896, 3. Davis was with Isham's *Oriental America* at the Brooklyn Bijou at the end of September of that year.

38. "Music Halls and Popular Songs," *The Cosmopolitan* 23, no. 5 (September 1897): 532. See also *Pleasanton Observer-Enterprise*, January 15, 1898, 1, and April 9, 1898, 1; *Yonkers Herald*, December 7, 1898, 1. If "A Hot Coon from Memphis" was released in late 1897 and the partners were still sharing clothing when it and the cake-walk photos were made, they were still in recovery from their journey east from Los Angeles. In addition, the "Hot Coon" image was featured in the September issue of *Cosmopolitan* magazine and was produced as a card for the American Tobacco Company that showcased the song and a few others in early 1898, including the Williams and Walker piece "I Don't Like No Cheap Man," made famous in part by McIntyre and Heath, who performed with them in Hyde's Minstrels. Therefore, the claim that "Williams and Walker Show How the Real Thing Is Done Before the [American Woman's Home] Journal Camera" may be hyperbole.

39. Walker, "Bert and Me and Them," 12. The idea may have originated with composer and performer Irving Jones (1874 to 1932), a former member of Sam T. Jack's aggregation, whose compositions "Get Your Money's Worth," released in 1897, and "Let Me Bring My Clothes Back Home," in 1898, were also issued as tobacco cards.

40. *INF*, January 31, 1903, 1. At least one image from this session survives, likely housed at the Yale Collection of American Literature, Beinecke Rare Book and Manuscript Library.

41. *Brooklyn Daily Eagle*, September 21, 1897, 7; *The Sun* (New York), October 3, 1897, 11; *Pittsburgh Press*, October 29, 1897, 11; *Evening Star* (District of Columbia), October 16, 1897, 24; *Indianapolis News*, November 10, 1897, 10; *Courier-Journal* (Louisville), November 14, 1897, 18; *Chicago Daily Tribune*, November 22, 1897.

42. *Los Angeles Times*, November 7, 1897, 19; *Washington Bee*, February 19, 1898, 5; *Evansville Courier and Press*, September 8, 1901, 7. Isham was reportedly institutionalized by December of 1899.

Chapter 5

Part of this chapter was previously published as Daniel E. Atkinson, "'Cake Walks and Culture': The Black Struggle for Sovereignty at the Dawn of Jim Crow," *Theatre History Studies* 43 (2024).

1. *The World* (New York), December 12, 1897, 24, and January 17, 1898, page unknown. "He Can Lead a Cake Walk: Vanderbilt Budding Forth as an All Round Society Clown," *Lewiston (ID) Teller*, January 21, 1898, 3; Tom Fletcher, *100 Years of the Negro in Show Business: The Tom Fletcher Story* (Burdge, 1954), 123. The term "Four Hundred" originally referred to the select group of people whom Caroline Astor could fit into the ballroom of her first of two mansions on Fifth Avenue.

2. "Dare Vanderbilt to a Cake-Walk Contest," *The World* (New York), January 17, 1898.

3. "Dare Vanderbilt."

4. "Dare Vanderbilt."

5. "Dare Vanderbilt."

6. See "Cake Walks and Culture," *The World* (New York), January 23, 1898, 33.

7. "Cake Walks and Culture," *The World*.

8. "Cake Walks and Culture," *The World*.

9. William Shakespeare, *Hamlet*, 1.5.167–68.

10. "Walkin' for Dat Cake," *Buffalo (NY) Evening News*, January 17, 1898, 5.

11. See *Buffalo (NY) Review*, April 22, 1899, 5; "I Don't Like No Cheap Man," received January 12, 1898, *Catalogue of Title Entries of Books and Other Articles: January 3–April 2, 1898*, vol. 14 (Library of Congress, 1898), 109.

12. "Nash Walker Here," *LDW*, May 16, 1898, 3; *LWW*, May 19, 1898, 5.

13. See *LDJ*, May 17, 1898, 4; *LDW*, May 27, 1898, 3 and 4.

14. Other biographies state 13 Cornelia Street and Twenty-Seventh Street between Sixth and Seventh Avenues in "Coontown."

15. *Trow's New York City Directories: For the Year Ending May 1, 1880*, vol. 93 (Trow City Directories, 1879), 1174; Richard Bruce Nugent, "Marshall's: A Portrait," *Phylon (1940–1956)* 5, no. 4 (1944): 317; 1860 census of Pasquotank County, North Carolina, p. 344, Family History Library microfilm 803909, certificate 5336; *New York, New York, U.S., Extracted Marriage Index, 1866–1937*, online database (Ancestry.com, 2014); Wills, 1720–1941, Pasquotank County Court of Pleas and Quarter Sessions, North Carolina.

16. "Ada Overton Walker," James Weldon Johnson and Grace Nail Johnson papers, JWJ MSS 49, box 67, folder 280, Yale Collection of American Literature, Beinecke Rare Book and Manuscript Library; *Denver Star*, October 24, 1914, 1; William Foster, *Memoirs of William Foster/ Pioneers of the Stage*, in *The Official Theatrical World of Colored Artists*, ed. Theophilus Lewis (Theatrical World Publishing, 1928), 40–49; Nugent, "Marshall's," 317.

17. "Ada Overton Walker," James Weldon Johnson and Grace Nail Johnson papers.

18. "Aida Overton Walker," *INF*, October 17, 1914, 5; Sylvester Russell, "The Mistakes of Williams and Walker," *INF*, April 14, 1906, 6.

19. "Welcome Death! Slogan of Robert Cole," *INF*, August 12, 1911, 5. See also Maureen D. Lee, *Sissieretta Jones* (University of South Carolina Press, 2013), 112–14.

20. Fletcher, *100 Years*, 181.

21. Foster, *Memoirs*, 40–49; Jayna Brown, *Babylon Girls: Black Women Performers and the Shaping of the Modern* (Duke University Press, 2008), 150–52. Foster mistakenly identified Ada Overton as one of the two women in the photo series. Brown noted that she was on tour with Black Patti's Troubadours' *A Trip to Coontown* when the photos were made. See also Jeanne Klein, "The Cake Walk Photo Girl and Other Footnotes in African American Musical Theatre," *Theatre Survey* 60, no. 1 (2019): 67–90; "Aida Overton Walker," *Pittsburgh Courier*, July 16, 1932, 7.

22. "Academy—Williams and Walker," *Washington (DC) Times*, October 9, 1898, 16. See also "Clorindy . . . ," *Theatre Arts* 31, no. 9 (1947): 61–65; *Boston Globe*, September 3, 1898, 10.

23. "Will Marion Cook on Negro Music," *NYA*, September 21, 1918, 6.

24. "Clorindy . . . ," *Theatre Arts* 31, no. 9 (1947): 61–62.

25. "Clorindy . . . ," 64. See also *Boston Globe*, September 18, 1898, 18; *The Sun* (Wilmington, DE), October 3, 1898, 2; *The Sun* (New York), October 23, 1898, 11; *CIO*, November 27, 1898, 15, and December 12, 1898, 5; *Chicago Tribune*, November 21, 1898, 5; *Kansas City Star*, December 29, 1898, 2; *St. Louis Post-Dispatch*, December 30, 1898, 5; *Los Angeles Evening Express*, January 28, 1899, 5. Rice's version of *Clorindy* embarked on a tour of mostly Keith's vaudeville houses in the East and Midwest until the end of the year and then went to the West Coast.

26. George W. Walker, "Bert and Me and Them," *NYA*, December 24, 1908, 12.

27. *Philadelphia Times*, August 14, 1898, 23, and October 2, 1898, 23; *Boston Globe*, September 9, 1898, 10.

28. *Brooklyn Citizen*, December 13, 1898, 6.

29. "Senegambians—The Grand," *Cincinnati Enquirer*, September 18, 1898, 17.

30. "News of the Theatres," *Buffalo Courier*, September 25, 1898, 16. See also *Brooklyn Daily Eagle*, December 11, 1898, 18.

31. *Cincinnati Enquirer*, September 20, 1898, 7; *INF*, October 1, 1898, 5, and October 17, 1914, 5; Fletcher, *100 Years*, 230–33.

32. "The Great Names He Knew Live On," *New York Herald*, September 8, 1936, 2.

33. *The Times* (Philadelphia), September 11, 1898, 23; Fletcher, *100 Years*, 230.

34. "The Hottest Coon in Dixie," words by Paul Laurence Dunbar, music by Will Marion Cook, Witmark and Sons, New York, 1898.

35. *Boston Globe*, September 6, 1898, 2; *Topeka Daily Capital*, April 19, 1903, 17; *Pittsburgh Daily Post*, March 5, 1905, 26.

36. "Academy—Williams and Walker," *Evening Times* (Washington, DC), October 11, 1898, 8.

37. Untitled caption, *Morning Times*, September 11, 1898, 14.

38. See "Bought Up the Show," *Washington (DC) Times*, October 13, 1898, 8; "Theatrical Gossip," *NYT*, October 20, 1898, 12; Waterbury *Democrat*, November 4, 1898, 6; *Sunday Leader* (New York), November 6, 1898, 10; *Brooklyn Daily Eagle*, December 11, 1898, 18.

39. "Last Week's Bill—Koster and Bial's," *New York Dramatic Mirror*, November 19, 1898, 18.

40. See *Brooklyn Citizen*, December 13, 1898, 6; *LDW*, December 23, 1898, 2.

Chapter 6

1. Chicot, "Wants Real Coon, Not Black and Tan," *Morning Telegraph*, January 4, 1899, 8. Chicot was the pen name of Epes W. Sargent (1872 to 1938), who went on to become the chief vaudeville reviewer for *Variety* in 1905. His use of "Black and Tan" implied an unlawful blending of Black and White culture that was a feature of a small but growing class of night spots in Manhattan and other large eastern cities.

2. "Great Congress of Colored Stars," *Morning Journal-Courier* (New Haven, CT), December 27, 1898, 3.

3. "Album of Gems, Introduced by Williams and Walker," sheet music cover, Hurtig and Seamon, New York, 1899, National Portrait Gallery, Smithsonian Institution; *Buffalo Review*, April 22, 1899, 5. See also *Evening Star* (Washington, DC), May 6, 1899, 24. Blenheim Palace has no record of the event. Several clippings from this tour also mentioned that the duo was part of Lou Johnson's Minstrels in California in 1894 as well as Neilson's Arial Ballet. Neither was true.

4. See *Cincinnati Enquirer*, March 3, 1899, 4; *New York Herald Tribune*, September 8, 1935, 2. See also "Recovered," *Cincinnati Enquirer*, April 6, 1899, 12. While they were engaged in Cincinnati, a diamond-encrusted matchbox was stolen from George and pawned by "an all-around crook, well known to the local police," named Shell Haywood. No charges were filed.

5. *Janesville Daily Gazette*, October 18, 1904, 5; *Seattle Post-Intelligencer*, March 26, 1899, 15.

6. *Philadelphia Inquirer*, May 5, 1899, 4.

7. "Academy—'A Lucky Coon,'" *The Times* (Washington, DC), May 7, 1899, 16.

8. "Academy of Music," *Evening Star* (Washington, DC), May 9, 1899, 10.

9. "Cold Weather Fails to Help Business," *The Times* (Washington, DC), May 14, 1899, 16; "Aida Overton Walker," *INF*, October 17, 1914, 5.

10. "The Great Names He Knew Live On," *New York Herald*, September 8, 1936, 2.

11. *New York Journal and Advertiser*, May 14, 1899, page unknown; "Mazet Sunday Was Just Like Others," *New York Journal and Advertiser*, May 22, 1899, 2.

12. "Mr. Neely and Not Ben Gay, All Coons Do Not Look Alike," *Morning Telegraph*, May 30, 1899, 4.

13. "Actors Draw the Color Line," *Standard Union* (Brooklyn), May 31, 1899, 12. See also *Morning Telegraph*, August 14, 1899, 3.

14. *LDJ*, June 12, 1899, 4; *LDW*, June 16, 1899, 2. The choice of a Pierce may have been an homage to Major Taylor (1878 to 1932), who became world champion on August 11, 1899, in Montreal, likely on a Pierce bicycle.

15. *The Sun* (New York), June 25, 1899, 4; *The Times* (Washington, DC), July 2, 1899, 13.

16. "Walker, of Williams and Walker a Benedict," *New York Journal and Advertiser*, June 24, 1899, 5.

17. Untitled caption, *Kansas City Times*, January 7, 1900, 11; "Funke Today, Matinee and Evening," *Nebraska State Journal*, January 20, 1900, 4. Another version of the story printed in *Current Comment and Kansas Register*, February 1, 1901, asserted the incident took place in Massachusetts Bay, Boston.

18. Tom Fletcher, *100 Years of the Negro in Show Business: The Tom Fletcher Story* (Burdge, 1954), 230.

19. *The Times* (Washington, DC), July 23, 1899, 12. Other copyrighted names: *The Policy Shop*, *The Policy Winners*, *The Policy Player's Ball*, *7-11-77*, and *Kings of the Policy Shop*.

20. See *Des Moines Register*, February 4, 1900, 20; *Indianapolis Journal*, February 13, 1900, 3. See also *The Times* (Washington, DC), December 10, 1899, 21.

21. *Norwalk Gazette*, September 23, 1899, 1.

22. Marriage certificate, *Vital Records*, New York Municipal Archives; Untitled caption, *The Sun* (New York), October 15, 1899, 19.

23. "Gay Burlesque on Negro Life," *New York Journal and Advertiser*, October 17, 1899, 5.

24. *Philadelphia Inquirer*, October 27, 1899, 2; *New York Dramatic Mirror*, November 4, 1899, 12; untitled caption, *Evening Star* (Washington, DC), November 11, 1899, 24.

25. "New Grand," *Evening Star* (Washington, DC), November 14, 1899, 16. See also "Notes from the Williams and Walker Co.," *INF*, November 25, 1899, 5.

26. Charles R. Douglass, "Where the Blame Belongs," *The Colored American*, November 25, 1899, 1.

27. "Manager Chase Had All He Wants of Negro Show Troupes," *Morning Telegraph* (New York), November 27, 1899, 5.

28. "A Principle at Stake," *The Colored American*, November 25, 1899, 4.

29. "Manager Harris' Sure Thing," *Kansas City Times*, January 21, 1901, 3. Reportedly, Harris took bets from doubtful White people who refused to believe such exclusive hotels would accept Black clientele.

30. *Detroit Free Press*, December 22, 1899, 4.

31. *CIO*, December 31, 1899, 30; *Chicago Tribune*, December 25, 1899, 5.

32. *Chicago Tribune*, December 26, 1899, 3; *INF*, December 30, 1899, 5.

33. "Williams and Walker," *INF*, March 12, 1910, 5, 6.

34. "They Arrive," *LDW*, January 15, 1900, 5.

35. "S.R.O. [Standing Room Only] Sign Was Out," *LDJ*, January 16, 1900, 4.

36. *LDJ*, January 16, 1900, 4; *INF*, January 27, 1900, 5.

37. *TSJ*, January 18, 1900, 4.

38. *Topeka Daily Capital*, January 17, 1900, 2; *The Topeka Plaindealer* (hereafter cited as *TPD*), January 12, 1900, 2; *Atchison Daily Globe*, January 17, 1900, 4.

39. "Orpheum," *Omaha Daily Bee*, January 22, 1900, 8.

40. *Des Moines Register*, February 11, 1900, 22.

41. "Bert Williams Doesn't Gamble 'No Mo,'" *The Times* (Washington, DC), August 9, 1908, 24.

42. *INF*, February 10, 1900, 5, and March 10, 1900, 5; *Weekly Leader* (Indianapolis), February 14, 1900, 1; *CIO*, February 18, 1900, 35.

43. "The Stage—Notes from the Williams and Walker Company," *INF*, March 10, 1900, 5.

44. "Bert Williams: Taking Him Away from the Williams and Walker Combination, and There Is Nothing to Commend it," *TPD*, March 23, 1900, 1; "Swelled," *Daily Review* (Decatur, IL), February 10, 1900, 2.

45. *Boston Globe*, March 11, 1900, 18; *Brooklyn Times Union*, March 17, 1900, 13; *Daily Morning Journal and Courier* (New Haven, CT), May 2, 1900, 2.

46. Untitled caption, *Meriden Daily Journal*, May 2, 1900, 12.

47. *Meriden Daily Journal*, May 2, 1900, 12; *INF*, May 12, 1900, 5. At this time, the team was made up of Shepard Edmonds, catcher; Richard Connor, pitcher; Clarence Logan, shortstop; Bert Williams, first base; Ed Thomas, second base;

W. H. Chappelle, third base; Ed Harris, right field; George Walker, left field; Billy Banks, center field; and Frank Mallory, manager. See also *INF*, May 12, 1900, 5.

48. *The Sun* (New York), May 6, 1900, 10; *The Colored American Magazine*, May 12, 1900, 5; *New-York Tribune*, May 13, 1900, 30. See also *Altoona Times*, September 15, 1904, 5; *Evening Capital* (Annapolis, MD), February 23, 1905, 4. *Policy Players* was revived in 1904 starring Ernest Hogan and in 1905 starring Salem "Tutt" Whitney (1875 to 1934).

49. *Trow's General Directory of the Boroughs of Manhattan and Brox, City of New York: For the Year Ending July 1, 1900*, vol. 93, Irmà and Paul Milstein Division of United States History, Local History and Genealogy, New York Public Library Digital Collections, pp. 1323, 1373; 1900 census of Manhattan, New York, New York, ED 0676, p. 6, Family History Library microfilm 1241111. Along with his apartment on 154 West Fifty-Third Street, George was listed in the 1900 census as a renter with Ada; her mother, Pauline; stepfather, Miles Reed; and a few chorus members (including Maggie Davis and James and Suzie Vaughn) at 505 Sixth Avenue in a racially mixed neighborhood.

50. Richard Bruce Nugent, "Marshall's: A Portrait," *Phylon (1940–1956)* 5, no. 4 (1944): 316.

51. *INF*, August 12, 1911, 5.

52. George W. Walker, "The Real 'Coon' on the American Stage," *The Theatre*, August 1906, 224–25. See also Marva Griffin Carter, *Swing Along: The Musical Life of Will Marion Cook* (Oxford University Press, 2008), 37–38.

53. James Weldon Johnson, *Along This Way: The Autobiography of James Weldon Johnson* (Viking Press, 1933), 172–73.

54. Lester Walton, "A Bit of Biography," *NYA*, October 9, 1913, 6.

55. "Williams and Walker," *INF*, March 12, 1910, 5.

56. Loften Mitchell, *Black Drama: The Story of the American Negro in the Theatre* (Hawthorn Press, 1967), 44.

57. Nugent, "Marshall's," 317–18.

58. "Revival of Rag," *Sunday Telegraph* (New York), September 4, 1904, 5.

Chapter 7

1. *NYT*, August 12, 1900, 10.
2. See James Weldon Johnson, *Black Manhattan* (Da Capo Press, 1991), 126.
3. "Editorials," *Denver Post*, May 29, 1907, 12.
4. Leslie M. Harris, *In the Shadow of Slavery: African Americans in New York City, 1626–1863* (University of Chicago Press, 2003), 280.
5. "West Side Race Riot," *New York Tribune*, August 16, 1900, 2.
6. Johnson, *Black Manhattan*, 127.
7. "The Stage," *INF*, September 1, 1900, 5.

8. Originally printed in the *New York Journal*, date unknown. Reprinted in "The Stage," *INF*, September 1, 1900, 5. The report indicated that George ran to the Hotel Marlborough, but it may have been conflated with Hogan's experience.

9. *New York Tribune*, August 16, 1900, 2; Ann Charters, *Nobody: The Story of Bert Williams* (Macmillan, 1970), 55.

10. Iver Bernstein, *The New York City Draft Riots: Their Significance for American Society and Politics in the Age of the Civil War*, ACLS Humanities EBook (Oxford University Press, 1990), 17–42.

11. *New York Tribune*, August 16, 1900, 2. The four men arrested in connection to what would now be called a lynching in the second degree were Henry Miller, John Smiliax, John Benson, and Henry Martin. See also *LDW*, August 17, 1900, 3; *TSJ*, August 16, 1900, 1; *NYT*, August 30, 1900, 12; *Evening World* (New York), December 8, 1900, 3.

12. *The Sun* (New York), August 19, 1900, 26, and August 21,1900, 7; *NYT*, August 20, 1900, 2; *INF*, October 27, 1900, 5.

13. Information provided in a 1972 oral history that is part of the Mike Montgomery collection, compact disc 2, track 10.

14. *Trow's General Directory of the Boroughs of Manhattan and Brox, City of New York: For the Year Ending July 1, 1900*, vol. 93, Irma and Paul Milstein Division of United States History, Local History and Genealogy, New York Public Library Digital Collections, p. 1040; "Race Gleanings," *INF*, November 5, 1904, 2. When the article was published in 1904, it claimed, "Today she has one of the largest dressmaking establishments in town." See also *Pittsburgh Daily Post*, February 26, 1905, 26.

15. *Chicago Tribune*, December 17, 1899, 40. Some historians cite the Great Northern Theatre, but period sources indicate McVicker's Theatre. See also *The Colored American Magazine*, September 1905, 496–502; "Brown's Grove Team," *LJG*, May 29, 1912, 8.

16. Johnson, *Black Manhattan*, 122.

17. *LJG*, January 9, 1902, 7; "Williams and Walker," *Boston Post*, May 5, 1901, 27. See also *INF*, October 6, 1900, 5.

18. "Harlem Sees 'The Sons of Ham' Presented by Black Comedians," *New York Telegraph*, April 7, 1901, 5.

19. *The Colored American Magazine*, October 6, 1900, 11; Marva Griffin Carter, *Swing Along: The Musical Life of Will Marion Cook* (Oxford University Press, 2008), 49. According to Marva Griffin Carter, the Cook–Mitchell wedding took place on October 21, 1900, in Manhattan. Some sources indicate the same date in Washington, DC, in 1899, but the company was not there during the month of October that year.

20. *Evening Bulletin* (Maysville, KY), November 24, 1900, 1; *Pittsburgh Daily Post*, November 25, 1900, 2, 24, and December 7, 1900, 7; *Pittsburgh Post-Gazette*, November 26, 1900, 9; *New York Tribune*, November 30, 1900, 1; *Cincinnati*

Enquirer, December 5, 1900, 8; *Muncie Daily Times*, December 24, 1900, 4; *St. Louis Republic*, December 30, 1900, 21. George Pickett's case was mild, and his roommate, Arthur Coates, presented no symptoms. Both were discharged after two weeks. Frank Sutton's and Harry Winfred's cases were more severe, and they remained hospitalized for a week or more.

21. *TSJ*, February 2, 1901, 10; "At the Play Last Night," *TSJ*, February 8, 1901, 4.

22. *LJG*, February 7, 1901, 2; *LDJ*, February 9, 1901, 4; *LDW*, February 11, 1901, 3.

23. "A Good Show and a Big House," *LDJ*, February 12, 1901, 4; *LDW*, February 11, 1901, 3; *TPD*, February 22, 1901, 3.

24. *INF*, May 4, 1901, 1.

25. "Announcement from Keith's," *Boston Globe*, December 10, 1901, 3; Tom Fletcher, *100 Years of the Negro in Show Business: The Tom Fletcher Story* (Burdge, 1954), 233.

26. *Boston Globe*, May 7, 1901, 4; "Briefly Told," *The Times* (Washington, DC), July 2, 1899, 13. For a synopsis of *Cannibal King*, see "Dunbar's Comedy," *Lexington Leader*, October 23, 1901, 7.

27. *Boston Globe*, May 26, 1901, 18; *New York Tribune*, June 11, 1901, 4; *The Times* (Philadelphia), June 30, 1901, 14; *Lima News*, November 29, 1901, 3; *The Press* (Kansas City), January 3, 1902, 8.

28. *Daily New Era* (Lancaster, PA), July 16, 1901, 2, and July 13, 1901, 2; untitled caption, *INF*, March 2, 1901, 5.

29. *The Colored American Magazine*, March 16, 1901, 6.

30. "Characteristics of the Colored Race," *Boston Post*, May 5, 1901, 28.

31. "Characteristics," 28.

32. *INF*, April 14, 1906, 6. The transition was mentioned on April 14, 1900, and became official in the September 4, 1900, issue (5).

33. "A Review of the Stage," *INF*, December 28, 1901, 15.

34. Sylvester Russell, "The Mistakes of Williams and Walker," *INF*, April 14, 1906, 6.

35. *New York Press*, July 6, 1905, 10; *Kansas City Star*, October 6, 1901, 17; *INF*, August 10, 1901, 5. The proposed cast consisted of Bob Cole, Ernest Hogan, Hen Wise, Billy Johnson, Coley Grant, J. Rosamond Johnson, Theodore Panky, Louis Salisbury, Reginald Burleigh, "Kid" Frazier, Abbie Mitchell Cook, Ada Overton Walker, Kate Milton, Mamie Grant, Muriel Ringgold, Cecil Watts, Anna Cook, Molly Dill, Odessa Warren, Nelly Dancy, Midget Price, Gertie Peterson, George Archer, John Boyer, the Alabama Comedy Four, and a chorus of forty.

36. "The Dark Soubrette," *INF*, October 12, 1901, 5. See also *Morning Telegraph* (New York), April 7, 1901, 5.

37. *Daily Argus* (Mount Vernon, NY), September 13, 1901, 5; *Brooklyn Daily Eagle*, September 29, 1901, 29.

38. *New York Dramatic Mirror*, October 19, 1901, 12. See also *Bert Williams: The Early Years, 1901–1909*, Archeophone Records, 2004. At the session, they recorded "I Don't Like That Face You Wear" (Victor Monarch no. 987), released as a 7 and 10 inch; "My Castle on the River Nile" (Victor Monarch no. 991); "The Phrenologist Coon" (Victor Monarch no. 992), 7 and 10 inch; "Where Was Moses When the Lights Went Out" (Victor Monarch no. 993), 7 and 10 inch; "All Goin' Out and Nothin' Comin' In" (Victor Monarch no. 994), 7 and 10 inch; "Junie" (Victor Monarch no. 995); "Good Morning Carrie" (Victor Monarch no. 997); "Her Name's Miss Dinah Fair" (Victor Monarch no. 999). On November 8, they recorded "She's Getting More Like the White Folks" (Victor Monarch no. 1085) and the smash hit "My Little Zulu Babe" (Victor Monarch no. 1086).

39. "Ada Overton Walker," James Weldon Johnson and Grace Nail Johnson papers, JWJ MSS 49, box 67, folder 280, Yale Collection of American Literature, Beinecke Rare Book and Manuscript Library.

40. *Morning Herald* (Lexington, KY), December 8, 1901, 6; *St. Louis Post-Dispatch*, January 2, 1902, 4; *The Press* (Kansas City), January 3, 1902, 8.

41. *TSJ*, January 14, 1902, 6; *LDJ*, January 15, 1902, 4; *LWW*, January 16, 1902, 4.

42. *Chicago Tribune*, January 19, 1902, 42. For the marriage announcement, see *INF*, February 8, 1902, 1; *Chicago Tribune*, January 29, 1902, 13. Green H. Tapley was mislabeled as "Breen." See also *Omaha Daily Bee*, March 29, 1902, 12; *San Francisco Call*, April 6, 1902, 15. On December 7, 1910, Daisy Robinson Talley and Carroll Clark (1885 to 1943) recorded "I Surrender All" for Columbia Records (A961). It is the oldest known commercial recording of a Black woman.

43. Guisard, "Comedian Asserts Colored Players Must Yield to Prejudice," *San Francisco Call*, April 20, 1902, 24. The subsequent quotation is from the same source.

44. *San Francisco Call*, April 17, 1902, 6.

45. "Sad Time for Williams," *Vancouver Daily World*, May 1, 1902, 2. See also Philip Sterling research materials, Billy Rose Theatre Division, New York Public Library (*T-Mss 1991-026). According to Lottie Williams's niece, Eunice Shreeves, Lottie's photo album of images from this and subsequent tours was given to Bill "Bojangles" Robinson after her death in 1929. The album has not resurfaced.

46. *Seattle Star*, April 29, 1902, 2. The meeting was probably more of a formality than anything else considering that George divulged the information in San Francisco a week before. See *San Francisco Call*, April 20, 1902, 24.

47. *The Province* (Vancouver, BC), April 29, 1902, 4; *Colorado Daily Chieftain*, May 23, 1902, 5; *Chicago Tribune*, June 9, 1902, 5; *Waterbury Democrat*, May 24, 1902, 6.

48. Douglass County Register of Deeds, deed book no. 72. See also *LDW*, June 25, 1902, 2, and July 5, 1902, 2; *LDJ*, May 15, 1902, 4, July 7, 1902, 2, and July 26, 1902, 4. Abe Levy was secretary of Elks Lodge no. 595 and was placed in charge of entertainment.

49. "Lawrence's Most Distinguished 'Son of Ham,'" *LJG*, July 24, 1902, 1; *LDJ*, July 26, 1902, 4; *LDW*, July 28, 1902, 3. Although the letter proclaims that he left Lawrence in 1893, it was likely an error because he had been working in California for a year by then.

Chapter 8

1. *Morning Telegraph* (New York), July 26, 1902, page unknown, and September 25, 1902, 12; *Kansas City Star and The Times*, December 30, 1902, 4.
2. *Brooklyn Daily Eagle*, July 27, 1902, 25; *New York Press*, July 6, 1905, 10.
3. "War Clouds Rise on Stage Horizon," *Morning Telegraph* (New York), July 1902, unknown date and page.
4. *Richmond Dispatch*, August 24, 1902, 6. See also *Morning Telegraph*, September 25, 1902, 12, where George was quoted, "We think we are ready for Broadway"; and *INF*, April 4, 1903, 9. Sylvester Russell recalled that around fifteen years earlier the Astor Place Company of Colored Tragedians opened at the Cosmopolitan Theatre at Broadway and Forty-First Street for a run of Shakespeare's *Hamlet* starring Hurle Bravado. Following *Hamlet*, Bravado withdrew, and *Othello* was produced with Benjamin F. Ford as Othello and J. A. Arneaux as Iago. The company ran for two weeks but closed due to bad business.
5. *INF*, September 20, 1902, 5.
6. *Washington (DC) Times*, August 26, 1902, 2; *St. Louis Republic*, August 26, 1902, 1; *Kansas City Star and The Times*, August 29, 1902, 8; *Pittsburgh Daily Post*, November 9, 1902, 28.
7. *New York Dramatic Mirror*, September 13, 1902, 17; *Stamford Advocate*, September 4, 1902, 4.
8. Both vehicles had scenes in Florida, focused on a lost box, and shared the songs "The Czar" and "Leader of the Colored Aristocracy."
9. *In Dahomey* (Cook) program, 1903, Billy Rose Theatre Division, New York Public Library.
10. *Denver Post*, June 8, 1902, 1, and June 9, 1902, page unknown, see also *Alexander's Magazine*, November 15, 1907, 17–19, and January 15, 1908, 66–67. In an early version of the script, Moses Lightfoot was a representative of the Dahomey Colonization Society, an example of art imitating life. Details remain elusive because almost nothing survives of George and Nashville's personal relationship, if there ever was one beyond 1885, when the elder Walker left Lawrence. Regardless, some communication likely took place when George traveled to Denver. If not, George surely would have learned of his father's exploits through mutual friends, and all Nashville had to do was read the entertainment section of his local paper to hear details of his more famous son's exploits.
11. *Boston Globe*, September 23, 1902, 8; *INF*, August 23, 1902, 5; *Harrisburg Telegraph*, October 31, 1902, 4.

12. Sylvester Russell, "Williams and Walker's Opening," *INF*, September 27, 1902, 5.

13. *Hartford Courant*, September 16, 1902, 5; *Boston Globe*, September 21, 1902, 33; *Boston Post*, September 21, 1902, 16.

14. *Philadelphia Inquirer*, September 30, 1902, 4. See also H. Harrison Wayman, "Sculptress," *The Colored American Magazine*, March 1903, 325–31; Judith N. Kerr, "God-Given Work: The Life and Times of Sculptor Meta Vaux Warrick Fuller, 1877–1968" (PhD diss., University of Massachusetts at Amherst, 1986), 145–47, 410, 438. "The Comedian" was not mentioned in a cursory inventory in *The Colored American*. There are no known photographs or castings, and the original was probably destroyed when her warehouse burned in 1910.

15. Sylvester Russell, "'In Dahomey' a Howling Success," *INF*, October 25, 1902, 5.

16. Russell, "'In Dahomey,'" 5.

17. *Harrisburg Telegraph*, October 31, 1902, 4.

18. Full-page advertisement in *San Francisco Examiner*, November 2, 1902, 47.

19. *Altoona Tribune*, October 27, 1902, 6; *Pittsburgh Daily Post*, November 2, 1902, 29; *Pittsburgh Press*, November 9, 1902, 36.

20. *Cincinnati Enquirer*, November 30, 1902, 34; Le Roi Antoine, *Achievement: The Life of Laura Bowman* (Pageant Press, 1961), 85–106.

21. *CIO*, December 15, 1902, 6; *Meriden Morning Record*, January 31, 1903, 2.

22. "Passed by the Office Window," *LDW*, January 5, 1903, 2.

23. *INF*, December 6, 1902, 6; *Kansas City Star*, December 26, 1902, 2; *The Press* (Kansas City, KS), December 26, 1902, 8; *American Citizen* (Kansas City, KS), January 9, 1903, 1; *Rising Son*, January 16, 1903, 1.

24. *LDW*, January 10, 1903, 3; *LDJ*, January 10, 1903, 4; untitled caption, *LDW*, January 12, 1903, 3.

25. "Record Is Broken," *TSJ*, January 10, 1903, 4. See also *Topeka Daily Herald*, January 10, 1903, 2.

26. *CIO*, January 25, 1903, 30.

27. *Indianapolis Journal*, January 26, 1903, 3. See also *NYT*, December 15, 1896, 7. George was introduced to the team in December of 1896 at a benefit for injured members of the National Guard, shortly after Williams and Walker made a hit at Koster and Bial's.

28. *INF*, January 31, 1903, 1, 5.

29. Sylvester Russell, "Doctrine of George W. Walker," *INF*, February 7, 1903, 5.

30. *LDG*, February 9, 1903, 3.

31. Unidentified clipping, Bert Williams vertical file, Schomburg Center for Research in Black Culture, New York Public Library.

32. "A Colored Actor's Work," *Pittsburgh Daily Post*, January 9, 1910, 30–31.

33. "Negro Mimes for Broadway," *NYT*, January 15, 1903, 9. See also *INF*, January 31, 1903, 1; Antoine, *Achievement*. Laura Bowman left a remarkable account of her time in the company just before the Broadway run and beyond.

34. "Broadway Likes Darktown Show," *Evening World* (New York), February 19, 1903, 5.

35. "Negroes Win Favor—New York Theatre," *New-York Tribune*, February 19, 1903, 9.

36. "A Health Cure in Three Acts," *The Sun* (New York), February 19, 1903, 7.

37. "We Are Broadway Stars," Billy Rose Theatre Collection, New York Public Library.

38. "Dahomey on Broadway," *NYT*, February 19, 1903, 9.

39. "Negroes Win Favor," 9.

40. *NYT*, February 22, 1903, 3.

41. "J. Harry Jackson Sends the Following from New York City," *INF*, February 28, 1903, 5.

42. "Notes of the Stage," *New-York Tribune*, February 23, 1903, 7.

43. Untitled caption, *Morning Telegraph* (New York), February 20, 1903, 4. For Charles Moore's letter and the resulting backlash, see "No Negroes Allowed on First Floor at Colored Comedy," *Baltimore Sun*, February 22, 1903, 5; "Business Manager Misquoted by New York Daily Paper," *INF*, March 7, 1903, 7; *Goodwin's Weekly*, March 7, 1903.

44. *Morning Telegraph*, February 23, 1903, page unknown.

45. "My Friend, Mrs. Paget," *Saint Paul Globe*, July 2, 1903, 7.

46. See *NYA*, October 11, 1917, 6. From this point, her name will be spelled *Aida*.

47. "Mrs. Walker is on Good Terms with the New York Four Hundred," *St. Louis Republic*, March 16, 1903, 5.

48. *Chanute Daily Sun*, March 27, 1903, 1.

49. *St. Louis Republic*, March 14, 1903, 1, and March 16, 1903, 5; *Saint Paul Globe*, July 2, 1903, 7.

50. "Mrs. Walker," 5.

51. "Mrs. Walker," 5.

52. "A Negress in Society," *Charlotte Observer*, March 18, 1903, 3; *Gastonia Gazette*, March 20, 1903; *Wilmington Messenger*, March 22, 1903, 9; *Semi-Weekly Messenger* (Wilmington, DE), March 31, 1903, 3.

53. "A Negress in Society," 3; *Gastonia Gazette*, March 20, 1903; *Wilmington Messenger*, March 22, 1903, 9; *Semi-Weekly Messenger* (Wilmington), March 31, 1903, 3.

54. "Williams and Walker's Last Week," *Daily Standard* (Red Bank, NJ), March 28, 1903, 4.

55. *NYT*, November 26, 1905, 17.

56. W. E. B. Du Bois, *Souls of Black Folk* (A. C. McClurg, 1903), vii.

57. *Cincinnati Enquirer*, March 22, 1903, 25; *Indianapolis News*, March 28, 1903, 16.

Chapter 9

1. Sylvester Russell, "Dahomey in New York," *INF*, April 4, 1903, 9.
2. *The Observer* (London), April 19, 1903, 6; "Heard in the Green-Room," *The Sketch* (London), April 22, 1903, 33. See also *Morning Telegraph* (New York), March 24, 1903, 10.
3. See *LDJ*, April 28, 1903, 4; "Emperors of Ragtime and King Edward VII," *Morning Telegraph* (New York), May 3, 1903, 7.
4. Bert Williams, "Fun in the Land of J. Bull," *The Green Book Album*, July 1909, 73.
5. *TPD*, May 22, 1903, 1; *Morning Telegraph* (New York), May 3, 1903, 7; Mabel Rowland, *Bert Williams: Son of Laughter: A Symposium of Tribute to the Man and to His Work* (English Crafters, 1923), 50–52.
6. *Board of Trade: Commercial and Statistical Department and Successors: Inwards Passenger Lists, 1903–1904*, class BT26, piece 212, 1903, National Archives, Kew, UK; "The Dawn of New Music—Negro Aspirations," *The Daily News* (London), May 15, 1903, 6; *LDJ*, May 21, 1903, 1; *The Tatler*, May 20, 1903, 300.
7. Quoted in Rowland, *Bert Williams*, 52. See also *Rising Son*, November 11, 1904, 1.
8. See *Illustrated London News*, May 23, 1903, 806; *Illustrated Sporting and Dramatic News*, May 30, 1903, 489; *The Tatler*, October 28, 1903, 133.
9. *The Tatler*, May 13, 1903, 246A.
10. Williams, "Fun in the Land of J. Bull," 75.
11. See "Written, Composed and Played by Coloured Coons: A Chat with the Composer of 'In Dahomey,'" *The Tatler*, May 20, 1903, 300.
12. Williams, "Fun in the Land of J. Bull," 77.
13. Williams, 77.
14. "'In Dahomey' and the Gordian Knot," *The Sketch*, May 27, 1903, 198.
15. "A Lawrence Boy's Annual Chat with Home Folks," *LDG*, May 28, 1904, 2.
16. "Shaftesbury Theatre," *The Observer* (London), May 17, 1903, 6; "Shaftesbury Theatre, 'In Dahomey,'" *The Globe* (London), May 18, 1903, 8.
17. "Shaftesbury Theatre, 'In Dahomey,'" 8.
18. See "Shaftesbury Theatre," *The Daily News* (London), May 18, 1903, 12.
19. "In Dahomey," *St. James' Gazette* (London), May 18, 1903, 15.
20. "In Dahomey," *Illustrated Sporting and Dramatic News*, May 30, 1903, 489.
21. "The Stage from the Stalls," *The Sketch*, May 27, 1903, 198.
22. See *Bolton Evening News*, May 23, 1903, 4; *The Evening Post* (Dundee, UK), June 16, 1903, 6.

23. "In Dahomey at the Shaftesbury Theatre," *The Playgoer* 4, no. 20 (June 1903): 466, 469.

24. "In Dahomey at the Shaftesbury," *Illustrated London News*, May 23, 1903, 776; "'In Dahomey' at the Shaftesbury," *The Graphic*, May 23, 1903, 698; "In Dahomey at the Shaftesbury Theatre," *The Playgoer*, 465.

25. *St. Louis Republic*, May 31, 1903, 4; *The Observer* (London), May 31, 1903, 6; *Omaha Daily Bee*, June 28, 1903, 12; Williams, "Fun in the Land of J. Bull," 77.

26. "Explaining that 'Colossal Piece of Impudence,'" *CIO*, October 23, 1904, 39.

27. *The Observer*, June 21, 1903, 5; *The Gazette* (Montreal), June 24, 1903, 1; *The Daily News* (London), June 24, 1903, 7.

28. "Williams and Walker Back Home," *Evening World* (New York), June 23, 1904, 10.

29. George W. Walker, "How the 'King of Dahomey' Met the King of England," *Rising Son* (Kansas City), July 10, 1903, 1.

30. Rowland, *Bert Williams*, 54–56.

31. From an interview with Abbie Mitchell on July 9, 1959, Philip Sterling research materials on Bert Williams (*T-Mss 1991-026), 1. See also *Topeka Daily Capital*, August 1, 1903, 4.

32. *The Gazette* (Montreal), June 24, 1903, 1; "Royalty Dance Cake Walk," *Minneapolis Journal*, June 25, 1903, 2; *CIO*, July 12, 1903, 1; *Cincinnati Enquirer*, July 13, 1903, 4; *Billings Gazette*, July 17, 1903, 3.

33. Quoted in Rowland, *Bert Williams*, 57.

34. "Saw the Coons," *The Gazette* (Montreal), June 24, 1903, 1.

35. "King and Coons," *The Daily News* (London), June 24, 1903, 7.

36. *TSJ*, June 24, 1903, 3.

37. "In Prince Eddie's Honor," *The Gazette* (Montreal), June 24, 1903, 1.

38. Walker, "How the 'King of Dahomey' Met the King of England," 1.

39. "Evah Dahkey Is a King," words by Paul Laurence Dunbar and Eddie Moran, music by John H. Cook, music supplement of *Hearst's Chicago American*, October 26, 1902.

40. *Topeka Daily Capital*, August 1, 1903, 4.

41. "Dahomey Moved to Buckingham Palace," *INF*, July 4, 1903, 5.

42. "Dahomey Moved," 5; "King Approves the Cake Walk," *CIO*, July 5, 1903, 9; "The Negro as a Society Leader," *Washington Standard*, July 17, 1903, 2.

43. *The Sun* (New York), June 24, 1904, 7; *Boston Globe*, March 19, 1905, 34; *Winnipeg Tribune*, March 28, 1912, 10.

44. See *New-York Tribune*, August 2, 1903, 9; *St. Louis Palladium*, October 24, 1903, 1; *The Era* (London), March 26, 1904, 7.

45. "Plays and Players," *The Globe* (London), October 1, 1903.

46. *Illustrated Sporting and Dramatic News*, October 10, 1903, 242; *The Observer* (London), November 8, 1903, 6; *Daily Telegraph* (London), December 19, 1903, 10; *Broad Ax* (Washington, DC), October 14, 1905, 1.

47. *The Observer* (London), December 20, 1903, 6; and *The Afro-American* (Baltimore), January 23, 1904, 1.

48. See Karl Jacoby, *The Strange Career of William Ellis: The Texas Slave Who Became a Mexican Millionaire* (W. W. Norton, 2016); *San Francisco Chronicle*, December 17, 1903, 1; *The Mitchell (SD) Capital*, January 1, 1904, 13; *Board of Trade: Commercial and Statistical Department and Successors: Outwards Passenger Lists*, BT27, National Archives, Kew, UK; Robert P. Skinner, *Abyssinia To-Day: Tan Account of the First Mission Sent by the American Government to the Court of the King of Kings (1903–1904)* (Arnold, Longmans, Green, 1906), 7–10; Amanda Kay McVety, "The 1903 Skinner Mission: Images of Ethiopia in the Progressive Era," *The Journal of the Gilded Age and Progressive Era* 10, no. 2 (April 2011): 187–212.

49. *Pittsburgh Daily Post*, January 13, 1907, 31.

50. *Hull (UK) Daily Mail*, February 2, 1904, 4; *St. James Gazette* (London), March 8, 1904, 16; *The Observer*, March 6, 1904, 6; *Western Daily Press* (Bristol, UK), March 22, 3; *The Era*, March 26, 1904, 7; *LDG*, May 28, 1904, 2; Aida Overton Walker, "Colored Men and Women on the Stage," *The Colored American Magazine* 9, no. 4 (October 1905): 571–75.

51. *INF*, April 9, 1904, 5, and May 14, 1904, 5; *NYT*, April 27, 1904, 2.

52. See Rowland, *Bert Williams*, 62. The Grand Lodge of Ancient Free and Accepted Masons of Scotland listed them as Egbert Austin Williams (127 West Fifty-Third Street, NYC; thirty years old), George William Walker (505 Sixth Avenue, NYC; thirty-one years old), Henry Troy (250 Stewart Street, Montgomery, AL, twenty-eight years old), John Edwards (910 Sciato Street, Indianapolis; thirty-six years old), George Catlin (100 West Twenty-Third Street, NYC; thirty-seven years old), Peter Hampton (329 West Thirty-Fifth Street, NYC; thirty-three years old), Green Henri Tapley (3428 Dearborn Street, Chicago; thirty-three years old), John Lubrie Hill (505 Sixth Avenue, NYC; thirty years old), James Escort Lightfoot (Hamilton, Ontario, Canada; thirty years old), and Alexander Rogers (18 West 134th Street, NYC; twenty-eight years old).

53. *LDJ*, May 16, 1904, 4.

54. For the entire letter, see "A Lawrence Boy's Annual Chat with Home Folks," *LDG*, May 28, 1904, 2.

55. *Passenger and Crew Lists of Vessels Arriving at New York, NY, 1897–1957*, 1904, microfilm T715, line 6, p. 6.

56. See Rowland, *Bert Williams*, 50.

57. *Deseret Evening News* (Salt Lake City), June 11, 1904, 16; *Hull (UK) Daily Mail*, August 16, 1904, 4; *New York Dramatic Mirror*, August 13, 1904, 18; *Sheffield (UK) Independent*, September 3, 1904, 9; *Belfast (UK) News-Letter*, November 8, 1904, 11; *Daily Telegraph* (London), October 4, 1905, 8.

Chapter 10

1. "Williams and Walker Back Home," *Evening World* (New York), June 23, 1904, 10.

2. "Williams and Walker Are Home," *The Sun* (New York), June 24, 1904, 7. Subsequent quotations are also from this source.

3. *The Sun* (Kansas City), June 24, 1904, 7; "New Kings of the Black Belt," *Morning Telegraph* (New York), June 24, 1904, 10.

4. *LDJ*, July 21, 1904, 4, and July 29, 1904, 4; *LDW*, July 30, 1904, 3; *TPD*, July 22, 1904, 3, and July 29, 1904, 2. Reportedly, "Cub Langston" was hospitalized following a stoning with green apples and peaches and suffered an eye injury after falling into a rosebush. See also *TPD*, November 10, 1905, 5. Cub Langston's father, James N. Hughes (1871 to 1934), traveled to Topeka from Mexico City during the week of November 12, 1905. Following a series of adventures with his father throughout the United States and Mexico, Langston Hughes succeeded Paul Laurence Dunbar as poet laureate of Afro-America until his death in 1967.

5. "The King of Colored Comedians," *LDG*, July 29, 1904, 2.

6. Shubert Archive, box 81, Shi–Shiz; *LDW*, August 1, 1904, 1; *INF*, August 20, 1904, 5.

7. *INF*, August 13, 1904, 5; "Revival of Rag," *Sunday Telegraph* (New York), September 4, 1904, 5. See also Thomas Bauman, *The Pekin: The Rise and Fall of Chicago's First Black-Owned Theater* (University of Illinois Press, 2014), 30–32. Established in 1903, the short-lived Pekin Publishing Company, started by Joe Jordan and Robert Motts, was likely the first Black-owned music publisher.

8. *NYA*, March 9, 1905, 1; *The State* (Columbia, SC), March 12, 1905, 24; *Colorado Statesman*, March 17, 1905, 2; *Broad Ax* (Washington, DC), August 12, 1905, 3.

9. "Princes of Comedy," *The Colored American Magazine*, September 3, 1904, 5. See also *The Sun* (New York), August 28, 1904, 5; *San Francisco Dramatic Review*, May 16, 1908, 3.

10. *Evening World* (New York), August 29, 1904, 7.

11. *Baltimore Afro-American*, September 17, 1904, 8; *INF*, September 24, 1904, 5.

12. Sylvester Russell, "A Word Endowed Prominent Stage Factors and Renown," *INF*, October 1, 1904, 2.

13. Russell, "Word," 2.

14. *Rising Son* (Kansas City), September 30, 1904, 5; *St. Louis Republic*, October 2, 1904, 7; *St. Louis Post-Dispatch*, October 9, 1904, 31.

15. *Rockford Morning Star*, October 16, 1904, 7; *Janesville Daily Gazette*, October 18, 1904, 5.

16. *Chicago Live Stock World*, October 22, 1904, 2; *INF*, October 22, 1904, 5; *CIO*, October 24, 1904, 6.

17. "Show Stopped by a Fight," *The Kansas City Star and The Kansas City Times*, November 16, 1904, 1. See also *Rising Son* (Kansas City), November 18, 1904, 1.

18. *LDW*, November 15, 1904, 4, November 19, 1904, 4, November 21, 1904, 1, and November 22, 1904, 1; *LDG*, November 19, 1904, 3, and November 21, 1904, 3. See also *Evening Herald* (Ottawa), February 20, 1912, 1. Officer Monroe used that pistol to stop Mexican bank robbers in 1912.

19. "Williams and Walker, Colored Comedians," *Topeka Daily Capital*, November 16, 1904, 5.

20. *TSJ*, November 17, 1904, 4; *TPD*, November 18, 1904, 3; *Topeka Daily Capital*, November 19, 1904, 8; "The Play Last Night," *Topeka Daily Capital*, November 23, 1904, 8; *TSJ*, November 23, 1904, 4.

21. "Williams and Walker Delight in Musical Comedy," *San Francisco Call*, December 5, 1904, 5.

22. *Evening Bee* (Sacramento), December 24, 1904, 3; *Spokane Chronicle*, January 4, 1905, 4, and March 25, 1905, 2.

23. *Manitoba Morning Free Press* (Winnipeg), January 28, 1905, 27; *Saint Paul Globe*, January 22, 1905, 19; *Minneapolis Journal*, February 16, 1905, 7.

24. H. G. Davis, "Future of the Negro on the American Stage," *Minneapolis Journal*, February 10, 1905, 15.

25. Courtesy of the Shubert Archive, box 81, Shi–Shiz. See also *Hartford Courant*, August 17, 1905, 6.

26. See *New York Clipper*, December 12, 1896, 3.

27. Addressed in a letter from George Walker to A. L. Erlanger, November 24, 1905. Shubert Archive, box 81, Shi–Shiz. See also *The Colored American Magazine* 14 (April 1908): 226–30.

28. *INF*, September 9, 1905, 5. The other members of the syndicate were Charles Frohman, J. Fred Zimmerman Sr., Samuel F. Nixon, Al Hayman, and, to some extent, William Harris.

29. *Minneapolis Journal*, June 13, 1905, 6; *Star Tribune* (Minneapolis), Jun 14, 1905, 7, and June 15, 1905, 7; *Spokane Chronicle*, Jun 21, 1905, 1; *TSJ*, Oct 28, 1912, 6. Rivers fell into relative obscurity as a performer. He died at the age of thirty-five in the Kansas State Hospital, Topeka, on October 27, 1912, likely of syphilis, and was buried at Mount Auburn Cemetery, Topeka.

30. George Walker to Abe Erlanger, February 23, 1905, Shubert Archive, box 81, Shi–Shiz.

31. "In Dahomey at the Globe," *Boston Herald*, March 21, 1905, 10.

32. *Harrisburg Telegraph*, February 19, 1906, 1; *Pottsville Daily Republican*, May 6, 1905, 3.

33. *NYT*, May 14, 1905, 44; *The Sun* (New York), May 28, 1905, 21.

34. "Even Umpire Can't Tell Who Won the Game," *Sunday Telegraph* (New York), May 28, 1905, 16. See also *New York Dramatic Mirror*, May 27, 1905, 14; *NYA*, June 8, 1905, 3.

35. *LDJ*, June 9, 1905, 4.

36. *Philadelphia Inquirer*, April 23, 1905, 34; *Harrisburg Daily Independent*, May 3, 1905, 9; *Leader-Telegram* (Eau Claire, WI), June 18, 1905, 3; *NYT*, August 16, 1905, 7.

37. *San Francisco Chronicle*, April 9, 1905, 9; *The Province* (Vancouver, BC), April 15, 1905, 9; *The Pilot* (Blair, NE), April 19, 1905, 2; *Daily Independent* (Hutchinson, KS), April 21, 1905, 6; *Chattanooga Daily Times*, May 28, 1905, 28.

38. *Cincinnati Enquirer*, June 11, 1905, 35; *Colorado Statesman*, August 19, 1905, 1.

39. *NYT*, January 1, 1904, 9. Ellis provided his account of King Menelik's court on October 16, 1903.

40. "Two Colored Comedians," *Pittsburgh Daily Post*, January 13, 1907, 31.

41. "May Go with Dockstader," *New York Tribune*, August 16, 1905, 7. See also *Buffalo Enquirer*, June 16, 1905, 2; *Meriden Daily Journal*, July 6, 1905, 5. See also *Benjamin H. Hurtig and Jules Hurtig and Harry Seamon v. Bert A. Williams and George W. Walker*, June 19, 1905, 5, New York City Municipal Archives.

42. "The Business Side of Dockstader," *Hartford Courant*, August 17, 1905, 6.

43. *NYT*, July 6, 1905, 9; Wayne D. Shirley, "The House of Melody: A List of Publications of the Gotham-Attucks Music Company at the Library of Congress," *The Black Perspective in Music* 15, no. 1 (Spring 1987): 79–112.

44. Untitled caption, *Buffalo Enquirer*, July 8, 1905, 2; untitled caption, *Philadelphia Inquirer*, July 9, 1905, 8; *Buffalo Evening News*, July 15, 1905, 5.

45. *Boston Evening Transcript*, March 22, 1905, 17; *Boston Globe*, March 24, 1905, 2, and July 20, 1905, 11; *NYT*, July 2, 1905, 38; *Philadelphia Inquirer*, July 9, 1905, 10; *Boston Evening Transcript*, July 29, 1905, 22; *NYA*, August 3, 1905, 7; *Brooklyn Life*, July 1, 1905, 3.

46. "The Williams and Walker Glee Club," *Boston Evening Transcript*, July 29, 1905, 22.

47. *LDJ*, July 12, 1905, 4, and July 17, 1905, 4.

48. *Boston Globe*, July 31, 1905, 10. See also *NYA*, August 3, 1905, 7; *INF*, August 19, 1905, 5; *Broad Ax* (Washington, DC), August 26, 1905, 1. For a complete schedule of events of the National Negro Business League meeting, see *Brooklyn Citizen*, August 13, 1905, 10.

49. *LDJ*, August 26, 1905, 1; *Kansas City Star*, October 21, 1906, 41.

50. *The Colored American Magazine* 9, no. 3 (September 1905): 496–502; *INF*, September 9, 1905, 5; *Atchison Daily Globe*, April 18, 1906, 5; *LDG*, April 24, 1906, 3.

Chapter 11

1. *LDW*, September 8, 1905, 1; *INF*, September 9, 1905, 5; *NYT*, September 20, 1905, 9; *The Sun* (New York), September 20, 1905, 5.

2. *Broad Ax* (Washington, DC), August 12, 1905, 3; *INF*, August 12, 1905, 8, and September 9, 1905, 5; *Iowa State Bystander*, August 18, 1905, 1; *TPD*, September 22, 1905, 6; *Wilkes-Barre Times*, September 12, 1905, 5.

3. "Why There Are No Colored Playwriters," *INF*, April 10, 1909, 5.

4. *INF*, October 14, 1905, 5. For one surviving example, see the Shubert Archive, box 81, Shi–Shiz, ca. September 1905. See also *NYT*, September 20, 1905, 9; *LDW*, June 10, 1907, 2; *INF*, June 22, 1907, 6.

5. *INF*, September 9, 1905, 5; *Plain Dealer* (Cleveland), September 15, 1905, 5; *Lewiston Evening Journal*, January 2, 1906, 10; Shubert Archive, box 81, Shi–Shiz. The attempt was confirmed in a letter from George to Abe Erlanger on November 24, 1905.

6. *The Sun* (New York), September 20, 1905, 5; *NYT*, September 20, 1905, 9; *NYA*, September 21, 1905, 1; *LDW*, June 10, 1907, 2; *INF*, June 22, 1907, 6.

7. Shubert Archive, New York, box 81, Shi–Shiz.

8. "'Abyssinia' Postponed," *The Colored American Magazine* 9, no. 5 (November 1905): 607–8.

9. Sylvester Russell, "George Walker of Williams and Walker," *INF*, January 14, 1911, 7.

10. *The Era* (London), October 7, 1905, 12.

11. Aida Overton Walker, "Colored Men and Women on the Stage," *The Colored American Magazine* 9, no. 4 (October 1905): 571–75; *Broad Ax*, October 14, 1905, 1.

12. *INF*, October 14, 1905, 5, October 21, 1905, 6, and November 25, 1905, 5; *Alexander's Magazine* 1, no. 6 (October 15, 1905): 28; *Broad Ax*, October 28, 1905, 2.

13. Sylvester Russell, "The Stage," *INF*, October 28, 1905, 5.

14. "Sylvester Russell Notes," *INF*, November 4, 1905, 5.

15. "Nobody," words by Alex Rogers, music by Bert A. Williams, Attucks Music Publishing, New York, 1905.

16. The first version may have been Columbia 33011, a wax cylinder. *The Chat* (Brooklyn), October 7, 1905, 3. Columbia 3243 / Marconi 0303, a subsequent shellac disc recording, was made sometime in April 1906, likely for ease of reproduction.

17. "'Abyssinia' Postponed," 607–8.

18. "Goes Tomorrow," *LDW*, June 22, 1907, 3.

19. "Goes Tomorrow," 3. There are several letters from theater managers that attest to that fear in the Shubert collection.

20. *INF*, November 18, 1905, 5, 8.

21. Alice Rohe, "Rediscovery of George ('Nash') Walker," *Evening World* (New York), November 1, 1905, 11. Subsequent quotations are from the same source.

22. *Broad Ax* (Washington, DC), November 4, 1905, 3; *Lewiston Evening Journal*, January 2, 1906, 10; *Anaconda Standard*, January 7, 1906, 22; *Chattanooga News*, January 10, 1906, 7; *INF*, January 14, 1911, 7.

23. "Negro on Stage Can't Be Serious," *Chicago Tribune*, November 12, 1905, 72; *INF*, November 18, 1905, 5.

24. "Monologist Drew Color Line," *Baltimore Sun*, November 15, 1905, 10. See also *Daily Press* (Newport News, VA), November 16, 1905, 3; *NYA*, November 23, 1905, 1; *Brooklyn Times Union*, December 30, 1905, 6.

25. "The Colored Actor in Vaudeville," *INF*, December 16, 1905, 5. See also *Star Tribune* (Minneapolis), March 10, 1907, 25. Kelly's resolve was tested again in March of 1907 when he was placed on the same bill as Avery and Hart at the Orpheum in Minneapolis.

26. George Walker to Abe Erlanger, November 24, 1905, Shubert Archive. See also *INF*, November 25, 1905, 5; *Broad Ax*, November 4, 1905, 1.

27. See "Sheriff Tied Up Cash," *TSJ*, October 26, 1907, 14; "Wilkerson Attaches Door Money," *Topeka Daily Capital*, October 26, 1907, 5; *The Gazette* (York, PA), November 19, 1905, 7; *Evening Bee* (Sacramento), November 25, 1905, 20; *Seattle Republican*, December 8, 1905, 3.

28. *INF*, November 25, 1905, 5; *Brooklyn Times Union*, November 25, 1905, 6; *NYT*, November 26, 1905, 35. See also Shubert Archive, box 81, Shi–Shiz, for surviving letters from Walker to Erlanger dated November 30, December 2, and December 11, 1905.

29. *Brooklyn Times Union*, December 9, 1905, 7; *Brooklyn Citizen*, December 27, 1905, 4.

30. *Cincinnati Enquirer Sun*, December 24, 1905, 18; *Brooklyn Times Union*, December 30, 1905, 6, 7; *Omaha Daily Bee*, December 31, 1905, 3; *Franklin (NE) Free Press*, January 12, 1906, 3.

31. "Pretty Desdamone," Star 2251; Columbia mx. 3410. See also *Alliance Semi-Weekly Times*, February 23, 1906, 1.

32. For the entire piece, see George W. Walker, "The Colored Performers on the American Stage," *INF*, January 13, 1906, 5. For greater detail of George's theater plans, see *Evening Review* (East Liverpool, OH), January 26, 1906, 3.

33. *INF*, November 5, 1904, 2; *New York Tribune*, February 10, 1906, 7. Dunbar contracted pneumonia in late summer 1899 and was chronically ill ever since. However, he continued to work until just before Christmas of 1905, putting the finishing touches on his final book, *Howdy Honey Howdy*. He was buried at Woodland Cemetery in Dayton.

34. *Brooklyn Times Union*, February 5, 1906, 2, and February 17, 1906, 6; *Brooklyn Citizen*, February 7, 1906, 12, and February 15, 1906, 3.

35. "Last Night's Play," *LDW*, October 23, 1906, 4.

36. Loften Mitchell, *Black Drama: The Story of the American Negro in the Theatre* (Hawthorn Press, 1967), 50.

37. *New York Tribune*, February 18, 1906, 7; *NYA*, February 22, 1906, 1.

38. "Williams and Walker," *Buffalo Morning Express and Illustrated Buffalo Express*, March 4, 1906, 34; *Kansas City Star*, March 4, 1906, 9.

39. "Williams and Walker Again," *NYT*, February 21, 1906, 9.

40. Acton Davies, "Playhouses of the Metropolis," *Deseret Evening News* (Salt Lake City), March 3, 1906, 16. A similar sentiment was expressed in other reviews as well. See "A Negro Play on Broadway," *Evening Bee* (Sacramento), March 3, 1906, 19; *News-Journal* (Mansfield, OH), March 3, 1906, 7.

41. *Buffalo Morning Express and Illustrated Buffalo Express*, March 4, 1906, 34.

42. Untitled column, *Philadelphia Inquirer*, March 4, 1906, 4.

43. Sylvester Russell, "The Mistakes of Williams and Walker," *INF*, April 14, 1906, 6.

44. "Sylvester Russell Notes," *INF*, May 26, 1906, 5.

45. "Greater New York Stage Notes," *INF*, March 10, 1906, 6.

46. *Evening Star* (Washington, DC), April 29, 1906, 60, and May 2, 1906, 18; *Washington Post*, May 2, 1906, 9; *Washington Times*, May 2, 1906, 10.

47. *Washington Post*, May 1, 1906, 12; *Brooklyn Times Union*, May 8, 1906, 12; *Pittsburgh Press*, May 13, 1906, 33, and May 27, 1906, 37.

48. *The Appeal* (Saint Paul), June 30, 1906, 4. Lineup: George Walker, pitcher; Jas. Thomas, catcher; Bert Williams, first base; William Elkins, second base; C. H. Foster, third base; Charles Gilpin, shortstop; G. H. Tapley, center field; C. Randall, left field; and A. Henderson, right field.

49. *Chicago Tribune*, May 27, 1906, 75, and May 29, 1906, 8.

50. Mabel Rowland, *Bert Williams: Son of Laughter: A Symposium of Tribute to the Man and to His Work* (English Crafters, 1923), 72–75.

51. D. W. Griffith adapted the book/play for the silver screen as *The Birth of a Nation* in 1915.

52. "What Williams and Walker Think of the Clansman," *CIO*, June 24, 1906, 34; *Dayton Herald*, June 28, 1906, 11. Subsequent quotations are from the same source.

53. *Broad Ax*, June 23, 1906, 2; *Alexander's Magazine*, September 15, 1905, 8, 9.

54. "A Scandal in the Williams and Walker Show," *TPD*, June 29, 1906, 5. Original unavailable.

55. "Scandal," 5. See also *Cleveland Gazette*, June 30, 1906, 2.

56. Sylvester Russell, "From New York City," *INF*, July 21, 1906, 5.

57. *Broad Ax*, July 6, 1907, 2; *New York Dramatic Mirror*, July 7, 1906, 12; *Variety*, July 7, 1906, 3; *NYA*, July 12, 1906, 6, and July 26, 1906, 6; *Muskogee Times-Democrat*, August 4, 1906, 7.

58. George Walker, "The Real 'Coon' on the American Stage," *The Theatre*, August 1906, 225.

59. Walker, "Real 'Coon,'" 226. Reprinted in *LDJ*, August 9, 1906, 1; *LDG*, August 9, 1906, 3; *The Colored American Magazine* 11, no. 4 (October 1906): 243–48.

60. "Williams and Walker in Abyssinia," *The Colored American Magazine* 11, no. 3 (September 1906): 165–66.

61. *New York Tribune*, July 29, 1906, 53; *Standard Union*, September 2, 1906, 18; *Brooklyn Citizen*, September 4, 1906, 5.

62. *New York Dramatic Mirror*, September 29, 1906, 12; *Pittston Gazette*, September 12, 1906, 3; *The Sun* (New York), September 13, 1906, 7, and September 23, 1906, 38; *New York Tribune*, September 19, 1906, 7; *NYA*, September 20, 1906, 6, and June 27, 1907, 6.

63. *Courier-Journal* (Louisville), October 3, 1906, 9; *Indianapolis News*, October 3, 1906, 14.

64. "Williams and Walker," *INF*, October 6, 1906, 7. See also *Topeka Daily Capital*, October 22, 1906, 6.

65. "Abyssinia's Star Actress," *Dayton Herald*, December 15, 1906, 9. See also *Pittsburgh Press*, January 6, 1907, 35.

66. Untitled caption, *Indianapolis Star*, October 10, 1906, 9. See also *The Green Book Album*, June 1912, 1180.

67. "Personal and Social," *LDW*, October 16, 1906, 1. See also *LDG*, October 15, 1906, 2; *LDW*, October 20, 1906, 4; *LDJ*, October 31, 1906, 1; *Colorado Statesman*, December 15, 1906, 1. On December 12, the editor of the *Detroit Informer* notarized George and Aida's signatures for a $5,000, eight-roomed house for George's mother and grandmother at 401 Indiana Street at the corner of Elliott. For Sanford Hayden's obituary, see *LDJ*, May 11, 1906, 1.

68. "The Big Show," *LDG*, October 23, 1906, 2.

69. *LDW*, October 23, 1906, 4; *Topeka Daily Capital*, October 29, 1906, 5, and November 1, 1906, 7; *TPD*, November 2, 1906, 1; *St. Louis Post-Dispatch*, November 4, 1906, 5.

70. *NYA*, November 15, 1906, 1; *St. Louis Palladium*, November 17, 1906, 4; *NYT*, January 12, 1907, 11; *Kansas City Star*, July 4, 1907, 3.

71. *Brooklyn Life*, February 16, 1907, 47; *New York Tribune*, March 8, 1907, 7. Quotation from *Baltimore Sun*, April 28, 1907, 1.

72. *Morning Examiner* (Ogden, UT), February 24, 1907, 11; *Atlantic Review*, May 7, 1907, 2; *Nashville Globe*, May 10, 1907, 8.

Chapter 12

1. "Black and White," *INF*, March 9, 1907, 6.

2. *Buffalo Times*, February 11, 1907, 3; *Cincinnati Enquirer*, March 17, 1907, 26.

3. Untitled caption, *Pittsburgh Post-Gazette*, March 17, 1907, 31.

4. Untitled caption, *News-Journal* (Mansfield, OH), March 20, 1907, 7.

5. *NYT*, April 26, 1907, 9; *Baltimore Sun*, April 28, 1907, 8; *INF*, April 6, 1907, 6; *Colored American Magazine*, April 1908, 229. See also "He'll Settle Down Here," *LDW*, April 6, 1907, 4; *LWW*, April 11, 1907, 2.

6. *The Gazette* (York, PA), May 13, 1907, 4; *NYA*, May 16, 1907, 6; *Morning Call* (Paterson, NJ), July 3, 1907, 11.

7. Advertisement in *Pittsburgh Post*, June 2, 1907, 33; "Voice of Press Is the Voice of the People," *Pittsburgh Gazette Times*, June 9, 1907, 28.

8. "Williams and Walker, On the Road to Bandanna Land," *Variety*, May 18, 1907, 11.

9. *Pittsburgh Press*, May 29, 1907, 4; *Pittsburgh Daily Post*, June 2, 1907, 33.

10. "Theatrical People and Their Well Earned Successes," *NYA*, June 27, 1907, 6. For the announcement of Walton's addition to *The New York Age*, see *NYA*, September 20, 1906, 2.

11. *NYT*, July 4, 1907, 7; *Kansas City Star*, July 4, 1907, 3. See also "Prospects of the Next Comedy Season," *INF*, June 29, 1907, 5. Sylvester Russell mentioned Cole and Johnson's *Shoo-Fly Regiment* lost as much as $5,000 during the previous season.

12. "George Walker on Philosophy," *Scranton Republican*, September 8, 1907, 6.

13. *LDW*, June 10, 1907, 2, and June 12, 1907, 1; *LDJ*, June 12, 1907, 1; *INF*, June 22, 1907, 6.

14. "The Simple Life," *LDW*, June 18, 1907, 2.

15. *LDW*, July 11, 1907, 4.

16. *LDW*, June 22, 1907, 3; *TPD*, November 8, 1907, 3, and September 10, 1909, 5.

17. *LDW*, October 9, 1907, 1.

18. "Goes Tomorrow," *LDW*, June 22, 1907, 3. The "somebody" Nash referred to was likely the Shuberts, whom he lobbied to purchase the Bowersock and build a much larger theatre on the site.

19. *Advocate* (Charleston, WV), July 18, 1907, 1; *LDJ*, June 22, 1907, 1.

20. *LDW*, June 22, 1907, 3; *Atchison Daily Globe*, December 9, 1908, 2. The names of Lawrentians include Neil Carter; Bill Hayden, Nash's uncle; Jim Strode; Jack Dimery; and Jim Harper.

21. Junius Mordecai Allen, *Rhymes, Tales and Rhymed Tales* (Crane, August 1906); *TPD*, July 5, 1907, 7, and July 12, 1907, 3. See also January 30, 1903, 4. The two poets may have met on January 24, 1903, when Dunbar spent a few hours in Topeka while on a speaking tour.

22. *NYA*, July 25, 1907, 6.

23. *LDJ*, August 22, 1907, 1, and September 12, 1907, 1; *LDW*, August 23, 1907, 4, and September 12, 1907, 1; *Daily Register* (Red Bank, NJ), August 21, 1907, 10; *LDG*, August 27, 1907, 2; *NYA*, August 8, 1907, 7.

24. "Goes Tomorrow," 3.

25. *Times Recorder* (Zanesville, OH), October 1, 1907, 6.

26. *Asbury Park Press*, August 30, 1907, 3; *The Press* (Kansas City), October 11, 1907, 4; *Kansas City Star and The Kansas City Times*, October 16, 1907, 4; *LWW*, October 17, 1907, 1; *LDW*, October 21, 1907, 4; *LDJ*, October 23, 1907, 4.

27. *LDW*, October 25, 1907, 4.

28. "Williams and Walker Have Grown Greatly in the Last Year," *LDJ*, October 25, 1907, 3.

29. "Nash Walker," *LDJ*, October 22, 1907, 3.

30. "At the Theatres," *TSJ*, October 18, 1907, 3.

31. "Bandanna Land," *Variety*, February 1908, 15.

32. "Williams and Walker," *Akron Beacon Journal*, October 1, 1907, 2.

33. Lester Walton, "Two Theatrical Successes," *NYA*, October 17, 1907, 1.

34. *Song Libretto of Williams & Walker's New Musical Comedy Creation Bandanna Land*, Gotham Attucks Music Company, 1907.

35. "Bon Bon Buddy, The Chocolate Drop," words by Alex Roger, music by Will Marion Cook, Gotham-Attucks Music, New York, 1907. George's depiction of "Buddy" was the inspiration for the character Sportin' Life, first played by John W. Bubbles (1902 to 1986) in George and Ira Gershwin's *Porgy and Bess*.

36. *Omaha Daily News*, December 20, 1908, 6.

37. "Bandanna Land," *Chicago Tribune*, November 11, 1907, 8. See also *INF*, November 30, 1907, 1.

38. *Pittsburgh Press*, December 19, 1907, 3.

39. "George Walker Tells of His Flashy Clothing," *Pittsburgh Press*, December 22, 1907, 33. For the complete statement, see "George Walker," *INF*, March 14, 1908, 5.

40. Lester Walton, "Bandanna Land," *NYA*, February 6, 1908, 10.

41. Franklin Fyles, "That Merry Widow Waltz," *Washington Post*, February 9, 1908, 2.

42. "'Bandanna Land' Scores at Majestic, Manhattan," *Standard Union* (Brooklyn), February 4, 1908, 3. See also *Brooklyn Citizen*, February 4, 1908, 5; *Brooklyn Daily Eagle*, February 4, 1908, 14; *NYT*, February 4, 1908, 7; *The Sun* (New York), February 4, 1908, 7; *Evening World* (New York), February 5, 1908, 15.

43. Tom Fletcher, *100 Years of the Negro in Show Business: The Tom Fletcher Story* (Burdge, 1954), 239–40; *Lincoln Star*, October 23, 1906, 10. When Williams and Walker were engaged at the Oliver Theatre in Lincoln in 1906, Bert visited an unnamed friend in the hospital, where he observed the mentally ill man playing an imaginary poker game.

44. *NYA*, February 6, 1908, 10; *Billboard*, February 8, 1908, 12; *Buffalo Evening News*, October 29, 1905, 9. Robert Motts opened the Pekin Theatre on South State Street, Chicago, in June of 1905. It was the first major Black theatre in the US and an example of what George envisioned in every major city with a sizable Black population in the country.

45. "Bandanna Land to Stay," *NYA*, February 13, 1908, 6.

46. "Booker T. Washington Sees 'Bandanna Land,'" *INF*, February 15, 1908, 5. See also *NYA*, February 20, 1908, 6.

47. For the entire letter, see "George W. Walker's Letter to the Thirteen Club," *NYA*, February 20, 1908, 6; *LDG*, February 25, 1908, 1; *LDW*, March 4, 1908, 3; *TPD*, March 13, 1908, 8; *LDJ*, July 25, 1908, 3.

48. "Theatre for Colored Folk," *Evening World* (New York), February 28, 1908, 3.

49. *NYT*, March 26, 1908, 1; *Standard Union* (Brooklyn), March 1, 1908, 18; *Brooklyn Citizen*, March 13, 1908, 4.

50. *Buffalo Sunday Morning News*, March 15, 1908, 10; *Chicago Tribune*, March 22, 1908, 17; *Brooklyn Daily Eagle*, April 16, 1908, 22.

51. *Boston Evening Transcript*, January 7, 1908, 13; *Boston Globe*, January 13, 1908, 6; "Bob Cole Freezes Ear by Taking Advice from Ernest Hogan," *NYA*, March 12, 1908, 6. See also *NYA*, March 26, 1908, 6.

52. *The Sun* (New York), March 7, 1908, 3; *Colorado Statesman*, March 21, 1908, 1; *LDW*, March 31, 1908, 1.

53. *News-Journal* (Mansfield, OH), February 29, 1908, 7; *Brooklyn Citizen*, March 4, 1908, 4; *NYA*, January 12, 1911, 6, and February 27, 1908, 6. See also *LDW*, March 10, 1908, 3. Among others were David Warfield, E. H. Southern, Lew Fields, Joe Weber, Victor Moore, Olga Nethersole, Mrs. Patrick Campbell, Dan Froham, Margaret Illington, and Kyrle Bellew.

54. "Anniversary Celebration of Williams and Walker a Gala Event," *NYA*, April 2, 1908, 6.

55. *Brooklyn Citizen*, March 25, 1908, 2; *NYA*, March 12, 1908, 6, and April 2, 1908, 6; *Brooklyn Daily Eagle*, March 22, 1908, 27; *NYT*, April 1, 1908, 7; *The Sun* (New York), April 1, 1908, 7; *New-York Tribune*, April 2, 1908, 7, and April 5, 1908, 2.

56. "Her String of Pearls a Wriggling Serpent," *Brooklyn Citizen*, April 18, 1908, 10. See also *Brooklyn Daily Eagle*, May 22, 1908, 20.

57. *Meriden Morning Record*, May 4, 1908, 2; *NYA*, May 21, 1908, 6, and May 28, 1908, 2; *NYA*, June 4, 1908, 6. The lineups were as follows: Williams and Walker—H. Turner, shortstop; E. Thomas, catcher; J. Shipp, left field; H. Troy, second base; R. Craig, pitcher; M. Housley, right field; B. Williams, first base; W. Elkins, third base; W. Chappelle, center field; G. H. Tapley, utility; A. M. Payne, manager. Colored Vaudevillians—W. Robinson, shortstop; Samuel Cook, second base; Harry Prampin, left field; Harry Scott, first base; Leon William, right field; Paul Floyd, captain; "Bob" Slater, manager.

58. *NYA*, May 21, 1908, 6, and June 11, 1908, 6; *INF*, May 23, 1908, 5, and January 20, 1912, 5; *Philadelphia Inquirer*, July 5, 1908, 3. See also *Berkshire Evening Eagle* (Pittsfield, MA), September 11, 1908, 8. King and Bailey were renamed "The Crazy Coons" and continued to tour as a solo act.

59. Untitled caption, *Nashville Globe*, April 17, 1908, 4. See also *Brooklyn Times Union*, April 6, 1908, 6; *NYA*, April 9, 1908, 6, and April 23, 1908, 6; *Variety*, April 11, 1908, 7; *New-York Tribune*, June 14, 1908, 2.

60. *NYA*, April 23, 1908, 6.
61. *NYA*, April 23, 1908, 6; May 28, 1908, 2; and June 25, 1908, 2; *Des Moines Register*, June 7, 1908, 28; *Washington Herald*, June 7, 1908, 19.
62. *NYA*, June 11, 1908, 6; June 18, 1908, 6; "The Hogan Testimonial Benefit," *NYA*, June 25, 1908, 6.
63. *NYA*, November 12, 1908, 6.

Chapter 13

1. *TPD*, July 24, 1908, 3.
2. "Well Known Performers Organization the 'Frogs,'" *NYA*, July 9, 1908, 6. See also *NYA*, May 17, 1906, 1; "Notes from Lester Walton, August 1, 1959," Philip Sterling research materials on Bert Williams (*T-Mss 1991-026); "Constitution, Rules and Bylaws of the Frogs," (D. E.) Tobias Press, 117 West Thirtieth Street, New York, 1908, J. Rosamond Johnson Foundation.
3. *NYA*, July 9, 1908, 6.
4. Justice John W. Goff quoted in "Won't Join 'Frogs' and Art," *NYT*, July 31, 1908, 5.
5. *NYT*, July 31, 1908, 5; *Brooklyn Daily Eagle*, August 1, 1908, 4; *NYA*, August 6, 1908, 6.
6. Indicated in a letter from Jack Shoemaker to Sol. Manheimer of the Shubert office, Shubert Archive, New York, box 81, Shi–Shiz. See also *NYA*, July 9, 1908, 6.
7. *TPD*, May 29, 1908, 2, and July 17, 1908, 5; "Nash Walker Is Here," *LDJ*, July 13, 1908, 1.
8. For the entire piece, see "The Fly in the Ointment," *LDW*, July 15, 1908, 3. See also "New Theatre Proposition," *Lawrence Daily Democrat*, May 1, 1909, 4; "Nothing to It," *LDJ*, May 14, 1909; "Opera House Work," *LDG*, June 4, 1910. The Shubert brothers built a theatre in Kansas City in 1906. When they became managers of the Williams and Walker company, rumors floated (likely from Nash) that they might do the same in Lawrence. However, J. D. Bowersock, owner of the Bowersock Opera House, quashed the idea and later announced his plans to remodel his theatre as a ground-floor opera house. After the venue burned to the ground in February 1911, Bowersock updated the theatre and reopened a year later.
9. *LDJ*, July 13, 1908, 1; *LDW*, July 16, 1908, 5; "The Coming Season," *NYA*, July 30, 1908, 6; *INF*, August 22, 1908, 5.
10. *Baltimore Sun*, August 8, 1908, 9, August 9, 1908, 10, and August 13, 1908, 9; *NYA*, August 13, 1908, 6, and August 20, 1908, 6; *New-York Tribune*, August 25, 1908, 7.
11. "The Frolic," *NYA*, August 20, 1908, 6.
12. "The Frolic," 6.

13. *NYA*, August 27, 1908, 7, and October 22, 1908, 6.
14. *NYA*, July 30, 1908, 6, and August 27, 1908, 6.
15. *Boston Evening Transcript*, September 8, 1908, 13.
16. "Salome," *NYA*, August 27, 1908, 6.
17. "Salome," 6. "The Play Not Always Reflected by the Title," *Salt Lake Herald*, August 30, 1908, 20; *Chicago Tribune*, August 30, 1908, 45; *Boston Evening Transcript*, September 8, 1908, 13.
18. *Fall River Herald*, August 28, 1908, 4, and September 5, 1908, 4; *Fall River Daily Globe*, August 31, 1908, 5; "Police Accept Defi," September 1, 1908, 1; *Fall River Daily Evening News*, September 1, 1908, 3; *Boston Globe*, September 12, 1908, 4, and September 18, 1908, 5.
19. Lester Walton, "About the Stars and Shows," *NYA*, October 8, 1908, 6.
20. *Boston Globe*, September 24, 1908, 2; *Boston Evening Transcript*, September 24, 1908, 7.
21. "Williams and Walker and Merry 'Bandanna Land,'" *Boston Globe*, September 13, 1908, 39.
22. Loften Mitchell, *Black Drama: The Story of the American Negro in the Theatre* (Hawthorn Press, 1967), 53. How he contracted the disease remains unknown, as does whether or not he passed it to Aida or anyone else. Surely, he must have known for some time, possibly a decade or more.
23. *Boston Globe*, September 27, 1908, 41, September 30, 1908, 8, and October 2, 1908, 6, 9; *Boston Evening Transcript*, September 29, 1908, 13; *Boston Herald*, September 30, 1908, 7; Tom Fletcher, *100 Years of the Negro in Show Business: The Tom Fletcher Story* (Burdge, 1954), 234.
24. *New York Dramatic Mirror*, October 10, 1908, 10; *Brooklyn Citizen*, October 15, 1908, 5.
25. "Theatrical Comment," *NYA*, February 4, 1909, 6; *The Chat* (Brooklyn), February 6, 1909, 35; *Dayton Herald*, February 20, 1909, 1.
26. "Bert Williams Tells of Walker," *INF*, January 14, 1911, 7.
27. *Dayton Herald*, February 20, 1909, 1.
28. *Brooklyn Daily Eagle*, October 20, 1908, 11; *Brooklyn Citizen*, October 21, 1908, 7; *NYA*, November 12, 1908, 6, and November 26, 1908, 6; *Pittsburgh Daily Post*, November 3, 1908, 5.
29. "High Prices Unpopular," *INF*, November 28, 1908, 5.
30. See Fishell's correspondence with the Shuberts, Shubert Archive, box 81, Shi–Shiz. See also *NYA*, November 26, 1908, 6; *Perrysburg Journal*, November 6, 1908, 4; *St. Louis Post-Dispatch*, November 9, 1908, 7.
31. *St. Louis Post-Dispatch*, November 19, 1908, 3, November 29, 1908, 2, and November 30, 1908, 16; *St. Louis Globe-Democrat*, November 24, 1908, 7; "High Prices Unpopular," 5; *LDG*, December 5, 1908, 2.
32. "Hi Nash," *LDJ*, December 9, 1908, 1.
33. "Nash Walker Home for Annual Visit," *LDW*, December 9, 1908, 1.

34. *LDG*, December 10, 1908, 2; *LDJ*, December 10, 1908, 1; *TPD*, December 4, 1908, 5, and January 15, 1909, 1; "Snapshots," *TSJ*, December 11, 1908, 14.

35. "At the Play," *TSJ*, December 11, 1908, 9.

36. Untitled caption, *Kansas City (KS) Globe*, December 18, 1908, 4.

37. George Walker, "Bert and Me and Them," *NYA*, December 24, 1908, 12.

38. *Chicago Eagle*, January 2, 1909, 4; "Two Dusky Salomes," *Chicago Tribune*, January 6, 1909, 8; *NYA*, January 21, 1909, 6; *Broad Ax* (Washington, DC), February 6, 1909, 2.

39. "Williams and Walker Pack the Northern," reprinted in *Broad Ax*, January 9, 1909, 1.

40. *NYA*, January 14, 1909, 6.

41. Sylvester Russell, "Eighth Annual Review," *INF*, January 9, 1909, 5. Subsequent quotations are from the same source.

42. *Broad Ax*, January 16, 1909, 2.

43. George Walker, "The Dramatic Stage as an Upbuilder of the Race," interview by Veronica Adams, *CIO*, January 17, 1909, 28. See also Walker, "Bert and Me and Them," 12.

44. *Star Press* (Muncie, IN), January 17, 1909, 4.

45. "Great Northern," *Chicago Eagle*, January 30, 1909, 4.

46. *Broad Ax*, January 16, 1909, 2, January 23, 1909, 2, and January 30, 1909, 1.

47. "Society Sees Negro Actors," *Chicago Tribune*, February 3, 1909, 1.

48. "Society Sees Negro Actors," 1; *Marion Star*, February 3, 1909, 1; *CIO*, February 3, 1909, 1; *INF*, February 6, 1909, 5, and February 27, 1909, 5.

49. Sylvester Russell, "Williams and Walker Appear at Mrs. Borden's Function," *INF*, February 27, 1909, 5.

50. *Indianapolis Star*, January 31, 1909, 39, February 9, 1909, 6, and February 13, 1909, 5; *Indianapolis News*, February 10, 1909, 7, and February 3, 1909, 13.

51. Sylvester Russell, "Sam S. and Lee Shubert to Down Klaw & Erlanger," *INF*, February 6, 1909, 5.

52. *TPD*, February 12, 1909, 3; *Kansas City Times*, March 11, 1909, 14.

53. "Walker Taken to Sanitarium," *Dayton Herald*, February 20, 1909, 1.

54. See Tim Brooks, *Lost Sounds: Blacks and the Birth of the Recording Industry, 1890–1919*, 1st ed. (University of Illinois Press, 2004), 481.

55. *Dayton Herald*, February 11, 1909, 3; "Walker Taken to Sanitarium," 1.

56. "Walker Taken to Sanitarium," 1. See also *Fort Wayne Daily News*, February 22, 1909, 11; *Cincinnati Post*, February 22, 1909, 1; *Marion Star*, February 22, 1909, 4, and February 23, 1909, 3; *Winchester News*, February 23, 1909, 4; *LWW*, February 18, 1909, February 24, 1909, 1, and February 25, 1909, 4.

57. Untitled captions, *NYA*, February 18, 1909, 6.

58. "Nash Walker Coming Home to Rest," *LDW*, February 22, 1909, 1; *LDJ*, February 22, 1909.

59. Untitled caption, *INF*, February 20, 1909, 5. See also *Dayton Herald*, February 20, 1909, 1; *INF*, February 27, 1909, 1.

60. Sylvester Russell, "Cullud Team," *INF*, February 27, 1909, 1. Clarice Vance also performed a version of the Salome dance.

61. "Walker of Williams and Walker Taken to Asylum," *St. Louis Post-Dispatch*, February 21, 1909, 17; *New Bern Sun*, February 27, 1909, 3; *Washington Post*, February 22, 1909, 5; *Washington Bee*, February 27, 1909, 1; *Chicago Tribune*, February 28, 1909, 49.

62. *Trenton Evening Times*, February 22, 1909, 3; *Dayton Herald*, February 20, 1909, 5; *TSJ*, February 24, 1909, 7; *INF*, February 27, 1909, 1.

63. "Won't Break Up," *LDW*, February 24, 1909, 1; *Kansas City Times*, February 24, 1909, 4; *INF*, February 27, 1909, 5.

64. "His Mind Failing," *LDG*, February 23, 1909, 2; *LJG*, February 24, 1909, 1.

65. "Geo. Walker Ill," *Billboard*, March 6, 1909, 17.

66. "The Great Names He Knew Live On," *New York Herald Tribune*, September 8, 1935, 2. See also *NYA*, February 25, 1909, 6, and March 4, 1909, 6; *INF*, February 27, 1909, 1.

67. Indicated in surviving correspondences, Shubert Archive, box 81, Shi–Shiz. See also *New York Clipper*, July 17, 1897, 318.

68. "Great Names," 2.

69. *NYA*, February 25, 1909, 6; *LDG*, February 26, 1909, 1; *Topeka Daily Capital*, February 26, 1909, 2; *LDW*, February 26, 1909, 1.

70. George Walker, "This Kansas Air Is Great," *LDW*, February 26, 1909, 1. See also "Nash Is Here," *LDJ*, February 26, 1909, 1.

71. "The Stage," *INF*, February 27, 1909, 5.

72. *Cincinnati Enquirer*, February 21, 1909, 30, and March 1, 1909, 8; Langston Hughes, *The Big Sea* (Alfred A. Knopf, 1940), 22–23. See also Dorthy Pennington, *The Histories and Cultural Roles of Black Churches in Lawrence, Kansas*, 1982, Kansas Collection, RH MS P508, Kenneth Spencer Research Library, University of Kansas, 6.

73. "'Nash' Walker Home Again," *Kansas City Times*, March 16, 1909, 4; *Sedalia Democrat*, March 1, 1909, 4.

74. *LDW*, February 27, 1909, 4; "Corinda," *Petaluma Argus-Courier*, July 14, 1909, 1; *Oroville Daily Register*, August 16, 1909, 1; "Walker Needs Rest," *Variety*, March 1909, 4.

75. "Colored Comedians," *Cincinnati Enquirer*, March 1, 1909, 8. See also "Theatrical Jottings," *NYA*, March 4, 1909, 6.

76. "Dorothy," "Women and Overwork," *INF*, February 27, 1909, 2.

77. *Evening Herald* (Ottawa, KS), March 6, 1909, 2; *Hutchinson News*, March 9, 1909, 2.

78. "Nash Is Resting," *LDJ*, March 5, 1909, 2; *LDW*, March 6, 1909, 3.

79. "Bandanna Land at the Grand," *Philadelphia Inquirer*, March 9, 1909, 4; "Paragraphic News," *Washington Bee*, March 6, 1909, 1.

388 | Notes to Chapter 14

80. *Colorado Statesman*, March 6, 1909, 5, March 13, 1909, 9, and March 20, 1909, 5; *TPD*, March 12, 1909, 5.

81. *LDW*, March 15, 1909, 4; "Back to Work," *LDW*, March 18, 1909, 2; *LDJ*, March 17, 1909, 4; *Billboard*, March 6, 1909, 17; *NYT*, March 14, 1909, 58; *NYA*, March 18, 1909, 6.

82. Lester Walton, "Williams Without Walker," *NYA*, March 18, 1909, 6.

83. "Williams and Walker in 'Bandanna Land' at the Majestic," *Brooklyn Citizen*, March 23, 1909, 5.

84. "Back to Work," 2.

85. *LDJ*, March 23, 1909, 1; *NYA*, March 18, 1909, 6; *Colorado Statesman*, April 3, 1909, 1; *Brooklyn Daily Eagle*, March 23, 1909, 22.

86. "Theatrical Jottings," *NYA*, March 25, 1909, 6.

87. *American Medical Directory*, vol. 2 (American Medical Association Press, 1909), 702–3. Other information gathered from the archives of the Sisters of St. Joseph, Brentwood, New York.

88. Juli Jones, "The Nervous Breakdown of Mr. George Walker, the Famous Comedian," *INF*, March 20, 1909, 5.

89. *NYA*, April 1, 1909, 6.

90. *NYA*, August 13, 1908, 6, and December 10, 1908, 6.

91. Untitled caption, *Colorado Statesman*, March 6, 1909, 5.

92. *TPD*, April 9, 1909, 7; *NYA*, April 22, 1909, 6, and May 27, 1909, 6.

Chapter 14

1. *Kenosha Evening News*, April 10, 1909, 8; *NYA*, May 13, 1909, 6, May 27, 1909, 6, July 1, 1909, 6, August 12, 1909, 6, and September 16, 1909, 6; *New York Dramatic Mirror*, July 10, 1909, 19, and July 17, 1909, 18; *Variety*, July 10, 1909, 17. See also *Broad Ax*, February 12, 1910, 2; *NYA*, September 22, 1910, 6, January 5, 1911, 6, and January 4, 1912, 6. In February 1910, "Williams and Walker's Chocolate Drops" became *The Chocolate Drops with King and Bailey* and continued to work in anticipation of a European tour in September of 1910. However, Eugene King died on November 22, 1912, in Copenhagen from an unusually severe cold.

2. *NYA*, April 15, 1909, 6, May 6, 1909, 6, and July 15, 1909, 6; *Brooklyn Daily Eagle*, May 16, 1909, 54, and May 25, 1909, 20; *The Sun* (New York), July 11, 1909, 7; *New York Dramatic Mirror*, July 24, 1909, 20.

3. *NYA*, April 29, 1909, 6; *Boston Globe*, May 9, 1909, 43; *Variety*, May 22, 1909, 5; *Sioux City Journal*, May 9, 1909, 8.

4. "The Great Names He Knew Live On," *New York Herald Tribune*, September 8, 1935, 2.

5. "Williams Alone Next Season," *Variety*, May 22, 1909, 5; *NYA*, May 20, 1909, 6, May 27, 1909, 6, and June 3, 1909, 6; *Detroit Free Press*, June 13, 1909, 58.

6. "Frogs Annual Frolic a Success," *NYA*, June 17, 1909, 6; *INF*, June 26, 1909, 5; *Colorado Statesman*, July 3, 1909, 1; *New York Dramatic Mirror*, July 3, 1909, 10.

7. *NYA*, June 3, 1909, 6; "Licking into Shape a Theatrical Company," *Brooklyn Daily Eagle*, August 29, 1909, 44; *Detroit Free Press*, June 14, 1909, 4; *TPD*, June 18, 1909, 5.

8. "Temple," *Detroit Free Press*, June 20, 1909, 46; *NYA*, July 1, 1909, 6; "The Stage," *INF*, July 3, 1909, 5.

9. *INF*, July 10, 1909, 5; "What the Colored Vaudeville Artists Are Doing in the East," August 28, 1909, 5; *NYA*, July 15, 1909, 6.

10. Lester Walton, "Theatrical Jottings," *NYA*, July 15, 1909, 6.

11. Sylvester Russell, "A Review of the Stage," *INF*, July 17, 1909, 6.

12. *NYA*, July 15, 1909, 6, and July 22, 1909, 6; *INF*, July 17, 1909, 5, 6; *New York Dramatic Mirror*, September 4, 1909, 23.

13. *NYA*, July 29, 1909, 6, August 5, 1909, 6, and August 12, 1909, 6; *American Medical Directory*, vol. 2 (American Medical Association Press, 1909), 702–3, 734; *Colorado Statesman*, August 14, 1909, 1.

14. *NYA*, August 5, 1909, 6, and September 16, 1909, 6; *Brooklyn Daily Eagle*, August 29, 1909, 44.

15. See correspondence between Fishell and J. J. Shubert on August 23, 1909, Shubert Archive, box 81, Shi–Shiz.

16. *NYA*, August 26, 1909, 6; *St. Louis Globe-Democrat*, August 29, 1909, 31.

17. W. Bob Holland, "Bert Williams at the Garrick," *St. Louis Post-Dispatch*, September 6, 1909, 6.

18. *Daily Times* (Davenport, IA), September 4, 1909, 9; *Des Moines Register*, September 4, 1909, 4, and September 17, 1909, 7; *Quad-City Times* (Davenport, IA), September 17, 1909, 8; *Cleveland Gazette*, September 18, 1909, 3; *Kansas City Star*, September 19, 1909, 32; *INF*, September 25, 1909, 6.

19. Transcript of an interview with Abbie Mitchell on July 9, 1959, 3, Philip Sterling research materials on Bert Williams (*T-Mss 1991-026), New York Public Library.

20. *LDG*, September 10, 1909, 3; *NYA*, September 16, 1909, 6; *LDJ*, September 23, 1909, 1.

21. "Walker off the Stage," *LDW*, September 18, 1909, 1. See also "Nash Walker Retires from Stage for Year," *Topeka Daily Capital*, September 19, 1909, 17; "Lawrence Comedian Leaves the Stage," *Hutchinson Gazette*, September 20, 1909, 3.

22. "Nash Is Coming Home," *LDJ*, September 23, 1909, 1.

23. "Bert Williams Cancels," *LDJ*, September 22, 1909, 2.

24. "Two Negroes Meet," *Kansas City Times*, September 21, 1909, 5.

25. "Great Names," 2.

26. Untitled caption, *LDW*, September 25, 1909, 2.

27. Sylvester Russell, "Bert A. Williams in Mr. Lode of Koal," *INF*, October 16, 1909, 5.

28. "At the Masonic," *Courier-Journal* (Louisville), October 26, 1909, 4.

29. "Williams and Walker Long Ago Parted," *INF*, February 5, 1910, 5. See also *Indianapolis News*, October 29, 1909, 5.

30. Franklin Fyles, "Gotham Theatre News," *Salt Lake Herald-Republican*, November 7, 1909, 4. See also *Star Tribune* (Minneapolis), November 7, 1909, 25; *Daily Arkansas Gazette* (Little Rock), November 7, 1909, 30; *Montgomery Advertiser*, November 7, 1909, 17.

31. *Philadelphia Inquirer*, December 14, 1909, 6; *NYA*, December 16, 1909, 6, December 23, 1909, 6, and December 30, 1909, 6.

32. *NYA*, December 30, 1909, 6, January 6, 1910, 6, January 13, 1910, 6, February 10, 1910, 6, and March 10, 1910, 6; *Brooklyn Citizen*, February 27, 1910, 20.

33. Untitled caption, *Colorado Statesman*, March 5, 1910, 9.

34. Uncle Rad Kees, "Williams and Walker, or the Passing of Two of the World's Greatest Entertainers," *INF*, March 12, 1910, 5.

35. "Williams Won't Come," *Lawrence Daily Democrat*, September 23, 1909, 2. See also *NYA*, October 14, 1909, 6; *Colorado Statesman*, October 30, 1909, 1.

36. *NYA*, September 16, 1909, 6; reprinted from the *Detroit Informer*, "Doings of the Race," *Cleveland Gazette*, September 25, 1909, 1, and December 18, 1909, 1.

37. "Nash Walker Is Here," *LDW*, December 1, 1909, 1. See also *TSJ*, December 2, 1909, 10.

38. *LDW*, December 18, 1909, 3; *LJG*, December 22, 1909, 3; Langston Hughes, *The Big Sea* (Alfred A. Knopf, 1940), 22–23, *TPD*, January 7, 1910, 4.

39. *TSJ*, January 8, 1910, 15, and January 15, 1910, 7; *Topeka Daily Capital*, January 9, 1910, 2.

40. "Nash Walker Is Seeing the Sights," *Topeka Daily Capital*, January 16, 1910, 16.

41. *Daily Times* (Davenport, IA), April 9, 1910, 10; *Quad-City Times* (Davenport, IA), April 10, 1910, 12; *La Crosse Tribune*, June 29, 1910, 3; *Oshkosh Daily Northwestern*, September 17, 1910, 10; *Joliet Evening Herald-News*, November 30, 1910, 2.

42. "The Play Last Night," *LDW*, January 22, 1910, 1.

43. "Have Williams and Walker Separated?," *NYA*, January 27, 1910, 6.

44. "Have Williams and Walker Separated?," 6.

45. *Chicago Defender*, May 14, 1910, 4; *Colorado Statesman*, July 2, 1910, 1; *NYA*, June 23, 1910, 6; New York City death certificates: Brooklyn, 1910, New York City Department of Records and Information Services.

46. Sylvester Russell, "George W. Walker of Williams and Walker Whose Mind Is Now Blank," *Chicago Defender*, July 2, 1910, 5; *TPD*, July 15, 1910, 2.

47. Russell, "George W. Walker," 5; *TPD*, July 15, 1910, 2.

48. *NYA*, June 23, 1910, 6.

49. *NYA*, July 7, 1910, 7, July 14, 1910, 6, and November 10, 1910, 6; *INF*, August 27, 1910, 6.

50. *New York Dramatic Mirror*, May 7, 1910, 13; *Chicago Defender*, May 14, 1910, 4; *NYA*, March 17, 1910, 6, June 16, 1910, 6, and June 23, 1910, 6.

51. "The Greatest Comedian on the American Stage," *The Green Book Album*, June 1912, 1180–81. While Williams and Walker were engaged at the Grand in Washington, DC, in November of 1899, Gans met his future wife, chorus member Madge Warren. To gain stage-door access, Gans agreed to give Bert boxing lessons. See also *INF*, November 25, 1899, 5; *American Citizen* (Kansas City), May 04, 1900, 1. Gans and Warren married on April 9, 1900, at the home of her uncle and the father of her cousin Odessa Warren, another member of the chorus.

52. "Great Names," 2.

53. *NYA*, March 26, 1908, 6; Ann Charters, *Nobody: The Story of Bert Williams* (Macmillan, 1970), 89.

54. *New-York Tribune*, May 31, 1908, 48; George Jessell, *Elegy in Manhattan* (Holt Rinehart and Winston, 1961), 43–45; Andrew L. Erdman, *Queen of Vaudeville: The Story of Eva Tanguay* (Cornell University Press, 2012), 113–16. There is a note in the Sterling papers from someone named Betty that reads "Herschell says Williams and Eva Tanguay were real chummy when he played here." Exactly where "here" was remains unknown, as does the full identity of "Herschell." Philip Sterling research materials on Bert Williams (*T-Mss 1991-026).

55. "About the Colored Shows," *NYA*, July 21, 1910, 6. See also *Chicago Defender*, July 30, 1910, 3.

56. *Colorado Statesman*, July 16, 1910, 12; "George Walker Insane," *Colorado Statesman*, September 10, 1910, 12.

57. "'Bob' Cole Breaks Down," *NYT*, October 12, 1910, 9. See also *NYA*, October 13, 1910, 6, and October 20, 1910, 6.

58. Lester Walton, "The Passing of the Triumvirate," *NYA*, October 20, 1910, 6.

59. Louis Armstrong Collection, object ID 1987.3.116. Reel-to-reel tape recorded by Louis Armstrong, LAHM tape 117 / Louis tape 71, track 1, 32:29. Louis Armstrong mistakenly attributed the song to George rather than Aida during an interview with former Williams and Walker cast member Laura Bowman in the early 1950s. Armstrong's March 9, 1931, recording of the song (OKeh Records, catalog no. 41486) paid homage to "Bon Bon Buddy" with the orchestra's punctuation of the musical phrase "Bon Bon Buddy, the chocolate drop," which set up Armstrong's vocal introduction, "Oh the Chocolate Drop, that's me!" before launching into the chorus of "Shine." The song received an extended lease when Dooley Wilson (1886 to 1953) performed it in the 1942 movie *Casablanca*.

60. *Evening Capital* (Annapolis, MD), September 3, 1910; *NYA*, October 13, 1910, 6, and October 20, 1910, 6; Lester Walton, "The Colored Stage Lamentations," *NYA*, October 20, 1910, 2.

61. *Colorado Statesman*, November 12, 1910, 12, and December 10, 1910, 1; *TPD*, December 9, 1910, 3; *Cincinnati Post*, January 2, 1911, 3.

62. "Comedian Walker Dead—Famous Partner of Bert Williams—Deranged by Prosperity," *Evening World* (New York), January 7, 1911, 2. See also *NYT*, January 8, 1911, 13; *The Sun* (New York), January 8, 1911, 5. In 1851, physician Samuel A. Cartwright asserted that Drapetomania was a mental illness that caused Black flight from bondage.

63. "George W. Walker, Actor . . . of the Famous Team . . . of Stars, Dead," *Chicago Defender*, January 14, 1911, 2.

64. *NYA*, January 12, 1911, 4, 6.

65. "To George Walker" and "Bye-Bye for a Little While," *NYA*, January 12, 1911, 6.

66. *NYA*, January 12, 1911, 6; Sylvester Russell, *INF*, January 14, 1911, 5; Sylvester Russell, "George Walker Laid to Rest," *INF*, February 4, 1911.

67. *NYT*, January 9, 1911, 13; *NYA*, January 12, 1911, 6.

68. *LDG*, January 12, 1911, 3; "A Boy Waif's Day at Home," *Fort Scott Daily Tribune and Fort Scott Daily Monitor*, January 13, 1911, 4; *Iola Register*, January 16, 1911, 4; *LJG*, January 18, 1911, 3. Howard made no mention of Nash Walker in his autobiography *Gay Nineties Troubadour* (Joe Howard Music House, 1956).

69. Hughes, *The Big Sea*, 23.

70. *LDG*, January 12, 1911, 3; *LJG*, January 18, 1911, 8; *INF*, February 4, 1911, 6. Rev. Jackson was assisted by Rev. Brown, Lawrence; Rev. Wilson, Topeka; Rev. W. W. Montgomery, Kansas City, Missouri; Rev. E. Arlington Wilson, Kansas City; Rev. J. M. Brown, Lawrence; Rev. Craw; and Rev. Hill. The choirs from the St. Luke AME, First Baptist of North Lawrence, and the Warren Street churches consolidated and sang "Rock of Ages" along with other selections.

71. Sylvester Russell, "George Walker of Williams and Walker," *INF*, January 14, 1911, 5.

72. *LJG*, January 18, 1911, 8. Following the funeral, Green Henri Tapley retired from public life. Other than his registration card for the draft on September 12, 1918, he was not mentioned in any known newsprint, and the date of his death remains unknown. He separated from his wife Daisy shortly after the cast returned from England and she likely began a domestic partnership with Minnie Brown. United States, Selective Service System, World War I draft registration cards, 1917–1918, Manhattan City, 144, draft card T, National Archives and Records Administration, imaged from Family History Library microfilm, M1509, New York.

73. Lester Walton, "Death of George W. Walker," *NYA*, January 12, 1911, 6.

74. "The Passing of George Walker," *TPD*, January 20, 1911, 4, 5.

75. "The Stage," *INF*, February 25, 1911, 5; "Sports and the Stage," *Colorado Statesman*, March 4, 1911, 12.

76. Sylvester Russell, "Why Aida Overton Walker Should Be Made a Star Next Season," *INF*, May 27, 1911, 5, 6.

77. Sylvester Russell, "The Williams and Walker of the Future," *Chicago Defender*, April 22, 1911, 4.

78. *NYA*, May 4, 1911, 6, May 18, 1911, 6, May 25, 1911, 6, and June 22, 1911, 6; *INF*, May 27, 1911, 5. Along with Aida, the performers slated to appear included S. H. Dudley, J. Rosamond Johnson, S. Tutt Whitney, "Strut" Payne, Harry T. Burleigh, James Reese Europe, J. Homer Tutt, Sissieretta Jones, Andrew Tribble, the Jeter Quartet, Minnie Brown, Felix Weir, Lottie Gee, Edna Gordon, Jacob Jones, "Jolly" John Larkins, and others.

79. *Lawrence Daily Journal-World* (hereafter cited as *LDJ-W*), April 6, 1911, 5; *INF*, May 20, 1911, 6; *Chicago Defender*, May 20, 1911, 4; *NYA*, May 18, 1911, 6, and May 25, 1911, 6; *Colorado Statesman*, May 6, 1911, 8. When venue managers heard that Bert wanted to leave the Follies in San Francisco to rehearse for the coming 1911 vehicle and attend the benefit, they refused to pay for the show unless he was in the cast. Bert was ordered to stay for another two weeks, and he obliged. Subsequently, managers in Salt Lake City and Denver followed suit, which meant that he could not reach New York until June 8, shortly before the Frolic of 1911.

80. *Leavenworth Post*, April 1, 1911, 6; *LDJ-W*, April 6, 1911, 5; *NYA*, June 8, 1911, 6, and September 21, 1911, 6; *INF*, June 10, 1911, 5, 6; *Pittsburgh Courier*, July 1, 1911, 1; *Broad Ax* (Washington, DC), July 1, 1911, 3; *Baltimore Afro-American*, July 1, 1911, 2; *Colorado Statesman*, July 1, 1911, 1.

81. "Editor's Notes," *TPD*, December 13, 1918, 2. The small marble marker that rests on the grave was likely financed by Bill "Bojangles" Robinson during the summer of 1926 when he also purchased a home for Alice. More than a century of exposure and neglect left the marker untethered and often on the ground. Thanks to the advocacy of Dr. Jeanne Klein, that marker was secured to a limestone base in June of 2024.

Chapter 15

1. *NYA*, July 6, 1911, 6, and August 3, 1911, 6; "Welcome Death! Slogan of Robert Cole," *INF*, August 12, 1911, 5. Quote from a conversation with K. Mélanie Edwards, granddaughter of J. Rosamond Johnson.

2. "How It Feels to Be a Negro," *Canadian Courier: The National Weekly*, March 27, 1909, 20.

3. *NYA*, September 7, 1911, 6.

4. Jack Shoemaker, "White Is as White Does," *NYA*, July 25, 1912, 6.

5. Aida Overton Walker, "Respect Memory of the Dead," *NYA*, August 1, 1912, 6. The subsequent quotations are from the same source.

6. *NYA*, February 20, 1913, 6. See also William Hyder, "Eubie Blake Story," *Sunday Magazine*, MHS 2800, box 11. An edited version was published as "The Roaring Ragtime Odyssey of Eubie Blake," *Baltimore Sun Magazine*, October 15,

1972, 5, 7. The same tactic was used by Major League Baseball when Jackie Robinson (1919 to 1972) was drafted by the Brooklyn Dodgers in 1947. His singular acquisition signaled the destruction of the Negro Leagues because it empowered White teams to freely pick and choose the players they found suitable (temperament over skill), as though the Negro Leagues were an à la carte menu—assimilation, falsely labeled as integration.

    7. *NYA*, January 9, 1913, 6; "Big Vaudeville Show," *NYA*, April 17, 1913, 6.

    8. Lester Walton, "Bert Williams and Miss Walker to Head Big Bill," *NYA*, July 24, 1913, 6.

    9. *NYA*, July 20, 1911, 6.

    10. *NYA*, October 16, 1913, 6; *Broad Ax*, October 25, 1913, 3, and November 22, 1913, 2; *Chicago Defender*, November 1, 1913, 6, and November 8, 1913, 1; "Aida Overton Walker Dazzles at the Pekin," *INF*, November 8, 1913, 5.

    11. *NYA*, July 23, 1914, 6; *NYT*, August 2, 1914, 42; *Washington (DC) Post*, October 4, 1914, 3.

    12. *Evening World* (New York), October 15, 1914, 9; *NYA*, October 15, 1914, 1; *Broad Ax*, October 17, 1914, 4; "Aida Overton Walker as the Public Knew Her," *Chicago Defender*, October 24, 1914, 1, 4; *INF*, October 24, 1914, 4, 5.

    13. *Evening World* (New York), October 15, 1914, 9; *NYA*, October 15, 1914, 1; *Broad Ax*, October 17, 1914, 4; *Chicago Defender*, October 24, 1914, 1, 4; *INF*, October 24, 1914, 4, 5; *New York Tribune*, October 27, 1914, 9; *NYT*, October 27, 1914, 5. The pallbearers were Robert T. Givens, John E. Nail, James Lightfoot, James Reese Europe, Richard Clark, Green Henri Tapley, Charles Harper, and Alex Rogers. In 2025, the Overton Nation provided a marker for Aida. Her plot is section 15, Locust Grove, block 16, division 2, grave 12811. See also Robert E. Weems Jr., "A Man in a Woman's World: Anthony Overton's Rise to Prominence in the African American Personal Care Products Industry," *The Journal of African American History* 101, no. 4 (Fall 2016): 407–35. Aida's cousin John Overton (1864 to 1946) founded the Overton Hygienic Company in 1898. He moved to Chicago in 1911 and marketed vanishing cream and pomade with Aida's name sometime around 1916.

    14. *NYA*, March 19, 1908, 6; Edmonds v. Attucks Music Publishing, 117 App. Div. 486 (N.Y. App. Div. 1907); *The Record Changer*, December 1947, 14.

    15. For example, see *Buffalo Times*, August 30, 1908, 46; *Knoxville Sentinel*, September 1, 1908, 8; *Fremont Daily Herald*, October 18, 1908, 3; *Boston Globe*, October 25, 1908, 71; *Chronicle-Telegram* (Elyria, OH), November 4, 1908, 6; *Akron Beacon Journal*, November 14, 1908, 6; *St. Joseph Gazette*, December 26, 1908, 5; *Beatrice Daily Express*, December 24, 1908, 3; *Marion Daily Mirror*, January 28, 1909, 4; *Nebraska Press and the Nebraska City Daily Tribune*, January 24, 1909, 4; *Atchison Daily Champion*, February 3, 1909, 5; *Morning Post* (Camden, NJ), March 8, 1909, 5; *Green Bay Press-Gazette*, April 2, 1909, 19; *Meriden Morning Record*, April 5, 1909, 9; *Neenah Daily Times*, April 9, 1909, 3; *Evening Star* (Washington, DC),

April 17, 1909, 8; *Call-Leader* (Elwood, IN), May 5, 1909, 3; *Bristol Herald Courier*, May 12, 1909, 3; *Brazil Daily Times*, June 5, 1909, 7; *Ottawa Daily Republic*, July 13, 1909, 3; *Indianapolis Star*, August 15, 1909, 61; *Post-Crescent* (Appleton, WI), August 16, 1909, 2; *Der Deutsche Correspondent* (Baltimore), August 20, 1909, 4; *Leavenworth Post*, August 28, 1909, 8; *Fort Scott Republican*, September 10, 1909, 2; *Omaha Daily News*, October 3, 1909, 21; *McPherson Daily Republican*, October 8, 1909, 3; *Perry Daily Chief*, October 11, 1909, 3; *LDJ*, June 28, 1909, 2.

16. *NYA*, January 21, 1909, 6, and April 29, 1909, 6; *Broad Ax*, January 30, 1909, 2; Wayne D. Shirley, "The House of Melody: A List of Publications of the Gotham-Attucks Music Company at the Library of Congress," *The Black Perspective in Music* 15, no. 1 (Spring 1987): 79–112; *Variety*, August 22, 1933, 47; "Nobody," words by Alex Rogers, music by Bert Williams, Edward B. Marks Music Corporation, New York, 1932.

17. *INF*, October 16, 1909, 5.

18. *NYA*, November 30, 1911, 6. Thomas Johnson (formerly of Klaw and Erlanger), president; Harry Kraton, vice president; Fred R. More, treasurer; Lester A. Walton, secretary; and G. L. Young, B. D. Wilkins, and Maurice, board members.

19. *NYA*, January 4, 1912, 6, January 18, 1912, 6, January 25, 1912, 1, 6, February 1, 1912, 6, February 8, 1912, 6, February 15, 1912, 6, February 29, 1912, 6, March 7, 1912, 1, 6, March 14, 1912, 6, March 21, 1912, 6, and May 2, 1912, 6; "Walker's Mother Writes," *NYA*, March 28, 1912, 6.

20. *NYA*, June 13, 1912, 6, July 4, 1912, 6, and August 1, 1912, 6; *The Sun* (New York), July 12, 1912, 11, and July 20, 1912, 13.

21. Mabel Rowland, *Bert Williams: Son of Laughter: A Symposium of Tribute to the Man and to His Work* (English Crafters, 1923), 32–33; "Hotel Marshall, Place of Unique Entertainment Closes," *NYA*, October 9, 1913, 6.

22. Tom Fletcher, *100 Years of the Negro in Show Business: The Tom Fletcher Story* (Burdge, 1954), 243.

23. *NYA*, February 20, 1913, 6, May 22, 1913, 6, and June 19, 1913, 1.

24. Sylvester Russell, "Ghosts of Hogan Haunts Williams' Mercenary," *INF*, August 1, 1914, 5.

25. Fletcher, *100 Years*, 242.

26. *Detroit Free Press*, February 19, 1922, 73, and February 28, 1922, 7; *NYT*, March 5, 1922, 1; Camille F. Forbes, *Introducing Bert Williams: Burnt Cork, Broadway, and the Story of America's First Black Star* (Basic Civitas, 2008), 319–20. In reference to Lottie Williams, see *NYA*, May 2, 1912, 7, and March 23, 1929, 1.

27. *Denver Post*, June 8, 1902, 11, and June 9, 1902, page unknown; *Windsor Beacon*, August 2, 1902, 7; *Denver, Colorado, City Directory, 1903 and 1904*.

28. *Colorado Statesman*, April 8, 1911, 2; *Fort Collins Express*, June 15, 1911, 5; *Emporia Weekly Gazette*, February 17, 1916, 5; *New York Amsterdam News*, June 16, 1926, 6; *Colorado Statesman*, November 18, 1922, 5; death certificate no. 11280, Colorado State Archives.

29. *LJG*, May 15, 1912, 3, and September 10, 1913, 1; *LDJ-W*, September 10, 1913, 5, and November 11, 1912, 1; *LDG*, May 14, 1913, 3; *INF*, October 17, 1914, 5; *Chicago Defender*, June 5, 1926, 1.

30. City directories, Lawrence, Kansas, 1915, 1917, 1923, and 1925. See also *Population Schedules and Statistical Rolls: Cities (1919–1961)*, reel 31984_245823, Kansas State Historical Society, Topeka, Kansas; *Kansas City Star*, December 15, 1920, 6; *University Daily Kansan*, December 13, 1920, 3. On December 14, 1920, Alice was the guest of Jim McIntyre of McIntyre and Heath for their performance at the Bowersock.

31. "Big Benefit for Walker's Mother," *New York Amsterdam News*, June 2, 1926, 5, June 16, 1926, 6, June 23, 1926, 6, and June 30, 1926, 1, 6; "Launch to Rescue Mother of World-Famous Showman from Poorhouse," *Chicago Defender*, June 5, 1926, 1; *LDJ-W*, June 8, 1926, 4; *NYA*, June 12, 1926, 6; *Billboard*, June 19, 1926, 12; *Variety*, June 30, 1926, 20.

32. City directories, Lawrence, Kansas, 1927 and 1930; *LDJ-W*, May 8, 1928, 6, and May 30, 1931, 2; Missouri death certificates, 1910–1969, Missouri Office of the Secretary of State, Jefferson City, Missouri.

33. *NYA*, May 26, 1910, 6, January 26, 1911, 6, April 25, 1912, 3, and June 19, 1913, 1.

34. *NYA*, June 18, 1914, 6, July 2, 1914, 6, August 20, 1914, 6, August 27, 1914, 6, September 10, 1914, 7, and May 10, 1917, 1.

35. *NYA*, July 24, 1926, 1, and May 28, 1927, 6.

36. Jack L. Cooper, "Coop's Chatter," *Metropolitan News* (Chicago), February 20, 1937, 9.

37. *Broad Ax*, March 4, 1911, 2, and March 11, 1911, 1; *INF*, November 8, 1913, 5, and November 22, 1913, 5; *Chicago Tribune*, October 10, 1930, 26; *Pittsburgh Courier*, October 11, 1930, 18; Alex Rogers's obituary, *NYA*, September 20, 1930, 1.

38. Eubie Blake, interviewed by Mike Lipskin and Rudi Blesh, March 30, 1969, recorded in the house of Marion and Eubie Blake, 284A Stuyvesant Avenue, Brooklyn.

39. Quoted in "Dorothy," "Unbidden Thoughts," *INF*, November 24, 1906, 6.

40. "Benefit Show at Alhambra Theatre a Success," *New York Amsterdam News*, June 30, 1926, 1, 6. See also *Pittsburgh Courier*, December 11, 1926, 13.

Bibliography

Abbott, Lynn, and Doug Seroff. *Out of Sight: The Rise of African American Popular Music, 1889–1895.* University Press of Mississippi, 2009.

Allen, Junius Mordecai. *Rhymes, Tales and Rhymed Tales.* Crane, ca. 1906.

American Medical Directory. Vol. 2. American Medical Association Press, 1909.

Anderson, Jervis. *This Was Harlem: A Cultural Portrait, 1900–1950.* Farrar, Straus and Giroux, 1982.

Antoine, Le Roi. *Achievement: The Life of Laura Bowman.* Pageant Press, 1961.

Asbury, Herbert. *The Barbary Coast: An Informal History of the San Francisco Underworld.* Garden City Publishing, 1933.

Athearn, Robert G. *In Search of Canaan: Black Migration to Kansas, 1879–80.* Regents Press of Kansas, 1978.

Atkinson, Daniel. "'Cake Walks and Culture': The Black Struggle for Sovereignty at the Dawn of Jim Crow." *Theatre History Studies* 43 (2024).

Atkinson, Daniel. "George 'Nash' Walker: The Unsung Favorite Son of Lawrence, Kansas." In *Embattled Lawrence,* vol. 2, *The Enduring Struggle for Freedom,* edited by Dennis Domer. Watkins Museum of History, 2022.

Badger, Reid. *The Great American Fair: The World's Columbian Exposition & American Culture.* Nelson Hall, 1979.

Badger, Reid. *A Life in Ragtime: A Biography of James Reese Europe.* Oxford University Press, 1995.

Bauman, Thomas. *The Pekin: The Rise and Fall of Chicago's First Black-Owned Theater.* University of Illinois Press, 2014.

Berlin, Edward A. *Reflections and Research on Ragtime.* ISAM monograph 24. Institute for Studies in American Music, Conservatory of Music, Brooklyn College of the City of New York, 1987.

Bernstein, Iver. *The New York City Draft Riots: Their Significance for American Society and Politics in the Age of the Civil War.* ACLS Humanities EBook. Oxford University Press, 1990.

Berson, Misha. *The San Francisco Stage: From Golden Spike to Great Earthquake, 1869–1906.* San Francisco Performing Arts Library and Museum Series, no. 2. San Francisco Performing Arts Library and Museum, 1989.

Blake, Eubie, and Eileen Southern. "Conversation with Eubie Blake: A Legend in His Own Lifetime." *The Black Perspective in Music* 1, no. 1 (1973): 50–59.

Blesh, Rudi, and Harriet Janis. *They All Played Ragtime*. 4th ed. Oak Publications, 1971.

Bond, Frederick Weldon. *The Negro and the Drama: The Direct and Indirect Contribution Which the American Negro Has Made to Drama and the Legitimate Stage, with the Underlying Conditions Responsible*. Associated Publishers, 1940.

Brooks, Tim. *Lost Sounds: Blacks and the Birth of the Recording Industry, 1890–1919*. University of Illinois Press, 2004.

Brown, Jayna. *Babylon Girls: Black Women Performers and the Shaping of the Modern*. Duke University Press, 2008.

Campney, Brent M. S. *This Is Not Dixie: Racist Violence in Kansas, 1861–1927*. University of Illinois Press, 2015.

Carter, Marva Griffin. *Swing Along: The Musical Life of Will Marion Cook*. Oxford University Press, 2008.

Charters, Ann. *Nobody: The Story of Bert Williams*. Macmillan, 1970.

Chude-Sokei, Louis Onuorah. *The Last 'Darky': Bert Williams, Black-on-Black Minstrelsy, and the African Diaspora*. Duke University Press, 2006.

Cook, Will Marion. "Clorindy . . . ." *Theatre Arts* 31, no. 9 (1947).

Cook, Will Marion. *In Dahomey; a Negro Musical Comedy: Book by J. A. Shipp, Lyrics by P. L. Dunbar & Others*. Keith, Prowse, ca. 1902/3.

Cordley, Richard. *A History of Lawrence, Kansas: From the First Settlement to the Close of the Rebellion*. E. F. Caldwell / Lawrence Journal Press, 1895.

Curtis, Susan. *Colored Memories: A Biographer's Quest for the Elusive Lester A. Walton*. University of Missouri Press, 2008.

Davis, Angela Y. *Blues Legacies and Black Feminism: Gertrude "Ma" Rainey, Bessie Smith, and Billie Holiday*. Random House, 1999.

Du Bois, W. E. B. *Souls of Black Folk*. A. C. McClurg, 1903.

Dunbar, Paul Laurence. *Lyrics of Lowly Life*. Dodd, Mead, 1896.

Emery, Lynne Fauley. *Black Dance: From 1619 to Today*. 2nd rev. ed. Princeton Book, 1988.

Erdman, Andrew L. *Queen of Vaudeville: The Story of Eva Tanguay*. Cornell University Press, 2012.

Fletcher, Tom. *100 Years of the Negro in Show Business: The Tom Fletcher Story*. Burdge, 1954.

Forbes, Camille F. *Introducing Bert Williams: Burnt Cork, Broadway, and the Story of America's First Black Star*. Basic Civitas, 2008.

Foster, William. *Memoirs of William Foster/ Pioneers of the Stage*. In *The Official Theatrical World of Colored Artists*, edited by Theophilus Lewis. Theatrical World Publishing, 1928.

Fowler, Paul E. "Athens of the West: African American Associational Life in Lawrence, Kansas, 1861–1948." Master's thesis, University of Kansas, 2016.

George-Graves, Nadine. *Royalty of Negro Vaudeville: The Whitman Sisters and the Negotiation of Race, Gender, and Class in African-American Theatre, 1900–1940.* St. Martin's Press, 2000.

Gilbert, David. *The Product of Our Souls: Ragtime, Race, and the Birth of the Manhattan Musical Marketplace.* University of North Carolina Press, 2015.

Gilbert, Douglas. *American Vaudeville: Its Life and Times.* Whittlesey House, McGraw-Hill Books, 1940.

Gildea, William. *The Longest Fight: In the Ring with Joe Gans, Boxing's First African American Champion.* Farrar, Straus and Giroux, 2012.

Harris, Leslie M. *In the Shadow of Slavery: African Americans in New York City, 1626–1863.* University of Chicago Press, 2003.

Harris, M. A. *A Negro History Tour of Manhattan.* Greenwood Publishing, 1968.

Haskins, James, and N. R. Mitgang. *Mr. Bojangles: The Biography of Bill Robinson.* Welcome Rain Publishers, 2000.

Howard, Joseph Edgar. *Gay Nineties Troubadour.* Joe Howard Music House, 1956.

Hughes, Langston. *The Big Sea.* Alfred A. Knopf, 1940.

Hughes, Langston. *Not Without Laughter.* Scribner Paperback Fiction, 1995.

Jacoby, Karl. *The Strange Career of William Ellis: The Texas Slave Who Became a Mexican Millionaire.* W. W. Norton, 2016.

Jasen, David A., and Gene Jones. *Spreadin' Rhythm Around: Black Popular Songwriters, 1880–1930.* Schirmer Books, 1998.

Jessel, George. *Elegy in Manhattan.* Holt, Rinehart and Winston, 1961.

Johnson, James Weldon. *Along This Way: The Autobiography of James Weldon Johnson.* Viking Press, 1933.

Johnson, James Weldon. *Black Manhattan.* Da Capo Press, 1991.

Kerr, Judith N. "God-Given Work: The Life and Times of Sculptor Meta Vaux Warrick Fuller, 1877–1968." PhD diss., University of Massachusetts at Amherst, 1986. ProQuest.

Kimball, Robert, and William Bolcom. *Reminiscing with Noble Sissle and Eubie Blake.* Cooper Square Press, 2000.

Klein, Jeanne. "The Cake Walk Photo Girl and Other Footnotes in African American Musical Theatre." *Theatre Survey* 60, no. 1 (2019): 67–90. https://doi.org/10.1017/S0040557418000509.

Krasner, David. *A Beautiful Pageant: African American Theatre, Drama, and Performance in the Harlem Renaissance, 1910–1927.* Palgrave Macmillan, 2002.

Krasner, David. *Resistance, Parody, and Double Consciousness in African American Theatre, 1895–1910.* St. Martin's Press, 1997.

Lee, Maureen D. *Sissieretta Jones.* University of South Carolina Press, 2013.

Levine, Lawrence W. *Black Culture and Black Consciousness: Afro-American Folk Thought from Slavery to Freedom.* Oxford University Press, 2007.

Lewis, David Levering. *When Harlem Was in Vogue.* Penguin Books, 1997.

Lindfors, Bernth, editor. *Africans on Stage: Studies in Ethnological Show Business.* Indiana University Press, 1999.

Lipsky, William. *Images of America: San Francisco's Midwinter Exposition.* Arcadia Publishing, 2002.

Lott, Eric. *Love and Theft: Blackface Minstrelsy and the American Working Class.* Oxford University Press, 1993.

Low, Denise, and T. E. Pecore Weso. "Langston Hughes in Lawrence: Photographs and Biographical Resources." *The Langston Hughes Review* 20 (2006).

Lowery, Debby, and Judy Sweets. *African Americans in the 1865 Kansas State Census (Douglas County).* Published by the authors, 2006.

Mahar, William J. *Behind the Burnt Cork Mask: Early Blackface Minstrelsy and Antebellum American Popular Culture.* University of Illinois Press, 1999.

Manchel, Frank. *Every Step a Struggle: Interviews with Seven Who Shaped the African-American Image in Movies.* New Academia Publishing, 2007.

Mitchell, Loften. *Black Drama: The Story of the American Negro in the Theatre.* Hawthorn Press, 1967.

Moon, Krystyn R., David Krasner, and Thomas L. Riis. "Forgotten Manuscripts: A Trip to Coontown." *African American Review* 44, no. 1/2 (2011): 7–24. https://doi.org/10.1353/afa.2011.0012.

Morgan, Thomas L., and Williams Barlow. *From Cakewalks to Concert Halls: An Illustrated History of African American Popular Music from 1895 to 1930.* Elliott & Clark Publishing, 1992.

Nathan, Hans. *Dan Emmett and the Rise of Early Negro Minstrelsy.* University of Oklahoma Press, 1962.

Nugent, Richard Bruce. "Marshall's: A Portrait." *Phylon (1940–1956)* 5, no. 4 (1944): 316–18.

Pennington, Dorthy. *The Histories and Cultural Roles of Black Churches in Lawrence, Kansas.* 1982. Kansas Collection, RH MS P508, Kenneth Spencer Research Library, University of Kansas.

Peterson, Bernard L., Jr. *A Century of Musicals in Black and White: An Encyclopedia of Musical Stage Works by, About, or Involving African Americans.* Greenwood Press, 1993.

Peterson, Bernard L., Jr. *Profiles of African American Stage Performers and Theatre People, 1816–1960.* Greenwood Press, 2001.

Phillips, Caryl. *Dancing in the Dark.* Knopf, 2005.

Rafiner, Tom A. *Caught Between Three Fires: Cass County, Mo., Chaos, and Order No. 11, 1860–1865.* Published by the author, 2010.

Reed, Christopher Robert. *"All the World Is Here!": The Black Presence at White City.* Indiana University Press, 2000.

Rice, Edwin. *Monarchs of Minstrelsy: From Daddy Rice to Date.* Kenny Publishing, 1911.

Riis, Thomas L. *Just Before Jazz: Black Musical Theater in New York, 1890–1915.* Smithsonian Institution Press, 1989.

Riis, Thomas L., editor. *The Music and Scripts of "In Dahomey."* A-R Editions for the American Musicological Society, 1996.

Rowland, Mabel. *Bert Williams: Son of Laughter: A Symposium of Tribute to the Man and to His Work.* English Crafters, 1923.

Rydell, Robert W. *All the World's a Fair : Visions of Empire at American International Expositions, 1876–1916.* University of Chicago Press, 1984.

Sampson, Henry T. *Blacks in Blackface: A Source Book on Early Black Musical Shows.* Vols. 1 and 2, 2nd ed. Rowman & Littlefield, 2014.

Sampson, Henry T. *The Ghost Walks: A Chronological History of Blacks in Show Business, 1865–1910.* Scarecrow Press, 1988.

Shirley, Wayne D. "The House of Melody: A List of Publications of the Gotham-Attucks Music Company at the Library of Congress." *The Black Perspective in Music* 15, no. 1 (Spring 1987): 79–112.

Smith, Eric Ledell. *Bert Williams: A Biography of the Pioneer Black Comedian.* McFarland, 1992.

Smith, Leland George. "The Early Negroes in Kansas." PhD diss., University of Wichita, 1932.

Smith, Shawn Michelle. *Photography on the Color Line: W. E. B. Du Bois, Race, and Visual Culture.* Duke University Press, 2004.

Sobel, Bernard. *A Pictorial History of Vaudeville.* Bonanza Books, 1961.

Sotiropoulos, Karen. *Staging Race: Black Performers in Turn of the Century America.* Harvard University Press, 2006.

Southern, Eileen. "Ada Overton Walker, Abbie Mitchell, and The Gibson Girl: Reconstructing African American Womanhood." *International Journal of Africana Studies* 13, no. 1 (Spring 2007).

Southern, Eileen. *The Music of Black Americans: A History.* 2nd ed. W. W. Norton, 1983.

Stearns, Marshall, and Jean Stearns. *Jazz Dance: The Story of American Vernacular Dance.* Da Capo Press, 1994.

Toll, Robert C. *On with the Show! The First Century of Show Business in America.* Oxford University Press, 1976.

Tuttle, William M., Jr. "Separate but Not Equal: African Americans and the 100-Year Struggle for Equality in Lawrence and at the University of Kansas, 1850s–1960." In *Embattled Lawrence: Conflict and Community*, edited by Dennis Domer and Barbara Watkins, 139–52. University of Kansas Continuing Education, 2001.

Walker, George W. "The Real 'Coon' on the American Stage." *The Theatre*, August 1906.

Washington, Booker T. *Up from Slavery.* Open Road Media, 2016.

Webb, Barbara L. "The Black Dandyism of George Walker: A Case Study in Genealogical Method." *The Drama Review* 45, no. 4 (2001): 7–24.

Weems, Robert E., Jr. "A Man in a Woman's World: Anthony Overton's Rise to Prominence in the African American Personal Care Products Industry." *The Journal of African American History* 101, no. 4 (2016): 407–35.

Wells, Ida B. *The Reason Why the Colored American Is Not in the World's Columbian Exposition: The Afro-American's Contribution to Columbian Literature*. Published by the author, 1893.
Williams, Bert. "The Comic Side of Trouble." *The American Magazine* 85 (January–June 1918): 33–35, 58, 60–61.
Williams, Carmaletta M., and John Edgar Tidwell, editors. *My Dear Boy: Carrie Hughes's Letters to Langston Hughes, 1926–1938*. University of Georgia Press, 2013.
Woll, Allen L. *Black Musical Theatre: From Coontown to Dreamgirls*. Louisiana State University Press, 1989.
Woll, Allen L. *Dictionary of the Black Theatre: Broadway, Off-Broadway, and Selected Harlem Theatre*. Greenwood Press, 1983.
Work, Monroe N. "The Origin of 'Ragtime' Music." *Negro Year Book: An Annual Encyclopedia of the Negro, 1925–1926*. A.M.E. Sunday School Union, 1926.
Young, Harvey. *The Cambridge Companion to African American Theatre*. Cambridge University Press, 2012. https://doi.org/10.1017/CCO9781139062107.

Index

Page numbers with an *f* refer to a figure or a caption; *n* refers to an endnote. Williams or Walker in a subentry refers to Bert Williams or George Walker (Nash). Aida or Lottie in a subentry refers to Aida Overton Walker or Charlotte Thompson Williams.

Abraham Lincoln (silent film), 318
Abyssinia: origin, 195; cast and tour schedule, 336–39; audience, 219; condensed version of, 214; first-class theatre as goal for, 195; at Grand Theatre, New York, 226; opening at Majestic Theatre, 216; photo, *218f*; plot, 216–19; postponement of production, 203; recovery from, 233; retirement of, 233, 235; reviews, 219–20; size/cost, 201; ticket sales, 220
Abyssinio (housing for mother/grandmother): furnishings, 239; party, 241; photo, *240f*; after Walker's passing, 319
Accooe, Will: death of, 179; in Williams and Walker company, 44; at Williams and Walker gathering spot, 111
Adams, Veronica, interview with Walker, 270–71
African royalty, 178
"Africque—the Kara Kara," 285

Aida Overton Walker's Abyssinian Maidens/Girls, 204, 219
Alexander, Charles (writer), 198
Alexander, Charlie (chorus), 98
Alexandra, Queen of England, 173
"All Coons Look Alike to Me," 53, 54, *55f*
Allen, Junius Mordecai (J. Mord.): as dialect lyricist, 241, 260, 381n21; poetry, 302–4; removal from *Big Smoke* production, 286; *Rhymes, Tales and Rhymed Tales*, 241
American Tobacco, images produced by, 72, *72f*, 358n38, 358n39
American Woman's Home Journal: cake walk dance feature in, *69f*; Williams and Walker feature in, 67
Amphion Theatre, 214
Anderson, Al, 39
Anti-Black Police Riot, 117–20
"Any Old Place in Yankee Land Is Good Enough for Me," 261–62
Arcade Minstrels, *19f*, 20

404 | Index

Archer, George, 316
Armstrong, Louis, 391n59
"As I See You on the Stage" (poem), 104
Atlantic City performances, 189, 256, 260–61, 298
Attucks Music Company, 187, 189
Avery, Dan and Hart, Charles 128, 155f, 182–83, 204, 257, 267, 283, 287, 345–46, 378n25 Avery, Lizzie, 155f, 333

Babbage, Dora Dean, 39, 44
"Baby Will You Always Love Me True?," 44
Bailey, Leo, 257, 267
Baltimore performances, 189, 261
bandanna as hallmark of minstrelsy, 241
Bandanna Land: adaptation for vaudeville/silent film, 318; attendance, 265; closing, 282; Deas, Reed, and Deas production of, 295; elite White patronage, 254; encores, 251; hindrance to Black progress as theme, 241; "Merry Widow" waltz, 250–51, 252f; opening, 261; pantomime of mentally ill man, 251, 382n43; photo, 244f, 266f; plot, 241, 242–43, 381n20; reuse for other purposes, 285; reviews, 245, 246; at Shubert-owned Majestic Theatre, 250; success of, 253
Barclay, Arthur, President of Liberia 319
Barton, James D., as receiver for Williams and Walker, 228, 231
baseball teams, 98, 109, 193, 194, 220–21, 230, 256, 261, 265, 266, 363n47
Beau Brummel persona, 58, 224
Belasco, David, 229

Belmont, Alva, 160
benefit performances/shows: at the Elks Club, 197; for a granite memorial for Walker, 309, 393n78; for Hogan, 257; for the National Guard, 369n27; for the Seaman's Fund, 168; for St. Philip's Parish Home, Grand Central Palace, Manhattan, 285; for Walker's mother, 320; for the White Rose Industrial Association Home for Colored Working Girls, 257
Bien, Franklin, 268, 286
Big Smoke, 288. See also *Mr. Lode of Koal*
Bijou Theatre, Manhattan, 288
"Bill Simmons' Sister," 258
Bimberg, Meyer (Bim the Button Man), 253, 254
Black Patti: about, 44–46; baseball prowess of, 98; poster, 45f; *A Trip to Coontown*, 85; vocal qualities, 35; "The Williams and Walker Fresh Kids," 257
Black Patti's Troubadours: about, 46; Hogan signed with, 90; Wiley with, 358n37
Black performances: absence of love scenes, 210, 215, 229, 242; cake walk dance. *See* cake walk dance coon songs, 53–57, 54–55f; in Lawrence, Kansas, 66–67; New York success, 58–62, 73; publicity, 67–74
Blake, James Hubert "Eubie," 31, 120, 313
Blake, Shout, 31
Blind Boone, 291
"Bon Bon Buddy, the Chocolate Drop": Armstrong's use of, 391n59; as biggest hit, 348n16;

inspiration for *The Chocolate Drops with King and Bailey*, 388n1; inspiration for the Gershwins, 382n35; sung by Aida, 274, 276, *276f*, 277; sung by Walker, 235, 243, 245, 246–47, 261, 262, 265, 267, 269–70, 272; use by the Mitchells, 285
bootblack stand, 11–12, *12f*, 136
Borden, John, 271–72
Bowersock Opera House, Lawrence: brisk ticket sales, 152, 245; *His Honor, the Barber*, 295; poster, *19f*; renaming of Liberty Hall, 15; show cancellation, 291; updating, 384n8; Williams and Walker reception at, 106, 128
Bowman, Laura, 150, 183, 335, 338, 343, 345, 370n33, 371, 391n59
Bradley, Ruth, 306
Britain, Joe and Sadie, 257
Broder & Schlam, publisher, 39
Brooks, Mazie, 90, 98, 327–28
Brown, Minnie, 191, 257–58, 335, 338, 343, 392n72, 393n78
Brown, Phil H., 354n21
Brown, Tom, 257–58, *263f*, 340, 342
Brymn, James T., *126f*, 152, 187, 300
buck and wing dancing, 37–38, 51, 88, 255, 271, 330, 353n3
Buckingham Palace royal command, 173–78
"Build a Nest for Birdie," 226
Burleigh, Harry T., 111, 273, 327, 393n78
Bush, Mazie, 271, 333

C. W. Pringle's Original Georgia Minstrels, 15
Cake Walk Carnival, 128
cake walk dance: at Buckingham Palace, 175; origin 57; photos of, 67, *69f*, *73f*, *170f*; steps/wardrobe for, 61; Vanderbilt-Williams and Walker challenge, 77–84; Williams and Walker as image for promotional materials, 71–72
Callendar, Harry, 62
Canary, Thomas and Lederer, George, 49–51
Cannibal King, 128, 131, 135, 142, 148, 366n26. See also *In Dahomey*
Carter, Cornelius, 12, 16, 115–16, 136, 139
Carter's Little Liver Pills, 115–16
Caruso, Enrico, 254
Cassin, Stephen, 120
Castle, Irene and Vernon, 314, *315f*
"Castle Lame Duck Waltz," *315f*
Chappelle, Thomas Ernest "Chappie," 91, 99, 277–78, 286, 291, 298–99, 308, 330, 340, 343, 364n47, 383n57
Chicago's Columbian Exhibition (1893): Colored People's Day, 27, 29, 43; Dahomeyans arrival/departure of, 27–28
Chicot, 97, 361n1
The Chocolate Drops with King and Bailey, 285, 342, 344, 383n58, 388n1
churches: Church of St. Benedict, the Moor, 283; Mount Zion Baptist Church, 243; St. Luke African Methodist Episcopal (AME) Church, 295; St. Philip's Church, 100; Warren Street Baptist Church, 17, 187, 242, 306, 319
Cincinnati performances, 256
Circle Theatre, Manhattan, 215
The Clansman (Dixon), 221–24, 379n51
Clark, Carroll, 367n42

Clark, John W., 230
Clef Club, 305, 322
Clifford, Billy and Huth, Maude, 37, 39, 40*f*, 357n24
Clorindy: origin, 88–90; at the Boston Theatre, 90–91; plot, 91; at vaudeville houses, 360n25
Coates, Sherman, 267
Cole, Bob: 27, 70–71*f*, 85–86*f*, 88, 93, 110, 129, 149, 227*f*, 254, 259, 262–63*f*, 272, 283, 288, 294, 297, 299–300, 309; death, 311–12, 314; W-H-C theatre, 317, 365n35
Cole and Johnson, Billy, 44, 46, 59, 111, 366n35, 355n26
Cole and Johnson, Rosamond, 44, 100, 117–18, 120, 187, 228, 329, 233–35, 257–58, 272, 277, 288, 297, 329, 333, 366n35, 381n11
Colorado African Colonization Company, 13, 145, 148*f*, 319
Comstock, F. Ray: contractual obligations, 246; as manager/producer, 234, 253; on Walker, 296
Conn, Malcolm, 137
Connors, Richard, 175, 192, 197, 328, 330, 333
Cook, Abbie Mitchell, 124, 158, 174, 177, 242–43, 257, 288, 290, 330, 365n19, 366n35
Cook, Mercer, 158–59
Cook, Will Marion, 27, 29–30, 44, 88–91, 93, 98, 108, 111, 121, 124, 128, 131, 134–35, 152, 155, 168–69, 188, 241, 260, 275, 316, 328, 330, 365n19, 248*f*
Cook and Dunbar: *Cannibal King*, 128; *Clorindy (Origin of the Cake Walk)*, 91; *In Dahomey*, 135; press interaction with, 168–69

coon songs, 53–57
"Coontown," Manhattan, 58–59
Cooper, George, 257–58
Cooper, Jack L., 323
Copeland, Andrew A., 256
Copeland, Theodore C., 306
Copeland, Will, 17
Corinda (Clorindy), 279
Corker, Sam, Jr., 120, 150, 263–64*f*, 307, 322
Craig, Marshall, 149, 155*f*, 333
The Crazy Coons (King and Bailey), 383n58
Cremorne, Jack, 24, 37
The Creole Black Prince, 285
Creole Burlesque Show, 44
Crowdus, Ernest Reuben. *See* Hogan, Ernest
"The Czar of Dixie," 172

Dahomeyan Villages, 27–28, 31–37, 32*f*, 148, 254
Dailey, Peter, 52
"Dance of the Veiled Mugs," 288
Dante, "Black," "The Prince" Carl, 90, 316, 327, 330, 344
Davies, Acton, 219, 365n40
Davis, Belle, 44, 67 73*f*
Davis, Gussie L., 282
Davis, H. G., 191
Davis, Harry, 52, 59
Davis-Shipp, Maggie, 96, 237, 271, 314, 328, 330, 333, 336–37, 339, 343, 364n49
de Young, Michael H., 28
Deas, Ella, 295
Deas, Lawrence, 295, 299
Deas, Reed, and Deas, 295
Delmonico's, Aida's appearance at, 159–60
Dixon, Thomas: *The Clansman*, 221–24, 379n51

Dixon, Walter H., 120, 344
Dockstader, Lew, 191, 194–96, 201–3, 206, 209, 211–14, 194–95, 355n35
"I Don't Like No Cheap Man," 83, 358n38, 359n11
"Dora Dean: The Sweetest Gal You Ever Seen," 39–42, 44, *40f*, 83, 256
Dougherty, Romeo L., 324
Douglass, Charles R., 102–3
Douglass, Frederick (activist), 88–89, 27
Douglass, Fred (actor), 109, 150, 328, 330, 345
Douglass Club, 77–79, 110
"Down Among the Sugar Cane," 271
Draft Riot (1863), 58, 119
"A Dream of the Orient," 245–46
"Drinking," 271
Du Bois, W. E. B., 160, 162, 350n0
Dudley, S. H., 232, 257, 275, 295, 297, 300, 323, 393n78
Dunbar, Paul Laurence, 27, 88–93, 111, 119, 128, 131, 134–35, 168, 216, 241, 350n0, 374n4, 378n33, 381n21
Duncan, Isadora, 263
Duryea, Etta Terry, 313
Dvorak, Antonin, 89

Easton, Sidney, 115
Edmonds, "Shep" Shepard, 30, 187, 316, 330, 363n47
Edward, Prince of England, 173
Edward B. Marks Music Corporation, 316
Edward VII, King of England, 173, 178
Eldridge House, 10–11, 13–15, 106, 137, 279
"Elegant Darky Dan," 124

Elkins, William C., 109–10, 197, 292, 305, 327–28, 333, 336–37, 343, 379n48, 383n57
Elks Carnival/parade, 137–38
Ellis, Jesse, 333, 336, 338, 343
Ellis, William H., 178–79, 193, 195, 376n39
Emperor Jones, 318
"Enjoy Yourselves," 73, *74f*
Enoch, May, 117–18
Erlanger, Abraham, 152, 154, 157, 187, 191–94, 202, 211–14, 226–27, 234, 254, 272, 298, 317–18
"Evah Darhkey Is a King," 176–77
"Exhortation," 243

Fiddler, Harry, 287
Fish, 318
Fishell, Dan, 268, 288
Fisk Jubilee Singers, 29, 183
Fletcher, Tom, 38, 56, 88, 101, 317, 344, 353–54n3
"The Fortune Telling Man," 131
Foster, Charles "Bass," 292, 343–44, 379n48
Foster, Jeanette, 299
"Four Hundred," 77, 80–81, 83, 97, 157–66, 359n1
Fred Neddermyer's Orchestra, 98
Freeman, George, 16
Freeman, Mark, 13
Frogs, 259–61, *263f–64f*, 270, 285–86, 295, 313, 316, 321–23
Fyles, Franklin, 219, 251, 292

Gans, "The Old Master" Joe, 249, 296, 298, 391n51
Gerber, David, 231
"Get Your Money's Worth," 358n39
"A Ghost of a Coon," 255
Gilliam, Charles, 323

Gilpin, Charles, 305, 318, 337, 379n48
Glee Club. *See* Williams and Walker
   Glee Club
God's Trombones, 322
Goff, John W. (Justice), 260
Goggins, Ed, 90, 98, 201
The Gold Bug, 49–51
The Golf Links, 129, 329, 331, 333
"Golly, Ain't I Wicked," 300
"Good Afternoon Mr. Jenkins," 124
"Good Morning Carrie," 132, *133f*
Goodwin, N. C., 190
Gotham music company, 188, 196
Gotham-Attucks, 188, 196, 204, 206,
   248f, 256, *301f*, 316, 376n43
Grady, Lottie, 288, 342
Green, J. Ed, 129
Grey, Odessa Warren, 109, 318
"The Guardian and the Heir," 257
Guiguesse, Ada, 158–59, *159f*, 177,
   257, 337, 340, 343
Guilbert, Yvette, 60
Guisard, 134–35

Hackett, James K., 194, 212
Hall Studios, 71–72
Halliday, Grace, 85, 88, 324, 327–28
Halliday Sisters, 44
Hammerstein, Oscar, 183, 204, 207,
   209–11, 254, 286, 298, 309
Hampton, Pete, 124, 149, 150, 183,
   330, 345, 373
Hampton Quartet, 29
Hanford, Edwin, 300
Hargous, Robert, 159, 161–62
Harris, Arthur, 117–18
Harris, George H., 103–4, 190, 330
Harris, George W., 190, 363n29
Harry Callendar's Minstrels, 62
Hart, Charles, 126, 142, 155, 182–83,
   204, 257–58, 283, 287, 345–46,
   378n25

Hart, George, 16
Harvey, Sherman, 107
Hayden, Alice (mother). *See* Myers,
   Alice
Hayden, Sarah (grandmother), 9–10,
   12, 67, 96, 132, 136, 154, 181,
   196, 230, 234, 239, 241–43,
   246, 307, 319, 347n4, 358n34,
   360n67
Hayden, Sanford (uncle), 9, 230, 307,
   319
Hayden, Will (uncle), 9, 319, 349n36,
   381n20
"He Ain't Got No Mamie," 189
"Hello! Ma Baby," 17
"Here It Comes Again," 217, 219
Herman (carpenter), 46, 221
"He's a Cousin of Mine," 316
"He's Up Against the Real Thing
   Now," *95f*
Hill, J. Leubrie, 255, 333, 339, 342
Hill, Walter, 24
Hill Opera House, Petaluma,
   California, 279
Hines, Isaac, 322
His Honor, the Barber, 295, 300
historically Black colleges and
   universities, 29, 352n35
Hodges, Joe, 38, 42, 327, 328
Hodges and Launchmere, 38, 42, 43,
   50, 62, 90
Hoffman, Gertrude, 263, 264
Hogan, Ernest, 35, 44, 53–58, *54f*,
   55f, 89–90, 92, 117–20, 141–42,
   152, 201, 206, 233, 235, 254–55,
   257–58, 263, 272, 275, 283, 287,
   294, 300, 311, 314, 316–17,
   356n4, 360n5, 364n48, 365n8,
   366n35
Holland, W. Bob, 290
Hopkins-Chenault, Hattie, 223–24,
   292, 333, 337, 342

"A Hot Coon from Memphis," 70, 71f, 92, 358n38
Hotel Laughland, 287
Hotel Marshall, 109–16, 209, 317
"The Hottest Coon in Dixie," 92
"The Hottest Coon in Town," 72
"The House of Melody," 188, 316
Howard, Joe, 17, 152, 306, 350n38, 392n68
Hughes-Clark, Carolyn (Carrie), 13, 187
Hughes, James M., 374n4
Hughes, Langston, 10, 13, 279, 295, 306, 374n4

Huld, Franz, 72, 358n37
Hunn, Ben, 120, 344
Hunn, Charles, 47
Huntingtons, 254
Hurtig and Seamon, 91–92, 97, 102, 131, 141, 159, 165, 166, 174, 177, 182, 191–96, 204, 228, 287
Huth, Maud, 37. *See also* Clifford and Huth
Hyde and Behman, 64f, 67, 89, 90, 93
Hyde's Comedians, 73, 83
Hyde's Minstrels, 358n38
Hyers Sisters, 16, 44, 349n29

"I May Be Crazy, but I Ain't No Fool," 189
"I Stood on the Bridge at Midnight," 258
"I Surrender All," 367n42
"I'll Keep a Warm Spot in My Heart for You," 226, 227f
"I'm a Cooler for the Warmest Coon in Town," 94f, 95
"I'm a Jonah Man," 150, 151f
In Dahomey, 117f, 134, 135, 141–58, 159, 165–83, 189–95, 219, 234, 319, 333, 335, 345

"In Far Off Mandalay," 288
Isham, John (Octoroons), 43–44, 67, 73, 85, 90, 101, 120, 332, 354n21, 358n37, 359n42
Isham, Will: *King Rastus* company, 120, 128
"The Island of By-and-By," 226
"It's Hard to Find a King Like Me," 219–19
"It's Hard to Love Somebody . . ." 243

Jack, Sam T., 39, 44
Jackson, Billy, 44
Jackson, G. N., 306
Jackson, J. Harry, 130–31
Jim Crow dance, 14
Johnson, Billy, 44, 85, 88, 111, 366n35
Johnson, Charlie, 39, 44
Johnson, (Babbage) Dora Dean, 92–93
Johnson, J. Rosamond, 27, 149, 198, 227f, 258, 262, 283, 299, 302, 322, 366n35, 393n78, n1
Johnson, Jack, 160, 194, 220, 298, 313
Johnson, James Weldon, 24, 27, 44, 84, 85, 111, 118, 120, 132
Johnson, Mary, 314
Johnson Amusement Company, 316
Johnson and Dean, 39, 44
"Jonah Man," 172, 175
Jones, Irving, 44
Jones, Juli, 282–83
Jones, Matilda Sissieretta. *See* Black Patti
Joplin, Scott, 30
Jordan, Joe, 39, 257, 264, 374n8
"Jump Back, Honey, Jump Back," 92–93
"Jump Jim Crow," 14
"Just the Same," 243

Kees, Uncle Rad, 33–34, 293–94
Kelly, W. C., 210–11, 378n25
Kemp, Bobby and May, 257–58
Kersands, Billy, 15, *19f,* 20
King, Eugene, 257, 388n1
King, Ike, 16
King Rastus company, 120, 128
"Kinky," 243, 272
Klaw, Marc, 152, 154, 157–58, 187, 191–94, 202, 211–13, 226–27, 234, 272, 317–18, 395n18
Klein, Jeanne, 393n81
Knapp-Herr, Barron, 160
Knox, George L., 220, 275
Koster and Bial's, 59, 62, 66, 67, 323, 369n27

La Sylph, 263, 264
The Land of Monkeys, 299
Langston family, 10, 13, 128
Langston, Charles, 10, 17
Langston, Mary, 10
Langston, Nat Turner, 13
Larkins, "Jolly" John, 257–58
"Late Hours," 243, 251, 271
Launchmere, Nina. *See* Hodges and Launchmere
Law, Mrs. George, 160
"The Leader of the Ball," 124, 255
Lederer, George. *See* Canary and Lederer
Lemonier, Tom, 187
Leslie and Shattuck, 50
"Let Me Bring My Clothes Back Home," 358n39
Lett, Charles, 110
Levy, Abe, 13, 18, 136, 139–40, 198, 367n48
Lightfoot, James Escort, 107, *197f,* 333, 336, 337, 339, 342, 373, 394

The Lime Kiln Club (skit), 285
Lime Kiln Club Field Day (silent film), 317–18
Logan, Clarence, 119–20, 344, 363n47
"Love Will Find a Way," 323
Lucas, Eli, 120
Lucas, Sam, 16, 44, 201, 288, 313, 349n29
"A Lucky Coon," 95–98, 327, 344
lynching (lynch mob), 16, 33, 58, 118, 365n11

"Ma Angeline," 39–40
Mack, Cecil (Charles McPherson), *125f, 133f,* 152, 187–88, *263f,* 285, 300, *301f,* 318
Mallory, Edward, 73
Mallory, Frank, 44, 88, 99, 210, 327, 328, 364
Mallory Brothers, 44, 73, 120
"Maori," 272
Marshall, James L., 110
Marshall, Lillian, 257
Marshall-Lett Hotel, 110
Martin and Selig's Mastodon Minstrels, 23
Matheny's Cafe, Harlem, 317
Mauvais Music Company, 39–40
Mazet rules, 100
McClain, Billy, 141–42, 148, 152
McClure, Bennie, 190
McConnell, Will A., 59, 89–91, 93, 192
McIntosh, Tom and Hattie, 44, 257, 305, 333, 337, 339, 342
McIntyre, James, 15, 349n25, 396n30
McIntyre and Heath, 15, 62, 83, 358n38, 396n30
"Me an' da Minstrel Ban'," *188f,* 189
"The Medicine Man," 104, *105f*
Melvin, Carrie, 44

Menelik II, King of Abyssinia, 178, 195, 216–17, 337, 376n39
"Merry Widow" waltz, 250–51, *252f*, 266
Midwinter Fair, 26–29, 31, *32f*
Mierisch, Ferdinand E., 316
Miller and Lyles, 323
Mills, Jack, 316
minstrelsy, 14–16
"Minuet," 243
"Miss Hannah from Savannah," 124, *125f*, 131
Mitchell, Abbie. *See* Cook, Abbie Mitchell
Mitchell, Jesse and Cordelia: *The Creole Black Prince*, 285
Monroe, Jim, 16, 190, 375n18
Montgomery, David, 52
Mores, J. F., 255
Morris, William, 285
Motts, Robert, 251, 307, 311, 314, 374n7, 382n44
Mr. Lode of Koal, 286–94, *289f*, 296, 313, 316, 342
Mull, Grant, 139, 179–80, 187
"My Castle on the Nile," 124, 131
"My Little Zulu Babe,"117, *126f*, *127f*, 131, 333, 367n38
Myers, Alice (mother), 9–10, 17, 67, 84, 96, 132, 136–37, 154, 168, 181–82, 198, 230, 234, 239, 242, 243, 259, 261, 269, 270, 271, 273, 275, 281, 290, 294–96, 302, 305–7, 309, 317, 319–21, *321f*, 347n4, 358n34, 380n67, 393n81, 396n30
Myers, Frank, 67, 182, 319

Nail family (Edward, Grace, and Jack), 58, 201, 257, 260, 357n12
Nash. *See* Walker, George

National Exhibition and Amusement Company, 322
National Negro Business League, 198, 262, 376n48
The Natural Born Gambler, 318
Near the Nile, 261, 271
Negro anthem, 198
Negro Republican Club, 187
Neilson, Mrs. Frederick, 160
New York Draft Riot (1863), 58, 119
"Nobody," 194, 205–6, 217–18, 251, 272, 285–86, 316
Nugent, Richard Bruce, 110, 115

O'Brien, Charles Sydney, 39–41
Octoroons, 43–44, 67, 73, 85, 101, 120
"Oh, I Don't Know, You're Not So Warm," 46–47, *48f*, 50–51, 65, 73, 156
Olcott, Vera, 263
Oriental America, 44, 358n37
Oriental Troubadours, 128–29
Overstreet, Marie, 306
Overton, Ada. *See* Walker, Aida Overton
Oyster Man, 263

Paget, Mary, Lady, 159–60
The Passing Show, 49
Payne, Arthur "Strut," *197f*, 287–88, 302, 336, 337, 340, 343, 383, 393
Pekin Publishing Company, 374n7
Pekin Theatre, Chicago, 228, 253, 299, 305, 311, 313–14, 323, 374n7, 382n44
Pené, Xavier, 27, 28, 31–32
Percy G. Williams' theatres, 299, 309
Peter Dailey's *A Good Thing* company, 52

"The Phrenologist Coon," 124, 131
Physioc, Joe, 120
Bell Brothers, 136, 139
Pickering, Albert, 254
Pickett, George, 124
Pickett, Jesse, 30
Pierce bicycle, 100, 362n14
Pinchback, P. B. S., 254
Piper, Fred, 44
Plessy v. Ferguson, 53
Plimmer, Walter J., 43
The Policy Players, 73, 101–2, 109, 120, 255, 328, 344, 362n19, 364n48
"Porto Rico," 300
"Pretty Desdemone," 207, 215, 273
Primrose and West Minstrels, 43, 92
Pringle, C. W., 15

ragtime music, 29–31, 42, 51–58
Raymond, Melville B., 214, 227–28, 231, 235
"Red, Red Rose," 243
Red Moon, 288, 294
Reed, Dave, Jr., *74f*
Reed, Harry, 295
Reed, Pauline, 84–85, 120, 267, 272, 274, 300–1
Rex, Sterling, *197f*, 257, 336, 337, 339, 342
Rhymes, Tales and Rhymed Tales (Allen), 241
Rice, Ed, 90, 360n25
Rice, T. D., 14
"A Rich Coon's Babe," 189
Richard and Pringle's Georgia Minstrels, 187
"Right Church, but the Wrong Pew," 261
Ringgold, Jennie and Muriel, 256, 263, 338, 366

Rivers, James "Ike," 192, 196, 197, 352–53n36, 375n29
Robertson, George, 16
Robinson, Bill "Bojangles," 257–58, 320, *321f*, 367n45, 393n81
Robinson, Daisy. *See* Tapley, Daisy Robinson
Rogers, Alex, 34, 111, 150, *151f*, 187, *188f*, 194, 241, *248f*, 249, *263f*, 271, 277, 283, 286, 288, 323, 333, 337, 339, 342, 348, 373n52, 394n13, 396n37
Rohe, Alice, 207–8
Roosevelt, Theodore, 158
Rucker, John, 257–58
Ruhl, Arthur, 47–48
Russell, D. E., 104
Russell, Sylvester, 43, 85, 88, *130f*, 149–50, 152–53, 165, 189, 203–4, 220, 224, 235, 270, 272, 275, 287, 291–92, 297, 299, 305, 306–7 309, 313, 318, 322, 323, 368n4, 381n11

Salome, 262–64, 277, *277f*, 300, 387n59
Sam T. Jack's *Creole Burlesque Show*, 39, 44
Sandow, Eugene, 51–52
Sargent, Epes W. *See* Chicot
Saulsbury, L. H., 271, 333, 337, 340, 343
Schimpf, Charles, 37
Schlam, Hugo V., 39–41
Schwab, Charles, 141
Seamon, Harry, 91, 160
"See Yer Colored Man," 24
The Senegambian Carnival, 90–91, 93–96. See also *"A Lucky Coon"*
Shattuck, Truly, 50, 355n40
"The Sheath Gown in Darktown," 261–62, 272

Shelton, Byron, 287
"She's Getting More Like the White Folks Every Day," 131
Shipp, Jesse Allison, *43f*, 43–44, 59–60, 91, 99, 101, 111, 120, 150, 152, 168, 173–74, 187, 195, 216, 237, 241, 243, 260, *263f*, 271, 277, 286, 288, 305, 309, 314, 327, 328, 330, 333, 337, 340, 343, 383n57
Shipp Jr., Jesse Allison, 265
Shoemaker, Jack, 228, 266, 267, 273, 285, 312–13, 343, 384, 393
Shoo-Fly Regiment, 228, 381n11
Shuberts, 192, 216, 233–34, 246, 250, 265, 268, 272, 277–78, 293, 296, 377n19, 381n18, 384n8
Shuffle Along, 323
Simmons, Susie, 272
Siren and Navarro, 292
Sissle and Blake, 320, 323
Skinner, Constance, 269–70
smallpox, 124–26, 128, 365n20
Smart Set, 152, 194, 295, 297, 300, 308
Smith, Joe, 102
Smith; Ed, 104
Society for the Suppression of Ragtime, 104
"Somewhere," 243
Sons of Ham, 117, 120, *122–23f*, 124, 129, 131, 132, 134–35, *155f*, 330, 332
Souls of Black Folk, 162
Southern Enchantment, 152
The Southerners, 177
St. Cloud Hotel café, 100
Stair and Havlin, 234, 297
The Standard, 67
Standard Quartet, 29
Stewart, Harrison, 35–36, 256–57
Stone, Daniel and Curtis, 13
Stone, Fred, 52
Sweet, William, 24
"The Syndicate Four Big Shots," 150
Syphilis, 73, 254, 266, 286, 299, 311, 314, 375n29

"Tain't Gwine to Be No Rain," 243
Tapley, Daisy Robinson, 132, 333, 338, 367n42, 392n72
Tango Picnic, 314
Tanguay, Eva, 263, 299, 391n54
Tapley, Green Henri "High G," 120, *121f*, 132, 187, *197f*, 272, 274, 278–79, 281, 297, 305–7, 330, 333, 336, 337, 340, 343, 367n42, 373n52, 379n48, 383n57, 392n72, 394n13
Tetrazzini, Mme. Luisa, 254
Texas Medley Quartet, 30
"That's Why They Call Me Shine," 300, *301f*, 316
"The Harbor of Lost Dreams," 288
"The Lament," 288
"The Leader of the Ball," 131
The Southerners, 177
Theatrical Exchange, Chicago, 43
Thompson, Charlotte "Lottie." *See* Williams, Lottie Thompson
Thompson, Noah D., 316
Thorpe, Robert, 117–18
Thurston, Willie, 137
Tin Pan Alley publishing houses, 58–59
Tobias, D. E., 246, 254
Tolliver, Ed, 292
touring
  1899–1900: *A Lucky Coon*, 97–101; *The Policy Players*, 101–10
  1901–1902, 131–36; *Sons of Ham*, 120–29

touring *(continued)*
  1902–1903: *In Dahomey*, 142–54
  1903–1904: departure from New York, 166, 168; in England, 165–72, 177–78; performance/success at Buckingham Palace, 173–77; performer changes, 177–78
  1904–1905: *Abyssinia*, 195–98; return to US, 185–95
  1905–1907: *Abyssinia* production, 215–20. See also *Abyssinia* in Chicago, 221–26; management problems, 201–14
  1907–1908: *Bandanna Land*, 241–58; in Lawrence, Kansas, 237–41; management issues, 233–37
Trevathan, Charles, 50–51, 355n41
A Trip to Coontown, 85, 128–29
Troy, Henry, 256, 333, 340, 342, 373n52, 383n57
Tuck, Sam, 100, 104, 107, 109, 132, 134–35, 328, 330
The Uncalled, 89
Uncle Tom's Cabin, 16, 29, 134, 318
Under the Bamboo Tree, 318
United States Amusement Company, 234
"Until Then," 243
"The Upper Ten and Lower Five of Blackville," 73
Ussugah, 28

Vanderbilts, 77–84, 97, 101, 111, 142, 160, 162, 172, 254, 272
Vaughn, James, *151f*, 177, 190, 292, 364n49
Victor Monarch, 132, 367n38
Victor United booking agency, 285
Vinegar, Pete, 16
Vodery, Will, 241

Walker, Aida Overton (wife): background, 1–2, 77–84; birthday present for, 108–9; on cake walk dance, 57–58; childhood clothing styles, 84; childhood dance busking, 85; on death of Halliday, 324; family tree, 84; footrace, 109; as influence, 228–29; in Lawrence, Kansas, 181–82, 237; marriage, 100–1; name change, 159; as performer, 124, 131–32; personifying the "Negro Problem," 160; photos, *87f*, *159f*, *163f*, *225f*; in the public eye, 161–62; response to "Honorary Whiteness" nomination for Williams, 312–13; response to infidelity, 223–24; Russell on, 149, 153; at Thorpe dancing studio, 85; wardrobe, 166
Walker, Aida Overton (wife), business elements: as essential to Williams and Walker company, 226; relationship with Williams and Shipp, 308–9; rift with Williams, 283–84, 287–88; separation from Williams and Walker company, 287–88; Smart Set as option, 297, 308; trademark assumed by, 273; Williams and Walker company role, 88
Walker, Aida Overton (wife), end of life: burial, 314; death of, 314; health issues, 313; pallbearers for, 394n13
Walker, Aida Overton (wife), husband's end of life: benefit for granite memorial, 309, 393n78; nurse hired for, 302; after the passing, 313; visit, 294
Walker, Aida Overton (wife), performances in/with: all-star event at the Pekin Theatre, 313; *Bandanna Land*, 242, 243; *Big Smoke*, 287; Black Patti's Troubadours, 85; "Bon Bon

Buddy, the Chocolate Drop," 276, *276f*, 277; costume for, 274; *In Dahomey* (opera), 158; Delmonico's, 159–60; *His Honor, the Barber*, 300; in London, 172; "Shine" act in male attire, 313; *Tango Picnic*, 314; Vanderbilt summer ball, 142; vaudeville, 285; "Vision of Salome" (dance), 262, 263–64, *277f*

Walker, Aida Overton (wife), publications: "Colored Men and Women on the Stage," 204; "Opportunities the Stage Offers Intelligent and Talented Women," 269; "Women and Overwork," 279–80

Walker, Aida Overton (wife), skills: choreography, 177; dancing, 245–46, 249, 300, 314; language, 239; teaching, 158, 160–61; teaching British royalty, 177

Walker, George: as Accepted Mason of Scotland, 179, *180f*, 373n52; on *Bandanna Land*, 242; "Bert and Me and Them," 269; on Buckingham Palace performance, 176; on *The Clansman*, 221–23; contributions, 324; correspondence with Mull, 179; dance skills, 249; Deas, Reed, and Deas production viewed by, 295; in drag, 44, *127f*; drawing of, *224f*; Dvorak similarities, 89; earnings, 210; education/training from other musicians, 15; figurine of, 149; gift of pearls "wriggling like a snake," 255–56; gold cap affixed to right incisor, 247; at Great Northern Hotel in Chicago during the Columbian Exposition, 351n14; Hogan visit, 254; indiscretions/infidelity, 209, 223–24, 299; insecurity about his voice, 273; in Lawrence, Kansas, 66–67, 150, 230, 280–81; *Lawrence Weekly World* comments on, 66–67; photos of, *73f*, 95–96, *112–14f*, *167f*, *225f*, *238f*, *263f*, *303f*; poem by, 182; portrait for Howard University, 309; on racial bias, 208–9, 229–30; on racism discussion without inclusion of Blacks, 253; "The Real 'Coon' on the American Stage," 224–26, *225f*; request for female chorus members for Pekin Theatre, 251, 253; stag party for, 179; stardom trappings of Jim Crow America, 235–37; as target of rioters, 118; theft charge dropped, 60; unexplained absence, 275; at Vanderbilt summer ball, 142; visits to Lawrence, Kansas, 137–38, 181–82, 187; on what Negroes want, 222–23; Williams compared with, 245

Walker, George and Aida: "Merry Widow" waltz, 250–51, *252f*, 266

Walker, George, business instincts: business ability, 203–4; contracts/business negotiated by, 59–60; on Dockstader. *See* Dockstader, Lew efforts at second company, 287; property purchase in Lawrence, 151; rags-to-riches story, 190; on retirement, 260; Williams and Walker company connection severed, 290

Walker, George, childhood/teen years: about, 1; birth in 1872, 10; Black nationalism exposure, 11; blown across the street in Lawrence, 15, 349n25; childhood experiences, 12–13; early musical exposure, 13; employment. *See* employment,

Walker, George *(continued)*
childhood/teen years family tree, 9–10, 347n4, 348n6; image in Lawrence, 11–12; inter-racial play groups, 16–17; jail time for theft conviction, 17; in Lawrence, Kansas, 8–13; minstrelsy exposure, 14–16; truancy, 16

Walker, George, fashion: fashion sense, 249–50; wardrobe, 60, 62, *63f*, 67, 107, 111, *112–14f*, 166, 185, 189, 238–39, *238f*, 246, 249, 251

Walker, George, illness: depression, 266–67; deterioration, 6–7, 262, 265–66, 297, 299; in Homeland Sanitorium, Lakewood, New Jersey, 282, 286, 290; medical care, 273; parting from Williams, 278; physician's opinion, 286; plight compared to other actors, 286; return to Lawrence, 278–79; St. Joseph Sanitarium, Mount Clemens, Michigan, 273, 290, 294; at St. Joseph-affiliated hospital, Far Rockaway, Long Island, 288; at State Hospital, Central Islip, Long Island, for end-of-life care, 297; syphilis, 266, 385n22; West Baden (care facility), 290

Walker, George, passing: clergy (Hutchins C. Bishop), 302; death, 302; eulogies, 307; funeral in Lawrence, 306, 392n70; funeral in New York, 302; funeral train and burial in Oak Hill Cemetery, 307; grave marker, 309, 393n81; lying in state, 302; memorial concert, 302; train station ceremony, 305; tribute by Howard, 306

Walker, George, publications/interviews: "The Colored Performers on the American Stage," 215; "The Dramatic Stage as an Upbuilder of the Race," 270–71; "The Fly in the Ointment," 260–61; "Negro on Stage Can't Be Serious," 209

Walker, Jerry Nashville (father): about, 9–13; death of, 319; military employment, 348n7; as president of Colorado African Colonization Company, 145, 148, *148f*

Walker-Hogan-Cole (W-H-C) Theatre, 316–17

Walters, Gustav, 37

Walton, Lester A., 42, 62, 111, 235, 246, 250, 258, 259–60, 262, *263f*, 264–65, 267, 270, 281, 286–87, 295–96, 300, 301–5, 307, 313, 322, 381n10, 395n18

Ward, Charles B., *74f*

Warren, Madge, 391n51

Warren, Odessa, 109, 118, 320, 328, 330, 366, 391n51

Warren Street Baptist Church, 17, 187, 242, 306, 319, 392n70

Warrick, Meta Vaux, 149, 369n14

Washington, Booker T., 22, 158, 198, 208, 253, 270

Watson, Harry, 298

"We Wear the Mask," 27–28

Weatherless, Nelson E., 103

The Wedding of King Booloolum and Queen Razzerina, 117

Wells, Ida B., 27

West, Mae, 314

W-H-C (Walker-Hogan-Cole) Theatre, 316–17

"When I Was Sweet Sixteen," 243

"When It's All Goin' Out and Nothin' Comin' In," 131

"When Miss Maria Johnson Marries Me," 191

"When the Moon Shines on the Moonshine," 189, 192
"When Zacharias Leads the Band," 131
White, William Allen, 13
White Rats, 129
Whitman, Albery Allson, 67
Whitman, Essie, 58, 67
Whitney, Salem, 364n48
Who's Stealin,' 323
"Why Adam Sinned," 189, 191, 255
"Why Don't You Get a Lady of Your Own," 97
The Wild Rose company, 142
Wiley, Stella, 44, 67, *73f*, 358n37
Wilkes, Mattie, 44, 120, 328, 336, 340
William Morris booking agency, 285
Williams, Bert: as Accepted Mason of Scotland, 179, *180f*, 373n52; acquaintance with Walker, 21, 23, 350n43, 351n8, 351n14; Aida's relationship with, 308–9; arrest of, 135; automobile, 141, 166; background, 22–23; as Bahamian by birth, 22, 176; boxing skills, 298, 391n51; contractual obligations, 393n79; dance skills, 47; death of, 318; drawing of, *224f*; as film star, 317–18; and Grey as costar, 318; "Honorary Whiteness" nomination, 312; infidelity evidence, 299, 391n54; in Lawrence, Kansas, 181–82; "Nobody," 194; ongoing feelings for Walker, 317; photos of, *73f, 225f, 263f, 303f*; on rabbits hunted for Nash's larder, 16; rift with Aida, 283–84, 287–88; Shuberts contract, 293; as sole Black member of Ziegfeld Follies, 298; stag party for, 179; summer employment, 285; at Vanderbilt summer ball, 142; "Vision of Salome" (dance), 264; on voting rights, 222; Walker compared with, 245; on Walker's rest requirements, 275; Walker's termination stated as business agreement', 292; wardrobe, 166
Williams, Bert, health/lifestyle issues: drinking/alcohol use, 298–99, 312; driving while intoxicated, 286; grief, 302; mood problems, 286, 290; throat issues, 271
Williams, George, 256
Williams, Lottie Thompson: background, 92–93; Chicago as home, 98; death of, 319; family tree, 92; Guiguesse as replacement for, 257; illness, 256, 312; in Lawrence, Kansas, 181–82; marriage to Bert Williams, 102; role in *Bandanna Land*, 243; tree-climbing contest, 109; at Vanderbilt summer ball, 142; wardrobe, 166
Williams, Percy G.: theatres, 299, 309; vaudeville contract with, 257
Williams and Walker brand, 285
Williams and Walker company: Aida as addition and influence, 88, 228–29; attendance records, 128, 132, 277; British audience response, 65, 172; business ability, 60, 100; challenge to Vanderbilt, 77–84; discord/disintegration within, 204, 284, 291; dispute with Hogan and McClain, 141–42; eastern tour success, 109; field day, 109; final show, 288; financial problems/receivership, 228, 231; gambling, 107–8; games on royal grounds, 174;

Williams and Walker company *(continued)*
in Indianapolis, 108; intellectual property rights, 39–41; Mallory as stage manager, 88; management issues, 293; members of, 44; New York arrival, 186–87; photos of, *63f, 68f,* 71–72, *303f;* praise for, 165; recovery from *Abyssinia,* 116; Reed as seamstress, 120; renamed as Williams Company, 290; response to segregated theatres, 158; reviews, 37–38, 171; revival attempts, 295; silver loving cup presented to, 107; staff acquired from *Octoroons* cast, 88; theatre planned for, 253–54; vaudeville contract, 257; Walker's connection severed, 290; western tour success, 109; White acceptability, 149; White management problems, 299; working relationship, 35; Zulu warriors as ambition, 254. *See also* first-class theatres

Williams and Walker company, performances: *Big Smoke,* 286–87; as buck and wing dancers, 37–38, 353n3; cake walk expertise/popularity, 58, 60–61, 62, 72, *73f; Chocolate Drops with King and Bailey,* 285; "command performance" for Borden, 271–72; musical comedies, 44; as Two Real Coons, 35; Williams and Walker roles, 33, 47

"The Williams and Walker Fresh Kids," 257

Williams and Walker Glee Club, 196–98, *197f,* 204, 257, 285, 336, 341

Williams and Walker partnership: celebration of, 266; in Harlem, 257; at Hogan benefit, 257–58; invitation to Hyde Park award service, 178; meeting with collaborators, 233; at Midway in San Francisco, 37; Negro Republican Club membership, 187; in New York, 58–62; at Orpheum theatre, Los Angeles, 37–38; publications featuring, 67; residence as gathering spot for Black entertainers, 110–11; sixteenth anniversary, 255; social norms upended by, 65; theatres for Black plays under Black control, 198; trip with Schwab, 141

Williams and Walker Quartet, 109–10, 196

Williams and Walker, second company, 120, 128

"Williams and Walker's Bon Bon Buddies" (vaudeville), 256

Wilson, Effie, 102

Wilson, "Griff," 24

Winfred, Harry, 124

Wonderland Theatre, Detroit, 46

Woolworth building, 128–29

Work, Monroe Nathan, 29

Yorkville Theatre, Manhattan, 228, 282

Young, George M., 235

Young's Casino, Manhattan, 313

Ziegfeld Follies, Williams's role in, 298, 312, 317